Lecture Notes in Computer Science 1519
Edited by G. Goos, J. Hartmanis and J. van Leeuwen

Springer

Berlin
Heidelberg
New York
Barcelona
Hong Kong
London
Milan
Paris
Singapore
Tokyo

Toru Ishida (Ed.)

Community Computing
and Support Systems

Social Interaction in Networked Communities

 Springer

Series Editors

Gerhard Goos, Karlsruhe University, Germany
Juris Hartmanis, Cornell University, NY, USA
Jan van Leeuwen, Utrecht University, The Netherlands

Volume Editor

Toru Ishida
Department of Social Informatics
Kyoto University, 606-8501 Kyoto, Japan
E-mail: ishida@i.kyoto-u.ac.jp

Cataloging-in-Publication data applied for

Die Deutsche Bibliothek - CIP-Einheitsaufnahme

Community computing and support systems : social interaction in network
communities / Toru Ishida (ed.). - Berlin ; Heidelberg ; New York ; Barcelona ;
Hong Kong ; London ; Milan ; Paris ; Singapore ; Tokyo : Springer, 1998
(Lecture notes in computer science ; 1519)
ISBN 3-540-65475-5

CR Subject Classification (1991): I.2.11, I.6, C.2, J.4

ISSN 0302-9743
ISBN 3-540-65475-5 Springer-Verlag Berlin Heidelberg New York

Typesetting: Camera-ready by author
SPIN 10692786   06/3142 – 5 4 3 2 1 0   Printed on acid-free paper

Table of Contents

Overview

Towards Computation over Communities 1
Toru Ishida

Methodology for Large Scale Experimentation: A Discussion
Report 11
Toyoaki Nishida, Geoffrey Bowker, Jon Mason, Toshiaki Miyashita,
Katashi Nagao, Toshikazu Nishimura, Takeshi Ohguro,
Charanjit Sidhu, Yasuyuki Sumi, Peter van den Besselaar, and
Makoto Yokozawa

Models and Concepts

Complexity and Adaptation in Community Information
Systems: Implications for Design 16
Michael D. Cohen and Robert Axelrod

How TRURL Evolves Multiagent Worlds for Social Interaction
Analysis 43
Takao Terano, Setsuya Kurahashi and Ushio Minami

Agent Based Approach for Social Complex Systems
– Management of Constructed Social World – 61
Hiroshi Deguchi

Awareness – The Common Link Between Groupware and
Community Support Systems 77
Johann Schlichter, Michael Koch and Chengmao Xu

Social, Psychological and Artistic Aspects of the Human
Interface 94
Ryohei Nakatsu

Methodologies for Large Scale Trials

Demographics and Sociographics of the *Digital City* 108
Peter van den Besselaar and Dennis Beckers

Groupware, Community, and Meta-Networks:
The Collaborative Framework of EdNA (Education Network
Australia) 125
Jon Mason

C-MAP: Building a Context-Aware Mobile Assistant for
Exhibition Tours 137
Yasuyuki Sumi, Tameyuki Etani, Sidney Fels, Nicolas Simonet,
Kaoru Kobayashi and Kenji Mase

**Managing Large Scale Online Discussions: Secrets of the Open
Meeting** 155
Roger Hurwitz and John Mallery

**Social Pattern Development Analysis: A Case Study in a
Regional Community Network** 170
Toshihiko Yamakami and Gen-ichi Nishio

Sharing Knowledge and Preference in Communities

**CoMeMo-Community: A System for Supporting Community
Knowledge Evolution** 183
Toyoaki Nishida, Takashi Hirata and Harumi Maeda

**IKNOW: A Tool to Assist and Study the Creation, Maintenance,
and Dissolution of Knowledge Networks** 201
Noshir S. Contractor, Daniel Zink and Michael Chan

**Building Agent Community toward Business Knowledge Base
Generation** 218
Toshiaki Miyashita, Yosuke Takashima, Yoshihide Ishiguro,
Takayoshi Asakura and Koji Kida

**Building Information Infrastructures for Social Worlds –
The Role of Classifications and Standards** 231
Geoffrey C. Bowker and Susan Leigh Star

Supporting Social Interaction in Communities

**Interactional Resources for the Support of Collaborative
Activities: Common Problems in the Design of Technologies
to Support Groups and Communities** 249
Paul Luff and Marina Jirotka

**Interactive Consultation System with Asymmetrical
Communications between People in Different Electronic
Communities** 267
Hiroshi Yajima, Tadashi Tanaka, Hiroshi Tsuji, Hirotaka Mizuno and
Norifumi Nishikawa

**Communities through Time: Using History for Social
Navigation** 281
Alan Wexelblat

**Reflections of Communities in Virtual Environments:
The Mirror** 299
Charanjit K. Sidhu

Silhouettell: Awareness Support for Real-World Encounter 316
Masayuki Okamoto, Hideyuki Nakanishi, Toshikazu Nishimura and
Toru Ishida

Agent Technologies in Communities

Supporting Network Communities with Multiagent Systems 330
Fumio Hattori, Takashi Ohguro, Makoto Yokoo, Shigeo Matsubara and
Sen Yoshida

Agent Augmented Community: Human-to-Human and Human-to-Environment Interactions Enhanced by Situation-Aware Personalized Mobile Agents 342
Katashi Nagao and Yasuharu Katsuno

Community Formation via a Distributed, Privacy-Protecting Matchmaking System 359
Leonard N. Foner

SYMBIOT: Personalizing Agents in Social Contexts 377
Chisato Numaoka

Author Index 393

Towards Computation over Communities

Toru Ishida

Department of Social Informatics, Kyoto University
Kyoto 606-8501, Japan

Abstract. With the advance of global computer networks, a dramatic shift in computing metaphors has begun: from *team* to *community*. Understanding that the team metaphor has created various research fields including groupware and distributed artificial intelligence, it seems that the *community* metaphor has the potential to generate new directions in research and practice. Based on this motivation, we organized the *Kyoto Meeting on Social Interaction and Communityware* in June 1998. This article reports the background and results of the meeting.

1. Introduction

With the advance of global computer networks like the Internet and mobile computing, discussion of *virtual community* [26] has become more active worldwide. People realized that the Internet and other network technologies could affect not just industries and economies but also our everyday life.

According to Webster's Dictionary, the word *community* is defined as "a body of individuals organized into a unit or manifesting usually with awareness some unifying trait." More specifically, Hillery reported that there were at least 94 definitions for this word even in the early 1950s [8]. His summary of the factors of community showed that they include *locality, social interaction* and *common tie*. MacIver also pointed out that the concept of community is based on the locality of human life, and is the counter concept of *association*, where people share a common goal [15].

Recently the term *community* is being used as a metaphor for the next stage of computing technologies, including the methodologies, mechanisms and tools for creating, maintaining, and evolving social interaction in human societies. We believe there will be a dramatic shift in computing metaphors: from *team* to *community*. Given that the team metaphor has created research fields like groupware and distributed artificial intelligence, it is quite possible that the community metaphor will generate new fields both in research and practice. Based on the above motivation, we organized the *Kyoto Meeting on Social Interaction and Communityware* from June 8 to 10, 1998 in Kyoto, Japan.

Figure 1. Kyoto Meeting

The rest of this article includes a summary of the meeting, but a large part is used to describe our view of the community computing metaphor. Though the field has not been established, readers are encouraged to be simulated to tackle this new research paradigm.

2. Extending Groupware for Communities

We first address how we extend groupware for human community support. Research into groupware was triggered by advances in local area networks. Various tools have been developed for communication between isolated people, such as desktop electronic meeting systems. Though there is no specific definition of the term *group*, previous research and practice of groupware mainly addressed the collaborative work of already-organized people. A typical example is that project members in the same company synchronously / asynchronously works using workstations connected by local area networks.

Community computing is for more diverse and amorphous groups of people [12]. We think that the metaphor of community has become important given the advance of global computer networks such as the Internet and mobile computing. Our goal is to support the process of organizing people who are willing to share some level of mutual understanding and experiences. In other words, compared to current groupware studies, *we focus on an earlier stage of collaboration: group formation from a wide variety of people.*

Every community has rules that can be represented logically. The rules may specify how to elect leaders, make decisions, collect monthly fees and so on. Groupware technologies can provide tools for supporting these formal procedures. In the case of communities, however, people require more than logical support. MacIver pointed out that, for communities, it is essential for members to share feelings such as *we-feeling*, *role-feeling* and *dependency-feeling*. The obvious problem is whether community feelings can be established within a virtual space. A similar question is whether the use of personal digital assistants (PDAs) really encourages people to develop these feelings. *Thus, the challenge is to extend the human community beyond physical localities through the use of public computer networks.*

3. Supporting Social Interaction in Communities

The community metaphor can create five different functions for encouraging social interaction in communities as follows [13]:

1. Knowing each other;
2. Sharing preference and knowledge;
3. Generating consensus;
4. Supporting everyday life;
5. Assisting social events.

The papers in this volume can be also classified using the above functions.

Various MUD systems have been developed for socialization via global computer networks. Chat systems using avatars might be useful for maintaining human relations among people who already know each other. However, the lack of reality sometimes seriously hinders the emergence of community feelings if the users are strangers. Various face-to-face meeting environments have been developed to support informal communication. For example, FreeWalk [20] provides a 3D community common where everybody can meet and can behave just as they do in real life. This volume also includes various approaches for knowing each other. IKNOW [5] and Silhouettell [25] encourage people to encounter each other based on their common interests. Yajima *et al.* propose interactive consultation for different electronic communities [32]. Wexelblat proposes to use history for social navigation for communities distributed in time [31].

In a community, people want to know what the others know, and sometimes to do what others are doing. To share preferences among people in a community, recommender systems are being studied to select items appropriate to each individual [16]. There are two ways to generate recommendations. One is called *content-based recommendation*, where the system selects items based on user's previous behavior: if the user selected *A*, and if *B* is thought similar to *A*, the system recommends *B* to the user. The other is called *collaborative filtering*, where the system selects items based on the preferences of the community: if the user selected *A*, and if other members who select *A* tend to select *B*, the system recommends *B* to the user. Yenta is a typical example of this approach [7].

In this context, we have the research issue of *community awareness*. Since the role of community computing is helping people to develop their own community, it is important to encourage people to develop *mutual knowledge* (to know what others know) and *mutual preference* (to do what others do). The question is how to increase mutual preference, knowledge, and activities without infringing on people's privacy. In supporting community awareness, the more information is provided about personal activities, the more people can become aware of the whole activity of the community. However, the possibility of infringing people's privacy increases at the same time. For example, using live video to observe the activities of colleagues without any restriction can be abused as a peeping hole to watch their movements closely. This dilemma is a serious design problem, since private communication occupies a more important role in community computing than is true for traditional groupware systems.

To share knowledge among people in a community, we need an open and informal representation of heterogeneous information. The goal of the *knowledgeable community project* [23] is to develop a computational framework for facilitating the knowledge acquisition process by humans and computers. Through an analysis of information systems in medical communities [3], Bowker and Star argue that community system designers must necessarily build for multiple social worlds simultaneously. They draw some design implications from this observation: notably arguing for sensitivity to the nature of the work of representing a community to itself. Miyashita *et al.* discussed how to build agent communities toward business knowledge base generation [18].

For generating consensus over communities, the Open Meeting environment [10] is intended to support discussions by large numbers of people. One such meeting was actually held on the Internet for a United States national performance review. Around 4000 people joined the network discussion. The proposals from government consisted of *recommendations* that represented goals and strategies, and *actions* that denoted *tactics*. People could add their comments to the hypertexts denoting the proposal. The hypertext links provided included *Agree, Qualify, Alternative, Disagree, Example, Question,* and *Answer*. The number of accesses made during the meeting period (two weeks) was around 35000, and there were 1300 comments. The human moderator accepted 1013 comments with the aid of a workflow management system.

Community networks have been developed to support everyday life. During the last decade, various software systems have been created to support local communities and shared interest groups. Knowledge about the use, users, and effects of these new systems is needed to create better designs and implementations. The results of a survey completed by the inhabitants of the *Amsterdam Digital City*, a large 'virtual community' can be seen in [1]. Related activities include EdNA (Education Network Australia) which is described in [17], and the Mirror, an experiment in virtual reality technology over the Internet, which provides a vehicle for exploring how to support evolving communities and enhance communication [29]. Yamakami and Nishio investigate how social patterns are developed though a case study involving a regional community network [33].

Internet services are often provided at large social events. However, it seems that people use the services mainly for reading and writing e-mail messages. More intimate computing is needed to assist socialization. The challenge here is to apply mobile computing to assist social events, and also to explore mobile computing with a large number of terminals. The ICMAS'96 Mobile Assistant Project was the first such experiment in an actual international conference; 100 personal digital assistants (PDAs) and cellular phones were used [22]. C-MAP is a mobile assistant for exhibition tours, and is more advanced than earlier experiments in terms of context-awareness: a personal guide agent in the mobile assistant directs users with exhibition maps that are personalized based on the physical and mental contexts of the users [30].

4. Community Metaphor in Social Information Systems

As an interesting trend, various large-scale social information systems are being developed: they include digital libraries, collaboratories, digital museums, digital democracies, digital economies, and telecommuting systems. Many books and papers have been published on these systems. Though we do not discuss a particular social information system in this volume, we believe all systems include (or will include) some of the five functions described above.

For example, the digital library project of the University of Illinois reported an interesting observation [2]. They questioned people in their university as to how they got the information required for research. It appears that "most novices search by keywords and topics." Undergraduate students typically perform keyword searches for retrieving material. "More advanced users did more browsing of a directed sort, for example reading through all recent issues of a particular journal, and did more snowball searching, chasing the references made in one article." Graduate students and young professors interleave searching and evaluating information of particular interest to them. The most interesting observation is that "experts built their own information infrastructures; they refined their systems to the point that the information came to them." It seems that professors do not perform keyword search or browsing. Their social relations yield sufficient information.

This observation suggests that the community computing metaphor is applicable to future digital libraries, so that people can yield and maintain social relations in their communities. Table 1 describes some of the relations between the listed functions and several social information systems. The aim of this table is to provide a uniform view of the community metaphor in social information systems; a view that is missing in previous research and development.

Table 1. Community Support Functions for Social Information Systems

	Telecom muting	Digital Library	Collabor atory	Digital Democracy	Digital Economy
Knowing Each Other	√	√	√		
Sharing Preference and Knowledge	√	√	√	√	√
Generating Consensus	√		√	√	
Supporting Everyday Life	√	√		√	√
Assisting Social Events			√	√	

5. Modeling, Design and Large Scale Trials

Organizations can be classified from the viewpoints of *openness* and *profit*. Since companies are well-organized, typically closed and for-profit organizations, collaboration can be easily established. Workflow management tools have been proposed for assisting people to work together. On the other hand, inter-company relations are more open. Each company is often modeled as a utility maximizer, and collaboration emerges as a result of competition. However, communities are not always for-profit organizations. Collaboration cannot be modeled as in companies, nor can it be expected to emerge from competition between members. This discussion shows that we need a different approach from traditional groupware or distributed artificial intelligence to understand and create collaboration in networked communities.

Table 2 summarizes a comparison of three computing metaphors: *team*, *market* and *community*. Teams often use local area networks as their infrastructure; the number of agents in each team ranges from 10 to 100; organizations are typically closed and participants are ready to cooperate. In markets or communities, however, wide or global networks are assumed as the infrastructure; the number of agents might reach 10^5; organizations are open, markets are competitive, while communities are collaborative. We already have a well-defined computational model for teams and markets: distributed cooperative problem solving has been studied in the area of distributed artificial intelligence ([11] for example); market-based computing (or economics-based computing) is currently studied. While there is no comprehensive computational model for communities, Cohen and Axelrod analyzed the complexity and adaptation in community information systems [4]; Terano *et al.* [27] and Deguchi [6] are applying their computational approaches to building models for communities.

Table 2. Team, Market and Community

	Team	Market	Community
Network	LAN	Extranet/Internet	Internet
Agent number	10^1-10^2	10^2-10^5	10^2-10^5
Organization	Closed Collaborative	Open Competitive	Open Collaborative
Computation	Distributed Problem Solving	Market-Based Computing	Adaptive Complex System
Application	Sensor Net Groupware	Network Auction Information Market	Community Network Digital City

For designing community support systems, Luff and Jirotka discuss how to support the early stage of interaction and collaboration [14]. Schlichter *et al.* propose awareness as a common base for community support systems, to improve contact building, as well as for groupware, to maintain group work at a high performance level [28]. Since people require more than logical support, Nakatsu discusses the importance of interdisciplinary research between engineering and social, psychological and artistic areas for future human interface technologies [21]. From the technological point of view, autonomous agents can take an important role in designing virtual communities. Hattori *et al.* applied multiagent systems to community support [9]. Numaoka proposes to introduce personalized agents in a 3D virtual environment. Nagao combines agent technologies and mobile computing technologies to augment the real world environment through actively integration with an information world [19].

Large scale trials have to be performed to confirm community support systems. The research issue lies in the evaluation of community interaction. In software engineering areas, the *rapid prototyping model* has been widely accepted as a way of developing application software. However, this model assumes that prototypes can be easily evaluated. For example, in the case of window applications, though it is hard to know all specifications in detail in advance, we can assume that their evaluation is possible at a glance. The problem in community computing is, however, that we cannot evaluate software in such a manner. The difficulty is in evaluating the systems embedded in human organizations. Measuring computation / communication efficiencies is not enough for evaluating software for networked communities. For example, people who are interested in digital cities cannot easily determine whether or not the systems are really useful. This is because community support systems are used by a variety of people, not just one person. Therefore, *rapid and community-wide evaluation* is as important as rapid prototyping.

6. Summary

This article discusses the *community* metaphor as the next stage of network computing. The first meeting in Kyoto was blessed with lovely weather. Though we did not organize a formal committee for this meeting, a number of social and computer scientists joined. Since the meeting was semi-closed, besides a variety of invited presentations, a number of papers were submitted to the meeting from the US, Europe and Pacific Rim countries. The mixture of invited and selected papers made the meeting moderately open and attractive. Most of presentations made at the meeting are included in this volume. We also had plenty of discussion time during the meeting. Some of the discussion results are also included. From these papers, readers can get a clear image of the actual meeting.

I would like to express my great appreciation of the co-organizers, Toyoaki Nishida, Takao Terano and Fumio Hattori and all the participants who contributed to the meeting. I also wish to thank the local arrangement people of the meeting: they are Toshikazu Nishimura, Hirofumi Yamaki, Hideyuki Nakanishi, Keiki Takadama, Shoko Miyagawa and Yoko Kubota. Special thanks to Hirofumi Yamaki and Masayuki Okamoto, who did tremendous work for editing this volume.

I also thank Andre Durand for a discussion on the term *communityware*. Though we have independently used this term, it appears that the term is a trademark of Durand Communication Inc. After long discussion at the meeting and via e-mail, we have decided not to encourage the use of the term *communityware* in this volume except for the names of papers or meetings that have been already realized. The term in this volume, if any, is thus used as a common noun like groupware.

References

1. P. van den Besselaar and D. Beckers, "Demographics and Sociographics of the Digital City," *CCSS*, Springer-Verlag, pp. 109-125, 1998.
2. A. Bishop, E. Ignacio, L. Neumann, R. Sandusky and L. Star, "John and Jane Q. Engineer: What About Our Users?" *DLI Social Science Team Report*, November 15, 1995.
3. G. C. Bowker and S. L. Star, "Building Information Infrastructures for Social Worlds - The Role of Classifications and Standards," *CCSS*, Springer-Verlag, pp. 232-249, 1998.
4. M. D. Cohen and R. Axelrod, "Complexity and Adaptation in Community Information Systems: Implications for Design," *CCSS*, Springer-Verlag, pp. 16-43, 1998.
5. N. S. Contractor, D. Zink and M. Chan, "IKNOW: A Tool to Assist and Study the Creation, Maintenance, and Dissolution of Knowledge Networks," *CCSS*, Springer-Verlag, pp. 202-218, 1998.

6. H. Deguchi, "Agent Based Approach for Social Complex Systems - Management of Constructed Social World -," *CCSS*, Springer-Verlag, pp. 62-77, 1998.

7. L. N. Foner, "Community Formation via a Distributed, Privacy-Protecting Matchmaking System," *CCSS*, Springer-Verlag, pp. 360-377, 1998.

8. G. A. Hillery, "Definitions of Community: Areas of Agreement," *Rural Sociology*, Vol. 20, pp. 111-123, 1955.

9. F. Hattori, T. Ohguro, M. Yokoo, S. Matsubara and S. Yoshida, "Supporting Network Communities with Multiagent Systems," *CCSS*, Springer-Verlag, pp.331-342, 1998.

10. R. Hurwitz and J. Mallery, "Managing Large Scale On-line Discussions: Secrets of the Open Meeting," *CCSS*, Springer-Verlag, pp. 156-170, 1998.

11. T. Ishida, *Parallel, Distributed and Multiagent Production Systems*, Lecture Notes in Artificial Intelligence 878, Springer-Verlag, 1994.

12. T. Ishida, "Towards Communityware," Invited Talk, *International Conference and Exhibition on the Practical Application of Intelligent Agents and Multi-Agent Technology (PAAM-97)*, pp. 7-21, 1997.

13. T. Ishida Ed., *Community Computing: Collaboration over Global Information Networks*, John Wiley and Sons, 1998.

14. P. Luff and M. Jirotka, "Interactional Resources for the Support of Collaborative Activities: Common Problems in the Design of Technologies to Support Groups and Communities," *CCSS*, Springer-Verlag, pp. 250-267, 1998.

15. R. M. MacIver, *Community*, Macmillan, 1917.

16. P. Maes, "Agents that Reduce Work and Information Overload," *Communications of the ACM*, Vol. 37, No. 7, pp. 30-40, 1994.

17. J. Mason, "Groupware, Community and Meta-Networks: The Collaborative Framework of EdNA (Education Network Australia)," *CCSS*, Springer-Verlag, pp. 126-137, 1998.

18. T. Miyashita, Y. Takashima, Y. Ishiguro, T. Asakura, and K. Kida, "Building Agent Community toward Business Knowledge Base Generation," *CCSS*, Springer-Verlag, pp. 219-231, 1998.

19. K. Nagao and Y. Katsuno, "Agent Augmented Community: Human-to-Human and Human-to-Environment Interactions Enhanced by Situation-Aware Personalized Mobile Agents," *CCSS*, Springer-Verlag, pp. 343-359, 1998.

20. H. Nakanishi, C. Yoshida, T. Nishimura and T. Ishida, "FreeWalk: Supporting Casual Meetings in a Network," *International Conference on Computer Supported Cooperative Work (CSCW-96)*, pp. 308-314, 1996.

21. R. Nakatsu, "Social, Psychological and Artistic Aspects of the Human Interface," *CCSS*, Springer-Verlag, pp. 95-108, 1998.

22. Y. Nishibe, H. Waki, I. Morihara, F. Hattori, T. Ishida, T. Nishimura, H. Yamaki, T. Komura, N. Itoh, T. Gotoh, T. Nishida, H. Takeda, A. Sawada, H. Maeda, M. Kajihara and H. Adachi, "Mobile Digital Assistants for Community Support," *AI Magazine*, Vol.19, No.2, pp.31-49, 1998.

23. T. Nishida, T. Hirata and H. Maeda, "CoMeMo-Community: A System for Supporting Community Knowledge Evolution," *CCSS*, Springer-Verlag, pp.184-201, 1998.

24. C. Numaoka, "SYMBIOT: Personalizing Agents in Social Contexts," *CCSS*, Springer-Verlag, pp. 378-392, 1998.
25. M. Okamoto, H. Nakanishi, T. Nishimura and T. Ishida, "Silhouettell: Awareness Support for Real-World Encounter," *CCSS*, Springer-Verlag, pp. 318-330, 1998.
26. H. Rheingold, *The Virtual Community*, Addison-Wesley, 1993.
27. T. Terano, S. Kurahashi and U. Minami "How TRURL Evolves Multiagent Worlds for Social Interaction Analysis," *CCSS*, Springer-Verlag, pp. 44-61, 1998.
28. J. Schlichter, M. Koch, and C. Xu, "Awareness - The Common Link Between Groupware and Community Support Systems," *CCSS*, Springer-Verlag, pp. 78-94, 1998.
29. C. K Sidhu, "Reflections of Communities in Virtual Environments: The Mirror," *CCSS*, Springer-Verlag, pp. 300-316, 1998.
30. Y. Sumi, T. Etani, S. Fels, N. Simonet, K. Kobayashi, and K. Mase, "C-MAP: Building a Context-Aware Mobile Assistant for Exhibition Tours," *CCSS*, Springer-Verlag, pp. 138-155, 1998.
31. A. Wexelblat, "Communities through Time: Using History for Social Navigation," *CCSS*, Springer-Verlag, pp. 282-299, 1998.
32. H. Yajima, T. Tanaka, H. Tsuji, H. Mizuno, N. Nishikawa, "Interactive Consultation System with Asymmetrical Communications between People in Different Electronic Communities," *CCSS*, Springer-Verlag, pp. 268-281, 1998.
33. T. Yamakami and G. Nishio, "Social Pattern Development Analysis: A Case Study in a Regional Community Network," *CCSS*, Springer-Verlag, pp. 171-183, 1998.

Methodology for Large Scale Experimentation:
A Discussion Report

Toyoaki Nishida[1], Geoffrey Bowker[2], Jon Mason[3], Toshiaki Miyashita[4],
Katashi Nagao[5], Toshikazu Nishimura[6], Takeshi Ohguro[7], Charanjit Sidhu[8],
Yasuyuki Sumi[9], Peter van den Besselaar[10], and Makoto Yokozawa[11]

[1] Nara Institute of Science and Technology, Nara, Japan,
Kansai Advanced Research Center, Communications Research Laboratory, Japan
nishida@is.aist-nara.ac.jp,
WWW home page: http://ai-www.aist-nara.ac.jp/doc/people/nishida/
[2] Graduate School of Library and Information Science, University of Illinois at
Urbana/Champaign
[3] Education.Au Ltd
[4] Human Media Research Laboratories, NEC Corporation
[5] Sony Computer Science Laboratory Inc.
[6] Department of Social Informatics, Kyoto University
[7] Computer Science Laboratory, NTT Communication Science Laboratories
[8] Human Factors Unit, BT Laboratories
[9] ATR Media Integration & Communications Research Labs.
[10] Social Science Informatics, University of Amsterdam
[11] Information Technology Research Dept., Nomura Research Institute, Ltd.

Abstract. Issues in community computing and support systems (CCSS)
are roughly categorized into academic / pedagogical ones concerning
social and information sciences, methodological ones including design
and evaluation of experiments, and pragmatic ones such as fund raising.
We have focused on the methodological aspects in CCSS, and discussed
how our methodology will be applied in the real world environment and
insights extracted.

1 Background of the Discussion

The purpose of this group is to identify critical issues in community computing
and support systems (CCSS) and discuss methodologies to develop and test
ideas in real world environments. The background of the participants spans an
interesting range of expertise. Major ones include:

- education
  - EdNA (Mason)
  - Education On Line (Sidhu)
  - distant education system (Bowker)
- pleasure and entertainment
  - MIRROR (Sidhu)
- everyday life

- Digital City (Besselaar)
- scientific context
  - environmental hydraulic modeling scientific teams (Bowker)
- academic meeting support
  - mobile assistants for an international conference (Nishimura, Nishida)
  - mobile assistants for an open house demo (Sumi)
  - Community Organizer (Ohguro)
  - community communication facilitators (Nishida, Nishimura)

The distribution is diverse in terms of the application field and the degree of penetration into the real world (i.e., from exploratory prototyping to real world experimentation with thousands of users.)

2   Questions Raised

After all participants explained her/his background and research interest, we talked about the issues to address. Interesting remarks were made during the initial discussions, such as:

- Generating data is easy, but how do we analyze them?
- We have classic analysis methods, but they are not stabilized set of tools.
- Community building contains political aspects. We have an implicit assumption that community building is good. Is it always true?
- Modeling communities with respect to communication: active vs passive, deep vs shallow.
- There are potential communities such as a (potential) community of cancer patients that come only true using networks.
- How to transmit real world information (e.g., I am a woman) in virtual world communication, and how much? Privacy issue is also relevant here.

After discussion, we agreed to focus on the following three questions:

- How do we understand the nature of communities?
- What is a methodology for designing community information systems?
- How do we evaluate the effectiveness of community information systems?

For the three questions raised, we mainly obtained results for the latter two questions. For the first question, it turned out it contains a lot of deep issues that should be answered in a long run. In the following section, we overview the major results.

3   Major Results of the Discussion

As a result of discussions, we were able to identify some key issues concerning a methodology for large scale experimentation of CCSS and figure out a shared perspective of the field. To base our discussion on a concrete ground, we conducted a brief case study on existing CCSS systems.

3.1 Application of methodology during the system development

A conventional model of system development comprises the following sequence of activities:

requirement capture → design → implementation → delivery.

Evaluation proceeds in parallel to the process. Usually, various kinds of loops, either small or large, are included which cause re-implementation, re-design, or even re-capture, slowing down system development. Can we employ a classical methodology as a reference model for designing CCSS as well?

Most participants considered that methodologies having been undertaken for CCSS so far are quite different from the classic water-fall models. This is mainly because it is very hard to capture requirements in advance. Many requirements (e.g., whether classify certain information as public or private) are tacit and are only captured after a certain period of trial and errors. Participants with actual development and deployment experiences mentioned that cycles of (partial) scrap-and-build are unavoidable and the actual development process might be called an evolutionary spiral of development and evaluation. Throughout the process, such notions as standardization, interoperability, and evolution are critical. An interesting point raised during the discussion is a notion of network externality, which roughly means that phenomenon encountered in a large scale network is quite unpredictable and different from small scale network. This means that rapid evolutionary prototyping is a critical part of the methodology for CCSS development, to capture the real requirements in a large community.

We also discussed about platforms for CCSS. Issues such as security, functionality, or openness are critical features of the platform. On the other hand, it was pointed out that one might able to experiment a lot with conventional tools, such as WWW-based systems with database facility.

3.2 Evaluation

Evaluation of CCSS is hard in various ways. It is hard to conduct controlled experiments on CCSS, for the aim of some community might not be consistent with that of its members. Interdependency makes measurement problematic. For example, economic and political factors can act as forces which may compel individuals, groups, or organizations to collaborate. Therefore, 'collaboration' is not necessarily a category 'intent'.

In spite of these difficulties, we have an inventory of measurement and evaluation methods that have been applied elsewhere. For example, office work support systems for business communities might be evaluated by such measures as:

- frequency of communication among workers/month
- productivity of documents/month
- frequency of E-mail sending/month
- frequency of saving E-mails/month
- increase in the speed of knowing or making relationships other workers.

In contrast, evaluation of public services for a citizen community might be made with such measures as:

- the number of getting new information or notices from a government
- the number of new generated citizen groups
- the number of responds to citizen's requests or questions.

For the analysis of MIRROR, a comparison of actual (objective) behavior and perceived (subjective) feedback makes up the overall assessment.

- Objective analysis includes:
  - usage data: performance statistics of interaction between users and the community. E.g., frequency of access, movement in space, total session time, time spent in different worlds, and
  - interaction record between users and the community: analysis of the text files of communication between users and recordings of visual content.
- Subjective analysis includes:
  - observed behavior: actual observation within the worlds. Researches can access and study the community as passive and/or active participants.
  - on-line questionnaires: target sample of users to obtain feed back related to key dimensions in communities and specific aspects of the trial
  - helpline data: problems and issues raised via support, e.g., WWW Helpline. Both technical and usability related issues included.
  - focus groups/cyberfocus groups: Focus groups carried out both face to face and within the community.

3.3 Case study

As a summary of the group discussion, we conducted a brief case study of existing CCSS systems. We chose EdNA, Digital City, and MIRROR, for they are typical examples of CCSS, and some participants have real experience of having been involved with development and experiments with these systems. It might be interesting to include chat rooms and MUD if there is another opportunity of such comparative study. Table 1 summarizes the comparison of these systems in terms of development / evolution, requirement capture, platform, delivery, and evaluation.

4   Future Issues

We consider evaluation and prediction are two issues that are hard enough to deserve further study in future. We have some experiences with evaluating CCSS using classical qualitative and quantitative methods, while they do not always conform with our intuition. Continuous study is required on better methods of evaluation.

Prediction of the effect of CCSS is needed in planning and designing phases of CCSS. Prediction is hard due to the uncertain operation of network externalities – in particular whether or not a sufficient number of people will join the system to arouse other people's participation.

Table 1. Comparison of typical community computing and support systems in use

	EdNA	Digital City	MIRROR
development / evolution	[initially] - information delivery service - the process for developing the information delivery service was itself collaborative and cooperative. [later] - communications technologies gaining in importance.	[initially] - small group hackers [now] - organization has developers in cooperation with advanced users	- multidisciplinary team, involving 3D designers, TV producers, human factors, software designers
requirement capture	[initially] - diversity of stakeholders - to provide Internet services to schools and training organizations as well as universities. - to screen / regulate content so quality ensured [later] - ongoing but has 'scaled down' to specific projects aimed at specific enhancements	[initially] - none, other than designers view [now] - designers and user interaction	- stakeholders technical team - BBC program designers - potential user requirements: e.g., Internet users, TV viewers - platform: security, remote access, speed of system, line to webpages, etc.
platform	- Oracle D/B and Netscape Severs	- Unix and WWW-based system	- has to meet requirements
delivery	- metadata specification and implementation, important for adding value to overall resource plus for each 'sub' community	- free subscription - not anonymous - kicked out after no use for three months	
evaluation	- ongoing, project based	- "by feel": people enter and leaves - discussion meetings of users - debate in bbs - survey and other research	- objective + subjective

Complexity and Adaptation in Community Information Systems: Implications for Design

Michael D. Cohen

School of Information
University of Michigan
Ann Arbor, Michigan, 48109 USA
(mdc@umich.edu)

Robert Axelrod

School of Public Policy
University of Michigan
Ann Arbor, Michigan, 48109 USA
(axe@umich.edu)

Abstract. Recently we have developed a framework for analyzing systems that are complex and adaptive. These properties are characteristic of community information systems. This paper sets out an abbreviated version of our framework. We then apply it to the case of community information systems, with special emphasis on extracting implications for design.

Introduction

How should community information systems be designed? It is not easy to point to principled guidance on such a question. In older fields, such as the design of individual user interfaces, there are now large bodies of research-based literature to rely on. This is not to assert that the interface design process has become mechanical as a result. There will always be important contributions of human inspiration to any activity properly called "design". But still we can see that for individual use of information systems there are systematic principles that can be written and taught, and one finds them in the curricula of the many higher educational institutions that offer training in HCI ("human computer interaction").

For the case of community information systems a whole new realm of difficult issues arises. Many of the phenomena being reported involve the interesting social dynamics that occur as information moves through populations of individuals. Indeed, such movement of information often proves crucial in constituting some portion of a population as a community. Research is beginning to accumulate quite a lot of evidence on what can occur. What is needed now is a usable framework for systematically ordering the observations that are pouring in.

Toward that end, we have found it instructive to consider community information systems as a special case of complex adaptive systems (CAS). We have been working for several years to draw together in a useful form insights about CAS that have developed in scientific work of the last few decades. Our intention in this paper is to apply the framework we have developed for the analysis of complex adaptive systems to the case of community information systems.

We must first set out the framework. We do this, in a highly condensed version, in the next section of the paper. We then use the framework to consider the core notions of this application domain: 'community' and 'information'. Thereafter we develop an example analysis of the use of distribution lists that applies important ideas from the framework, such as: *exploration vs. exploitation* , *norm promotion*, or *interaction proximity*. Throughout the paper we try to orient our remarks toward issues that are of interest to those designing and deploying community information systems, or formulating policies that affect their operation.

A Framework for the Analysis of Complex Adaptive Systems[1]

Design and Policy Making in "Interesting Times"

Our society is enmeshed in a major social transformation, driven in part, and getting much of its distinctive character from, the amazing advances in technologies of information. The rate of technical change in processing, storage, bandwidth, sensing, and effecting is dizzying. The technical changes in turn facilitate large shifts in most of our fundamental institutions: in nation states, communications industries, churches, armies, factories, friendship networks, and more. The rate of social change is intoxicating, disorienting, and probably accelerating.[2]

An Information Revolution invites -- seems to demand -- new system designs at every level of social organization. What shall nation states do about encryption or boundary-spanning financial crimes? What shall families do about the materials their children can easily read? What shall armies do to prepare for attacks on "info-structure"? What shall charitable organizations and firms do about the privacy of records kept on their clienteles? In all these cases and thousands more, deep questions are being asked about interventions that will steer future developments in beneficial directions. In an era where so many customary social, political, and economic arrangements seem up for grabs, what interventions will bring us to a future we would prefer? How can we foresee the likely consequences of the new systems we contemplate?

The approach in this document departs sharply from conventional efforts to foretell our future and draw policy implications for the unfolding Information Revolution. We begin, as have many others, by acknowledging the difficulty of prediction. But we do not proceed by setting those difficulties aside and then doing our best to extrapolate from available theories.

---

[1] This section is adapted from a portion of "A Complex Adaptive Systems Approach to Information Policy", a report presented by Robert Axelrod and Michael Cohen at the Highlands Workshop, Washington D.C., June 8, 1997.

[2] We will refer to the transitions underway as the "Information Revolution", although we hasten to point out that other forces are deeply involved. Transportation, biotechnology, marketing, and a host of other technologies have expanded dramatically in the last half-century. Information technology has fueled these expansions and been shaped by them. Transport in particular has always been intertwined with information, from royal postal roads to express mail and fiber optic cables. While acknowledging these complications, we concentrate here on the Information Revolution, the aspect of our era that seems to us to have the most novel and transforming properties. We use the phrase "Information Age" to indicate a time in the future, perhaps several decades hence, when the effects of current transformations will be more well-established.

Instead, we consider why at this historical and technological juncture we should *expect* the future to be especially difficult to discern. Our answer lies in the *complexity* of the social and technical processes whose rates of change are accelerated. We argue that theories of complex systems are beginning to provide some guidance to those who must make design decisions in a hard-to-predict Information Revolution.

We mean "complexity" in a special sense that requires some careful explanation. After providing that, we go on to show that theories of complex systems -- and particularly complex *adaptive* systems -- are beginning to provide us with better ways of thinking about situations like the ones we confront. Such theories do not currently provide sharp predictions of future states of the world. (Our own interpretation -- not shared by all -- is that they will not do so even when much developed beyond their current infancy.) But in their current form they do give us a grounded basis for inquiring where the "leverage points" and significant tradeoffs of a complex system may lie, what kinds of situations may be resistant to policy intervention, when small interventions may be likely to have large effects, and which kinds of interventions may be surprisingly inconsequential. For guidance to designers such insights into the right questions to be asked can be very valuable, even if the theories are too multiple and too preliminary to support any claim that *the* theory of complexity implies any sharply etched expectation about a future scenario and how a particular intervention will guarantee it.

In the remainder of this section we offer a quite different response to the widespread sense of the unpredictability of our era: an analysis of the reasons why prediction is hard. In the next section, we provide a set of insights into systemic complexity that are consistent with prediction difficulty, and an effort to extend those insights into some useful methods of thinking through policy problems.

In the final section of the paper we apply our proposed methods by examining a series of issues related to the design of community information systems. Our hope is that these applications will have direct value in casting important problems in new light, and will also have two indirect results:

> 1) that our analyses will stimulate others to a treatment of the substantive issues that improves upon ours (We surely do not have "the best perspective" on each issue we discuss.)

> 2) that responses to our analyses will feed back to improve the complexity-oriented analytic approach we have developed.

The starting point of our approach is the difficulty of prediction. Although we all do our best to foresee important consequences, there is widespread acknowledgment that this is extraordinarily hard in the current circumstances of dramatic change. Some of the most famous stories of the half century center on managers and board members at companies like IBM and Intel who were unable to grasp the world-changing character of their own potential products. Industry thought leaders are frank enough to say in 1997 that they first saw the Mosaic Web browser as an inconsequential toy.[3] The National Science Foundation remarks that its panel of distinguished information technology scientists and engineers is consistent in its unwillingness to predict the future.[4] The experience of the unanticipated World Wide Web explosion is fresh in our memories. Sections of the U. S. National Information Infrastructure report were hopelessly out of date less than 18 months after its publication. We have strong reasons to suppose that we may not be able to foretell what is to come.

This wary attitude to prediction is probably healthy, but it presents a severe roadblock to the normal processes of formulating and implementing policies or designs. The standard procedure of design is to develop expectations (predictions) of how the future will unfold, and to define actions we could take or structures we could implement that lead to more desirable predicted futures. This stance can be stretched to accommodate some uncertainty by bringing in Bayesian or other technology for dealing with probability distributions on possible futures. But all the usual approaches grind to a halt if we don't believe we can envision the likely effects of proposed interventions.

A second line of response to the difficulty is offered by various forms of scenario generation.[5] This approach explores what are thought to be major driving forces, looking for policies that are robust over variation in dominant factors and gaining the benefits of preparation for responding to the unexpected as it unfolds. The scenario approach still requires an ability to correctly identify what the major driving forces are, and how they will affect the questions of interest. It can also be hobbled if we cannot say, for example, how a development like fragmentation of social structure will be affected by a technology like low-orbit satellite telephony.

We believe that difficulty of prediction does not make the situation hopeless, although it does require a large shift in the conceptual tactics of social system design. We hope the approach we develop here will complement and strengthen conventional and scenario-building approaches to the future.

When experts are asked to write about the future and its requirements their customary response to this roadblock is to acknowledge the difficulty and then do the best they can with their particular expertise. This is entirely sensible. And retrospection shows that in hard-to-predict moments there often was *someone* who was right about what might happen and had an appropriate sense of what could have been done.[6] But a careful observer of such moments also sees that there were usually many conflicting expert predictions in play, even for the effects of a single factor.

---

[3]Donald Norman, public lecture, School of Information, Ann Arbor, MI, April 23, 1997.

[4]*New York Times* Sunday magazine Special Supplement, April 20, 1997.

[5]A useful brief account of the approach is Lawrence Wilkinson's "How to Build Scenarios" at http://www.wired.com/wired/scenarios/build.html.

[6]In the domain of information technology a nice example is the now "ancient" essay by Vannevar Bush, "As We May Think", in *Atlantic Monthly*, July 1945. (http://geneva.crew.umich.edu:80/~mdc/611/AsWeMayThink.html). One can see him glimpsing something like our World Wide Web fifty years ago, though he thought it would come much sooner than it has.

And, before the fact, there was generally no reliable way to discern which would turn out to be right.

Fortunately we can be confident that many others will take a more tried course of arguing for their best estimates or generating plausible scenarios. We therefore have the luxury to "diversify the intellectual portfolio" by stopping to examine the roadblock that experts usually must bypass. We can ask two questions that are normally set aside:

> 1) "What makes the future of the Information Revolution and the impacts of possible policies so hard to predict?" and

> 2)"Do the causes of the difficulty suggest any new ways of responding to it?"

Our argument is that much of the difficulty of prediction relates to the complexity of the current situation, where, as mentioned, we use the term "complexity" in a special sense that requires a bit of explication.

We do not mean merely that the "Age of Information" is being shaped by many simultaneous factors -- although this is certainly true. This property of "having many moving parts" we propose to render with the word "complicated", and we certainly do think that word applies to the current situation. But there are many systems with lots of moving parts that are nonetheless quite easy to predict -- think of the gigantic number of colliding molecules in a perfect gas. By "complexity" we want to indicate something else: that the system consists of multiple parts and/or processes each of which interacts significantly, and perhaps nonlinearly, with some of the others. Ecologies and brains seem to be well-described as systems that are "complex" in this more specialized sense. Spin glasses are good examples of such systems from physics.[7]

What makes prediction especially difficult in these settings is that the forces shaping the future do not act additively, but rather their effects are via nonlinear interactions among system components. In such worlds events change the probabilities of other events --sometimes dramatically. This is a world of avalanches, of "founder effects" (where small variations make large differences), of self-restoring patterns (in which there can be large disturbances that don't ultimately matter), of apparently stable regimes that suddenly collapse. A collection of complex systems is a kind of dynamical zoo, a "wonder-cabinet" of processes that change (or resist change) in patterns wildly unlike the smoothly additive changes of their simpler cousins. It is not strictly necessary for complexity that there be large numbers of parts or subprocesses, or even that the components follow different laws of action. Some

---

[7]There is still no agreement on precisely defined measures of complexity. Many proposals are review by Seth Lloyd, "Physical Measures of Complexity" in E. Jen, (ed.), *1989 Lectures in Complex Systems* (New York: Addison-Wesley, 1990). A popular review of current debates is provided by George Johnson, "Researchers on Complexity Ponder What It's All About", *New York Times*, May 6, 1997, page B4. Despite this contention, there is enough commonality in examples and approaches to allow us to extract recurring principles and concepts that are useful in considering policies.

very difficult-to-predict complex systems consist of a modest number of identical elements, each of which is simple to describe in isolation, but which become formidable to predict as an interacting ensemble. For example, as few as two Prisoner's Dilemma strategies, each capable of only two actions, can go on for dozens of periods without stabilizing their collective pattern.[8]

We cannot say that there is convergence among theorists who have begun to study complex systems as a class. It is not a field where a crisp and unified theory has already been developed, or is expected in the next few years. But there are recurring themes in the work of complexity researchers, and we think a number of them can be distilled and brought to bear on the problem of analyzing policy and design possibilities in a world that is hard to predict because it is complex.[9] The yield of the enterprise is not a theory that predicts the details of what is to come. We would liken the results instead to the artificial selection principles of animal husbandry (a field that much interested the youthful Darwin). These are methods that do not assure specific outcomes, but do tend to foster increasing value of populations over time -- whether the populations are of livestock, of technical innovations, or new community information systems.

Complex Adaptive Systems

Many complex systems (but by no means all) can be further characterized as being "adaptive". By this we mean that events trigger changes within the system that alter its response to subsequent similar events in ways that change the system's survival chances or improve its performance on some other chosen metric, such as profit or response time. So, classically, the death before reproduction of an organism with certain disadvantageous phenotypic characters reduces the frequency in the subsequent population of the responsible genotype. Subsequently the population has a different response to its environment. It will either have higher viability or be further on its way to extinction as a result of the death. Or, to take an example from an artificial rather than a natural system, a signal that stops an assembly line when a defect is noticed is a standard event in a factory committed to quality improvement. It triggers a process for finding and eliminating the defect's source. Thus it may eventually improve the quality measures that are the chosen metric in this case.

---

[8]Research in recent years has provided the starting components of a literature on the properties of complex systems as a class. Accessible accounts of this work are listed in the Appendix. An interesting entry point to contemporary and classic pieces in the technical literature is the volume edited by R. K. Belew and M. Mitchell (*Adaptive Individuals in Evolving Populations: Models and Algorithms*, (Reading, MA: Addison-Wesley,1996).

[9]A world that is hard to predict because it is complicated can be attacked in quite a different way. Nearly additive contributions of factors means that independent studies of the important factors can later be merged at acceptable cost. As an example, the human genome project is a large bet that much can be understood via such a divide and conquer strategy.

It is worth noting that the highly interactive character of complex systems prepares a fertile ground for adaptiveness. Complex systems are already situations in which events can strongly alter the probability of subsequent events. The property of adaptiveness itself becomes more likely, since systems in which such changes enhance survival will, on average, be around to be observed more than others where this does not occur. Thus there can be said to be a kind of "selection for adaptiveness", even in non-biological settings.

For a system to exhibit adaptive mechanisms that enhance survival (or another chosen metric), it must resolve, either implicitly or explicitly, a very difficult problem of *credit assignment* . If adaptive value is to arise when present events alter the likelihood of future events or patterns, the changes must be the "right" --survival enhancing -- ones, at least to a useful approximation. When an animal (phenotype) loses out to a predator or disease, all copies of the responsible gene set are typically destroyed, and its frequency therefore reduced. This linkage is so tight in evolution that we hardly dwell on it. But a different system could "keep the plan back at the factory". Then destruction of an instance of the plan would not cause the automatic future gene frequency adjustment. Sperm banks are a case of just such a variation in the mechanism of credit assignment, allowing social processes to assign credit along with direct success of the corresponding phenotype in reproductive competition.

While the tightness of the linkage in the ordinary gene pool case is one of the strengths of evolutionary mechanisms in achieving credit assignment, it is still important to see that the problem is only approximately solved. For, in the usual case, only a small portion of the genetic material of the animal is responsible for its fatal defects. (On some occasions of random accident no part may be responsible.) But the individual's entire gene set is destroyed, reducing the frequencies of many worthy genes in the process. So the credit assignment is still approximate, though good enough, it turns out, for the "genetic algorithm" to be able, in many circumstances, to steadily improve the survival prospects of evolving populations.

A. The Relevance to the Information Revolution We see work on complex systems -- and especially on those that are adaptive -- as highly relevant to design and policy deliberations. Our view can be grounded in a little more detail by considering three arguments:

1) It has become widely accepted that a major source of prediction difficulty is the multiplicity of *interacting* forces that are determining the unfolding the Information Revolution. For example, the hard lesson has been learned that technologies are adopted not only as a function of cost, but also as a function of numbers of others adopting (so that inferior technology with a small market lead may become dominant, as in the stories of VHS versus Beta and the QWERTY keyboard).[10] Effectiveness of technology has been observed sometimes to depend on deployment of other

---

[10]Paul David, "Clio and the Economics of QWERTY", *American Economic Review*, vol. 75, 1985, pp. 332-35.

technologies, such as Internet service provision depending on the installed base of telephones.

There have been striking cases of process surprise, such as an (originally expensive) way of replacing carbon paper (xerography) that can upset the security mechanisms of nations as well as altering the conduct of basic office procedures. And cultural variables have been shown to set a controlling context for technical developments, as in rural areas of developing countries that may leap-frog wired communications to go directly to wireless, or when countries with non-alphabetic languages have sharply different approaches to "word-processing". Reaping the benefits of new technology has turned out often to require collateral resources, so that innovations imagined to favor equality can turn out to accelerate differences between social classes. We have learned that the absence in electronic media of socially controlling status cues can unleash embarrassing episodes of "flaming".[11]

These lessons, and many more, have taught us all that virtually every important force in collective life affects the way the Information Revolution plays out: scale economics, technological preconditions, national developmental sequencing, social status, economic inequality, internal security postures, cultural context, and many more forces work to *condition* the development of information technology impacts. This is not unique to our episode of the Information Revolution. The historian William McNeill points out that the Chinese empire, Islam, and the Christian West each gave its own distinctive shape to the movable type revolution in printing. Roughly speaking, the Chinese used printing to reinforce central authority, while Islam suppressed the technology. The Western case is one we will discuss in more detail below. But here we want to point out that these *interactions* are just the kind of non-linear contextual effects that distinguish complex dynamic regimes.

2) If complexity is often rooted in interaction effects, then we might expect systems increasingly to exhibit complex dynamics when changes occur that increase the extent of interaction among their elements. But this, of course, is exactly what information technology advances are doing: reducing the barriers to interaction among processes that were previously isolated from each other in time or space. Information can be understood as the mediator of interaction. Decreasing the costs of its propagation and storage increases possibilities for interaction effects, almost by definition. An Information Revolution is therefore likely to beget a complexity revolution.

3) Reflection on the Information Revolution to date, and on previous waves of major change, shows that adaptation plays a major shaping role. Indeed, buried in the detailed mechanisms of many of the conditioning factors mentioned above there is often an adaptive mechanism. Some are simple, such as network externalities of fax machines, making each new one more valuable than the last. Others are elegant accomplishments of human intellect, such as the propagation of encryption methods by members of subcultures intent on fostering individual liberty at the expense of government potency.

---

[11]Lee Sproull and Sara Kiesler, *Connections: New Ways of Working in the Networked Organization* (Cambridge, MA: MIT Press, 1992).

Adaptive interactions are especially strongly implicated in the Information Revolution. Improvements in processing, storage, transmission, and sensing make it possible for us to know the state of a system with far greater speed and precision. We want this knowledge because it allows us to be more adaptive, and that in turn can vastly increase performance. Anti-lock brakes allow adaptation to road conditions at a time scale faster than native human capabilities. Financial networks allow buying and selling based on global knowledge of price movements that could not earlier be assembled. Effects of military attacks can be known from sensors and satellites allowing adjustments to later attacks. Effects of policies in business and government can be assessed much more accurately and quickly, allowing for adjustments to policies (such as monetary rates, inventory acquisitions, or licenses of new pharmaceuticals) that were unthinkable in previous generations. Much of the promise of the Information Revolution rests on the possibility of increasing the valued adaptiveness of our (often complex) social and technical systems.

Together these three features argue strongly that theories of complex adaptive systems (CAS) promise to be relevant to our Information Age for deep and intrinsic reasons. Dramatic growth in information technology implies, in turn, sharp increases in interaction, complexity and adaptation. To explore this potential relevance we proceed by characterizing a series of patterns that are frequently observed in the study of complex adaptive systems. Then we make use of those patterns in analyzing a set of specific issues where they suggest new approaches to designing community information systems.

B. Fundamentals Complex systems studies are being conducted across a wide range of traditional fields. To note just a few examples: physics (Per Bak on avalanche dynamics), archaeology (George Gummerman on settlement patterns in the ancient southwest), epidemiology (Carl Simon on the spread of HIV via non-random contacts), brain research (Christoph Koch and Francis Crick on the phenomena of consciousness), economics (Brian Arthur on positive scale economies), and computer science (Stephanie Forrest on computer immune systems).

In the typical areas of complexity research, the systems under study have many elements (sometimes referred to as "components", "actors" or "agents"). Those elements are usually seen as instances of several different "types" (e.g., buyers and sellers; Bosnians and Serbs). The elements are connected to each other by relations such as magnetic attraction, organizational authority, electrical stimulation, combat unit loyalty, genetic cross-over, or incentives for economic exchange. The elements are treated as having local patterns of action, based on their individual circumstances. The questions of interest center on the emergent global dynamics of the system. How (or when) does a system of locally trading agents develop prices that will cause market-wide inventories to clear? How does a brain made of interconnected neurons learn? How does a pile of sand generate its characteristic mix of large and small avalanches? How does a gene pool remix itself over time to create and retain genotypes that will be fit for a changing environment? How does a network of trust grow that permits informal credit mechanisms to lubricate trade efficiencies?

It is usual in this approach to view the global properties of the system as emerging from the actions of its parts, rather than seeing the actions of the parts as being imposed from a dominant central source. This is not a denial that there are times when systems have central authorities or dominant influences. But the project of complexity theories in such cases is to understand how those dominant influences come about, what sustains (or undermines) them, and how local action responds in the face of global constraints. An excellent example is the work of Padgett and Ansell on the emergence of the state from marital and commercial networks of medieval Florence.[12]

Complexity research and its focus on emergent system-level properties has received considerable attention recently, in some measure because advances in computation have enabled progress on a number of problems that had long been too difficult for conventional mathematical tools. But it is important to remember that the fundamental orientation of complexity research is actually rooted in long traditions. Adam Smith's hidden hand, the "blind watch-making" of Darwinian evolution, the cell-assembly neuro-psychology of Hebb, and the self-reproducing cellular automata of von Neumann are earlier intellectual developments breaking the same path, uncovering system-level properties produced by the structured interaction of simpler components.

This brief description exhibits much of the working vocabulary of our subsequent discussion. We will focus repeatedly on some *system* of *multiple elements*, which are instances of various *types* enmeshed in a structure of *interactions* that foster the *emergence* of its *system-level properties*.

C. The Usefulness for Design and Policy Analysis Why might this perspective and its associated vocabulary be useful for design of systems or policies in our hard-to-predict Information Age? This is a natural question to ask. After all, the research questions that are being studied may sometimes seem remote. (Do the neurons fire in synchronized waves or incoherently? Are the magnetic poles of particles oriented like those of their near neighbors or are they disarrayed? Do most of the animals in a population continue to exhibit a certain useless trait, or has this type vanished over time?) However, the social issues that can involve many of the same dynamics do not seem remote. (Do similar transactions across the economy take place at one price or many? Does animal husbandry improve the agricultural value of an animal population? Does an infection -- or use of the Internet -- become endemic in certain subpopulations? Do citizens remain loyal to a single large state, or transfer their loyalties to several smaller ones?)

What can be observed here is one fundamental reason that the approach is relevant: the occurrence in social systems of dynamic patterns analogous to those of other systems -- physical, biological, and computational.

A second basis of the approach's value is the fact that many social policy instruments are directed, at least in substantial part, toward controlling the interaction

---

[12]J. Padgett and C. Ansell, "Robust Action and the Rise of the Medici, 1400-1434", *American Journal of Sociology*, 1993.

of types: segregation (and integration) of races; visa and immigration rules; entry qualifications to religious and social organizations; "cultural revolutions" and "peace corps" that send the highly educated to less developed areas; political (re)districting; zoning restriction of commercial, industrial and residential activities; film, television and Internet ratings to facilitate matching of audiences and contents; or foster care systems that place children with adults different from their parents.

Many other policies have important or interesting side effects that are related to interactions of types: e.g., imprisonment that mixes experienced criminals with rebellious adolescents; public transit patterns that separate urban center residents from suburban jobs; armies of occupation that result in children of intermarriage; computer networks for defense and science that increase communication of parents with college-distant children and facilitate finding of long-lost friends; and so on.

D. Change Mechanisms and Design Principles Our aim is to exploit the resemblance of change processes often seen in CAS scientific work to those of social systems that are now occurring in the Information Revolution. It is our argument that principles derived from working with CAS research problems shed valuable light on the issues confronting designers and policy makers in the Information Revolution.

We can begin to develop this argument by characterizing a set of CAS change mechanisms. We cannot hope to provide any sort of exhaustive catalog. But it will be useful to show how an array of examples fall into a few useful clusters. A key to simplifying our task is the observation that most of the mechanisms and related principles that have policy relevance, center on:

1) changes in the number and/or relative frequency of the system's types, or

2) the way that type variability is channeled over time through the network of interactions among the elements.

3) the operation of credit assignment and adaptation mechanisms to alter the existence and frequencies of types.

These are necessarily rather abstract issues. We can put some intuition into them by expanding them in turn. In each case we provide examples from complex systems studies, along with examples from social systems with more intuitive connections to policy and design concerns. (For example, we discuss similarities between crossover mechanisms that recombine genetic materials and deliberate invention activities that recombine high order concepts -- such as "horseless carriage" and "engine horse-power".) We go on in each section to summarize observations about the recurring useful concepts that have developed as a result of CAS research in the area.

1. Mechanisms That Alter Frequencies Complex systems, whether adaptive or not, generally have a population of agents that are instances of various possible types, and they have mechanisms that create, destroy and transform agents. The prototypical case of this is probably a breeding population of organisms each instantiating some genotype. Death is the most obvious mechanism, destroying agents and possibly destroying a genotype if all its instances die.

In this genetic case, *mutation* is an important source of variance, and it can function to create new types, as well as to alter the relative frequencies of existing types. It is striking that many kinds of CAS have mechanisms that function similarly to mutation. For example, *temperature* in systems where the elements have energy levels, such as annealing of metals, also functions to "mutate" atomic arrangements into new configurations. *Process errors* in factories and laboratories can have this same impact of creating new types (as with the accidental discovery of the inkjet principle in the "malfunction" of a research laboratory syringe). And there are many other processes that introduce *"noise"* into operations of copying or re-creation and thereby produce variants (sometimes novel ones).

The mechanisms mentioned in this group tend to have certain properties in common. They introduce variation into the system of interest from uncontrolled forces external to the system, such as radiation, external heat, or disruptions of quality control. As a result of the uncorrelated, exogenous source of variation in types, most of the variants introduced into orderly systems by such processes are deleterious -- with a sprinkling of very rare spectacular advances. Exploring for new possibilities by nearly random variation, can therefore be expensive. (In fact, it is even slower than enumerating all the possibilities, since random generation will add duplication. With random variation, you examine each piece in the haystack and put it back if it isn't the needle.)

By contrast, there are a number of other mechanisms that produce new types and change in relative frequencies in a more targeted, less uncorrelated, fashion. They tend to be endogenous, triggered by events internal to the system in which they operate. Some examples are: *selection* mechanisms that create copies of the better elements from some set and eliminate others; and *imitation* mechanisms that transform an element by making it into a copy of some other element. Both of these tend, over time, to reduce the variety of types in a finite system, although in the beginning they may increase the relative frequency of some rare types. Neither mechanism generates novel types (except through error in copying, as discussed above).

There are also endogenous mechanisms that do create new types. In biology one of the most studied is *crossover*, a process of recombining genetic contributions from each of two parents. This mechanism can also create novel types, but it is vastly different from mutation. It works with pieces of already viable genetic material, and so is far more likely to yield an improvement instead of a lethal mutation. It has long been noted that self-conscious activities of deliberate invention have similar properties. This can be seen clearly in early forms of inventions, such as the motor and wagon combinations of the first "horseless carriages" or the self-conscious decomposition used by the Wright brothers to define subproblems of airplane design that could be independently attacked.[13] *Constraint relaxation* is another such mechanism, frequently practiced in human problem solving. It seeks solutions to a hard problem by generating variants that violate some one of the situation's constraints. It introduces new variants by starting with materials of established feasibility and modifying them. A nice example is "slippery water", a chemical additive that increases water volume reaching a fire by reducing friction of water inside pipes and pumps, relaxing what had seemed to be a given physical constraint.

In crossover, constraint relaxation, and deliberate inventive recombination we have examples of mechanisms that can create new types or change relative frequencies, and that operate internally, in some degree of correlation with the system's other conditions. Mechanisms like these are commonly found in complex *adaptive* systems. They implicitly exercise criteria in their creation of new elements, and therefore have an improved chance of meeting the need for *credit assignment* characteristic of CAS.

1a. Exploration versus Exploitation

Work over the years with these various complex system mechanisms for creating, transforming, and destroying elements (and therefore types) has led an important tradeoff principle, usually referred to as: "Exploration versus Exploitation". It captures the tension in complex adaptive systems between creation of untested types that may be superior to what currently exists versus using copies of tested types that have so far proven best. This tradeoff characterization has turned out to be illuminating across a wide range of settings from simple genetics to organizational resource allocation, wherever the testing of new types comes at some expense to realizing benefits of those already available.[14] Two extremes illustrate the tradeoff:

"Eternal Boiling". Levels of mutation, temperature, or noise can be so high that the system remains permanently disorderly, any preliminary valuable formations being broken apart before they can be put to use. Exploration completely swamps exploitation.

"Premature Convergence". Needed variability can be lost, for example by very speedy imitation of an initial success, cutting off future system improvements. Exploitation quickly swamps exploration.

More generally, investments in options and possibilities associated with "exploration" frequently come at the expense of obtaining returns on what has already been learned, "exploitation". An early and striking exposition of the tradeoff occurred in the context of the "two-armed bandit problem", in which a player with a fixed

---

[13]M. D. Cohen, "The Power of Parallel Thinking", *Journal of Economic Behavior and Organization*, vol. 2, 1982, pp. 285-306.

[14]John Holland gave any early formalization of this point in *Adaptation in Natural and Artificial Systems* (Ann Arbor: University of Michigan Press, 1975). James March applies it to organizational management in "Exploration and Exploitation in Organizational Learning," *Organization Science*, vol. 2(1), 1991, pp. 71-87.

supply of coins plays two slot machines that have unknown and potentially different rates of payoff. To decrease sampling error in estimates of which machine pays more, and thereby increase long-run expected gains, coins should be played on both machines. But to maximize gain in the short run, coins should be played on the machine that is currently estimated as best-paying.

The tradeoff can be seen in many different practical situations. For example, companies must decide whether to invest resources, such as capital and management attention, in developing ideas for wholly new products or in marketing, refining -- or reducing costs of -- existing products. We apply the tradeoff idea below to design issues that arise in structuring asynchronous conversations.

1.b. Extinction

A second concept nicely illustrated by the mechanisms that destroy elements is the possibility of the total loss of a type in systems with discrete elements. Some researchers have taken to calling this the "nano-fox" problem after predator-prey theories that have continuous numbers of animals in them, growing and shrinking by proportionality constants. In these continuous theories a tiny fraction of a predator is always around, so that no matter how severe the starvation, the predator population will rebound as soon as prey return. There is no complete extinction in such models. But in real populations the difference between having a few animals and zero animals is usually not just a little extra waiting time. Recreating a lost type is very unlikely and occupation of the vacant ecological niche by another species is far more to be expected.

Again there are numerous analogs to design and policy settings. The legal system distinguishes death from the most severe and permanent incapacitation. Bankruptcy has quite different effects on a firm's history than mere extreme debt. These "zero-points" in social situations correspond to sharp changes in the later dynamics. Compare what can happen before or after a life-supported patient is declared legally dead.

A related notion is that all possible types already exist in tiny quantities. It is akin to Plato's notion of discovery as a form of remembering truths already dimly known. Again the discrete complex systems view is that a new idea may not be "waiting in the wings" for the circumstances that will bring it rapidly to prominence. It matters enormously whether the number of people who have thought of it is one or zero. We see this when we observe, once a theorem is known to be true, how readily theorists obtain the second and subsequent --shorter and more elegant -- proofs. The distinction has relevance for policy strategies such as "counting on the market to find a solution", which can be expected to work far more rapidly and reliably in domains where several approaches have been partially worked out, as opposed to domains in which a feasible approach is yet to be conceived.

The underlying source of this sharp effect of zero is that copying mechanisms generally work quite differently from synthetic mechanisms that have the power to create new types correlated with the context. So, for a social example, we have imitation in a traditional social system, where the procedure of others is carried out exactly, without explicit justification of details. It is a copying process that can rapidly spread an existing type, such as double entry bookkeeping or the Grameen banking system for micro-credit. But imitation of other procedures -- even with random error -- will only very rarely invent such types where they have never existed.

2. Patterns of Interaction Thus far we have focused on the mechanisms that create and destroy types in complex systems, and on principles associated with those mechanisms. But very often the events of interest within a system arise from the interactions of its components. Trades occur when buyer meets seller. New animals are created when a male and female breed. Religious communities grow as adherents proselytize the uninitiated. This observation suggests a second category of mechanisms that shape the dynamics of complex systems: the processes and/or structural factors that determine which elements (or types) will interact with which others.

CAS research suggests that it is useful to distinguish two classes of determinants of interaction: *proximity* and *activation*, how elements come to be near each other and how the sequencing of their activity is determined. The distinction, with good reason, roughly generalizes that between space and time.

Proximity is a general term that makes visible the commonalities among a range of factors that make particular elements likely to interact. The most obvious of these is the physical space in which buyers and sellers, frogs and flies, Democrats and Republicans, friend and foe, all play out their lives. Nearby location in 2- or 3- dimensional space makes interaction events more likely for a wide range of processes, from pollination and friendship formation to predation and enemy formation. Normally, we pay less attention to a host of other relational networks that establish "proximity", such as organizational hierarchies, old friendship ties, or community group affiliations. But these pseudo-spaces also determine which interactions are more likely, and thus profoundly influence the spread of rumor and disease, the finding of jobs and marriage partners, and the occurrence of crimes and kindnesses.

This substantial list of proximity factors -- though only a brief sampler -- has mostly been discussed as a set of static forms within which faster processes play out -- hunting prey in physical space, or finding jobs in friendship networks. But CAS research often shows that on larger time scales the relationship can be reversed. Neighborhoods may shape the choices of house buyers, but housing purchases may ultimately (re)shape neighborhoods. An exogenous given in a short time frame may be an endogenous result in a longer one. And just as with movement that alters spatial proximity, so most of the other proximity factors mentioned have associated change processes: business hierarchies are reorganized to make some groups closer together and to move others farther apart; friendship links form and dissolve; community groups are joined and left, formed and disbanded; barriers and boundaries are deliberately introduced into systems (physical and social) with the aim of altering the rates of interactions among types. Indeed, as work by Riolo has shown, even random numerical *tags* can provide an arbitrary pseudo-space in which model agents can relocate themselves to cluster with others who interact beneficially with them.[15]

Activation is a general term that groups together many different processes that affect the temporal structure of component activity. Just as many different factors can be analogs of space in determining interaction likelihoods, so many factors can alter the temporal structure of events. CAS research often shows that it is very valuable to distinguish systems with externally "clocked" activations, such as budget cycles or seasonally triggered agricultural processes, from endogenously activated processes in which results of the current event control which events may next occur. Some examples of endogenously activated processes are: the movement of a sand-grain in pile that makes other grains more likely to move, the activation of neuron that makes other neurons more likely to reach an activation threshold, and the mobilization of a citizen that increases the chances that those who are socially proximate to her will become active in her cause.

The distinction of exogenous from endogenous activations is again strongly relevant to the adaptive aspects of complex systems. Markets where every actor can trade one unit per session work very differently from markets where the actors with the strongest demands can trade much more frequently than others.[16] In Anglo-American intellectual traditions, it is typical to expect the adaptive capacity of a system -- especially a firm or market -- to be increased when events can be triggered locally and flexibly rather than globally and rigidly. But it is vital to point out that adaptive capacity is *two-edged*. As we saw in the simple case of population effects of organism death, adaptive capacity can speed extinction as well as increase of viability. Allowing traders to respond to local conditions can let them exploit short-lived arbitrage possibilities. But it can also let them make ever riskier trades to cover their own losses. In general, we have acknowledged this two-edged sword by defining adaptation neutrally, allowing for changes in system survival chances -- both up and down.

Once again there is an important tradeoff principle inherent in these observations. It is not identical to "explore versus exploit", but it has a similar flavor. Where structural arrangements affecting proximity or activation are designed or analyzed, a major question is often the extent to which positive feedback loops are possible in proximity and activation. Can elements move "nearer" to other elements that benefit them? Can elements be repeatedly active if they experience (or help create) extreme conditions? At issue is whether interactions will be concentrated among a few pairs of types or will be spread across a wide range of type pairings. The interactions might be accomplishing any mix of exploring and exploiting, which is why the tradeoff

---

[15]R. L. Riolo, "The Effects of Tag-Mediated Selection of Partners in Evolving Populations Playing the Iterated Prisoner's Dilemma," Santa Fe Institute Working Paper 97-02-016, February 1997.

[16] It is striking that in non-monogamous biological populations, females often follow the once-per-period principle while males can be active in proportion to fitness and fortune. Thus both designs are mixed in one system, blending the intense and diffuse interaction modes we will describe below.

involved is not identical. What is involved is rather the tradeoff between "intense versus diffuse" interactions among types.

So, for example, systems in which reproductive or copying activity is rapidly triggered by apparent success are highly responsive to current signals, but prone to loss of variety and premature convergence. Industries where firms that make decisions about new production technology on an annual cycle may look "stodgy" compared to industries where firms quickly imitate their competitors' production methods. But they run less risk of everyone "flocking" to the same method. This quick copying avoids waste if the new method is better in all circumstances than those abandoned. But it can be disastrous if the "winning type" turns out to have bad consequences in the long run and the suppliers for the alternative methods have meanwhile gone out of business. This particular illustration shows how greater activation intensity might foster excess exploitation. But there is nothing inherent about this alignment. Diffuseness of type interactions can also lead to insufficient exploration -- or, in other circumstances, insufficient exploitation. The point about the intense/diffuse tradeoff is that it generates a set of questions that need to be asked about how the channeling of proximity and activation in a complex adaptive system will affect the exploration-exploitation balance. Those questions do not have context-free answers.

"Edge of Chaos" arguments, have received wide attention for claiming that evolutionary systems tend to structure their interconnectedness so as to achieve a good balance between exploration and exploitation. A typical example of such arguments is work of Stuart Kauffman[17] arguing that evolutionary processes adjust what we are calling intensity of proximity and activation so that systems are likely to avoid both "premature convergence" and "eternal boiling". The claim is much debated,[18] but the debate is whether some parts of nature tend to a particular balance in the tradeoffs we have described, not whether the tradeoffs exist. Kauffman believes that systems tuned to a favorable balance between exploration and exploitation will tend differentially to survive. This brings us quite naturally to our third topic.

3. Credit Assignment We have looked in previous sections at the mechanisms that create and destroy types and at the processes and structures that govern interaction among types. These are two key clusters of concepts that support analysis of complex systems. But if the systems are adaptive, then we must consider a third cluster of concepts, dealing with what we have called *credit assignment* to types.

An important initial distinction is between implicit and explicit criteria in credit assignment. For example, if an organism is highly fit, credit is implicitly assigned to its genes by copying them -- or variations of them -- into many offspring. No theory

---

[17]Stuart Kauffman, *The Origins of Order: Self-Organization and Selection in Evolution*. (New York: Oxford University Press, 1993).

[18]M. Mitchell, P. Hraber, and J. P. Crutchfield, "Revisiting the Edge of Chaos: Evolving Cellular Automata to Perform Computational Tasks," *Complex Systems* vol. 7, 1993, pp. 89-130.

or alternate representation of the organism's world is involved in this process. On the other extreme, companies often allocate end of year performance bonuses to individuals whose contributions are determined by explicit criteria, such as total sales. This is intended to cause subsequent emulation of the rewarded action on the theory that the actions (such as sales) are good for the overall organization.

Our definition of "adaptive" has been that events alter future events so as to change the survival chances of the system. The main events of interest are creation, destruction and interaction among types. Credit assignment occurs when an event, like type creation, becomes more likely because of an event that altered (say, increased) system survival chances. So, for example, the birth of a population member good at obtaining food (which may favor survival), results in multiple offspring (creating more instances of a successful type). In this case, the reproductive process of the population has implicitly assigned credit to the genotype of this particular food-finder. In the year-end bonus example, an explicit credit assignment has been designed to encourage imitation of the type of the high-performing salesperson.

Typically, both implicit and explicit credit assignment mechanisms have serious limitations. If we spend a little time examining the two categories we can see that to some extent the weaknesses are complementary, and this introduces another tradeoff principle, this time between implicit and explicit credit assignment.

3.a. Implicit Credit Assignment Mechanisms

Many complex systems besides biological populations have implicit mechanisms that accomplish a credit assignment. A characteristic property of traditional practices, for example, is that they spread by imitation of the practice of successful individuals. Often there is not a detailed causal analysis of how the particular elements of a given practice might contribute to the success. Credit is assigned to the whole practice, which is repeated with as much detailed fidelity as possible. This gives rise to Little League baseball players who emulate the spitting habits of their Major League idols. When causation is not clear, individuals even imitate their own prior practices, as when a person develops an attachment to a lucky pair of socks. Because the fundamental logic of these processes is to copy successful types, the typical errors are to assign credit to the whole type when only a part is responsible, or to assign credit to a type when the result arises from an interaction of types. This kind of error results in what social psychologists call the "Fundamental Attribution Error", crediting an event to the disposition of an individual rather than to the situation.

An instructive biological case is "founder effects", such as an island populated by red-spotted birds descended from a red-spotted pair that were among the first to reach the locale. In the early history of a population an outstandingly fit individual has offspring that form a large portion of the next generation. Incidental traits of that "founder" are then carried widely through the population, although the traits themselves may not confer any reproductive value. But they co-occurred with traits that do have value, and the implicit mechanism of credit assignment works at a coarse-grained, whole-individual, level that does not distinguish the valuable traits from the incidental.

3.b. Explicit Credit Assignment Mechanisms

On the *explicit* side of credit assignment we have many examples in human systems: prices as signals of value; myriad theories of causal sequences -- some valid, some superstitious; learning processes that develop reputations of others for effectiveness or trustworthiness; detailed methods of program evaluation, experimental design, and statistical inference. None of these work perfectly either, though the more refined and expensive mechanisms may avoid some important errors.

A biological example of limitations in explicit credit assignment arises in mimicry -- as when another species takes on the coloration of monarch butterflies whose taste is repulsive to predator birds. This works because birds develop a "prediction" of taste from appearance and rely on it to avoid both monarchs and their imitators. One presumes that the capability to associate taste expectations with appearances, which is an explicit credit assignment mechanism, serves the birds well overall. But its occasional inaccuracies can also be exploited -- in this case by the implicit cleverness of differential survival for monarch look-alikes. Non-biological explicit credit assignment has similar limits, of course. The high performing sales person may receive a bonus and be emulated. Years later more careful cost accounting may show that most of the sales actually lost money for the firm because of eventual refunds or support costs.

We have seen that both implicit and explicit credit assignment mechanisms can make what an outsider might call "errors". From an intra-systemic point of view, however, it is not always possible to speak of "errors". If system survival is the objective function, then credit assignment mechanisms affect it as they do. And their effects define what is the system that does survive. Only when the representational capacities and agency of organisms come into play can there be explicit mechanisms, embodying representations of the system, its types, and its goals.

Credit assignment schemes are almost always imperfect. The implicit and explicit families of credit assignment mechanisms have somewhat complementary weaknesses. Limitations of implicit mechanisms stem from ignoring fine structure or context. Limitations of explicit mechanisms stem from focusing on wrong, insufficient, or poorly measured aspects of fine structure or context. Thus a designer or analyst of a CAS can be aided by attending to another tradeoff: between the problems caused by inaccuracies of implicit omission versus those of explicit commission. For example, in work teams there can be implicit assessment of individual's relative contributions formed over the course of doing the work together. There can also be explicit mechanisms of supervisors observing team members and rating specific attributes of their performance. Both systems can have problems, but they are different in character. Implicit evaluation can fail to give credit to individuals whose contributions are not readily visible. Retrospective studies of pharmaceutical R&D labs have found cases where a few unhonored individuals may have had a hand in most of the laboratory's important results.[19] On the other hand, explicit evaluation can be driven by supervisorial theories of the work that do not match the tacit knowledge skilled workers have of the actual tasks. The comparative strengths of implicit versus explicit evaluation will be at issue in our discussion below of criteria used in assessing community information systems.

Multiple Adaptive Processes

Finally, it bears mentioning that complex systems can often have multiple adaptive processes. This gives rise to another whole cluster of principles that center on the relative speeds of the adaptive processes. In most situations labeled *coadaptation* the processes are presumed to be acting at roughly comparable rates. This is a reasonable way to look at social processes. An off-beat example is the coadaptation of states that sell lottery tickets and citizens who buy them. Citizens learn to play or not to play, while states learn what fraction of the players to reward with what sized returns. Across many US states this coadaptation has converged on a similar shared implicit notion of a fair return on a wagered dollar (about 44 cents).[20]

When rates of adaptation differ widely among processes in one system, there can be many important consequences. Fast processes, like intense activation or proximity, can alter the balance of exploration and exploitation.

And it is often observed that in hierarchical complex systems, adaptive processes of varying rates tend to be associated with different hierarchical levels. Herbert Simon's beautiful essay on "The Architecture of Complexity" pointed this out thirty years ago, when he noted that goal setting, a major adaptive mechanism in firms, tends to operate slowly and on major long-term features of the goal structure at high levels of management, and rapidly on day to day aspects of performance at lower levels.[21] For example, top management may ask "What markets will we be in this year?" while supervisors on the floor ask "What should be today's production target?"

This catalog of concepts useful in structuring and managing the interactions within complex adaptive systems is necessarily brief and abstract. But it equips us with a tool kit we can bring to bear on a wide variety of issues that we must confront in designing systems and policies in the Information Revolution. We turn first to considering the concepts central to defining "community information systems". This is followed by a section that revisits major ideas from the framework, illustrating each one by applying it to design issues that arise in community information systems.

---

[19]J. N. Baron and K. N. Cook, "Process and Outcome Perspectives on the Distribution of Rewards in Organizations," *Administrative Science Quarterly*, 37, 1992, pp. 191-197.

[20]J. Cross analyzes this situation in *A Theory of Adaptive Economic Behavior* (New York: Cambridge University Press, 1983).

[21]Herbert Simon, *Sciences of the Artificial* (Cambridge: MIT Press, 1969)

Applying the Framework to 'Community' and 'Information'

Community In the approach we have outlined, a *community* can naturally be seen as a complex adaptive system. The patterned interactions among its members sustain themselves for some period of time. In this view, a community appears as a kind of breeding ground -- not accidentally, but essentially. Interactions among members are constantly giving rise to actions and ideas that entail further interactions. Those actions and ideas may be relatively unchanging or may rapidly evolve, but in any case they implicitly produce, maintain, modify, or dissolve the boundaries of the community.

On this view, an arbitrary subset of a larger population (say "all mothers of exactly four children") does not make a community. Such a subset may have some interactions among its "members". But what would move such a subset toward the status of a genuine community would be interactions that engender subsequent interactions among agents of this type. Examples might be recurring exchanges of useful information, identification of shared concerns, or the creation of a targeted communication channel such as a newsletter or a weekly support group meeting.

We do not see this for mothers of exactly four children, but we do for other subsets of mothers, such as those whose children have specific diseases or disabilities. Sometimes the definition of such a group is explicitly tied to a shared concern, as in Mothers Against Drunk Driving (MADD). Sometimes the communication is a side effect of other purposes, as among mothers of *any* number of children who come together via Parent-Teacher Associations. We note that mothers of four children could become a genuine community. It would only require something to make exactly four children especially significant (e.g., a tax ruling, or a superstition).

In the neighborhood where we live, parents gathering to support the production of school plays has spawned a group producing their own plays, "The Burns Park Players". A latent community of mothers (and fathers) who liked putting on plays came together and discovered itself in the process of supporting school activities. No doubt the budding off of this now separate community was made much easier by telephones, faxes, copying machines, and, increasingly, eMail. Differentiation of communities has an important resemblance to speciation from a CAS point of view.

In this perspective it seems clear why members of a logical category (such as mothers of exactly four children) are not necessarily a community. And we see how the residents of a geographical area may mistakenly be regarded as a community. Their common geography can be merely a logical grouping. They may be socially and politically inert. The art of community organizers (or labor organizers), is to bring such a subset of actors into a condition of self-sustaining and effective interaction.[22]

In part, community membership seems to be distinguished from membership in a logical or geographical category by some form of commitment. It does not make

---

[22]A classic statement is Saul Alinsky's *Rules for radicals; a practical primer for realistic radicals,* New York, Vintage Books, 1972.

sense to talk of a community of radio towers, even if they do bounce signals off each other. It might make sense to talk of a community of robots programmed to pursue a common goal.[23] It definitely makes sense to talk of the community of people who are working to elect a political candidate or who meet to enact a shared religion. These latter cases are distinguished by commitments, various forms of binding the self to the community.

The *objects of commitment* can vary widely across communities. There can be commitment: to activities (Friday nights in the corner pub); to specific others (survivors of a crash); to the -- possibly changing -- membership of an explicitly identified group (the trend-setting online conference, "The WELL"). And the *bases of commitment* can differ, and hence vary in their influence on an individual's actions: a simple expectation of gain (commitment to attending job training classes); a notion of what is valuable (commitment to the Shaker Furniture Club); an identity (commitment to a gay identity support group). As we shall see, the varying objects and bases of commitment that may play important roles in constituting communities, also enter into the allocations of credit that occur within those communities and give them distinctive dynamics.

Information In the view we have put forward, *information* takes on a community-based meaning. Faced as we are with the technology of the Information Revolution as an overwhelming source of metaphor, it is tempting to think of information itself as a kind of stuff. But pulses on a wire or letters on a page are an incomplete notion of information. The voltage on the wire and the alphabet are media within which patterns can be created and detected. But without detectors whose actions are conditional on the patterns, there is no point in regarding them as information. Our conversations on this point with our colleague George Furnas have pushed us to say that information is a detectable pattern on which action can be conditioned. (So we end up rewriting an old claim: "Beauty is in the conditional action system of the beholder.")

If one really pushes this view, there is information in any causal interaction, from the collision of billiard balls to a reading of the Gettysburg Address. An old tennis ball conveys information, once a dog has given it new meaning -- training her owner to throw it for her by bringing it back. It is less common to think of artifacts like a ball in this way, but notice that it reproduces detectable and meaningful patterns in both actors' (distinctive) sensory fields, and these patterns condition action.

For some purposes, this view of information might be too all-encompassing, but for our purposes it has two extremely useful consequences:

> 1) it directs our attention onto *detectable patterns*, and this has rich implications via our elaboration of the notions of *copies* and *types*; and
> 2) it emphasizes the role of the *community* in determining the *meaning* of the information that it generates and detects.

---

[23]Arthur W. Burks, *Robots and Free Minds*, Ann Arbor : College of Literature, Science, and the Arts, The University of Michigan, 1986.

Once information is defined as action-conditioning pattern, copying comes into play as the reproduction of pattern. Communities use information systems to propagate copies of significant patterns, whether those are bits of gossip, coordinating commands, or emotion-charged symbols. We can therefore ask the kinds of questions suggested by our framework: : what credit assignment processes in a community define ideas, action patterns, or actors as significant types? what processes in a community create copies of significant types?, what alters the frequencies of types? how are variations introduced among types?, how do community information systems affect the rates of interaction among types? These are among the questions that will be explored in our next section.

Information Systems   These views of community and information suggest that *information systems* almost always will be seen to play a crucial role in maintaining communities. The "systems" maybe as humble as the reciting of epic poems about ancestors, the whispering places that propagated the news in Cervantes' pre-newspaper Madrid, or Judaism's ritual cycle of reading aloud a from sacred text.[24] They may be as technically sophisticated as eMail distribution lists, ethnic cable stations, Internet "push channels", or "samizdat" underground publishing with photocopiers.

It is natural for us to think mostly of the more sophisticated cases.   Our contemporary era has focused heavily on explicit technology in self-consciously designed systems.   But it is useful to recognize that the idea of community information systems is far more general. The traditional cases, however "low tech", can still be highly instructive. Office water coolers still function like the whispering places in the plazas of old Madrid. The information that employees can get at their company's official website is often not half so interesting as what they may learn from meeting each other at the shared network printer.

Given the framework we have sketched, we now can summarize our characterization of a "community information system". We take this phrase as denoting the facilities that convey detectable and (potentially) meaningful patterns among a set of individuals within a larger population who (may) share some traits, pursuits or interests. This set of individuals is the (potential) community.   The facilities may rest upon structures that are accidental (visible distinctive footprints), traditional (songs of field hands), or thoughtfully designed (aliases for Internet distribution lists).   The commitments that may be orchestrated may be uniformly shared by all (fans of Marilyn Monroe), diverse but complementary (business operators along Main Street), or even constructively antagonistic (buyers and sellers of rare stamps).   But if there is to be a sustained pattern of interaction among the individuals that realizes, and perhaps transforms, their commitments, some kind of

---

[24]A rich account of an apparently simple information system is given by John Seely Brown and Paul Duguid, in "The Social Life of Documents", *first monday*, issue #1, 1996, http://www.firstmonday.dk/issues/issue1/documents/index.html .

information system is likely to play an essential role. And increasingly, it may be a system that is, in some part, deliberately designed.

Applying Ideas from the Framework to A Design Case

We can now illustrate a number of the framework elements by examining a hypothetical instance of community information system design: the introduction of new distribution list (DL) into and organizational eMail system. This is an extremely simple case, but it proves to be quite rich and demonstrates the implications of some of the principal ideas in the framework presentation.

Consider a set of colleagues -- say about half a dozen -- who work in several different divisions of a company, and have frequently found themselves attending meetings where parts of the discussion centered on ideas for new products. A number of pairwise eMail exchanges have occurred among members of the set, frequently with copies to some of the others via the eMail cc: capability. Now one member of the set is considering whether to establish a DL for the group within the company's eMail directory. This DL-founder must decide: whether to establish the list; who exactly to include; whether to allow the list to be one freely joined by others in the company, or joined only with her permission; and whether to use the default name for the list offered by the system ("DL674"), or choose another more meaningful name ("newProducts!"). What might be the ramifications of these simple choices?

The immediate expected effect of introducing the name is to alter the pattern of interactions among the group's members. Messages that were moving among pairs and triplets of individuals will now be seen, and subject to comment, by all the DL's members.[25] If the DL is used, it seems quite likely that for any member of the DL the number of message he sends that are seen by other members will rise, as will the number sent by other members that he will see. In this sense intra-list interaction intensity rises, and interaction *proximity* has been increased for the list members by the creation of the DL. In consequence, the extent of shared background and meaning among the DL members can be expected to rise as the list is used.

The principal intent of introducing the list, in this hypothetical case, was to increase exploration of new product possibilities. But we cannot say in general that DLs will favor *exploration* vs. *exploitation*. Even in the hypothetical setting, whether the effect would realize the intent would depend on the opportunity cost: the other interactions not engaged in as a result of the DL introduction. In order to be active in the new products DL its members might put less energy into searching for lower priced inputs to current products (so that the shift would be away from exploitation).

---

[25] The organization's mix of "near" and "far" network linkages will also have been changed. The large potential effects of such changes are studied in the recent doctoral dissertation of sociologist Duncan Watts: "The Structure and Dynamics of Small-World Systems", Cornell University Ph.D. Dissertation, August 1997. A related study of the alternative possible effects of such network changes is by Marshall van Alstyne and Erik Brynjolfssson: "Could the Internet Balkanize Science?" , *Science*, vol. 274, 29 November 1996, pp. 1479-1480. A later, longer version is at http://web.mit.edu/marshall/www/InfoAccess.html .

But they might put less energy into talking to dissatisfied former customers (so that the net shift would be neutral, or perhaps even away from exploration). The tradeoffs are not a property of DLs per se, but rather of the interaction of the mechanism with the situation into which it is introduced. This is the kind of difficulty of prediction that follows from the complex adaptive character of the community that is changing its information system. Our framework does not provide fixed predictions of the effects of particular mechanisms. Indeed, it makes us skeptical of many such predictions. It does bring into focus a coherent cluster of important questions to examine in an actual design setting.

Just as we cannot say in general that introduction of a DL will shift the community toward exploration of new product possibilities, so we cannot be sure that it will substitute interaction *intensity* for interaction *diffuseness*. Whether that will happen is again a situational matter, depending on the interaction of the DL mechanisms with the mental models and preexisting social structure of those working in the company -- both those in the DL and those outside it. Presumably, there are many other competing claims on the attention of all the members. Some of those claims will get less attention if the DL gets more (conservation of attention being a fundamental law of social life). A DL member might respond to the increase in messages it creates by filtering out or withdrawing from some other DL. Overall diffuseness of message interactions could actually increase in such a case. Some might adapt by replying more tersely to many other messages that they receive. This could have the effect of increasing rates of misunderstanding, an effect similar to the occurrence of additional random *errors of copying*.

Typically, a DL-founder cannot know what these responses to its resulting loads will be, and therefore must risk wide variation in the possible effects of the intervention (along with other interventions like it). This suggests that some control of information system design might usefully be located at another organizational level, where there might be better overview of the responsibilities and action patterns of the whole organization. This is a point to which we will return briefly below.

In the initial period after the introduction of the DL a number of events can be expected to occur that will importantly shape its eventual course. Members will become aware of it, perhaps by receiving an introductory message sent to the group. Then they will choose to use it, or to continue sending messages directly to smaller sets of individuals. Those groups may not be proper subsets of the membership named by the founder. Or they may be proper subsets, but some members may feel the DL membership is too inclusive so that content for the subset is not appropriate for all. Such misalignments of membership with the DL members' intentions will complicate its coming into reliable use.

But if the DL becomes frequently used, its existence may then alter the content of the messages composed. This is the normal dialectic of "structuration" in which short-lived actions may lay down long-term constraints.[26] Messages in the world with the DL established will be going to a wider audience than previously, and to some extent

---

[26]The structuration idea has been developed by Anthony Giddens. See *The Constitution of Society*, Cambridge, England: Polity Press, 1984.

message senders will take that into account, perhaps by choosing content that is more neutral or guarded if the DL membership is heterogeneous. At the same time, a larger group is seeing messages that are identical and at nearly identical times. The effect of this, as intended in the DL-founding, is to produce a wider base of shared knowledge among the DL-members. Over time their internal communication should become more efficient as shared assumptions and background increase.

As the DL becomes used, an important effect of its existence may occur among those who are not members. The name will appear in cc: fields of messages they receive. They may find themselves addressing it, perhaps without being sure just who is in it. Whether this will happen may depend in part on the name that was chosen. A non-DL worker in the company with a message on the subject "reasons for caution" may be willing to send it to "newProducts!" but not to "DL674". In the latter case it might go to selected individuals instead, even to a proper subset of "DL674". But some members of the list might not see it, or might see it later -- a difference in *activation*. And, as countless organizational experiences have taught, early knowledge of an event or opinion can have large downstream consequences, which makes organizational actors highly averse to "reading about it in the papers."

In many organizations, processes among non-members bring DL names into spoken currency, as shorthand for the groups or purposes associated with them. The creation of a DL thus appears as an opportunity to publish a newly coined collective noun and insert it into the community's discourse. This can be a very significant effect of a simple act of DL-founding.

The existence of an established DL changes the landscape of credit allocation. The DL's name, membership, and purpose are more available as *objects of commitment*. The successes and failures that occur in the organization's new product development will be associated with actors who seemed to be involved. Groups that appear to contribute to success will strengthen the identification of their members and gain credibility in the eyes of others. Once again it can make it a large difference whether the founder chose "DL674", "newProducts!" -- or "friendsOfSue. Each alternative, by its different suggestion of the nature of the group's commitment, will have its own influence on the meaning that the list-name takes on over time, and perhaps on the patterns of commitment that evolve in the community.

In the early stages of a DL's existence various forces previously latent will be unleashed in the resolution of questions on whether and/or how it is to be used. Precedents are set by members' choices to use -- or not to use -- the list for issues that fall into the gray border areas of its announced intent. Again, the name choice partially regulates these early events. Meta-conversations may ensue about appropriate use of the list. And these may happen over the list itself, or in side communications. DL members may take actions on behalf of the list in its early days, for example, by cc:'ing to it their answer to a message from a member who did not use the list. These are the events that bring the DL and its name into the working lexicon of its members -- and outsiders. It acquires in the process connotations that may dwarf its precise denotation as a simple alias for the addresses of a set of individuals.

The structure created by the DL enters into the credit allocations of its members. The group "identified" by the name may come to think of itself as a meaningful social entity. They may invite each other to parties. They develop *commitment* to their community -- its members, its purposes, or both.

As an established part of the mental maps of its members and non-members the list can serve to distribute credit or blame for subsequent events over its entire membership. In its absence, only individuals might have been implicated in a particular success or failure. Here again the process is sensitive to the scope of the name. A failed new product that came from members of the "newProducts!" group can be credited quite differently than one that hatched in conversations among the members of "DL674".

As mentioned earlier, the manifold consequences of a simple act such as registering a distribution list can be extremely rich and difficult to predict. We conclude with two observations about design issues in community information systems.

First, the difficulty of detailed ("point") prediction -- even in such a simple case -- is truly daunting. In communities that are complex adaptive systems it will often be true that general statements about effects of information system interventions will not be very reliable. Our framework offers a coherent cluster of questions that designers may want to consider in assessing the likely interaction of specific contexts and mechanisms.

Second, it is extremely useful to consider the location in the community of various design capabilities. In our simple example, the individual making the decision to introduce a DL may be the one best positioned to assess some of its possible consequences. If so, it may be good design to give individual users the power to restructure eMail flows that we studied in our hypothetical case, even if the larger system experiences some loss of control. But there is also the need to assess large-scale implications of many such restructurings. At the level of establishing the system within which actors play out their strategies, our framework offers a population perspective for designers. To take just one other element of the situation, suppose that many users will found distribution lists. Is it better for the system to require the memberships to be modifiable only by the founder, to default to that arrangement but allow voluntary joining to be enabled, or to default to voluntary joining? Here the designers of the overall eMail system are in the position we described in setting out our framework as analogous to animal husbandry. Our framework suggests a coherent set of questions, grounded in what is being learned about complex adaptive systems and subject to refinement by agent-based simulations, which may help the designers of community information systems to support the breeding of many thriving and productive communities.

How TRURL Evolves Multiagent Worlds for Social Interaction Analysis

Takao Terano [*1], **Setsuya Kurahashi** [*1,*2] **and Ushio Minami** [*1,*3]

[*1] The University of Tsukuba, 3-29-1, Otsuka, Bunkyo-ku, Tokyo 112-0012 Japan
Tel:+81-3-3942-6855 Fax:+81-3-3942-6829
Email: terano@gssm.otsuka.tsukuba.ac.jp
[*2] YD System Corp, 1-18, Kanda-Sudacho, Chiyoda-ku, Tokyo 101-0041, Japan
Tel:+81-3-3251-8110 Fax:+81-3-3251-8650
Email: kura@tokyo-densan.jp
[*3] Hakuho-do Corp., 3-1-8, Shibaura, Minato-ku, Tokyo 118, Japan
Tel:+81-3-5446-6483 Fax:+81-3-5446-6490
Email: usshi@hakudodo.co.jp

Abstract. TRURL is an agent-based simulation environment, which is designed to analyze social interactions among agents including software and people in community computing. The unique characteristics of TRURL are summarized as follows: (1) Unlike conventional simulation systems, TRURL has so many predetermined and acquired parameters with which TRURL is able to simulate very complex conditions of the societies. The former parameters have constant values during one simulation cycle, however, the latter parameters change during the interactions. (2) TRURL utilizes Genetic Algorithms to evolve the societies by changing the predetermined parameters to optimize macro-level socio-metric measures. This means TRURL solves large-scale inverse problems. This paper first describes basic principles, architecture, and mechanisms of TRURL. Then, it discusses how TRURL evolves the artificial societies by automated parameters tuning on both micro- and macro-level phenomena grounded in the activities of real worlds.

1 Introduction

Recently, a great deal of arguments have been devoted to the study of (1) distributed information systems such as Internet applications [15], [3], (2) behaviors of animats or social insects in the A-Life literature [7], [10] and (3) explainable and executable models to analyze the social interaction of human organizations [4], [2]. Researchers of the above categories often utilize techniques including multiagent systems and evolutionary computation. From the state-of-the-art literature, they frequently report that simple autonomous agents or artificial worlds are able to evolve global *interesting* social structures and behaviors [22]. These research will certainly contribute to uncover the issues related to *Community Computing* and its support systems.

However, many of the approaches seem to report too artificial results, because of the following three reasons: (I) Although many agent models are developed from the bottom-up, the functions the agents have are so simple that the models can only handle with difficulty to practical social interaction problems. (II) Although the functions are simple from the viewpoint of simulation experiments, the models have too many parameters that can be tuned and, therefore, it seems as if any *good* result a model builder desires is already built in. (III) The results seem to have a weak relationship with emerging phenomena in real-world activities. Thus, these studies have not yet attained a level necessary to describe the flexibility and practicability of social interactions in real organizations.

To overcome such problems, we have developed a novel multiagent-based simulation environment TRURL [25] * for social interaction analysis. In our simulation model, we have extended the ideas of artificial societies in [7], [10]) and computational organization theory [4], [22].

In this paper, we first describe the design of the agent architecture, the artificial world model, and algorithms to evolve the worlds. Then, we discuss socio-metric measures which were used in a survey study to analyze activities of electronic community-based forums in Japan. Based on this discussion, we report some experimental results which reveal the nature of both micro- and macro-level phenomena which often occur in face-to-face-, e-mail-, Net-News-, and mass-communication-oriented societies. Finally, concluding remarks and future issues are given.

2 Basic Principles of TRURL

In conventional simulation models, the simulation is executed straightforwardly: Initially, many micro-level parameters and initial conditions are set, then, the simulation steps are executed, and finally the macro-level results are observed. Unlike in conventional simulation models, TRURL executes these steps in the reverse order: set a macro-level objective function, evolve the worlds to fit to the objectives, then observe the micro-level agent characteristics. Thus, TRURL solves very large inverse problems. So far, it has been considered difficult to adopt such an inverse approach to social system simulation studies, however, here we succeeded by utilizing a Genetic Algorithms [11] to evolve the societies by changing the predetermined parameters to optimize macro-level socio-metric measures, which can be observed in such real societies as e-mail oriented organizations and electronic commerce markets. Thus, using TRURL, we automatically tune the parameters to observe both micro- and macro-level phenomena grounded in the activities of real worlds.

The basic principles of TRURL can be summarized as follows: To address point (I) in Section 1, the agents in the model have detailed characteristics with enough parameters to simulate real world decision making problems [9]; with respect to (II), instead of manually changing the parameters of the agents, we evolve the multiagent worlds using GA-based techniques [11]; as for (III), we set some socio-metric measures which can be observed in real world phenomena as the objective functions to be optimized during evolution. Using TRURL, therefore, we are able to analyze the nature of social interactions in artificial worlds,

---

* Trurl is a hero of science fiction: "The Seventh Sally or How Trurl's own perfection led to no good" by Stanisław Lem. Trurl developed a sophisticated micro world for an arrogant king.

which are based on such real-world activities as e-mail oriented organizations and electronic commerce markets.

2.1 Agent in TRURL

Roughly, an agent in TRURL has event-action rules [23]. Each agent exchanges knowledge and solves its own multi-attribute decision problems by interacting with the other agents. The agents move around in the world to form groups with similar attitudes in decision making. They also have the motivation or energy to send and receive messages. The messages are used to make and/or modify the decisions of each agent. To implement these functions, the agents have both predetermined and acquired parameters, by which the characteristics of micro levels of the agent activities are determined. The former parameters have constant values during one simulation cycle, and the latter parameters change during the interaction processes among the agents. Summing up the decisions of the agents, the total attitude of the artificial world is determined as the macro-level status.

More formally, agent A in TRURL is represented as the following tuples:

$$A = (\{Kd\}, D, M, C_p, C_c, P_s, P_r, P_a, P_c, \delta, \mu, n),$$

where $\{Kd\}$ is a set of knowledge attributes, D: decision level the agent makes, M: motivation value or energy level of behaviors, C_p: physical coordinates, C_c: mental coordinates, P_s: probability of message sending, P_r: probability of message reading, P_a: probability of replying attitudes for pros-and-cons, P_c: probability of replying attitudes for comment adding, δ: metabolic rate, μ is the mutation rate of knowledge attribute values, and n is the number of knowledge attributes the agent has.

The agent usually has some subset of knowledge only which the agent can use for decision making. The knowledge the agent has is a set of knowledge attributes, defined as:

$$Kd = (N, W, E, C),$$

where N is a knowledge attribute, W its importance value, E its evaluation value; and C its credibility value.

Knowledge attributes can be exchanged among the agents via message transformation activities, however, the values of W, E, and C are changed based on the conforming behaviors determined by the agents' predetermined parameters. The decision each agent makes can be changed by changing the knowledge Kds. W and E respectively correspond to the importance factor of Bass's model and the attribute evaluation factor of the Fishbein model both in consumer behaviors of marketing sciences (see, e.g., [17]) for a definition of these models). They are used to obtain the decision D_i of agent A_i using a multi-attribute additive function:

$$D_i = \sum_{K_j \in K_{A_i}} W_j E_j.$$

C corresponds to the belief factor of the Bass model, which determines the level of the agent's belief of a given knowledge attribute. It is also used to determine comforting behaviors of the agent, which will be described below.

The motivation value M changes during the simulation to measure how strong the agent is motivated in the artificial world. If M becomes zero, the agent is retired, and a new one with random acquired parameter values participates in the world.

The metabolic rate δ is subtracted from M at every simulation step, when the agent has no messages. Also, δ is added to M per message, when the agent received it from the other agents, and $2 * \delta$ is added to M per reply-message when the agent receive it.

C_p and C_c represent where the agent is, in both the physical and mental world in decision making. The probability values P_s, P_r, P_a, and P_c are used to determine the conforming behaviors and knowledge exchange, which affect the agent decision value D. The movement and conforming behaviors are determined by the action rules described below.

2.2 Predetermined parameters of the agent

Predetermined parameters define the agents' congenital characteristics. The parameters are not changed during one simulation, but are tuned by GA operations when the world evolves. The predetermined parameters are listed below. They have values between 0.0 and 1.0.

- Physical coordinates $C_p = (X_{ip}, Y_{ip})$: The initial physical position of the agent in the artificial world; The values do not change during the simulation;
- Probability of message sending P_s: The probability that agent A_i sends messages to other agents A_js at each simulation step; The probability of selecting a specific A_j is inversely proportional to the physical or mental distance between A_i and A_j;
- Probability of message reading P_r: The probability that the agent reads messages from other agents at each simulation step;
- Parameters for conforming behavior α, β, and γ: The parameters are used to change conforming behavior of the agent; α, β, and γ are respectively used to control the importance value W, evaluation value E, and credibility value C of the knowledge attribute;
- Probability of having certain reply attitude with respect to similar or opposing opinions P_a: The probability that the agent will reply to another agent with the same opinion Kd; The value 1.0 represents the attitude of replying to only agents that have similar opinions, while the value 0.0 represents the attitude of replying to only agents that have opposing opinions. An agent with a high (resp. low) P_a value has conforming (resp. self-righteous) characteristics. In our implementation, an agent A_i gives an additional comment regarding Kd_k to another agent A_j with the following probability: $Prob = P_a - (E_{ki} - E_{kj})^2$, where E_{k*} is the evaluation value of Kd by the agent A_*;

- Probability of sending additional comments with the reply P_c: The probability that the agent will send a message containing additional comments Kd_js, when it receives message Kd_i; the value 1.0 means that the agent always replies with additional knowledge, while the value 0.0 means that the agent never sends messages with additional knowledge; The agent with high (resp. low) P_c is talkative (resp. not talkative);
- Metabolic rate δ: The metabolic rate determines the unit of change of the agent's motivation;
- Mutation rate μ: The mutation rate determines the probability of random change of the number of knowledge attributes in order to simulate the random effects of the external environment;
- Number of knowledge attributes n: The number of knowledge attributes that the agent knows. It is natural to assume each agent knows only part of the knowledge necessary for decision making; Therefore, this parameter represents the concept of "bounded rationality" of agents' knowledge; At the initial step of the simulation, for Kds which A_i does not have, we set W, E, and C to 0.0, 0.5, and 0.0, respectively.

2.3 Acquired parameters and action rules

The acquired parameters of the agents will change at each simulation step. At the initial phase of the simulation, they have random values.

- Motivation M_i: The value indicates the agent's motivational level in the artificial world;
- Mental coordinates $C_c = (X_{ic}, Y_{ic})$: The initial mental position of the agent is given at random in the artificial world; The values are changed based on the conforming behavior during the simulation; When agent A_i increases its credibility value C by exchanging knowledge Kd with another agent A_j, A_i will approach A_j by one unit distance; When C is not increased, or when A_i receives bad messages, A_i will move away from A_j with the probability of 0.5 or randomly move away for one unit distance. By this behavior, the agents will form groups with high credibility.
- Parameters for conforming behaviors: importance value w^i_{Kd}, evaluation value e^i_{Kd} and credibility value c^i_{Kd}: These parameters are changed based on the following conforming behaviors, when agent A_i makes decisions by receiving knowledge attribute Kd.

Each agent A_i interacts with another agent A_j at every (discrete) simulation step based on the constraints of the agents and the artificial world. A_j is stochastically selected by A_i proportional in terms of the physical and mental distance between them. At the interaction, a knowledge attribute Kd is transformed between A_i and A_j. When A_i receives an unknown Kd, A_i will accept Kd as it is. However, when A_i receives a Kd which it already knows, the value of the knowledge attribute will change by the following rules of conforming behavior:

$$\Delta w^i_{Kd} = \sum_{j \in S} \alpha(w^j_{Kd} - w^i_{Kd}) \cdot \max(0, c^j_{Kd} - c^i_{Kd}),$$
$$\Delta e^i_{Kd} = \sum_{j \in S} \beta(e^j_{Kd} - e^i_{Kd}) \cdot \max(0, c^j_{Kd} - c^i_{Kd}),$$
$$\Delta c^i_{Kd} = \sum_{j \in S} \gamma(1 - 2|e^j_{Kd} - e^i_{Kd}| \cdot \max(0, c^j_{Kd} - c^i_{Kd})),$$

where w^i_{Kd}, e^i_{Kd}, and c^i_{Kd} are respectively the importance value, evaluation value, and credibility value of Kd which A_i has; α, β, and γ are parameters; S is the agent from which A_i receives the message Kd at simulation time t.

Using the rules of conforming behavior, in general, if Kd of A_j has a higher credibility value than that of A_i, the attitude of A_i with respect to Kd will become similar to that of A_j. A_i's credibility value c^i_{Kd} with respect to Kd becomes higher when the evaluation value e^i_{Kd} is similar to that of A_j, and c^i_{Kd} becomes lower when e^i_{Kd} is different from e^j_{Kd} and c^j_{Kd} is higher than c^i_{Kd}. If c^i_{Kd} is higher than c^j_{Kd}, A_i does not change the credibility c^i_{Kd}.

Based on the probability Pa and Pc, A_i will reply to messages from the other A_js. The interaction activities continue. and the agents move together based on the moving rules described above.

The social interaction and changes of behaviors of **TRURL** agents are summarized in Figure 1.

```
Function Agent-Interaction(predetermined_parameters) returns socio-metrics
    static acquired_parameters

    Set-Acquired-Parameters(all_agents)
    for each c in simulation_steps do
        for each a in agents do
            if random() > probability_of_message_reading(a from a') then
                if a reads messages_from(a') then
                    Transform-Knowledge-Attributes(a', Kds)
                    if credibility_value changes then Approach(a')
                    else Move-Random()
                    if random() > probability_of_replying_attitude(a) then
                        Give-Comments(a')
                        Give-Additional-Comments(a', probability_of_comment_adding)
                    New-Message-Send(a', probability_of_message_sending)
                else Calculate-Motivation(metabolic_rate)
                if motivation(a) <= 0 then Set-Acuired-Parameters(a)
                Mutaion(mutation_rate)
        end
    end
    return socio-metrics
```

Fig. 1. Social Interaction and Changes of Behaviors of the Agents

3 Four Models for an Artificial Society

As a conceptual model of computer mediated social networks such as the Internet society and/or electronic commerce, we characterize the world by both physical and mental spaces (D_p and D_c). D_p and D_c consist of two-dimensional grids forming a torus structure. In D_p, the coordinates of A_j represent the physical places where A_j is. In D_c, the coordinates of A_j represent the mental positions among the agents. The movements of agents in the world are learning processes to form groups with same attitudes. In the current implementation, the size of both D_p and D_c is $50 * 50$.

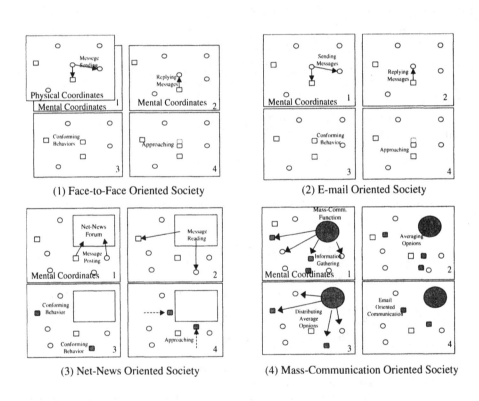

(1) Face-to-Face Oriented Society   (2) E-mail Oriented Society

(3) Net-News Oriented Society   (4) Mass-Communication Oriented Society

Fig. 2. Agents' Behaviors in FFS, EMS, NNS, and MCS

We design the following four artificial societies (Figure 2):

1. Face-to-Face communication oriented society (FFS)
   The communication among the agents are constrained by both the physical and mental coordinates.They interact with physical and mental neighborhoods. The ratio is parameterized.
2. E-Mail oriented society (EMS)
   The communication among the agents are constrained by the mental coor-

dinates.In this society, agents interact with each other one by one at each step.

3. Net-News oriented society (NNS)
   NNS is an extension of EMS. It has a virtual white board at the center of the world. Agents in the world send messages to the white board, and the white board distributes the messages to all the agents. The credibility value of the messages is the same as that of the senders.

4. Mass-Communication oriented society (MCS)
   MCS has one mass communication agent who gathers the decisions of all the agents at each simulation step. The decisions or attitudes are then averaged and are distributed with high credibility values. The mass communication agent acts as a monitor of the society.

```
Function Evolving-Society(predetermined_parameters) returns society
   static acquired_parameters

   Set-Predetermined-Parameters(random())
   for each c in generation_steps do
      for each s in societies do
         fitness(s) <- Agent-Interaction(predetermined_parameters)
      end
      Select_Elite(fitness, societies)
      Crossover(societies)  ;;; uniform corssover is used
      Mutation(societies, mutation_rate)
   end

   return society
```

Fig. 3. Algoritm to Evolving Artificial Societies

4 Parameter Tuning of a Society by GAs

As described in the previous section, the agents, their behaviors, and the world are controlled by many parameters. Therefore it is very difficult to make them in order to properly carry out social interaction. Thus, we apply Genetic Algorithms for this purpose. The outline is shown in Figure 3 and Figure 4 .

The predetermined 12 parameters of each agent ($C_p = (X_{ip}, Yip)$, P_s, P_r, α, β, γ, P_a, P_c, δ, μ, and n) can each be represented by integers between 0 and 9, which correspond to real numbers from 0.0 to 1.0. The predetermined characteristics of an agent are coded into a twelve integer string. Each initial world is coded into a gene, which consists of a sequence of agent codes with a fixed number specified by the user. The number represents the size of the agents.

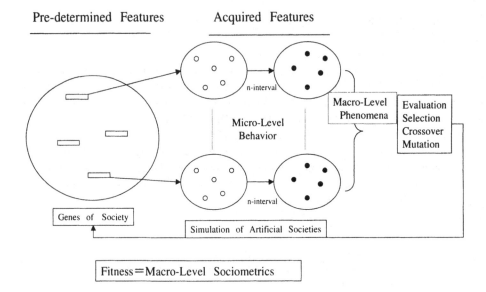

Pre-determined Features   Acquired Features

Genes of Society

Micro-Level
Behavior

n-interval

n-interval

Macro-Level
Phenomena

Evaluation
Selection
Crossover
Mutation

Simulation of Artificial Societies

Fitness＝Macro-Level Sociometrics

Fig. 4. Evolving Artificial Societies via GAs

In the simulation, we first specify the type of world (FFS, EMS, NGS, or MCS), and set the world's parameters, represented by the gene, to an initial state, then we execute simulation steps (for example, 100-200 steps) to evolve social behaviors by changing the acquired parameters. The resulting status is a phenotype of the world, which is represented by sets of both predetermined and acquired parameters of the agents.

Each world is evaluated by a specified evaluation function, which represents some of the socio-metric measures describe in the next section. Based on the function values, *good* worlds are selected. We use the size-two tournament selection method and the elitist strategy. For the reproduction, we adopt the uniform crossover operator and changing crossover rate from 10% to 0%, proportionally decreasing at each step of the reproduction.

In the current implementation, a maximum of 500 agents in each world is allowed. However, in most experiments, we evolve 100 generations for 20 worlds with 10 to 20 agents.

5 Discussion of Socio-Metric Measures

There are several studies in the literature that analyze social interactions among participants in computer mediated communities. Among them, an investigation carried out by our colleague [16] is very interesting because (1) he analyzed data of several network forums in Japan for several years and suggested that specific structures and leaders have evolved, and (2) he proposed five socio-metrics measures to reveal the characteristics of the network forums. These socio-metric measures can be evaluated in TRURL and reflect the characteristics of social interaction in real worlds. We adopted the proposed measures as the evaluation functions to be optimized in the evolution process of artificial societies. The definitions and brief descriptions of the measures are shown below.

Ratio of transmitters

This metric indicates the social structure where a small number of members (transmitters) sending one-way many messages to other members.

$$T = \frac{(\sum_{i=1}^{g}(Sd-rd_i)-\sum_{i=1}^{g}(Rd-rd_i)+g(g-1))Sd}{2g(g-1)^2};$$

Ratio of receivers

This metric indicates the social structure where a small number of members (receivers) receiving one-way messages from other members.

$$R = \frac{(\sum_{i=1}^{g}(Rd-rd_i)-\sum_{i=1}^{g}(Sd-sd_i)+g(g-1))Rd}{2g(g-1)^2};$$

Ratio of leaders

This metric indicates the social structure where a small number of members (leaders) acting as both transmitters and receivers. They will manage the society.

$$L = \left(\frac{\sum_{i=1}^{g}((sd_i \cdot rd_i)_{max}-sd_i \cdot rd_i)}{(g-1)((g-1)^2-1)}\right)^{1/2};$$

Ratio of local communication

The metric indicates the social structure where half of the members are active (they always send and receive messages) and the others are passive (they only receive messages).

$$D = \frac{\sum_{i=1}^{g}(\tilde{S}d-sd_i)^2)}{g(g-1)^2/4};$$

Ratio of activation The metric indicates the social structure where the participants are active (they always send and receive messages)

$$A = \frac{\sum_{i=1}^{g}(sd_i+rd_i)}{2g(g-1)}.$$

In the above equations, sd_i is the number of receivers to whom agent A_i sends messages, rd_i is the number of message senders to A_i, g is the number of members, Sd and Rd respectively mean the sd_i and rd_i of the agent A_i with the maximum value of $sd_i + rd_i$; and $\tilde{S}d$, $\tilde{R}d$ respectively mean the average values for senders and receivers. We omit the discussion on how to derive the measures. Instead, Figure 5 shows examples of the socio-metric measures applied to simple network structures to simplify understanding.

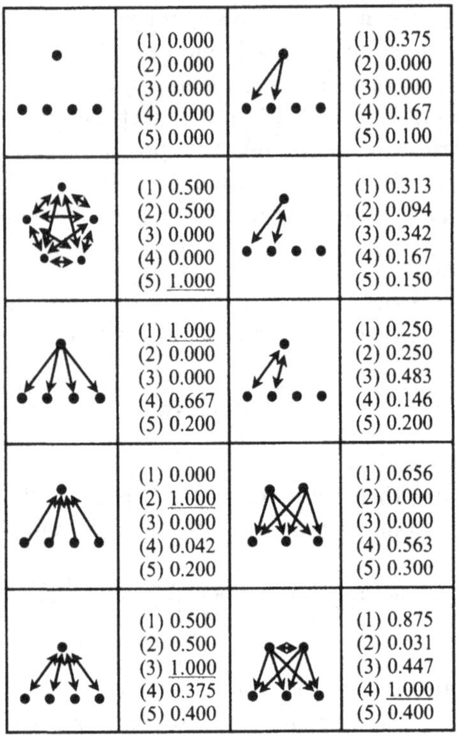

	(1) 0.000 (2) 0.000 (3) 0.000 (4) 0.000 (5) 0.000		(1) 0.375 (2) 0.000 (3) 0.000 (4) 0.167 (5) 0.100
	(1) 0.500 (2) 0.500 (3) 0.000 (4) 0.000 (5) <u>1.000</u>		(1) 0.313 (2) 0.094 (3) 0.342 (4) 0.167 (5) 0.150
	(1) <u>1.000</u> (2) 0.000 (3) 0.000 (4) 0.667 (5) 0.200		(1) 0.250 (2) 0.250 (3) 0.483 (4) 0.146 (5) 0.200
	(1) 0.000 (2) <u>1.000</u> (3) 0.000 (4) 0.042 (5) 0.200		(1) 0.656 (2) 0.000 (3) 0.000 (4) 0.563 (5) 0.300
	(1) 0.500 (2) 0.500 (3) <u>1.000</u> (4) 0.375 (5) 0.400		(1) 0.875 (2) 0.031 (3) 0.447 (4) <u>1.000</u> (5) 0.400

(1) Ratio of transmitters   (2) Ratio of receivers
(3) Ratio of leaders
(4) Ratio of local communication
(5) Ratio of activation

Fig. 5. The Characteristics of Socio-metric Measures

6   Experiments and Discussion

We have carried out intensive experiments on interactions in electronic medi-ated societies by **TRURL**. The experiments have been conducted by the following principles: (1) Using the four equipped societies, we have compared the charac-teristics of social interactions in each society, (2) Using the inverse simulation method, we have designed specific societies characterized by the socio-metrics, and (3) Changing the objective functions to be optimized, we have evolved arti-ficial societies with various characteristics. The detailed discusiions of the ecper-iments will be reported elsewhere, Figure 6 summarizes the experimental setup and results. In the following subsections, some of them are described.

6.1   General observation in the four different societies

In order to show general behaviors of **TRURL** simulation environment, this sub-section explains the attitude changes or the averages for the agents' decisions,

Comparing Social Interactions in Various Societies		
Objectives	Societies	Results
(I) Changes of Social Attitudes	Face to Face Oriented Society E-mail Oriented Society Net-News Oriented Society	Moderate Change Rapid Change Sig. Change; Stable
(II) Changes of Motivation	Face to Face Oriented Society E-mail Oriented Society	Higher difference Lower difference
Designing Specific Societies		
Objectives	Results	
(III) Society with a Leader	An evolved leader is not so strong, but it usually read messages, replies them with comments,, has wide knowledge.	
Evolving Artificial Societies		
Objectives	Results	
(IV) Conforming Society	Agents deeply rely on each other, reply to similar opinions, have narrow knowledge, and are influenced by each other.	
(V) Influential Leader	The characteristics of the leader is similar to the one in (III).	
(VI) Society against Conforming Attitudes	Agents usually read messages, and reply to various opinions with additional comments against the message senders.	
(VII) Society with Mass Communication	Mass comm. prevents the society from radical situations	

Fig. 6. Summary of the Experiments Using TRURL

in Face-to-Face, E-mail, Net-News, and Mass-Communication oriented societies. In the experiment, we give random predetermined parameters and one powerful agent, and then observe the simulation processes. We do not apply GAs in the experiment, because we need not evolve any new features for the worlds.

The results are shown in Figure 7. In each graph of Figure 7, the curves represent one typical epoch with 300 simulation steps. The horizontal and vertical axes respectively represent the simulation steps and the average value of agent attitudes ($\sum evaluation_i * weight_i$).

The results are clear. Each world shows its own characteristics. In FFS, since the communication capability is constrained by physical conditions, the attitudes are moderately changed. The same phenomena can be observed in real social interactions in daily life. However,

in EMS, the attitude change depends on the initial condition; some societies show a very rapid change while others show very little change. This depends on the general agents in the society has dependent characteristics with highly crediblilty or not. If the agents heavily rely on each other, they form a closer group and result in the situation where they have the same opinions. If they donot rely on each other, on the other hand, sir e the interests diverge, the total attitude change will become stable.

However, in the very earlier stages of the simulation for NNS, the attitudes are significantly changed, and then stabilized in the latter stages. This phenomenon is similar to the "techno bubble" in real electronic commerce activities that has

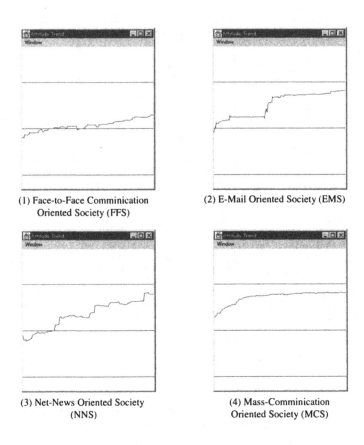

(1) Face-to-Face Comminication
Oriented Society (FFS)

(2) E-Mail Oriented Society (EMS)

(3) Net-News Oriented Society
(NNS)

(4) Mass-Comminication
Oriented Society (MCS)

Fig. 7. General Observation of Agents' Behavior in FFS, EMS, NNS, and MCS

been reported in literature. In the later stages of the simulation, on the other hand, since the knowledge they have become similar, they do not find valuable comments. Then, the society becomes less credible and less interesting.

In MCS, whether we can manage the "techno babble" phenomenon particularly in consumer behavior research is a very interesting problem. By mass communication, in the simulation, we mean that there is a special agent which gathers all the decisions or attitudes of the agents, and then distributes the average values, or public opinions, to all the agents. The timing of gathering and distributing is stochastically determined. Compared with the other graphs in Figure 7, where there is no mass communication, it is clear that the effects of mass communication suppress conforming behaviors.

6.2 Society with a leader

To analyze the characteristics of the society with leaders, which we often observe in real electronic mail based forums, we will optimize the function of ratio of leaders in EMS.

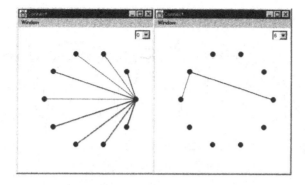

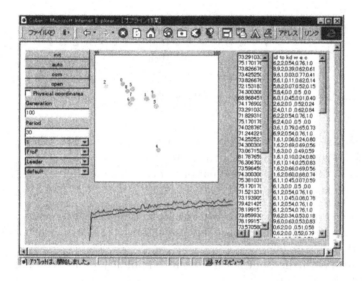

Fig. 8. Evolution of the Society with a Leader

The result is summarized in Figure 8. The upper two figures shows two types of the communication among agents. The lower figure displays the intermediate screen image of the simulation.

The circles represent the location of the agents in the world. Their radii and color represent the level of motivation and the decision made, respectively. The agents moves according to the behavioral rules.

Figure 9 shows how the society evolves during the GA cycle. The upper, middle, and lower curves respectively represent the fitness of the highest, mean, and lowest values of the evaluation function. The figure suggests that the GA design works well.

We can observe there are two types of agents: those who communicate with

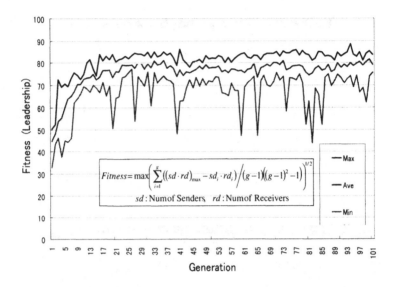

Fig. 9. Changes of Fitness during the GA cycle

every other agent, and those who communicate only with two other agents. We call the former types leaders and the latter types ordinary agents.

Analysis of the predetermined parameters of leader agents reveals the following characteristics:

– The leader agent usually reads messages and replies with comments;
– Leaders have larger, but not maximum number of knowledge attributes than the other agents; and
– Leaders have higher, but not maximum, credibility values with regard to the knowledge attributes.

The observations are slightly different from our original intuition that the leader should have maximum values knowledge attributes and credibility values.

6.3 Society with conforming attitudes

There are often cases where very subtle environmental changes cause a radical change of public opinions. To analyze the situation, we evolve an EMS society where the agents conform to the opinions of a single strong agent. The evaluation function is as follows:

$$\text{Fitness} = \sum_{i=1}^{n} \sum_{j=1}^{m} w_{ij} e_{ij},$$

where, n is the number of the agents and m is the number of knowledge attributes. To give an explicit chance of the conforming activities, we set the parameters so that only one agent (powerful agent) always has the decision or attitude $D_i = \sum_{K_j \in K_{A_i}} W_j E_j = 1.0$.

The characteristics or the predetermined parameters of the general agents in the world are summarized as follows:

– Evaluation parameter β of general agents is slightly higher than that of agents in other societies. This means they tend to rely upon each other;
– Probability of reply attitude P_a is nearly equal to 1.0. This means they tend to reply to the agents with similar opinions.
– They have smaller number of knowledge attributes n. This means they have interests in narrow topic areas.

The results suggest that in a conforming society, public opinion will be deflected, even if there are only a few powerful agents.

6.4 Society with a highly influential sgent

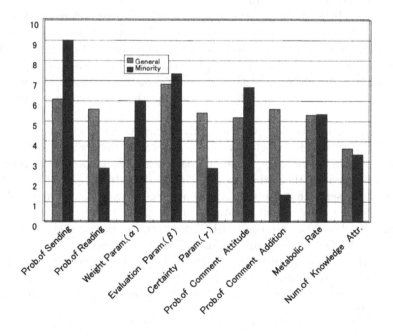

Fig. 10. Characteristics of Powerful and General Agents

Opposite to the previous world, in this experiment, we will observe a powerful agent, which has stronger influence over the behavior of other agents. In order to evolve the world, we first evolve a conforming EMS society, and then set the predetermined parameters of the powerful agent by GA operations. The results are summarized in Figure 10.

In Figure 10, the average values of 10 simulation are shown. The predetermined parameters are classified as those of a minority of powerful agents and those of other general agents.

The remarkable characteristics of the powerful agents are as follows:

- The agents often read messages and reply to them;
- The agents have interests in various knowledge attributes;
- The agents have a lower metabolic value; and
- The agents tend to reply to the agents with different opinions.

7 Concluding Remarks

This paper described a novel model for computational and mathematical organization theory (CMOT). The model and simulatot TRURL are originally intended to analize social interaction among agents including software and people. They also contribute to uncover both theoretical and practical issues in Community Computing and their information systems.

Although TRURL utilizes conventional CMOT oriented techniques, the principles are different from the literatures in the following manner: (I) the agents in the model have enough parameters to simulate real world decision making problems; (II) instead of evolving agents, GA-based techniques are applied to evolve appropriate worlds; and (III) some socio-metric measures which can be observed in the real world are defined as the objective functions to be optimized in the evolution.

Therefore, using TRURL, we can analyze various aspects of social interaction in artificial worlds, which have some grounds in the real world activities. The most remarkable feature of the approach is that it adopts an intermediate approach between mathematical models [6] and case studies [21]. The model is rigorous in the sense that it is operational or executable on a computer and that it describes the nature of real world phenomena [23].

Future work includes (i) using TRURL to carry out various social interaction experiments by further defining the 'useful' objective functions or socio-metric measures, (ii) analyzing micro-macro interactions between people, information systems, organizations, and societies [15], [5], [8], and (iii) extending our idea to general organizational problem solving and organizational learning models [20], [14], [24], [1], [12].

References

1. Aiba, H., Terano, T. 1996. A Computational Model for Distributed Knowledge Systems with Learning Mechanisms. *Expert Systems with Applications* 10: 417–427.
2. Axelrod, R. 1997. *The Complexity of Cooperation: Agent-Based Models of Competition and Collaboration.* Princeton University Press.
3. Bradshaw, J. M., ed. 1997. *Software Agents.* AAAI/MIT Press.

4. Carley, K. M. and M. J. Prietula, eds. 1994. *Computational Organization Theory*. Hillsdale, N.J: Lawlence-Erlbaum Assoc..
5. Cohen, M. D. and L. S. Sproull, eds. 1991. Special Issue: Organizational Learning: Papers in Honor of (and by) James G. March. *Organization Science* 2(1).
6. Cyert, R. M., March, J. G. 1963. *A Behavioral Theory of the Firm*. Prentice-Hall.
7. Epstein, J. and R. Axtell. 1996. *Growing Artificial Societies*. Brookings Institution Press, The MIT Press.
8. Espejo, R., Schuhmann, W., Schwaninger, M., and Bilello, U. 1996. *Organizational Transformation and Learning*. John Wiley & Sons.
9. French, S. 1986. *Decision Theory: An Introduction to the Mathematics of Rationality*. John Wiley & Sons.
10. Gaylord, R. J., and D'Andria, L. J.: *Simulating Society: A Mathematica Toolkit for Modeling Socioeconomic Behavior*. NY: Springer-Verlag.
11. Goldberg, D. E. 1989. *Genetic Algorithms in Search, Optimization, and Machine Learning*. Addison-Wesley.
12. Hatakama, H., Terano, T. 1996. A Multi-Agent Model of Organizational Intellectual Activities for Knowledge Management. in *Knowledge Management - Organization, Competence and Methodology*, edited by J. F. Schreinemakers. Ergon Verlag, p. 143–155.
13. Hraber. P., T. Jones, S. and Forrest. 1997. The Ecology of Echo. *Artificial Life* 3: 165–190 .
14. T. Ishida, L. Gasser, and M. Yokoo. 1992. Organization Self-Design of Distributed Production Systems. *IEEE Transactions on Knowledge and Data Engineering* 4: 123–134.
15. Kirn, S., and G. O'Hare, eds. 1996. *Cooperative Knowledge Processing – The Key Technology for Intelligent Organizations*. Springer.
16. Kobayashi, Y. 1996. *Structural Analysis of Electronic Community Created by Computer Mediated Communication*. Master Thesis of Grad. Sch. Systems Management, Tsukuba University (in Japanese).
17. Lilien, G. L., Kotler, P., Moorthy, K. S. 1992. *Marketing Models*. Prentice-Hall.
18. March, J. G., Sproull, L. S. 1991. Learning from samples of one or fewer. *Organizational Science, Special Issue: Organizational Learning* 2: 1–13.
19. Masuch, M., and Warglien, M., eds. 1992. *Artificial Intelligence in Organization and Management Theory*. North-Holland.
20. Morecroft, J. D. W., and J. D. Sterman, eds. 1994. *Modeling for Learning Organizations*. Productivity-Press.
21. Nonaka, I., Takeuchi, H. 1995. *The Knowledge Creating Company: How Japanese Companies Create the Dynamics of Innovation*. Oxford: Oxford University Press.
22. Prietula, M. J., Carley, K. M. and Gasser, L. eds. 1998. *Simulating Organizations: Computational Models of Institutions and Groups*. CA: Morgan Kaufman.
23. Russel, S., Norvig, P. 1995. *Artificial Intelligence A Modern Approach*. Prentice Hall.
24. Terano, T. et. al. 1994. A Machine Learning Model for Analyzing Performance of Organizational Behaviors of Agents. *Proc. of the Third Conference of the Association of Asian-Pacific Operational Research Societies (APORS)*, p. 164–171.
25. Terano, T., Kurahashi, S., Minami, U. TRURL: Artificial World for Social Interaction Studies. Proc. 6th Int. Conf. on Artificial Life (ALIFE VI), pp. 326-335, 1998.

Agent Based Approach for Social Complex Systems - Management of Constructed Social World -

Hiroshi Deguchi

Kyoto University, Graduate School of Economics
Yoshida-Honmachi, Sakyo-ku, Kyoto, 606-8501, Japan
deguchi@econ.kyoto-u.ac.jp
http://degulab.econ.kyoto-u.ac.jp/

Abstract. In this paper we focus on social complex systems that contain autonomous agents and on their indirect control principle. In a social complex system we can not assume any universal law that rules the system. For analyzing such a system we distinguish three layers of realities of the system such as theoretical, computational and social constructed ones. We investigate several types of agent societies depending on different layer of realities. We also discuss why agent based approach is essential for supporting community.

1. Introduction
1.1 Breakthrough in Complex Systems Study

First we pay attention to the three major breakthroughs in the study of complex systems. The first one is the cybernetics revolution. In cybernetics we formulated the concept of feedback. The concept of feedback makes it possible to use the word "purpose" as a scientific concept from an engineering point of view.

The second breakthrough comes from computer science. The concept of program plays an essential role in the study of complex systems. In complex systems we focus on hierarchical emergent properties on the higher layer of the systems. If we approach from the anti reductionist point of view we need the descriptive basis for the higher layer's activities. The concept of program provides the basis of non physical description of the systems law on the higher layers of complex systems. H. A. Simon stressed on the science of program and characterized the concept of "role" as programed procedures. The object oriented description of complex soft system comes from this paradigm.

The third revolution had arisen in the area of statistical physics. The paradigms are called synergetics or self-organization that characterize the change of structure by mathematical bifurcation theory of no linear dynamical systems[1,2]. The third revolution shows the importance of symbolic generalization in paradigms. Historically the concept of positive feedback, which is strongly related to bifurcation, is discussed in the context of cybernetics, The old paradigm is called second cybernetics by M.

Maruyama. It is also applied to social systems theory. The concept of second cybernetics only lacks a mathematical formulation.

Now we turn our attention to the arising of the fourth breakthrough. New paradigm will emerge in the area of autonomous multi agent systems[3]. Multi agent systems are systems in which several agents interact. The "agent" tries to accomplish their goals under the activities of communication, cooperation, competition, negotiation, transaction, control and management. The science for a system of homogeneous or heterogeneous autonomous agents is becoming more important. Most social sciences, robotics and the theories of software agents are included in this area.

If we shift our attention to a system of autonomous agents the former three paradigms are insufficient to analyze the multi agent system. For analyzing the structural change of a social complex system we have to develop the paradigm of multi agent system, because it is very difficult to apply the dynamical systems approach to a social complex system on which bifurcation is investigated.

The only exception comes from the area of evolutionary game theory that studies partly from agent oriented approach. We can induce a dynamical system that is called replicator dynamics from the game theoretical interaction between random matching agents in an agent society.

Now we should investigate the fourth breakthrough for a social complex system of autonomous agents. In the forthcoming paradigm we pay special attention to the systemic properties such as internal model, indirect control, Micro-Macro linkage and mutual reference activities among agents. In this paper we try to draw a rough sketch of the fourth breakthrough in perspective. We also explain how community supporting system is essential in social complex systems.

1.2 Reality Analysis for Agent Based Society

How we can manage an autonomous multi agent system. This is a key problem for analyzing complex systems with decision makers that is called a social complex system. For this purpose we pay attention to the structure of our "life world" and the construction of its reality.

In this century our "life world" has extended. In this extension many artificial concepts such as nation state, company and industrial products are introduced. In this decade more drastic changes have occurred in many aspects of our life world. For example several years ago no one could imagine the internet community that gave us a global digital life world on the network. It is insufficient to use traditional scientific methodology for analyzing this extended life world. Many autonomous agents interact according to their own action rules and evolve and learn their action rules in the world. We need a new methodology for supporting, managing and studying an agent based society.

For this purpose we pay attention to the layers of realities. We distinguish three different and important layers of realities for analyzing an agent based society. The one is a theoretical layer of reality where the mathematical models for a social complex system are developed. The second is a layer of computational reality where the facts on the computer are used for analyzing an agent based society. Our digital life world constructed by computer mediated communication is based on the computational reality. In the same way the community supporting system is also a technology that is based on the computational reality.

The third layer of reality is a social constructed reality. In this layer we pay attention to the subjective and intersubjective construction of reality on our wetware, i.e., human body. In other words the construction of cognitive class library and its management on our wetware should be analized. For designing this extended life world as a rich place we have to know how our social reality is constructed by communication which is supported by theoretical and computational realities. This kind of subjective approach is now used in the area of management science as a complementary approach to the hard systems approach like operations research. Soft systems methodology and structuration theory are typical examples of these kinds of soft and subjective approachs [4,5]. Gaming simulation is an another approach toward a construction of reality [6]. In this paper we pay attention to gaming simulation.

Our Methodology is shown in the following figure. Theoretical approach, agent based simulation and gaming simulation construct methodological triangle. These approaches support with each other. For designing society supporting system on the virtual world we need powerful methodology to understand the complexity of the multi agent society.

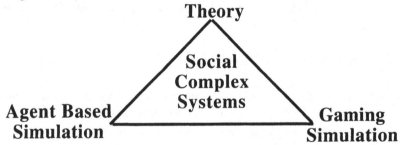

Fig.1. Methodological Triangle

2. Theoretical Analysis for Social Complex Systems
2.1 Modeling Framework

A social complex system consists of a number of autonomous agents and a certain macro functional agent. We introduce a new management concept called indirect control which is used to analyze the theoretical reality of social complex system.

For characterizing the indirect control concept we introduce replicator dynamics and its bifurcation analysis on the agent based society. The replicator dynamics is a population dynamics for multi agent system that is introduced by micro interactions between agents[7,8]. We also introduce gaming simulation for providing an experimental basis of theoretical analysis.

Our modeling framework is shown in the following figure 2 and figure 3.

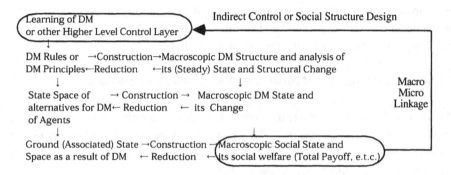

Fig.2. General Modeling Framework for Agent Societies

We have to unfold our modeling framework for a concrete mathematical model. For this purpose we use replicator dynamics and its bifurcation theory. The framework is shown as follows.

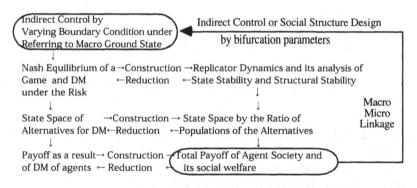

Fig.3. Replicator Dynamics Modeling for Agent Societies

We distinguish a state space of alternatives from a ground associated state space. For example a state space of alternatives consistes of alternatives of game theory and a ground state space consists of payoff of the game. A state of alternatives is determined by certain decision making rules or principles such as Nash equilibrium or a decision making principle under the risk. Micro agents select a satisfiable solution from the set of alternatives. A macro functional agent varies structural parameters for finding better social payoff of agent society. This variation of structural parameters is called indirect control of an agent society[9].

We use a replicator dynamics for the modeling of agent based societies. Replicator dynamics was introduced in the area of evolutionary game theory in biology at first. Now it is widely used in evolutionary economics. A replicator dynamics is formulated under the game theoretical framework basically. We extend the framework and introduce the dynamics from mixed model of game theory and decision making model under a monitoring risk. We also shift our attention to the model from the state stability point of view to the structural stability of dynamics.

2.2 Replicator Dynamics of random matching prisoner's dilemma

We introduce an agent society that consists of a random matching model of prisoner's dilemma. In the society agents make random matching pairs and play two person prisoner's dilemma shown in the following table. An agent can not appoint an opposite player under the random matching assumption.

Table 1. Payoff Matrix of prisoner's Dilemma

	C	D
C	(R,R)	(S, T)
D	(T, S)	(Q,Q)

We assume that $T>R>Q>S$ and $R>(T+S)/2$ from the condition of prisoner's Dilemma.

Let P be the ratio of the population of agents who select the cooperative alternative (C) on the game in the agent society.

$$E(C,C)=R, \ E(D,D)=Q, \ E(C,D)=S, \ E(D,C)=T$$
$$W[C]=PE(C,C) + (1-P)E(C,D)=PR+(1-P)S$$
$$W[D]=PE(D,C) + (1-P)E(D,D)=(1-P)Q+PT$$
$$W\tilde{} =PW[C]+(1-P)W[D]=PR+(1-P)S+(1-P)Q+PT$$

$$dP/dt=P(W[C]-W\tilde{})=P\{W[C]-PW[C]-(1-P)W[D] \}$$
$$=P\{(1-P)(W[C]-W[D]) \}$$
$$=P(1-P)\{P(R+Q-S-T)+S-Q \}=0 \text{, where } 0 \leq P \leq 1 \text{ hold.}$$

dP/dt=0 means steady states of the replicator dynamics. Then p=1 , p=0 and p=(Q-S)/(R+Q-S-T) are steady states of this dynamics.
Where $0< P=(Q-S)/(R+Q-S-T) <1$ is required. From the assumption $P=(Q-S)/(R+Q-S-T)>1$ holds. Thus there exist only two steady states such as p=1 or p=0. dP/dt<0 also holds. Thus only P=0 is stable.

Next we try to formulate an indirect control by varying boundary conditions of replicator dynamics. We introduce a decision making model under the risk over the prisoner's dilemma model.

We assume the macro agent such as a government or a manager who is monitoring agent activities with a certain probability. Let β be a probability of the monitoring. Let "a" be a compensation for a betrayed agent and "b" be a sanction for a betrayer. The payoff matrix is shown as follows.

Table 2. Payoff Matrix of prisoner's Dilemma with a monitoring risk

		C	D
β	C	(R,R)	(S+a, T-b)
	D	(T-b, S+a)	(Q,Q)
$1-\beta$	C	(R,R)	(S, T)
	D	(T, S)	(Q,Q)

Then the replicator dynamics is shown as follows.

$E[\beta](C,C)=R, E[\beta](C,D)=S+a, E[\beta](D,C)=T-b, E[\beta](D,D)=Q$

$Wr[\beta,C]=\beta\{PE[\beta](C,C)+(1-P)E[\beta](C,D)\}=\beta\{PR+(1-P)(S+a)\}$

$Wr[\beta,D]=\beta\{PE[\beta](D,C)+(1-P)E[\beta](D,D)\}=\beta\{P(T-b)+(1-P)Q\}$

$Wr[1-\beta,C]=(1-\beta)W[C]=(1-\beta)\{PR+(1-P)S\}$

$Wr[1-\beta,D]=(1-\beta)W[D]=(1-\beta)\{(1-P)Q+PT\}$

$Wr[C]=Wr[\beta,C]+Wr[1-\beta,C]$

$\qquad =\beta\{PR+(1-P)(S+a)\}+(1-\beta)\{PR+(1-P)S\}$

$Wr[D]=Wr[\beta,D]+Wr[1-\beta,D]$

$\qquad =\beta\{P(T-b)+(1-P)Q\}+(1-\beta)\{(1-P)Q+PT\}$

$W^{\sim}=PWr[C]+(1-P)Wr[D]$

$dP/dt=P\{Wr[C]-W^{\sim}\}=P(1-P)\{Wr[C]-Wr[D]\}$

$=P(1-P)\{\beta\{PR+(1-P)(S+a)\}+(1-\beta)\{PR+(1-P)S\}$

$\qquad -\beta\{P(T-b)+(1-P)Q\}-(1-\beta)\{(1-P)Q+PT\}\}$

$=P(1-P)[(\beta a+S-Q)+P\{\beta(b-a)+R-S+Q-T\}]$

Where $dP/dt=0$ means steady states of the replicator dynamics. Then $p=1$, $p=0$ and $P=(Q-\beta a-S)/\{\beta(b-a)+R-S+Q-T\}$ are steady states of this dynamics.

The followings are the examples of structural parameters for an indirect control.

(1)β =0.8, a=1,b=1.5　　0 o————>————◆ 1

(2)β =0.6, a=1,b=1.5　　0 o———>——◆——<————o 1

(3)β =0.4, a=1,b=1.5　　0 ◆————<—————————o

Where ◆ means stable state and O means unstable state and (β, a, b) become structural parameters of this dynamical system.

To lead the agent activities to the cooperative ones indirectly, dP/dt>0 is required. For the purpose (β a+S-Q)+P{β (b-a)+R-S+Q-T}>0 is necessary. If a$\leq$b then dP/dt>0 holds under the suitable indirect control parameter β. a=1 and b=1.5 satisfy the condition.

In the previous case a government can vary the parameter β under the conditions of a=1,b=1.5 to make agent activities become cooperative. β =0.8 is enough to change most of autonomous and rational activities of agents to cooperative one.

We will show another example with structural parameter β =0.4, a=1 and b=3. Where the stability of the states are shown as follows.

(4)β =0.4, a=1,b=3　　0 ◆————<————>————◆ 1

The convergence to the two different states depends on initial conditions as is shown in the next computer simulation.

3. Gaming Simulation for Social Constructed Reality Management

3.1 Gaming Simulation

In this section we introduce gaming simulation for managing social constructed reality. Gaming simulation gives good test beds to verify the validity of the model depending on theoretical and computational reality. Gaming simulation is not a computer simulation. It is a game designed for human players. Gaming simulation is also different from a role playing game in which the roles of players are given by subjective description. In gaming simulation the role for each agent (player) is defined concretely. In gaming simulation a player acts under the well defined boundary conditions of the roles.

We adopt a certain gaming simulation and compare the results with the theoretical and computer simulation models. We present the following gaming simulation.

3.2. Gaming for Random Matching Prisoner's Dilemma Society

We can design a gaming simulation corresponding to the agent society characterized by replicator dynamics. In this paper we show the case of prisoner's dilemma. The dilemma society consists of 10 human players in this case. The players play the game under the random matching environment. There is no handshaking possibility in this model.

The following is a result under the parameters as T=3, R=2, Q=1,and S=0.5. Where T>R>Q>S and R>(T+S)/2 hold.

In this simple case a random matching play among 10 players makes 5 pairs in each session. The following is a result of the session that was repeated three times. In this obvious case one player selected the alternative D in the first and the second session. In the third session all players selected "D" that is consistent with the theoretical analysis. In the third session total payoff of the society becomes 10 and average payoff becomes 1 for a player. In the corresponding replicator dynamics P=0 becomes stable that means all players select "D."

Next we introduce the indirect control mechanism by statistical monitoring. We can observe structural changes in the social payoff as well as the population of alternatives.

We add the special management agent called Government who acts as a macro micro linkage. The government is monitoring the activities of other agents and varies structural parameters for raising the total payoff of the society.

In the first case the government selects the structural parameters as a=1 , b=1.5 and β =0.4. Then all players will select "D" from theoretical point of view. The population of the selected alternative in the experiment is shown as follows. The results of the gaming are slightly different from the ones of mathematical model.

In the case of human agent society a player constructs a certain internal model. The model represents player's belief or his understanding of the environment. The internal model is referred and learned mutually. The internal models and its mutual learning make another mode of the indirect control. In this case the internal models are more cooperative than the replicator dynamics says. The players prefer cooperative attitude to no cooperative attitude because of its higher average payoff as is shown in figure 5. Statistical monitoring pattern helped such learning. Because the monitoring was done in the first 6 sessions because of statistical fluctuation. In many cases agents act more sensitive than the theory prospects. In figure 6 total social payoff becomes better than no monitoring case.

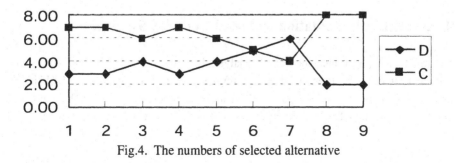

Fig.4. The numbers of selected alternative

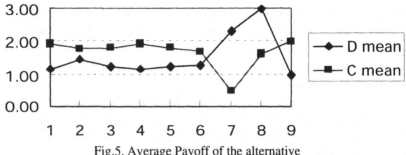

Fig.5. Average Payoff of the alternative

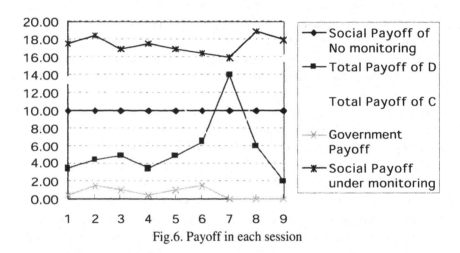

Fig.6. Payoff in each session

Varying Structural Parameters by the government means our indirect control in the agent society. Agents select their own alternatives under their own decision making principle and structural parameters determine its boundary conditions. When β, a or b are varied the macro state of the agent society may change drastically by the bifurcation of the steady state of the dynamical system.

Our experiment on the gaming simulation shows such bifurcation on this agent society. We notice that after the change of monitoring parameters the social payoff has changed drastically.

4. Agent Based Simulation on Social Complex Systems

It is difficult to introduce theoretical analysis for more complex cases. The Social dilemma such as the tragedy of the commons provides a typical case[10,11]. We assume that there are limited pasture land and shepherds on the land. The shepherds want to extend their flocks. However the land is limited. Thus there occures a social dilemma among agents. There is a dilemma between individual rationality and collective rationality as well.

It is difficult to analyze the case depending on the theoretical reality. There is a game theoretical analysis for the tragedy of the commons. But it is difficult to formulate the variety of the actions of the agents by game theoretical framework. We can analyze the variety by agent based simulation on the computational reality.

For this purpose we introduce the classifier system to describe the action rules of a shepherd. In the following case five shepherds are living on the pasture land.
In this case two types of indirect control are introduced on the pasture land. The one is a tax mechanism for rich agents. The other is a subsidy for bankrupts.

The results are shown in the following figures. Figure 7 and 8 are the case of commons with no indirect control as a policy. There survives only one dominant agent in the commons and the commons become non sustainable.

Figure 9 and 10 are the cases of the commons with a tax for rich agents. In this case the commons become sustainable and there survive one or two dominant agents in the commons. Figure 11 and 12 are the cases of the commons with a tax for rich agents and a subsidy for bankrupts. Then the common becomes more sustainable and a variety of activities is observed in the commons.

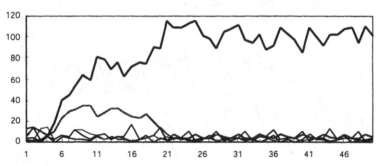

Fig.7. Change of the Number of Sheep (No Policy Case)

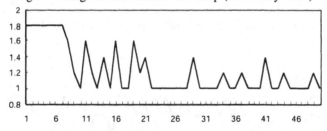

Fig.8. Change of the Reproductive Rate (No Policy Case)

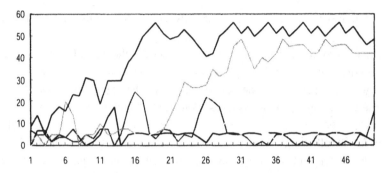

Fig.9. Change of the Number of Sheep (Tax Case)

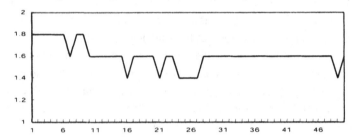

Fig.10. Change of the reproductive rate (Tax Case)

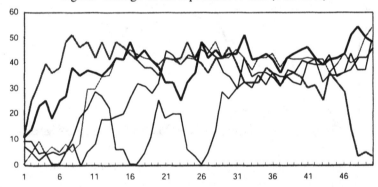

Fig.11. Change of the number of sheep (Tax & Subsidy Case)

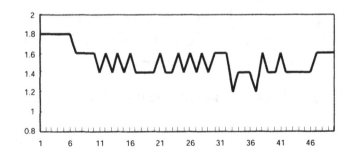

Fig.12. Change of the reproductive rate (Tax & Subsidy Case)

5. Gaming Simulation for Complex Agent Societies
5.1 Social Dilemma of the Commons

We compare the previous results of agent based simulation with the results of gaming simulation by the same condition. The same types of activities on human based gaming simulation is obtained. The results are shown as follows.

Figure 13 and 14 are the cases of the commons with non indirect control as a policy. There survive a number of dominant agents in the commons and the commons become non sustainable. The winner agents will become alone in the long run. Figure 15 and 16 are the cases of the commons with a tax for rich agents and a subsidy for bankrupts. In this case the commons become sustainable and the variety of activities is observed in the commons.

We learn about the meaning of an institutional framework that is regulating a social complex system through the experience of gaming simulation and agent based simulation . Community supporting systems should support these kinds of mutual learning mechanisms among agents in the society.

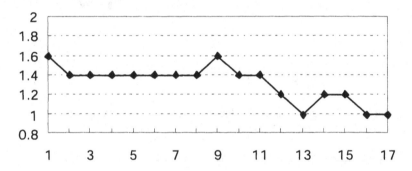

Fig.13. Change of the Reproductive Rate (No Policy Case)

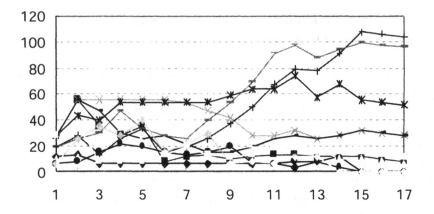

Fig.14. Change of the Total Assets (No Policy Case)

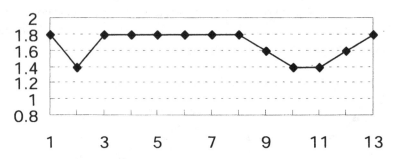

Fig.15. Change of the Reproductive Rate (Tax & Subsidy Case)

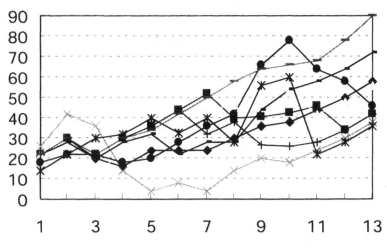

Fig.16. Change of the Total Assets (Tax & Subsidy Case)

5.2 Virtual Economy Gaming

Finally we introduce the virtual economy gaming that was developed by H. Deguchi [12]. Virtual Economy consists of nine agents such as Agriculture ,Milling Industry ,Bread Industry (Bakery), Steel Manufacture, Machinery Industry ,Government , Household, Bank and Central Bank. The model is illustrated as follows.

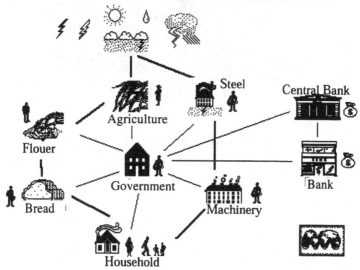

Fig.17. Virtual Economy

In the model economy agriculture grows wheat, milling industry makes wheat flour of wheat, bread industry (bakery) makes bread from flour, steel manufacture makes steel and machinery industry makes machinery from steel. In the model we assumed that there is no materials for steel industry. Household purchases and consumes bread. A machine is purchased by each industry as an investment and used for production. A machine is also purchased by government or household. The machines that are purchased by government or household are considered as an infrastructure and a house respectively. A machine is made depreciation on according to a scenario. Population increases by a scenario. Household supplies workers to each industry and a government and household receives a wage. A government can issue national bonds. A center bank issues a bank note and fixes the official bank rate. Household and industry deposit money in a bank. A bank lends money.

This virtual economy constructs an agent society as a total economic system. In the virtual economy gaming players act as economic agents such as government, agriculture. The following figure shows a case of the virtual economy gaming. The figure 18 and 19 show GDP growth contribution of each agent, nominal and substantial GDP growth respectively.

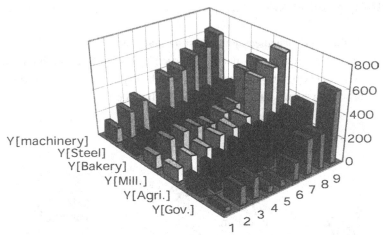

Fig.18. GDP Contribution of Agents

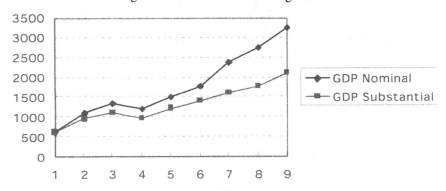

Fig.19 Nominal and Substantial GDP Growth

As the virtual economy gaming is too complex we can not construct agent based simulation in this stage. Virtual Economy Gaming was used for the training course of SNA at the Ministry of International Trade and Industry (MITI) of Japan in its educational program on 1995 and 1996. Virtual economy will becomes a good test bed of agent based simulations for complex agent societies. It will also becomes an effective supporting system to learn about the complexity of economic systems.

6. Conclusion

In our modeling of agent based society we assumed a macro functional agent on the society such as a government or a manager who controls monitoring activity. This agent plays the important role of micro macro linkage. The macro agent varies the structural parameters to attain a macro functional satisfaction criteria such as better social welfare. This is called indirect control of agent society that was shown in figure 2.

Our experimental results are differ slightly from the theoretical ones of replicator dynamics. In the theoretical model we only assumed the indirect control by bifurcation mechanism. In the experiment of gaming simulation we notice another modality of indirect control. A human player constructs a certain internal model that represents an understanding of the player and its environment. Internal models are referred to and learned mutually by players. It makes another modality of indirect control. The results of gaming simulation do not converge to the theoretical ones. To formulate the indirect control principle depending on the internal model we need more effort and an extension of our theoretical framework.

The agent based simulation also helps to analyze such a complex interaction among autonomous agents. In the case of the commons the results are full of interesting suggestions. Designing community supporting system in our extended life world requires a multiple analysis of the realities on the agent societies.

References

1. Haken,Herman: Synergetics An Introduction, Supringer(1978)

2. G.Nicolic,I.Prigogine: Self-Organization in Nonequiliblium Systems ,Wiley(1977)

3 Robert Axelrod: The Complexity of Cooperation - Agent-Based Models of Competition and Collaboration, Princeton University Press (1997)

4. Checkland, P.: Systems Thinking, Systems Practice, John-Wiley(1981)

5. Walsham G.: Interpreting Information Systems in Organization, John-Wiley(1993)

6. Greenblat C.: Designing Games and Simulations: An Illustrated Handbook, Sage(1988)

7. Esben Sloth Andersen: Evolutionary Economics -Post-Schumpeterian Contributions -, Pinter Publishers(1996)

8. Fernando Vega-Redondo: Evolution, Games, and Economics Behaviour,OXFORD UNIVERSITY PRESS(1996)

9. Hiroshi Deguchi: Complex Social Systems and Its Management, in Intelligant Autonomous Systems IAS-5, Edited by Y. Kakazu, M.Wada, T.Sato, pp.702-709, IOS Press(1998)

10. U. Schulz, W. Albers, U. Mueller (Eds.): Social Dilemmas and Cooperation, Springer-Verlag (1994)

11. Hardin, G.R.: The tragedy of the commons, Science, 162, pp.1243-1248(1968)

12. Hiroshi Deguchi: MULTI AGENT ECONOMICS AND ITS GAMING SIMULATION, in Modeling and Control of National and Regional Economies 1995, edited by Vlacic et al., pp.269-274, Pergamon Press(1996)

Awareness – The Common Link Between Groupware and Community Support Systems

Johann Schlichter[1], Michael Koch[2], and Chengmao Xu[1]

[1] Institut für Informatik, Technische Universität München, Germany
[2] Xerox Research Centre Europe, Grenoble, France
{schlicht,xu}@informatik.tu-muenchen.de, koch@xrce.xerox.com

Abstract. Due to the proliferation of computer networks the electronic support of geographically distributed groups has become increasingly important. With respect to groups we can distinguish between teams and communities. In general, team members know each other and collaborate to achieve a common goal while community members have just common interests or preferences. Often there is no personal contact between community members. The electronic support for both group types has developed independently. While community support systems concentrated mostly on the building process, i.e. finding people with similar interests, groupware focused on the collaboration process, i.e. the synchronization and exchange of information in the context of a specific team task. The paper proposes awareness as a common base for both community support systems to improve contact building as well as for groupware to maintain group work at a high performance level. We discuss communities and teams in educational settings and propose an architecture which integrates the awareness mechanism.

1 Introduction

Due to the proliferation of personal computers and computer networks the electronic support of geographically distributed groups has become feasible and in recent years increasingly important. The distribution may range from different floors within the same building to locations within different countries or even time zones. Furthermore, a group of people may also be distributed across organizational boundaries. Thus, the electronic support must include intra- and interorganizational interaction and collaboration as well.

With respect to groups we can distinguish between teams and communities. In general, team members know each other and collaborate to achieve a common goal while community members have just common interests or preferences. The team is often formed through a management decision selecting team members according to their skills, competencies and potential contributions to the specified team goal. Usually teams are tightly interacting groups with team interests dominating over personal interests of the individual team members.

Communities do not have a common goal and thus, the interaction between community members is usually loose. In most cases they do not know each other and personal interests dominate over community interests.

The electronic support for both group types has developed independently. While community support systems concentrated mostly on the building process, i.e. finding people with similar interests, groupware focused on the collaboration process, i.e. the synchronization and exchange of information in the context of a specific team task. Groupware systems are often targeted to a specific task domain. Teufel et al. [24] categorize groupware systems according to their communication, coordination and cooperation support. The major system categories are conferencing systems, e.g. E-mail and video conferencing, workflow management systems, e.g. FlowMark [13], workgroup computing systems, e.g. Iris [14,16] and shared information spaces, e.g. BSCW [2].

Typical software tools supporting the building and interaction process of communities are Internet Relay Chat [20], MUDS [4] and in more modern environments presence indicators and chat tools integrated into web pages. We define

- *community support system* as a medium for initiating contact with unknown collaborators who have similar interests and preferences, and
- *groupware* as a medium for contacting and interacting with known collaborators in order to achieve a shared goal.

Even though support systems for both group types have developed independently, both areas have something in common: the contact facilitation with unknown or known collaborators. We propose awareness as a common base for both community support systems to improve contact building as well as for groupware to maintain group work at a high performance level.

In Section 2 we present definitions of the terms community and team, and highlight the differences. Section 3 discusses possible support mechanisms for both group types, concentrating especially on awareness issues. Section 4 focuses on communities and teams within educational settings. Section 5 proposes an architecture which integrates the awareness mechanism supporting communities and teams as well as the transition between these group types.

2 Communities and Teams

The term "community" has been defined in the literature in different ways; for example Elisabeth Mynatt [17] sees a community as a *"social grouping which exhibit in varying degrees: shared spatial relations, social conventions, a sense of membership and boundaries, and an ongoing rhythm of social interaction"*.

For this paper we will further elucidate this definition based on the definition of the term 'community' in Webster's English Dictionary [25]: *"1) social group of any size whose members reside in a specific locality, share government, and often have a cultural and historical heritage; 2) a social, religious, occupational, or other group sharing common characteristics or interests and perceiving itself as distinct in some respect from the larger society within which it exists"*.

So our understanding of community is a set of people who share something (e.g. a language, a network access, ...) but who do not necessarily know each other or interact on a personal basis. Examples for communities are all students at an university, or all Java programmers speaking English. The main usefulness of comunities lays in its being a starting point for identifying a set of people one could interact with, e.g. to find some help for solving problems or to share experiences.

Groups According to our definition, community members do not necessarily know each other. It makes a difference for possible support mechanisms when the members of a grouping know each other. Therefore, we will use a different term for communities whose members know each other. We will refer to such groupings as "groups".

In contrast to teams which we will define in the next paragraph, groups do not necessarily cooperate. Thus, the interaction is loose because there is no shared task or common goal. Examples of groups are a group of friends or the members of a research institute.

Compared with communities contact building within groups for cooperation on a project or a task is easier because there is already a certain level of knowledge and understanding between group members.

Teams The most advanced form of a community is a "team". The members of a team know each other and are cooperating to achieve a common goal sharing some artefacts they are working on, e. g. a jointly edited document. This description corresponds with a definition found in Webster's Dictionary [25]: *"team: a number of persons associated in some joint action"*.

Fig. 1. Communities, groups, and teams

The main differences between these three group types are the level of interaction between the members and the existence of shared goals and artefacts. It should be noted that there is no clear separation between these group types. Seamless transitions occur between them and groups and teams can exist inside communities (see Figure 1).

3 Support Mechanisms for Communities and Teams

In the following we will discuss different support mechanisms available for groupings of people. Thereby we will not consider groups as a separate type of grouping
but concentrate on support for communities and teams.

3.1 Goal of Support for Communities and Teams

The basic questions concerning support mechanisms are the following: Does the
mechanism only support one individual in the community/team, can it only be
used for supporting the majority of individuals or is it restricted to supporting
interaction of two or more members of the community/team?

We will focus on communities and teams as an environment for cooperation.
Thus, there must be mechanisms to initiate and to carry on the cooperation process. Dividing the cooperation process into smaller stages might help to identify
possible support mechanisms. The following stages can be identified:

1. find someone to collaborate with
2. make contact with the selected people
3. build a common understanding; this includes trust building, the identification of a goal, and the negotiation about the way how this goal should be
   reached.
4. collaborate; collaboration usually consists of two alternating phases
   - the execution of individual work and
   - the communication between co-workers in order to coordinate activities
     and work plans.

The emphasis of *community support systems* is on the first two stages while
groupware concentrates on the last two stages.

3.2 Support for Communities

According to our definition in Section 2 a community is a set of people who share
something (e.g. a native language or an interest) but in general who do not know
each other personally. One potential benefit of being part of a community is the
easier identification of others who might provide some help for the appropriate
execution of an individual (or group) task. For example, to find a person who
has the required competencies and skills and who is willing to collaborate and
to exchange information.

Hence, the main aspect of community support is to facilitate the identification
and selection of potential collaboration partners. Collaboration can be as short
as posing and answering a question, but it can also lead to long-term cooperation
and even to the founding of business enterprises.

Contact Facilitation There are several ways of supporting contact facilitation. Here are three real life examples:

- In Usenet newsgroups one can identify partners by reading news articles or by analyzing answers after posting a request article.
- In a company which maintains an internal employee database one can find the relevant contact partners by querying the database.
- In a library one can find possible partners by looking at the lending history of a book one might be interested in.

Common to these examples is the goal of identifying and selecting the relevant individuals of a community for interaction. In order to support this process, attributes describing the individuals are required. This information can be obtained along different ways, e.g. by conversations (newsgroups), by querying a database which contains information about people with respect to skills, competencies and interests, or by watching objects where one assumes that access to these objects indicates certain characteristics of the user one is looking for (library). The monitoring of accesses to Web pages is a typical example of the latter category.

These examples already demonstrate a two-step approach to support contact facilitation. In the first step an object is specified whose access and use might identify potential contact partners. Object examples are newsgroups, the employee database or an arbitrary object, such as a document or a book. In the second step, the object is monitored with respect to its usage by other people. Thus, awareness of what is going on with the specified object is of major interest during contact facilitation.

Collaborative Use of Knowledge After the identification process a direct communication channel is established to that person. Thus, after contact a cooperation environment is set up similar to working environments of teams. Contact facilitation results in the establishment of a temporary team.

Indirect cooperation is another mechanism often found in the context of communities. Here people cooperate without knowing each other personally. Information provided by some people is used by other people to support their own work. Classic information systems where different users insert and retrieve data are typical examples of this support mechanism. Increasing the number of submitting people might lead to a larger, less specialized community and the pure database solutions no longer work efficiently. Another class of systems that can help to find interesting data in large databases (e.g. the Web) are recommender systems where people rate the information they read and other people use these ratings for filtering incoming information according to their interest level (e.g. Firefly[1]).

In recent work on recommender systems selection of users and recommendations are often combined, that is: the system does not incorporate the ratings

---

[1] see http://www.firefly.com/

of all users but only of those which have been selected as advisors (see KnowledgePump [9]).

For the rest of the paper we will concentrate on direct interaction rather the shared databases or recommender systems.

3.3 Support for Distributed Teams

Collaboration within teams requires the coordination of activities which are performed by the team participants in order to reach the shared goal. In general, coordination is achieved via communication between team members.

There are two different types of tasks which should be considered when discussing computer support for distributed teams: structured and unstructured tasks. The former are tasks which are performed according to a standard procedure, such as approving a business trip or processing bank loan applications. These tasks are often formalized by a detailed model that clearly describes the steps necessary for completing the task. Unstructured tasks are never standardized because they are inherently chaotic. Examples are creative work such as writing a paper for a conference or the production of a movie. In contrast to the first task type there is no obvious structure. Single steps inside the task can only be described in a very complex and often fuzzy manner.

For structured tasks explicit support for coordination is suitable. Workflow management systems are increasingly applied to handle the coordination of structured tasks as well as the execution of the individual steps associated with these tasks.

For unstructured tasks, however, there is no abstract work model that describes the steps necessary for performing a task. Instead, the system must offer as much flexibility as possible to team members so that they can do whatever they think is necessary to achieve a particular goal. This requires a high degree of group awareness where co-workers are aware of each other's past, current and possible future activities within the shared environment. The propagation and exchange of group awareness information results in "implicit coordination" of team work.

The exchange of information may be achieved by direct or indirect communication. There are several factors contributing to the success or failure of the collaboration between team members:

- For direct synchronous communication it is necessary to know when the communication partners are available, e.g. for spontaneous collaboration, for initiating direct communication or for explicitly coordinating activities or access to shared resources.
- In addition to planned direct communication there must be a method of supporting spontaneous direct communication. Therefore, awareness of who is around is needed.
- In order to enhance group awareness required for implicit coordination it is necessary to generate, distribute and display various information about the current state of the work and co-workers as well as about the history of past activities and events (indirect communication).

In the following paragraphs we give a brief overview of support technology for these areas. More information can be found in publications of the "Computer-Supported Cooperative Work (CSCW)" area (e.g. biannual ACM CSCW conferences).

Contact Facilitation / Media Spaces Contact facilitation in teams helps the user to determine when to communicate with someone he already knows, rather than finding a new partner. It provides awareness information concerning the absence of team members, availability of team members for conversation and social acceptability of initiating a conversation with any of them.

Several interface techniques have been developed for contact facilitation within teams. Media spaces are one way of providing distributed groups with informal awareness of each other. Video walls, for example, rely on continuous video and audio for information about who is around at other sites [1]. Video snapshots, such as Portholes provide periodically updated video snapshots of other people's offices [6]. Video glimpses, as in Montage give short video views into another person's offices without any additional audio channel. Minimalist awareness systems, such as PeepHoles [10] indicate how long a person has been absent from his computer.

Support for direct Communication Direct communication of a distributed team can be realized through standard synchronous and asynchronous methods of computer and network based communication: telephone calls, video and audio conferences, text talk, email/news.

In addition to these standard means we refer the interested reader to recent approaches to make video conferencing more conference like (e.g. MAJIC [11]) and the use of 3D virtual spaces which provide places for direct communication (text based: Blaxxun CommunityClient/Server[2] [21] - audio/video based: FreeWalk [18]).

Processed Awareness Information In general, Media Spaces only transmit pictures or audio information recorded at one site to all other connected sites. The interpretation is left to the user. It is not possible for the system to preprocess or filter the information.

Informal team awareness is the general sense of which of the team members is around and what others are up to. These are the kinds of things that people track when they work together in the same physical environment. This awareness is the glue that facilitates casual interaction, the spontaneous and one-person initiated meetings that form the backbone of everyday coordination and work [3,8].

The informal awareness and the casual collaboration triggered by informal awareness is an essential and highly productive part of the work experience [5].

---

[2] see http://www.blaxxun.com/

To summarize, one can say that awareness "is part of the *glue* that allows groups to be more effective than individuals" [10].

Media spaces and awareness systems intend to provide informal awareness for distributed teams which do not share the same physical environment. Besides media spaces awareness information can also be distilled from interaction with workspace objects and displayed in special views to the team members.

3.4 Awareness as a Common Base for Communities and Teams

The electronic support for communities and teams developed independently. While community support systems concentrated mostly on the building process, i.e. finding people with similar interests, groupware focused on the collaboration process, i.e. the synchronization and exchange of information in the context of a specific team task.

As we showed above there is one task needed in both settings: contact facilitation with unknown or known collaborators. Additionally, there is a need to seamlessly switch from community support systems (contact facilitation) to groupware (accomplishing group tasks). Hence, the two areas should grow together. In our opinion the notion of awareness is a common base to connect the two application domains. Making contact requires awareness of who is in the same (virtual) place and who is interested in the same data. For successful synchronization in teams it is essential to have some knowledge of what is going on in the team.

Most of recent CSCW research has emphasized awareness-oriented collaboration systems where users coordinate their work based on the knowledge of what the members of the collaborating group are doing or have done. Group awareness can be defined as "an understanding of the activities of others, which provides a context for your own activity" [6]. Pedersen describes awareness as an "ability to maintain and constantly update a sense of our social and physical context [19]".

An increase of awareness within a collaborating group has several advantages:

- It encourages informal spontaneous communication (e.g. via video conferences, phone calls, etc.), since people are more likely to contact others directly if they know their partner is at leisure and can be interrupted without interfering too much with his/her ongoing work.
- Awareness is important for keeping the group members up-to-date with important events and therefore contributes to their ability to make conscious decisions.

Awareness is needed for both, contact facilitation in communities and teams and for maintaining team work at a high performance level within teams.

The reason why recent awareness systems have focused on one of the two areas is caused by different needs of the different user groups. The main difference is that context is available in team work while not in communities (people do not know each other). Thus, in the latter case there is some need to establish context (e.g. information on which page both users are working upon, where the user is from, exchange of business cards, etc.). In teams there is more background information available on the team goals as well as on the characteristics of the team members. Therefore contact facilitation can work with less information displayed. Thus, it is enough to display an image of the co-workers; additional information, such as the individual interests and skills is not needed.

As a result, different information is required for providing awareness in teams as opposed to communities. However, it is possible to provide a seamless transitions between these two types.

In the following section we will present mechanisms of using awareness information in different educational settings. Educational environments comprise both group types, communities as well as teams. Our main goal has been to use the same services in all settings and to provide seamless transition between communities and teams.

4 Communities in Education Systems

4.1 Collaboration Entities of Educational Environments

At a university cooperation is a ubiquitous work form of interaction between students, professors and research assistants. Both learning and teaching can be regarded as a kind of cooperative process. Lectures, seminars and practical courses serve as places where cooperation is organized and takes place.

The collaborations occurring at different level of abstractions as well as between different entities lead to the forming of a variety of communities and teams. According to the organizational view (see figure 2) a university is organized into departments, chairs and project teams which respectively correspond to community, group and team as defined above. On the other hand, we will subsequently investigate another kind of view, the event oriented view.

Both views reflect the same relationships between communities, groups and teams. Interpreting the differences between the pyramid bottom and its top, one can observe the following trends from the bottom to the top: less members, but closer cooperative relationships between the members; informal spontaneous interactions dominate within a community (at the bottom of the pyramid) whereas the work in a team (at the pyramid top) is usually planned and goal-oriented.

4.2 Communities and Teams in Lecture 2000

The geographical distribution of a university often restricts and encumbers the cooperation between students, professors and research assistants. For example, the fourteen chairs in the Informatics department of the Technische Universität München (TUM) are located at six different sites requiring up to half an hour travel time by public transportation to go from one site to another. Students must shuttle between dormitories, chair locations and the main campus of the

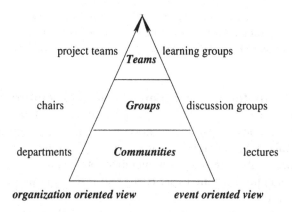

Fig. 2. Different views of communities, groups, and teams in educational systems

university to attend classes and to interact face-to-face with tutors and fellow students. The project Lecture 2000 [23] aims at supporting and enriching common university lecturing by applying the potential of new technologies and by designing and implementing an integrated multimedia based learning and teaching environment. It enables and facilitates the cooperation between students, professors and research assistants even when they are distributed across several locations.

Derived from the characteristics of the learning and teaching process Lecture 2000 distinguishes between the following collaboration entities (event oriented view): the class of a lecture as a community, learning groups for the lecture as teams, a discussion group and spontaneous groups facilitating the transition from the community to the teams inside the community.

Class as a Community attending a Lecture People who come to attend a lecture may come from different departments of a university, from other cities or other states of a country, and even from other continents. At present, such a group of people can either sit together in a classroom or attend the lecture remotely. As an effort to remove the geographical obstacle some lectures at the TUM are propagated to the wide area network via Mbone. The common interest in the lecture serves as a "glue" to unite people who often do not know each other personally. They constitute a community called "class". Notably, members of the community also include those who never actually make their appearance in class but are nevertheless interested in the content of the course.

The class exists only as a very loose and often only as virtual community. Experience shows that students prefer to participate in discussions in small groups composed of 2 to 5 persons in order to discuss course related issues. Normally, the work of a small group can lead to the answers to the issues arising from the learning process which can be stored as histories for future studies and examinations. Therefore, these small groups will be regarded as teams derived from the community. In section 3.1, we have considered it central for community support to facilitate the identification of potential collaboration partners. The following will discuss contact facilition in educational settings distinguishing between asynchronous and synchronous modes.

Discussion Group for asynchronous Contact Facilitation Associated with each lecture there is a discussion group available to all attending students providing asynchronous contact facilitation. The discussion group can be regarded as a public service which enables lecture participants to communicate with others more easily. Normally, the members of such a group share common interests in exchanging learning experiences and discussing problems connected with the learning process.

Under these circumstances people contact each other asynchronously and often anonymously using nick names. In practice, a discussion group of a lecture plays a similar role as the Usenet newsgroups mentioned before. As interactions mature people can establish a team for conducting a more efficient and closer cooperation. A discussion group represents a subgroup in a small community.

Spontaneous Groups for synchronous Contact Facilitation Informal spontaneous interactions have proven to be very important in communities. In a distributed community, where members do not know each other, this kind of "unintented" meeting plays a very important role in facilitating the identification of potential collaboration partners.

In [12] four categories of interactions have been distinguished: planned (prearranged meeting), intended (explicitly sought by one person), opportunistic (anticipated by one party but occurring only when the parties happened to see each other) and spontaneous (unanticipated by either party). These latter two types of interactions are called "unintented". The term "spontaneous (temporary) group" specifies a group formed by people when they meet each other in an "unintented" manner. These kinds of meetings lead to synchronous interactions. Previous research has shown that synchronous interactions provide people with better opportunities for developing a common understanding than asynchronous interactions.

Learning Groups Cooperation in education could be described as the specific cooperative relationships characterized by common goals and responsibilities shared by a group of people. The common goals and responsibilities can be better achieved and assumed in a small group than in a large one. Therefore, the interactions within loosely coupled discussion and spontaneous groups often lead to the creation of small groups for preparing and reviewing the lecture content in more detail. These small groups, called Learning Groups, distinguish themselves from the discussion groups by fewer members, closer relationships and clearer objectives. Mostly the members of learning groups communicate with each other synchronously. Learning groups are examples of teams as defined above.

5 The Lecture 2000 Environment

Lecture 2000 [23] provides a comprehensive information space and supports collaboration facilities. The following will focus on the latter aspect and discuss the support of communities and teams and the seamless transition between them. We will firstly describe our system design and then briefly show how this support is achieved in the system. Finally, some issues with respect to awareness support revealed by the design will be explored in more detail.

5.1 Architecture of Lecture 2000

Lecture 2000 is client/server based. For each lecture there is a separate server (see Figure 3) which after the initiation phase consists of a tutor studio, a discussion group and an entrance hall. As the lecture progresses new learning groups and spontaneous groups might be established. A server which is entered via the entrance hall represents a lecture community. From the entrance hall a student can go into the discussion group, one of the learning groups, the tutor studio, or initiate a spontaneous group with other people whom he encountered in the entrance hall.

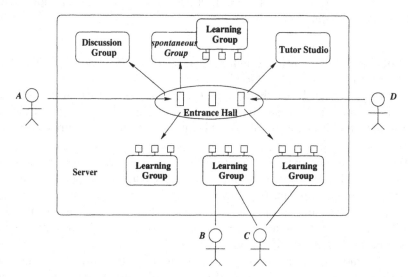

Fig. 3. The structure of a server in Lecture 2000. It consists of Discussion Group, Learning Group, Tutor Studio and Entrance Hall

Discussion Group A discussion group provides an asynchronous interaction mode for lecture participants to discuss and solve lecture related issues.

Learning Groups A learning group is a team that is composed of several students who meet regularly for preparing and reviewing the lecture. Entrance into a learning group is protected by a password selected by the owner of the group. However, the tutor of the lecture is allowed to take part in team discussions without providing a password.

A learning group exports the following information about itself: (1) current group state: there can be four possible states represented by a door sign: between sessions (a closed door), open to all (an opened door), closed to all (a closed door with a red light), and opened after contact (a closed door with a green light); (2) group membership and the contact information of group members; (3) data list of group activities. Based on the exported information members of the lecture community might interact with learning group members and thus participate in team discussions. It can even lead to the change of team membership.

Tutor Studio It is assumed that a tutor occasionally participates in learning group discussions. Additionally there is a tutor studio which aims at increasing the collaboration possibilities between students and the tutor. In practice a tutor studio is similar to an office. Entrance into the studio is restricted to pre-determined consulting hours.

Like a learning group, a tutor studio exports information to provide people with the current state of the studio, data lists and contact information such as the secretary's telephone number.

Entrance Hall The entrance hall is furnished with a variety of information about activities occurring in other places on the server, such as in learning groups and the tutor studio. In particular, one can learn about others who are also in the entrance hall at the same time. Then, the entrance hall provides a medium for awareness and it facilitates all possible interactions in the lecture community:

- With help of the exported information of a learning group people in the entrance hall can attempt to contact team participants. If possible, they can join a team and take part in its discussions.
- People in a learning group can notice those who appear in the entrance hall. When a user has found a potential collaboration partner in the entrance hall, he can invite him to join the group.
- People who happen to meet each other in the entrance hall can initiate a spontaneous (temporary) group. If they agree to form a team for a close and regular collaboration, they can also do so. Thus, the spontaneous group may change into a team (learning group).
- From the entrance hall one can also judge whether or not entrance to the tutor studio is permitted by checking the information on the door of the studio.
- Finally, one can enter into the discussion group to seek possible collaboration with others.

5.2 Support Mechanisms for Community and its Teams

In the design, we have mainly used two contact facilities (discussion group and entrance hall) in supporting the first two cooperation stages depicted in section 3.1. Compared with other methods such as the deployment of an internal employee database, the entrance hall supports synchronous interactions which provide much better opportunities for developing a common understanding among encounters.

Within a team, every place is equipped with groupware tools in supporting the collaboration work among the members of the team, for example multiuser editor [15], chat tool and so on. However, one of our main concerns in supporting the collaboration activities within a team is the link between the discussion process and the information space provided by Lecture 2000. The material stored in the information space serves as a basis for the discussion. Discussion results with respect to the issues can be stored in either private or public workspaces for the future use of the members, and the movement of results between the sites will also be supported.

5.3 Related Issues

In section 3 we have explored the idea that awareness provides a common base for both community and team support. As decribed above, people can use various groupware tools to do collaborative work. Without a doubt, awareness plays a key role in groupware tools. Here, we mainly focus on the investigation of issues related to the awareness support in a community.

Awareness and Privacy Control Awareness involves knowing who is around, what activities are under way, who is talking with whom; it provides a view of one another in the daily work environment [7]. In other words, it means that an individual must enter into public or private areas in order to learn as much as possible about others and their activities. Media space technology typically focuses on the use of direct audio and video connections as a means to obtain such information. However, it is difficult to distinguish between public and private spheres in some situations. Privacy is relative. Even in a public area (e.g. in a cafe), staring at someone is considered impolite. Privacy issues have often been a major concern when designing and installing media spaces.

To enable participation within a widely distributed community Lecture 2000 is designed to support people with audio-video equipment, audio only, or perhaps even text only devices. Furthermore, students have no permanent workplaces compared with workers in a company. Thus, the environment of Lecture 2000 does not depend on the media space technology to obtain awareness information.

Place for Awareness Support Lecture 2000 uses a variety of places to support awareness for the communities. Places, such as "rooms" in TeamWave and "virtual hallways" in the original design of the Cruiser media space [22] have become increasingly popular in collaborative systems. They facilitate and structure interaction between people.

The awareness provided by a place can be observed in two ways: within a place and outside of a place. Within a place, awareness reflects a kind of interest, preference, cultural background and rules implied by the place. For example, when somebody enters into a lecture room of a university, it means that he is interested in the content of the lecture and will comply with the university rules.

Outside of a place we pay particular attention to the ways people enter the place. Different people may use different ways. A place itself often implies the mechanism in which it should be entered from the outside. For example, a student should knock at the door before he enters into the professor's office whereas he can walk right into a lecture room.

Places in Lecture 2000 Thus, a place as a spatial metaphor can both provide awareness for a community and also serve as a workplace for a team. Furthermore, places which can easily be located will facilitate a variety of spontaneous interactions. However, a place which has no boundaries can also lead to unexpected annoyances and privacy violations. On the other hand, if a place provides very tight boundaries it can encumber the collaboration possiblities with those outside of the place.

Thus, Lecture 2000 provides places which have boundaries but which can export necessary information to the outside. This information may link both sides of a place. Additionally suitable privacy considerations make a place more open and more usable. The places of Lecture 2000 not only have boundaries for privacy protection but they can also export information for supporting a variety of spontaneous interactions.

6 Conclusion

In this paper we have presented a model that connects the application areas of community support systems and groupware. Taking this model as a starting point we have highlighted (group) awareness as the connecting point and then presented the Lecture 2000 example where these results are used in a system supporting different community types in an university setting.

The Lecture 2000 project started in 1996. Initially the project focused on the information space publishing and distributing the complete material of several courses electronically as well as teleteaching aspects for online courses. From the very beginning we tried to integrate support mechanisms, such as a study advisor, self assessment tests and chat tools for spontaneous interaction. Currently we are refining the design for the lecture server to support communities and teams as discussed above.

References

1. Abel M., Corey D., Bulick S., Schmidt J., and Coffin S. *The US West Advanced Technologies TeleCollaboration research project*, In Wagner G., editor, *Computer Augmented Teamwork*. Van Nostrand Reinhold, 1990.
2. Bentley R., Horstmann T., and Trevor J. The world wide web as enabling technology for cscw: The case of bscw. *CSCW: The Journal of Collaborative Computing*, 2(3), 1997.
3. Cockburn A. and Greenberg S. Making contact: getting the group communicating with groupware. In *Conf. on Organizational Computing Systems*, pages 31–41, Nov. 1993.
4. Curtis P. Mudding: Social phenomena in text-based virtual realities. In *Proc. Conf. on the Directions and Implications of Advanced Computing*, May 1992.
5. Donath J. S. Casual collaboration. In *Proc. IEEE Intl Conf. on Multimedia Compt. and Syst. (ICMCS)*, pages 490–496, May 1994.
6. Dourish P. and Bellotti V. Awareness and coordination in shared workspaces. In Turner J. and Kraut R. E., editors, *Proc. Intl Conf. on Comp. Supported Cooperative Work*, pages 107–114. ACM Press, New York, NY, Oct. 1992.
7. Dourish P. and Bly S. Portholes: Supporting awareness in a distributed work group. In Bauersfeld P., Bennett J., and Lynch G., editors, *Proc. ACM SIGCHI Conf. on Human Factors in Compt. Syst.*, pages 541–547. ACM Press, New York, NY, May 1992.
8. Fish R. S., Kraut R. E., Root R. W., and Rice R. E. Evaluating video as a technology for informal communication. In Bauersfeld P., Bennet J., and Lynch G., editors, *Proc. ACM SIGCHI Conf. on Human Factors in Compt. Syst.*, pages 37–48. ACM Press, New York, NY, May 1992.
9. Glance N., Arregui D., and Dardenne M. *Knowledge Pump: Supporting the Flow and Use of Knowledge in Networked Organizations*, In Borghoff U. and Pareschi R., editors, *Information Technology for Knowledge Management*. Springer Verlag, Berlin, 1998.
10. Greenberg S., Gutwin C., and Cockburn A. Using distortion-oriented displays to support workspace awareness. Technical report, Dept of Comp. Science, Univ. of Calgary, Canada, Jan. 1996.
11. Ichikawa Y., ichi Okada K., Jeong G., Tanaka S., and Matsushita Y. Majic videoconferencing system: Experients, evaluation and improvement. In Marmolin H., Sundblad Y., and Schmidt K., editors, *Proc. 4th European Conf. on Comp. Supported Cooperative Work*, pages 279–292. Kluwer Academic Publishers, Dordrecht, Sep. 1995.
12. Isaacs E., Tang J. C., and Morris T. Piazza: A desktop environment supporting impromptu and planned interactions. In Ackerman M. S., editor, *Proc. Intl Conf. on Comp. Supported Cooperative Work*, pages 315–324. ACM Press, New York, NY, Nov. 1996.
13. Kamath M., Alonso G., Guenthoer R., and Mohan C. Providing high availability in very large workflow management systems. Technical report, IBM Almaden Research Center, July 1995.
14. Koch M. *Kooperation bei der Dokumentenbearbeitung - Entwicklung einer Gruppeneditorumgebung für das Internet*. DUV, Wiesbaden, Germany, 1997. ISBN 3-8244-2083-X.
15. Koch M. *Unterstützung kooperativer Dokumentenbearbeitung in Weitverkehrsnetzen*. PhD thesis, Inst. für Informatik, Techn. Univ. München, Germany, 1997.

(also available as: 'Kooperation bei der Dokumentenbearbeitung - Entwicklung einer Gruppeneditorumgebung für das Internet', DUV, Wiesbaden, 1997).

16. Koch M. and Koch J. Using component technology for group editors - the iris group editor environment. In ter Hofte G. H. and van der Lugt H. J., editors, *Proc. Workshop on Object Oriented Groupware Platforms*, pages 44–49. Telematics Research Centre, Enschede, NL, Sep. 1997.

17. Mynatt E. D., Adler A., Ito M., and O'Day V. L. Design for network communities. In *Proc. ACM SIGCHI Conf. on Human Factors in Compt. Syst.*, 1997.

18. Nakanishi H., Yoshida C., Nashimura T., and Ishida T. Freewalk: Supporting casual meetings in a network. In Ackerman M. S., editor, *Proc. Intl Conf. on Comp. Supported Cooperative Work*, pages 308–314. ACM Press, New York, NY, Nov. 1996.

19. Pedersen E. R. and Sokoler T. Aroma: Abstract representation of presence supporting mutual awareness. In Pemberton S., editor, *Proc. ACM SIGCHI Conf. on Human Factors in Compt. Syst.*, pages 51–58. ACM Press, New York, NY, Mar. 1997.

20. Reid E. M. Electropolis: Communication and community on internet relay chat, 1991. Honours Thesis.

21. Rockwell R. An infrastructure for social software. *IEEE Spectrum*, 24(3), Mar. 1997.

22. Root R. W. Design of a multi-media vehicle for social browsing. In *Proc. Intl Conf. on Comp. Supported Cooperative Work*, pages 25–38. ACM Press, New York, NY, Sep. 1988.

23. Schlichter J. Lecture 2000: More than a course across wires. *Teleconference - The Business Communications Magazine*, 16(6):18–21, 1997.

24. Teufel S., Sauter C., Mühlherr T., and Bauknecht K. *Computerunterstützung für die Gruppenarbeit*. Addison-Wesley Publishing Company, 1995.

25. *Webster's encyclopedic unabridged dictionary of the English language*. Gramercy Books, New York, 1996.

Social, Psychological and Artistic Aspects of the Human Interface

Ryohei Nakatsu

ATR Media Integration & Communications Research Laboratories
2-2, Hikaridai, Seika-cho, Soraku-gun, Kyoto, 619-0288, Japan
nakatsu@mic.atr.co.jp, http://www.mic.atr.co.jp

Abstract: Human interface is defined as technologies for supporting human communications and, therefore, it has close relation with other areas concerning human communications. In this paper, the basic concept of human interface is examined and it is pointed out that interdisciplinary research between engineering and social, psychological, and artistic areas should be carried out for the development of future human interface technology. Also several examples of this type of research are described.

1 Introduction

In recent years, the meaning of "human interface" has been extended from the base concept of a "man-machine interface." It can now be taken to refer to research into how the computer can support communication both between humans and between humans and computers. For this reason, human-interface research must take into account social, psychological, and artistic aspects in addition to technological aspects, which were the sole concern of the conventional approach to this kind of research in the field of engineering. The problem then arises as to how best to proceed with human-interface research that includes these factors while using engineering as a base to work from. This paper examines what forms these aspects might take in the human interface and points out important problems that need to be addressed. It also presents examples of research being performed at the ATR Media Integration & Communications Research Laboratories that take into account these aspects from an engineering perspective.

2 Role of the Human Interface

2.1 The human interface and communication

In a narrow sense, "human interface" can be taken to mean a "man-machine interface." From this point of view, much research has been performed on how computers as representative of machines can be made easier for people to use. Considerable attention has therefore been placed on methods of communication between humans and computers. However, as computers come to play a significant role in our lives in a variety of forms, the problem goes beyond how to establish an effective interface between a single computer and a solitary human user. In particular, a multi-dimensional problem arises that involves how communication among people is developing and how it should be done in an environment characterized by the ubiquitous computer. For example, as communication between people connected to networks like the Internet goes beyond real-time speech and takes on an asynchronous character in the form of media like text and pictures, the narrow definition of the problem as one of how to construct an interface between a human and a computer no longer holds. We therefore view the human interface in the following manner.

(1) Researching the human interface means researching human communication activities. Communication in this case includes that between humans and between humans and computers.

(2) The central issue of human-interface research is determining how the computer should support human communication activities

Once the problem is set up in this way, the question as to how to treat the human interface becomes clear. In other words, the problem shifts from how to make it easier for a human to use a single computer to how to make a computer support human communication.

Next, from the viewpoint of communication, let's take a look at the way in which the human interface has been researched up to now mainly in the field of engineering. Here, we can point out that engineers have traditionally been focusing their research on robots, computer agents, and other entities that feature a function for communicating with humans. It can also be said that this research has for the most part concentrated on the language component of communication. On example of such research is voice recognition systems that aim to extract meaning from speech, or in other words, logical information. In recent years, however, it has come to be recognized that the conveyance of emotion and sensitivity, i.e., non-language communication, plays an important role in our daily lives. Speech, for example, includes both logical information and non-logical information, with examples of the latter being information related to the speaker (individual information) and information related to emotions (rhythm information). Technology associated with non-logical communication should become an important element of future research on the human interface.

2.2 Communication model

Figure 1 shows a diagram of a human communication model. The topmost layer controls communication functions based on the use of language. Researchers in the human interface and artificial intelligence (AI) fields have been studying the mechanisms of this layer. As mentioned above, typical examples of such research are voice recognition. In the field of voice recognition, research has been performed for many years on algorithms that could hopefully provide a high level of recognition. Nevertheless, actual performance has fell short of expectations, and the reason for this has sometimes been attributed to inadequate recognition algorithms. Could the real reason, however, be that the true nature of the problem has been ignored?

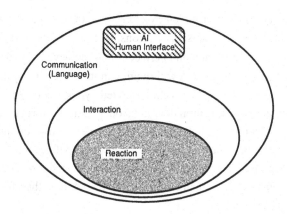

Fig.1. Communication Model

The objective of voice recognition has been to extract only logical information included in speech. As explained previously, though, logical information is merely one type of information making up speech. Also included are very rich forms of information associated with emotions and sensitivity. We can consider these types of information to be generated in the lower layers in the figure, specifically, the interaction layer and reaction layer. The interaction layer here controls actions like generating the speaker's rhythm and taking turns to speak in order to maintain a communication channel. This layer plays an important role in establishing smooth communication between people. Beneath this layer is the reaction layer, which controls basic human actions like turning one's head in the direction of an arriving sound and shutting one's eyes in response to a bright light. We can view such primal functions as being acquired deep in man's past during a time when he was still in an animal stage.

In the above way, we can say that low-layer functions, which differ from those that treat logical actions and logical information on a higher layer, play an important role in human communication, and that non-language information like emotions and sensitivity is generated and understood by these functions in the lower layers. We can postulate that the limit reached in voice-recognition performance resulted from the treatment of such essential information as noise and not worthy of attention. To therefore achieve comprehensive human communication functions that also include the transmission and reception of non-logical information, the mechanisms of the above interaction and reaction layers must be researched and eventually integrated with the functions of the top communication layer[1].

3 Aspects of the Human Interface

As described above, the broader meaning of the human interface requires that we think of it in terms of its ability to support human communication. Moreover, in contrast to the traditional engineering approach of dealing only with logical information among the various types of information exchanged in communication, non-logical information associated with the senses, emotions, and sensitivity will also have to be taken into account if a superior human interface is to be achieved. As described below, dealing with this type of information will require an interdisciplinary approach as opposed to past human interface research characterized by engineering work only.

To reiterate, human communication does not stop at logical information; it includes a wealth of non-logical information that plays a major role in daily communication. We can now pose the question: from what points of view should this kind of information be dealt with? In response, we can say that non-logical information is deeply related to various levels of behavior in human communication, and must therefore be treated in terms of the following aspects.

(1) Social behavior in human communication

It is said that man is a social animal. While engaged in person-to-person communication, a human being also communicates as a member of society. This gives rise to behavior in communication based on organizational and social rules that go beyond individual norms of communication. In addition, organizations and society tend to change with time as well as with progress in technology. Research of communication behavior must therefore take these two items into account. We will refer to this aspect of communication as the "social aspect of the human interface."

(2) Basic behavior in human communication

As indicated by the communication model presented earlier, basic actions in human communication are controlled by the paleocortex through a mechanism shared with the animal kingdom. Both humans and animals such as dogs and cats therefore react on the basis of whether intent has been communicated or not. To research this type of basic mechanism, the following method is adopted: focus on communication behavior when people are sending or receiving basic stimuli to or from the outside world; examine basic behavioral mechanisms by analyzing this type of behavior through psychological experiments; and create models. On the basis of this approach, we refer to this aspect of communication as the "psychological aspect of the human interface," and the information that is sent and received here as low-order sensory information.

(3) High-order behavior in human communication

In addition to communication that deals with non-logical information like that associated with the senses, humans can engage in communication having even higher orders of non-logical information. The impression felt when viewing or listening to a great work of art or music is clearly high-order information different from low-order sensory information handled by humans as an animal response. Such high-order information is a major element in distinguishing man from animals and will therefore be referred to here as high-order sensory information or "Kansei" information. Because this kind of information is typically handled by painters, musicians, novelists and other artists, we will refer to the aspect of communication related to the sending and receiving of high-order sensory information as the "artistic aspect of the human interface[2]."

The above discussion shows that research of the human interface can no longer be the sole domain of engineering but must take on an interdisciplinary character involving sociology, psychology, and art in addition to engineering. The following sections will describe the way that research should proceed for each of the above aspects, and will introduce studies now being performed at the ATR Media Integration & Communications Research Laboratories as concrete examples of research on the human interface.

4 Social Aspect of the Human Interface

4.1 Approach

Human communication actually includes a variety of social aspects. This section will point out those points considered most important to our discussion and will also propose a specific research approach.

In addition to human beings, future society will feature virtual entities created by computer. These entities, or "agents," are expected to play a big role in our lives, and as they take on a ubiquitous existence, human beings will have no choice but to coexist with them. The agent side in such a society will therefore have to act in a manner that satisfies the social nature of communication. In other words, we are entering an era that demands "social agents." Our response in this regard should be as follows.

(1) First, behavior under the social conditions present when people talk to each other must be examined, its basic model and mechanism determined, and that mechanism incorporated into agents. In this way, agent behavior can be made more human.

At the same time, we can imagine that communication behavior on the human side will change depending on whether the other party is another human or a computer agent. The approach is therefore not simply to model the communication behavior of people and incorporate it into agents, but must include the following step.

(2) The behavioral principles of humans when the other party is an agent must be modeled, an optimal agent model for this situation created, and that model incorporated in agents.

The analysis of communication between people in a social situation is a field of sociology, and for this reason, research with regard to step (1) above must be pursued in cooperation with sociology and related fields. On the other hand, communication behavior in a virtual environment corresponding to step (2) above is an area that has not been dealt with to any great extent in sociology. Nevertheless, how to go about establishing an agent society is a problem that cannot be ignored in the coming years. It will therefore be necessary for the fields of engineering and sociology to cooperate in determining the conditions for communication under a variety of virtual environments, and in observing and analyzing communication under such conditions.

4.2 Research example: rhythm in conversation

Based on the above ideas, the author and his colleagues are focusing certain research on:

(1) Observing and analyzing communication activities among people; and
(2) Establishing virtual communication conditions and observing and analyzing communication activities under such conditions.

Here, we describe the observation of rhythm in conversation between people as a specific example of research work[3]. While it has already been shown that two speakers in a conversation will mutually adjust their response time and speech rate, this has only been done in a qualitative manner. Here, we will focus on "rhythm" in conversation and observe the way in which rhythm is adjusted between two speakers engaged in a conversation. The target conversation of analysis is performed over the telephone whereby one speaker informs another speaker of a route on a map. Here, one unit of speaking delimited by an interval of silence is called a sub-utterance unit (SU), and the average mora duration (AMD) within a single SU is taken to be an evaluation standard when measuring rhythm. Two adjacent SUs are called a non-opening pair (NOP) when made up of elements like question/answer and request/consent, and an opening pair (OP) when a new topic of conversation begins. The difference in AMDs between two adjacent SUs are measured: a positive result indicates an utterance rhythm that is accelerating, and a negative result an utterance rhythm that is decelerating.

The problem here is to determine how NOPs and OPs accelerate or decelerate for a single speaker and for both speakers in the conversation. The results of analysis are shown in Fig. 2. It was found that: (1) The rhythm of conversation accelerates for NOP and decelerates for OP; and (2) This phenomenon is the same when measurements are made for either the same speaker or between two speakers. In other words, each of two speakers in a conversation adjusts his or her speech to the rhythm (speech rate) of the other party's speech. In addition, rhythm speeds up if the topic of conversation remains unchanged, and the rhythm resets and slows down when the topic changes. In short, two speakers in a conversation adjust their rhythm just like two dancers, and work closely together when speeding up and slowing down the conversation.

These findings indicate that such a mechanism must be incorporated in agents to make them more human like. It is not sufficient to simply understand the contents of the other party's speech; rather, the rhythm of the other party's speech must be detected and the agent's responding rhythm must be set based on the contents and rhythm of the other party's speech and on the appropriate reply to these. Although much research is being performed on agents having a function for conversing with humans by voice means, there is yet no example of incorporating such a function, and it remains a major research subject.

5 Psychological Aspect of the Human Interface
5.1 Approach

As described above, basic information such as that associated with the senses is referred to as low-order sensory information in this paper. Engineering that deals with this type of information is generally called "Kansei processing," and a variety of re-

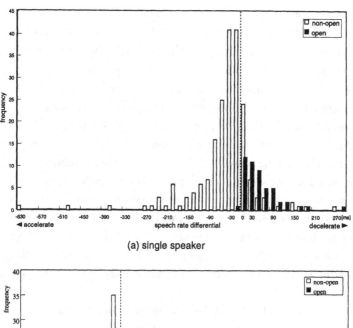

(a) single speaker

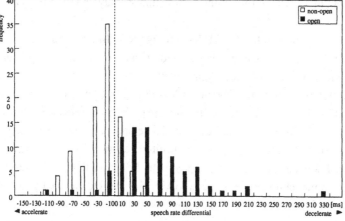

(b) cross speaker

Fig. 2. Speech rate and information openings

search has come to be performed under this name. It should be pointed out here that the information targeted by Kansei processing is limited to low-order sensory information. However, the term "Kansei" has often been associated with high-order sensory information to be described later, and misunderstandings can easily occur. As a result, research has been appearing that attempts to deal with high-order sensory information within the same framework as conventional engineering. In this regard, we point out that engineering still operates on the basis of Descartes' idea of mind and matter as separate, and it has advanced to its current state through the study of matter. High-order sensitivity belongs to the mind, so to speak, and the manner in which it is manifested is indefinite and unclear. It is therefore contradictory to deal with mind-associated high-order sensory information on the basis of engineering methodology that deals only with matter.

However, if we limit sensory information to low-order sensory information, much of it will be shared in common by people. This means that by clarifying the relationships between physical stimuli and the senses through psychological experiments and the like, human communication mechanisms can be researched at the level of low-order sensory information. The following points are significant with regard to this approach. (1) The basic format of this approach is "bottom-up" beginning with research of the relationship between simple stimuli and the senses and gradually shifting to research of compound stimuli and the senses. (2) Examining the relationship between real, complex phenomena and the senses using only the above methodology is difficult. Accordingly, when researching the relationship between complex, compound stimuli (like landscape images) and the senses, hypotheses will be formed and tested in parallel with the bottom-up methodology in an effort to clarify the relationship. (3) Emphasis will be placed on storing the high-order sensory information possessed by artists, designers, etc., as data in a reusable format instead of simply analyzing the information.

5.2 Research example: the COMI&CS image handling system

In communication, how to go about creating and transmitting images that one wants to convey to other people is becoming an important topic. We have been researching a system called the Computer Organized Media Integration & Communication System (COMI&CS) that performs these functions[4]. The configuration of COMI&CS is shown in Fig. 3. This system stores individual elements for creating images as components that users can freely manipulate and edit to generate a desired image. The system also stores knowledge and data associated with the senses that are possessed by experts in relation to media manipulation, creative techniques, etc., as an aid to non-expert users. System features are described below.

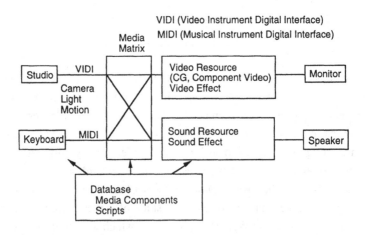

Fig. 3. Configuration of COMI&CS

(1) Multimedia component database

The system stores various kinds of image and sound data. Moreover, in addition to video and audio materials, which are most commonly associated with multimedia, the system also stores the various types of elements making up images and sounds as multimedia components. These might be the shape and movements of objects appearing inside an image, description of camera work, lighting conditions, etc. These components can be searched for, combined, and output so as to create one image, and information describing the combination of these components can be stored in a database in the form of scripts.

(2) Database processing by an impression-based language

The system allows a user to search for stored images most similar to the one that he or she wants to create and to search for components needed for that image. The user can also exchange components in the retrieved image and manipulate it in other ways to achieve the desired image. To perform these tasks, the system includes a function that enables the user to search for and process images on the basis of an impression-based language that includes expressions like "more refreshing" and "faster." In this way, users do not have to be an expert like an artist or designer to be able to create simple images to their liking.

To effectively implement the above, the relationship between the senses and color, texture, shapes, etc., must be clarified by psychological experiments. At the same time, in order to automatically associate impressions with compound images like landscapes and to search for images based on these impressions, research must be performed on the factors involved in determining what impressions are to be associated with a certain image.

(3) Storage of expert knowledge and reusability

In parallel with the above research, an important problem to be addressed is how to incorporate the intuition, feelings, etc., of artists, designers and other such experts into the system. Because intuition and feelings of such experts do not have properties that can be easily analyzed to clarify basic principles, these elements will instead be stored as knowledge in a form that can be reused. Specifically, by having actual experts operate COMI&CS to create various forms of content, records can be made of the way they search, manipulate, and combine media components, and these records can be stored in a database as scripts. Then, by having general users make use of these scripts, some of the work performed by experts can be reused. Figure 4 shows a scene of COMI&CS being used to manipulate various types of media.

6 Artistic Aspect of the Human Interface
6.1 Approach

As described above, research of human interfaces in the field of engineering has up to now focused on the treatment of logical information in human communication. As

Fig. 4. COMI&CS being used for image expression

research advances, however, it is now being recognized that behind this external form of communication lies a deeper level of communication mechanism based on human sensitivity or Kansei. In particular, high-order sensory information like impressions is very difficult to deal with by engineering only. On the other hand, artists have long been dealing with issues of sensitivity. To therefore deal effectively with high-order sensory information, we can expect research in the coming years to approach the problem from both engineering and artistic points of view.

At the same time, a field called interactive art is now developing as a new movement in the art world. In this regard, we first point out that the most important function of art is to convey an artist's idea or message by appealing to the emotional or sensitive cognitive abilities of the viewer or reader. During the long history of art, this technique of communication has become quite refined and advanced. In traditional fields of art, however, information in communication flows in a passive and uni-directional manner from artist to viewer via the work of art. In contrast, the new field of interactive art allows the art audience to change the artistic expression of the work by interacting with it. In this process, feedback is first generated from the audience to the work of art, and then from the work to the artist, who examines the modified work. In this way, information flows from the audience to the artist. In short, interactive art enables information to flow in a bi-directional manner thereby achieving a higher level of communication. Figure 5 shows a comparison between the flow of information in traditional art and new interactive art. Unfortunately, interactive art is still in a developing stage characterized by many primitive systems in which responses are generated through pushbutton interaction. Interaction techniques must therefore be enhanced and brought to a higher level of communication by incorporating advanced techniques, especially those associated with image and voice recognition.

In the above way, engineering is seeking the cooperation of the art world to enable high-order sensory information to be handled by computer. At the same time, the art

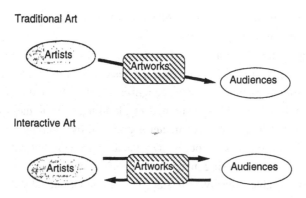

Fig. 5. From traditional art to interactive art

world is searching for new technologies to enhance current interactive art and to raise interaction to a higher level of communication. Since these objectives are mutually agreeable, we can say that the groundwork has been laid for advancing research through cooperation between art and engineering. These two approaches, moreover, are both contrastive and complementary. Engineering features an analytical approach in which phenomena are measured to provide a basis for constructing models. Art, on the other hand, adopts an approach based on the intuition and sensitivity possessed by artists. Because these two methodologies are contrastive and complementary, we can expect the cooperation of these two fields to yield beneficial results.

6.2 Research example: emotional agent MIC

Based on the ideas presented above, we have been engaged in collaborative research with engineers and artists with the goal of developing new means of communication. The following presents one example of this research.

In speech-based communication, emotions play an important role, some times playing an even bigger role than the logical information included in speech. This phenomenon can be observed in the way that a baby learns to recognize emotional information before understanding semantic information in mother's speech. Adults too recognize emotional information along with semantic information in speech, and by integrating the two, can come to understand what the other party is trying to say at a deeper level, which makes for smoother communication.

The solution to this sort of problem from a technical perspective lies in the research of emotion recognition technology. Here, however, "emotion recognition rate" has little meaning, and what might be of more significance is to create an agent having an emotion recognition function and to determine how humans evaluate this agent. With this in mind, we have created a pair of computer characters called MIC that recognize and respond to emotions[5]. This is a collaborative project with an engineer and an artist in which the emotion recognition section is developed by an engineer and computer graphics and response animation associated with these computer characters are created by an artist. MIC has the following features.

(1) MIC engages in non-language-based communication with humans using emotions, sensitivity, etc. MIC is a character that recognizes emotion in human speech and responds to it. Emotions that MIC can recognize are eight typical human emotions: delight, happiness, anger, sadness, fear, mockery, kidding, and calmness.

(2) The entire bodily image of the character is prepared by computer graphics and an emotional reaction is expressed not just by a facial expression but with action by the entire body. Moreover, by using images in the background that also respond to emotion, the audience is able to easily understand the current emotional state of these characters.

(3) Adoption of the following systems has enabled us to achieve high-level emotion recognition functions. Eight Neural networks corresponding to each of the above eight emotions have been prepared and arranged in parallel to form an emotion recognition system. A large amount of speech training data have been prepared on the basis of voice data spoken by multiple speakers with various emotions and consisting of multiple words lacking phoneme balance. Use of this training data makes emotion recognition possible for non-specific speakers and arbitrary content.

The total process flow is shown in Fig. 6 and a typical MIC response pattern is shown

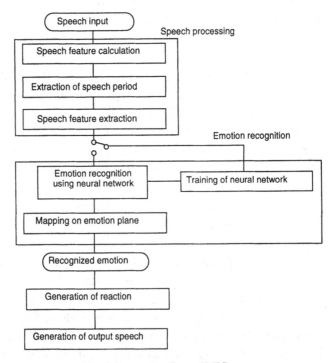

Fig. 6. Processing flow of MIC

in Fig. 7. At present, these characters are being presented at various art and technology exhibitions to allow the general public to interact with them, and favorable evaluations are being received.

Fig. 7. An example of MIC's reactions

7 Conclusion

The human interface, which in the past was often considered synonyms us with "man-machine interface," has come to be targeted by a wider range of research areas as the use of computers become widespread and the relationship between them and people takes on many forms. Nevertheless, it still appears that discussions on the human interface are for the most part held within the field of engineering. In this paper, we have presented a research area that reconsiders the meaning of the human interface and questions how the computer can support human communication on the basis of a new extended meaning. We have also shown that when considering the human interface from this point of view, social, psychological, and artistic aspects must be taken into account in addition to the engineering aspect, and that to study these aspects in future human interface research, an interdisciplinary approach including engineering, sociology, psychological, and art becomes vitally important. Examples of actual research in this area now being performed at the ATR Media Integration & Communications Research Laboratories have also been presented.

References

[1] Ryohei Nakatsu, "Nonverbal Information Recognition and Its Application to Communications," Proc. of the 3rd International Conference on Automatic Face and Gesture Recognition, pp. 2-7 (1998.4).

[2] Ryohei Nakatsu, "Image/speech Processing That Adopts an Artistic Approach -Toward Inte-

gration of Art and Technology," Proc. of ICASSP 97, Vol. I of V, pp. 207-210 (1997.4).

[3] Hanae Koiso et al., "Information Potentials of Dynamic Speech Rate in Dialogue," Proc. of the 19th Annual Conference of the Cognitive Science Society, pp.394-399 (1997.8).

[4] Seiki Inoue, "Mental Image Expression by Media Integration - COMICS (Computer Organized Media Integration & Communication System) -," Proc of International Workshop on New Media Technology, pp. 122-127 (1996.3).

[5] Naoko Tosa and Ryohei Nakatsu, "Life-like Communication Agent - Emotion Sensing Character MIC and Feeling Session Character MUSE -," Proc. of the International Conference on Multimedia Computing and Systems, pp. 12-19 (1996.6).

Demographics and Sociographics of the *Digital City*

Peter van den Besselaar & Dennis Beckers

University of Amsterdam, Department of Social Science Informatics
Roetersstraat 15, NL-1018 WB Amsterdam, The Netherlands
{peter, beckers}@swi.psy.uva.nl

During the last decade, various systems have been created to support local communities and shared interest groups. Knowledge about the use, users, and effects of these new systems is needed to inform design and implementation. In this paper we present the results of a survey among inhabitants of the *Digital City*, a large infrastructure for 'virtual communities'. The number of users, the range of facilities offered in the *Digital City*, and mutual interaction between the users does increase. At the same time, the original local (Amsterdam) base of the system has disappeared, and today's users are living all over the Netherlands. The population of the *Digital City* is fairly homogeneous, and therefore does not reflect the heterogeneous nature of a 'real' city. Use of the *Digital City* is mainly recreational, and not yet integrated with other aspects of daily life.

1. Introduction

Information and communication technology (ICT) is used intensively in the economy and in organizations. However, since the late eighties, it has been recognized that ICT also can be used to support *community life*, and *community networks* have emerged as extensions of public domain within cyberspace.[1] A community is an association between people, which is not coordinated by money (the market) or by power (formal organizations) but through communication based on shared norms and interests. Communities are often defined as *local* [7], but this locality can be in geography (villages and neighborhoods) as well as in information space (special interest groups, using the Internet as a medium). Community networks are meant for rebuilding community life by improving communication, economic opportunity, participation, and education. [16] To do so, community networks offer various functions, such as access to community services and information, tools for communication, and discussion platforms related to community issues. Early community networks used BBS technology, and during the mid-1990s, a transition to WWW-technology took place. More recently, new tools are being developed to increase the functionality of community networks. These include awareness tools, intelligent agents, and filtering tools [7].

---

[1] Literature on community networks is growing, e.g., [5, 8, 13, 15, 16, 17]. A useful overview from an activist point of view is [15]. For an overview from a computing point of view see [7].

The development of community networks and digital cities can be studied from the wider perspective of coordination mechanisms in society. In modern societies, various mechanisms exist for the coordination of social, economic, and political life. On a somewhat abstract level, three classes of mechanisms can be distinguished: markets, hierarchies (formal organizations), and social networks (or communities, e.g., families, neighborhoods, special interest groups). [18] Which of these mechanisms are appropriate in a certain situation depends on the transaction costs (coordination costs) involved. [2] As transaction costs are mainly for information and communication, they are expected to change because of the use of modern information and communication technologies (ICT). Markets are developing into *electronic markets* [10], using the new technology for reducing costs of gathering information and coordinating market transactions. At the same time organizations are changing into *virtual organizations* [11, 12]. And, because ICT influences the various transaction costs in different degrees, the relative efficiency and effectiveness of markets, hierarchies, and social networks may change. For example, Malone, Yates, and Benjamin [10] have argued that ICT reduces the transaction costs of markets more than of hierarchies. In other words, while electronic markets and electronic hierarchies are emerging and replacing traditional markets and hierarchies, the balance may shift to more market and less formal organization. Whether this tendency is dominant and irreversible, is of course highly dependent on the direction of technological development and on the way new technologies are adopted.

Also the role of communities and social networks in society depends on their relative efficiency. In pre-modern, traditional society, local communities carried all the different functions needed for the reproduction of the community. During the historical process of modernization and differentiation of society, traditional communities have lost many of their social functions, which have been taken over by the market, and by government. However, with the emergence of ICT-based community support systems, transaction costs in communities and social networks may decrease. Modernized, social networks may become more important again for society.[2]

Whether community networks succeed in improving community life, depends of course on the design of the community systems, but also on contextual factors. For example, Van Alsteyne and Brynjofsson have demonstrated that the use of the Internet by scientists can result in *widening access*, as well as in a *balkanization* of science [19]. Science, as other social systems, behaves as a *complex adaptive system* [4], and the effects of technological change therefore may be counter-intuitive. Community networks add additional layers of communication to existing communities, which may reinforce the social network, but also lead to new communities, and to a change or disintegration of existing communities. Therefore, it cannot be concluded from the mere *technological possibilities* that community life will benefit from adopting ICT-based community networks.

---

[2] It has been argued that the market and the state are no longer able to solve the unemployment problem. Advocates claim that community networks may strengthen local economy, and also support a 'social (non-monetary) economy' [15]. If this is true, community networks may become a useful tool in the creation of new forms of employment. [20]

This uncertainty opens up a whole research agenda into the use, the effects and the design of community networks, and other forms of *community computing*. Under what conditions will these new media for communication and interaction transform and create sustainable communities? What tools (for filtering, awareness, decision making, information search, chat) are useful in various situations? What infrastructures are appropriate in which contexts? Do modern means of communication create new 'hybrid' communities, less based on real space and more on information space? What does this imply for the design of community systems? Because it is uncertain how community networks and community support systems will influence society [4], it is relevant to study the functioning of existing community systems, and how these community systems affect social networks, and society at large. In this paper, we analyze the development of a large community system: the *(Amsterdam) Digital City*, as a contribution to this research program.

2. The *Digital City*: History and Organization

Early in 1994, the Amsterdam *Digital City* began as an initiative of hackers and cyberspace activists, the objective being to democratize access to the Internet. The organizers, funded by the local government, created a text based (BBS) system, accessible through telephone and modem. As the number of Dutch people with Internet connections and modems was very low in 1994, terminals were installed in public places, such as libraries and cultural centers, to improve access to the system. The main project was to use the *Digital City* for communication between citizens and local politicians and for the dissemination of political information among the citizens of Amsterdam. The DDS was founded shortly before the local elections in 1994 in Amsterdam, and the ten week experiment was planned to end after the elections. However, the *Digital City* was a large success, and it stimulated the interest for the Internet in the Netherlands enormously. The number of registered users increased very fast: during the first ten weeks, some 10.000 inhabitants were registered, and over 100.000 visits took place. Growth has continued ever since. In 1996, the population had increased to 48.000, with in average 8000 visits per day. Additionally, per day some 2000 (non-registered) 'tourists' were visiting the *Digital City*. In June 1998, the number of inhabitants had grown to 80.000, despite the fact that citizens who do not use the facility for more than three months, are expelled from the *Digital City*.

From a grass roots and subsidized initiative (in 1994), the Amsterdam *Digital City* (DDS[3]) evolved into a non-subsidized not-for-profit organization, with a turnover (in 1997) of about $ 500.000, and employing (in 1998) more than 25 persons (all together filling 17 full time positions). Its main objectives have become broader:
- Democratizing the electronic superhighway: creating an electronic sphere that allows for participation, discussion and information exchange. In other words, the creation of an electronic public domain, freely accessible, and with freedom of

---

[3] The acronym DDS stands for *De Digitale Stad*, Dutch for *The Digital City*.

expression. The DDS offers its inhabitants free email, the possibility to create a 'digital house' in the city (WWW-page), facilities for chat and discussion, and access to a myriad of information about all aspects of daily life.

- Innovation: development of knowledge, and conducting research and development about information and communication infrastructures, and disseminating this knowledge.
- Supporting small and medium sized firms in using the Internet and WWW, and improving the regional economic structure.

The DDS earns its income mainly through the second and third objectives: by advising other organizations about the use of the Internet and WWW, by providing computing facilities, by providing WWW services, and by providing digital office space and possibilities for advertising within the DDS. The local government in Amsterdam, which funded the start of the DDS, is now paying for services.

The fact that the DDS has to generate its own income, based on its expertise (consulting) and its sizable population (renting virtual offices as well as space for advertisement), also affects the way the DDS is organized. Although it started as a local grass roots movement, the DDS has lost its original democratic structure. In contrast to the dominant idea of community networks as bottom up activities, owned by the users, and often based on public funds [13, 15], the DDS is a 'not-for-profit company'. The digital citizens are 'customers', without a formal and organized representation in the DDS. An early plan to establish an 'advisory board' with users of the system, never materialized.

An example of an important top-down decision, initially not having support of the users, was a major change in the design of the system. When the DDS moved from a text-based interface to a WorldWideWeb interface, many 'digital citizens' opposed it as unnecessary. However, the leadership of the DDS felt that they had to use the most advanced technology (in 1995: WorldWideWeb) to remain attractive in the long run, even if users initially opposed the change.

On the other hand, the lack of formal influence has never resulted in questions of legitimacy. Several users of the *Digital City* participate in various design aspects, e.g., in an advanced users group, where new designs and tools are discussed and tried out. In this sense, the DDS is similar to traditional *participatory design projects*. [3]

3. The Design of the *Digital City*

The current (third) system of the *Digital City* is a WWW based system, in which the metaphor of the city is implemented quite literally. Figure 1 shows the map of the DDS, which can be found at http://www.dds.nl. The city consists of more than thirty squares with cultural, recreational, technological, civic, and political themes, providing a meeting place for ideas and information exchange. A list of the squares is added in appendix 1. The squares are the location for the commercial information suppliers, and for not-for-profit organizations. On the squares, companies and organizations can rent virtual offices, to provide information, and to sell products and services. For example, the 'Europe Square' houses the Dutch Office of the European Commission, and other organizations related to the European Union. They provide information to the public. Political debate around European issues takes place here.

Fig. 1. The map of the Digital City

The 'houses' of the digital citizens are located around the squares (in the form of WWW-pages). Digital citizens use their houses for presentation of themselves, and for information they feel may be of interest to the visitor. Some very interesting houses exist, such as a house that provides links to the homepages of various media (journals, magazines, movies, etc.) from the entire world. The main difference between the shops and offices and the private houses is, that the latter are free. Therefore, one is not allowed to provide commercial information in one's house. Private houses lack tools for communication.

Because the number of inhabitants increases faster than the number of squares, there is a shortage of building space for houses. A variety of measures have attempted, only with partial success, such as building 'skyscrapers'. It is also permitted to 'squat' houses that are not maintained by their inhabitants. By now, it is also allowed to build houses in the *Digital City* that are not properly located in the 'city structure'. In 1996, some 3300 inhabitants had their house, a number that doubled to 6500 a year later. Of these, some 1500 houses are properly located, that is, have a 'door'. The others can be accessed through an index.

A popular facility in the *Digital City* is the 'metro', a complex text-based Multi User Dungeon. Other facilities are the weekly DDS-magazine, various cafe's and kiosks, email, and discussion groups. Many 'billboards' for advertisements and announcements are spread over the DDS. Originally, the DDS provided free and full Internet access. This was terminated quite early, because of the costs involved, and because many Internet access providers entered the market in the Netherlands from 1995 onwards. The *Digital City* maintains both a text-based interface and a WWW-based interface; 82% of the users are using the WWW-based interface.

3.1 Innovation

In 1997, the *Digital City* started to experiment with 3D virtual reality. Dam Square has been built as a 3D model (http://dam.dds.nl/xdam/damBang.html), and citizens were invited to extend the 3D virtual space with their own buildings, streets, and squares. This experiment with 3D was a consequence of the need for the DDS to attract users, and to remain competitive in the WWW-advisory market and in the market for Web-commercials. However, the use of advanced technology may result in decreasing accessibility, because users need fast computers and especially fast tele-communication connections to use the 3D interface. Recently, the DDS decided not to move into the 3D direction, as it is still much too slow. An updating of the interface, and new awareness and communication tools, however, are being developed.

3.2 Community Networks and Digital Cities

What is the difference between a 'digital city' and a 'community network', as variants of 'community computing'? As already discussed, communities share geographical space or information space, and community networks can be designed for both types of communities – however, different architectures and different functions may be required. A digital city is simultaneously similar to and different from both types of community networks. The DDS does not see itself as a *local* community network, because the scope of the *Digital City* is much larger – the content is not restricted to the Amsterdam region, and the services are available for everybody who wants to register. In fact, the users of the DDS live all over the Netherlands. The DDS is also not a *topical* community network, as it covers a large number of different topics. This is clearly represented in its various squares, each focusing on a certain topic: Women's Square, Books square, Music square, Gay Square, Culture Square, Technology Square, and so on. On the other hand, the DDS does have a local component, as much information in the DDS is about Amsterdam.

In other words, the DDS aims at providing an *infrastructure* for many different thematic communities. The DDS is a community of communities, and, consequently, the city-metaphor has broader implications than simply as an interface. As in real cities, the DDS supports highly diverse activities. And, as a real city, the DDS attracts people from many places outside.

To what extent is the *Digital City* successful in realizing these goals? Does the new communication infrastructure of the DDS result in the emergence of sustainable (local and topical) communities? Does the DDS offer functions, which are useful, and integrated into peoples' everyday life? What is the connection between cyberspace and community space? [17] In this paper, we present results of surveys among users of the DDS towards answering these questions.

4. Data and Methods

Some months after the start (in January 1994) of the *Digital City*, a survey was held among the users (Schalken & Tops 1994). We organized a second survey (May/ June 1996) to investigate digital life in a more mature environment. We did not yet finish the analysis of the data from the third survey (May/June 1998), and therefore we can only present some preliminary results of the last survey. The research is a cooperation between the *Digital City* and the University of Amsterdam, and will be repeated on a regular basis. This may result in a growing body of knowledge about citizens and city life in digital cities.

Of course, a survey method is not sufficient to generate a complete picture of social relations and processes in digital environments. Therefore, we also undertake more detailed studies, based on interviewing and observing users. However, the surveys provide us with information about tendencies in use and users, which is the focus of this paper. Where appropriate, we will add information obtained from the more in depth interviews and observations.

4.1 The Questionnaire

The questionnaire, in the form of Web-pages, was announced at several localities in the *Digital City*. The questionnaire remained for about five weeks in the DSS, to enable more incidental users and tourists to participate, too. Apart from the 50 questions (included as appendix 2), we also asked respondents to (voluntarily) fill in their name and address, and about three quarters did so. We will use this database for interviewing, and for longitudinal research.

To become a citizen of the DDS, one needs to register. In 1996, at the time of our second survey, 7% of the registered citizens had either a house or a homepage in the DDS. This stands in contrast to 22% of our respondents who had this high level of involvement. As a consequence, the sample is not representative, and we expect the more active digital citizens to be over-represented, and the incidental visitors under-represented. After the first analysis of the data, we re-weighted the sample to match available population statistics: growth of the number of digital citizens, the share of users with a house. The results before and after the correction of the sample, however, are quite similar. We base our analysis on the data from the original sample.

4.2 The Analysis: Data and Method

After answering the questions, the respondents needed to click a button on the screen to send their responses. These were then automatically placed into a data file, accessible to SPSS. The analysis consisted of various steps. First the descriptive statistics were produced on users and use of the Amsterdam *Digital City*. In a second phase, we searched for relations between the independent variables (characteristics of the users, such as gender, age, education, experience with the Internet, and so on), and the dependent variables (indicating the use of the DDS). In a third phase, we used factor analysis to reduce the number of 'DDS-use' variables to underlying dimensions. This resulted in several identifiable factors, representing various use-dimensions. The analysis was aiming at 1) describing use and users of the DDS, and 2) trying to find out whether 'typical' groups of users and ways of using the DDS do exist.

Table 1. Some basic statistics

	May 1994	*May 1996*	*May 1998**
Total number digital citizens	10.000*	48.000*	80.000*
Average visits per day	2.000*	8.000*	
Tourists per day		2.000*	
Respondents	1.200	1.300	700
Of which: Male	91%	84%	79%
Higher education#	86%	86%	64%
Age 18-25	29%	48%	38%
Amsterdam based	45%	23%	22%
Working	49%	39%	40%
Unemployed, old aged	8%	0.5%	12%
Housewives	0.1%	0.6%	***
Student incl. high school	31%	56%	48%
Turn over in 1997		$500.000	
Number of employees		About 15	About 25

*	Provided by the *Digital City*.
**	Preliminary results.
***	Included in 'unemployed'.
#	Users studying at college or university, or with a degree.

5. Results: Use and users of the Amsterdam *Digital City*

An overview of some characteristics of digital citizens is given in table 1. As is clear, the digital citizens are male, young, high educated or trying to become so. The decrease (between 1996 and 1998) of the 'high educated'-group and the 'age 18 to 25'-group is due to the quickly increasing number of high school students in the DDS. Inhabitants with a job are mainly working in education, culture, business services, and public administration. Digital citizens are also increasingly distributed over the entire country: only 23% of the 1996-respondents were based in Amsterdam, and this share is even lower in the 1998-survey. Ethnic and cultural minorities (the language in the DDS is Dutch!), the lower educated, the elderly, the unemployed, housewives are all underrepresented, although their share in the DDS populations seems to increase again. However, the DDS is still a homogeneous community and not a modern heterogeneous *urban* community. The *Digital City* is more like a digital suburb, or a digital campus.

The figures reflecting the number of visits per day suggest a rather intensive use of the system. On average, these figures suggest that digital citizens visit the city a little more than once a week. This is corroborated by the answers in the questionnaire. However, our systematic 'ethnographic' observations over a three week period never found such large numbers in the DDS. This is most likely because the system does not register on-line use in a meaningful way. This is a problem that has been reported by the DDS, and has not been solved during the last two years. As a consequence, the possibilities of interaction in the system are not optimal: one cannot communicate online with fellow citizens if one is not aware of their presence.

5.1 Use of the Digital City: City Life

An important characteristic of communities is the level of interaction and communication. Are digital communities emerging within the DDS? To get a provisional answer to that question we asked whether digital citizens have contact with fellow digital citizens. The question was also asked in the 1994-questionnaire, and therefore we are able to see changes. Table 2 gives the results, suggesting that a digital community is emerging over time. The frequency of mutual contact clearly is increasing.

Table 2. Frequency of communication between digital citizens

	1994	1996
Often	3%	20%
Sometimes	18%	37%
Seldom	33%	22%
Never	46%	21%

As described above, the DDS offers various functions to its inhabitants. In the questionnaire, we distinguish the following functions: *information supply* (through WWW-pages), *information retrieval*, *debate* on political, social and other issues (discussion groups), *asynchronous communication* (electronic mail) and *synchronous communication* (web cafe's, chat).

Table 3. What do digital citizens do: use of various functions*

Activities:	1994	1996
Email	52%	95%
Information search	54%	85%
Information supply		55%
Debate	16%	40%
Virtual face-to-face	22%	30%

  *   % (very) important

We asked the respondents how they value these functions and how they use the functions (for private activities and/or professionally). As table 3 shows, email and search for information are the most important functions for the respondents, and the supply of information, debate and chatting are less important. Additionally, the use of these functions is predominantly private, rather than job related.

What kind of things are digital citizens doing and talking about? This may be indicated by the thematic squares that the respondents consider important. Table 4 shows a classification of the various squares in six categories: 1) Internet related squares; 2) culture, lifestyle and leisure related squares; 3) information and education; 4) politics and civic activities; 5) squares related to work and economy; and 6) miscellaneous. The distribution of information providers and discussion groups over these six categories is also exhibited. Finally, the table shows (on a ten points scale) how the respondents value the relevance of the various squares. Appendix 1 gives the scores per square.

Table 4. What do digital citizens do: fields of interest

Topics	Important Squares*	Information Providers**	Discussion Groups**
Technology, Internet, DDS	10	13%	12%
Culture, leisure, lifestyle	7.5	35%	64%
Information & education	7	15%	-
Politics & civic	4.5	20%	24%
Economy & work	3	12%	-
Miscellaneous	-	05%	-

*   1996-Survey
** Adapted from [6].

The figures suggest that the use of the DDS is Internet related and mainly recreational. This is also reflected in the distribution of information providers in the DDS and the distribution of the discussion groups. Although the DDS started as an activity aiming to improve local democracy, it is not very strong in political issues and civic activities. The DDS does not play a main role in the local political debates, and the political community is not very active in cyberspace. 'Traditional' communication media are still far more important here. It should be noted that civic organizations are only starting to use the DDS (and the Internet in general), and therefore their activities on the Web are still in their infancy.[4]

5.2 Patterns of Use

The above figures are averages. However, we are also interested in whether different groups of digital citizens use the DDS in different ways. For example, do men use the DDS differently from women? Do differences exist between use by older and by

---

[4] Kole [9] studied email use by women's organizations and NGO's in the context of developmental issues. She found that these organizations generally are just starting with email.

young citizens? Between students and workers? Between digital citizens with and without a house in the DDS? And, what is the link between community space and cyberspace; do users who live in Amsterdam use the DDS differently from others? Using *analysis of variance*, our data suggest the following similarities and (sometimes small) differences:

Men versus women. Female users have less experience with the DDS, use it more often, and stay a little longer on-line. They use the DDS somewhat less for professional purposes, although professional use by men is low as well. Women use the chat facility in the web cafe more than men, but a male user is more apt to have a house in the DDS. There are some indications that women have slightly more contact with fellow DDS citizens than men do. Finally, we saw a small difference in the way men and women navigate in the DDS. Men more often use URL's, and women more often the index and map of the DDS.

Student versus employed. Employed persons (of course) use the DDS more often professionally than students, however professional use is generally low as already mentioned. Students have more contact with other DDS-users. Chatting in the Web cafe is more important for students than for other users; for discussion groups the reverse is true.

Users with a 'house' versus other users. Digital citizens with their own house in the DDS have more contact with other users. They also make professionally use of the DDS more often, and are generally more experienced. They consider the information function as more important than do other DDS users, but this relation does not hold true for the communication and discussion functions.

Level of education. The more highly educated digital citizen uses the DDS more often for professional aims, has more experience with the DDS and the Internet, and has much more contact with others. Interestingly enough, he values 'information search' less than the less educated user does.

Age related use. Younger users have significantly more contact with others in the DDS. This is not surprising, as age strongly correlates with the student-employed distinction (see above). The relation holds when checking for gender.

Amsterdam based users versus others. Amsterdam based users arrived earlier with the DDS and later with the Internet than others, indicating that the DDS may have functioned as a learning tool for Amsterdam based users with respect to the Internet. There is no difference between the two groups with respect to the frequency in use of the DDS and the Internet. Also the frequency of contacts with others in the DDS is identical, as is the relative value they place on the communication and discussion functions. However, Amsterdam based users seem to place less value information search, the web cafe, and the chat facilities than do other users. On the other hand, they score higher on creating and accessing Web sites. Finally, the Amsterdam based user scores slightly higher on professional use. Summarizing, the differences between Amsterdam based users and others do not indicate strong relations between community space on the one hand and cyberspace on the other.

Frequent versus infrequent users. Frequent users have more contact with other users, and sign on for longer sessions in the DDS. They especially value making WWW-pages and use of email, but there is no difference with respect to their job related use of the various functions.

Experience and use. The longer one visits the DDS, the higher the various functions are valued, and the more the user communicates with others. New users are more apt to make professional use of the DDS.

Another way of approaching the question of differences in ways of using the DDS is based on a factor analysis of the 22 items in the questionnaire which are related to the use of the DDS. The analysis resulted in the following six 'use dimensions', that have been used to identify various 'typical users', and 'typical behaviors'.
- Degree of professional use;
- Contact with fellow DDS-citizens;
- Degree of substitution of other media by email;
- Use of chat facility;
- Use of the information function;
- Use of communication & discussion function.

Combining the results of the comparison of groups with the results of the factor analysis, we are inclined to distinguish five overlapping groups in three dimensions: main activity of the user (employed versus studying), type of use (professional versus recreational), and level experience of users (new users). Summarizing the findings results in the 'use map' (figure 2).

6. Conclusions and Discussion

On the basis of the first two surveys (1994 and 1996), a few preliminary results of the 1998 survey, and some additional observation and interviewing, we can now answer the question whether a virtual public space and cybercommunities are emerging in addition to 'real' space and local communities. The answer is 'yes and no'. Yes, in the sense that:
- An increasing number of DDS squares are built, with social, political, and civic topics, and related organizations.
- An increasing number of digital citizens have regular contact with fellow citizens.
- The DDS as a digital sphere is successful and sustainable, with many enthusiastic citizens, a rapidly growing population, and potentially a viable combination of 'civic' and 'economic' activities. Although the survey did not show the emergence of more or less stable communities within the DDS, it becomes clear from interviews that on a smaller scale some active communities are existing. Examples are groups of enthusiastic users of the MUD (the Metro), around the Chess Cafe and the Literature Cafe, the Motor Club and the Skeeler Club, and around Gay Square.
- Similar to a 'real' city, the DDS attracts a lot of people from the entire country.

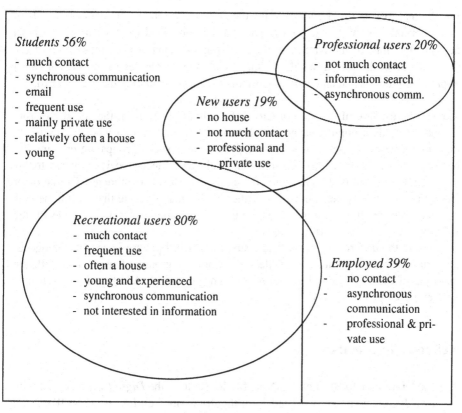

Fig. 2. Use map (1996)

However, also opposite tendencies were discovered:
- The DDS is mono-cultural and used in a mono-functional way, and does not reflect the social structure of 'real' urban communities.
- Although the DDS covers many civic topics, the actual level of activity around these topics is low. This is as well true of the organizations that are present on the civic squares. They probably are still unsophisticated users, and the DDS is not a part of their organizational culture. Alternatively, the DDS may not offer enough added value for these organizations.
- In sum, the level of economic, work-oriented, and professional activities is low. Much office space is empty. Digital citizens generally do not use the DDS for work related issues. In other words, the relevance of systems as the DDS is not (yet) clear for this type of use.

Different tendencies are visible simultaneously. *Existing* interest groups are only beginning to use network technology to improve their communication and information exchange. For these groups, the DDS may become a resource and a medium. However, although the mutual interaction within the DDS increases, it is less clear whether *new* (thematic) communities emerge from interaction within the DDS.

For the majority of the digital citizens, the *Digital City* does not seem to be part of their 'normal', every day activities. This can be concluded from what are the most popular functions of the DDS, and the most popular squares (i.e., topics), and from the valuation of the various available functions. For example, recreation sites are most popular, while the civic and economy oriented squares are among the least visited.

The social structure of the *Digital City* differs significantly from the social structure of the Amsterdam population and of the Dutch population as a whole. This is not uncommon with the use of new technologies: various social groups are entering cyberspace in stages. In 1996, university and college students received access to the Internet. More recently, this has been the case for high school students. On the other hand, to push the city metaphor a bit further, it also may indicate that within the new media landscape, digital communities are the garden cities, not yet accessible for the socially and culturally deprived citizens.

Despite the differences in use and users, the general picture is one of homogeneity. This may change with a possible arrival of new groups of users, and with the maturing of the medium and of its use (learning by using). Additional research may answer these open questions.

Acknowledgements

The cooperation of Joost Flint and Nina Meilof (both at the *Digital City*) is gratefully acknowledged. The paper benefited from the discussions during the *First Workshop on Social Interaction and Communityware* in Kyoto (June 1998) and from discussions with Doug Schuler in Barcelona (July 1998). Carolien Metselaar provided us with many useful comments on an earlier draft. We are indebted to Philip Galgiani for correcting our English.

References

1. Beckers, D.: Use and Users of the Amsterdam Digital City, Masters thesis. University of Amsterdam, 1998. URL results: http://swi.psy.uva.nl/beckers/results/digital city.html
2. Ciborra, C.U.: Teams, Markets and Systems. Cambridge, CUP, 1993.
3. Clement A., Van den Besselaar, P.: Participatory Design Project, A Retrospective View. Communications of the ACM 36 (1993) 6, pp. 83-91.
4. Cohen, M.D., Axelrod, R.: Complexity and Adaptation in Community Information Systems: Implications for Design. This volume.
5. Cohill, A.M., Kavanaugh, A.L. (eds.): Community Networks, Lessons from Blacksburg, Virginia. Boston: Artec House, 1997.
6. Francissen, L., Brants, K.: Virtual Going Places, Square Hopping in Amsterdam's Digital City. Tsagarousianon, Tambini, Bryan (eds.), Cyberdemocracy, Technology, Cities, and Civic Networks. London, Routledge, 1998.

122

7. Ishida, T. (ed.): Community Computing, Collaboration over Global Information Networks. John Wiley & Sons, 1998.
8. Kraut, R. (ed.): Internet@Home. Special Section. Communications of the ACM, 39 (1996), 12, pp. 33-74.
9. Kole, E.: Myths and Realities in Internet Discourse, Using Computer Networks for Data Collection and the Beijing World Conference on Women. The Gazette, The International Journal for Communication Studies, 60/4, August, pp. 343-360.
10. Malone, T.W., Yates, J., Benjamin, R.I.: Electronic Markets and Electronic Hierarchies. Communications of the ACM, 30 (1987), 6, pp. 484-497.
11. Mowshowitz, A.: Virtual Organization, a Vision of Management in the Information Age. The Information Society 10 (1994) pp. 267-288.
12. Mowshowitz, A. (ed.): Virtual Organization - Special Section. Communications of the ACM, 40 (1997) 9, pp. 30-64.
13. Rheingold, H.: The Virtual Community. Harper 1993.
14. Schalken, K., Tops, P.: The Digital City, A study into the backgrounds and opinions of its residents, 1994.
15. Schuler, D.: New community networks, wired for change. New York: ACM Press, 1996.
16. Schuler, D.: Community networks, building a new participatory medium. Communications of the ACM 37 (1996) 1, pp.52-63.
17. Schuler, D., Page, C.: Community Space & Cyberspace, what is the Connection? Proceedings 6th DIAC, March 1997. Seattle: CPSR, 1997.
18. Thompson, G., J. Rances, R. Levacic, J. Mitchell (eds.), Markets, Hierarchies & Networks; the Coordination of Social Life. London etc., Sage 1991.
19. Van Alsteyne M., Brynjolfsson, E.: Widening Access and Narrowing Focus: Could Internet Balkanize Science? Science, 274 (5292), 1997, November, 29, pp. 1479-80.
20. Van den Besselaar, P.: The future of Employment in the Information Society: a Comparative, Longitudinal and Multi-Level Study. Journal of Information Science 23 (1997) 5, pp. 373-392.

Appendix 1. The squares in the *Digital City* (1996)

Square	R*	Square	R	Square	R
Book Square	185	Gay Square	219	Park Square	27
BVE Square (educ.)	57	Health Square	48	Politics Square	84
Computer Square	346	IBM Square	52	Square 13 (Youth)	48
Culture Square	221	Internet Square	422	Sports Square	144
DDS Central Square	2119	Local Government Sq	46	Technology Square	73
Digital Cities Sq.	267	Metro Square	285	Tourism Square	22
Ecology Square	65	Movie Square	272	Travel Square	58
Education Square	118	Music Square	340	TV & Radio Sq.	131
Entrepreneurs Sq.	61	National Government	112	World Square	60
Europe Square	66	News Square	267	Work Square	28

* Respondents were asked to mention three squares most important to them. A first place is good for three points, a second place is good for two, and a third place for one point. The table (R) gives the total number of points per square.

Appendix 2: Questionnaire

Nr.	Variable	Values
Var1	Gender	Male / female
Var2	Age	0-99
Var3	Education	Highest school level
Var4	Main activity	Work/school/household/civic duties
Var5	Employment	Industrial sectors
Var6	Occupation	Management/professional/clerical/sales/ services/other
Var7	Income	Net income per month
Var8	Political orientation	Political parties
Var9	Political commitment	Do you vote – last elections
Var10	Civic duties	Yes / no voluntary work
Var11	Civic duties	Hours per week
Var12	Member DDS	Yes/no login name in the DDS
Var13	Internet experience before DDS	Yes / no
Var14	Entering DDS from	Home/school/work/public terminal/ other
Var15	Speed modem	Bautrate
Var16	Entering DDS through	Modem bank / internet provider
Var17	Which provider	Name
Var18	Since when internet	Date (half year periods)
Var19	Since when DDS	Date (half year periods)
Var20	How often in DDS	Number of times per week
Var21	Average stay in DDS	Minutes
Var22	Learned about DDS	Various media
Var23	Average stay in Internet	Minutes
Var24	Most important square	Names
Var25	Second square	Names
Var26	Third square	Names
Var27	Importance of information	5 points scale
Var28	Use of 27	Private / professional – 5 points scale
Var29	Importance of web-cafe	5 points scale
Var30	Use of 29	Private / professional – 5 points scale
Var31	Importance of IRC	5 points scale
Var32	Use of 31	Private / professional – 5 points scale
Var33	Importance www-making	5 points scale
Var34	Use of 33	Private / professional – 5 points scale
Var35	Importance www-browsing	5 points scale
Var36	Use of 35	Private / professional – 5 points scale
Var37	Importance of email	5 points scale
Var38	Use of 37	Private / professional – 5 points scale
Var40	Use of 39	Private / professional – 5 points scale
Var41	Does email influence phone use	5 points scale
Var42	Ibid. fax use	5 points scale
Var43	Ibid. letters	5 points scale
Var44	Ibid. face to face communication	5 points scale
Var45	Own house in the DDS	Yes / no
Var46	Contact with other inhabitants	4 points scale
Var47	Confrontation with sexism	3 points scale

Var48	Hinder from sexism	5 points scale
Var49	Confrontation with racism	3 points scale
Var50	Hinder from racism	5 points scale
Var51	Confrontation with rude behavior	3 points scale
Var52	Hinder from rude behavior	5 points scale
Var53	Type of interface	Text / graphics
Var54	Ability to navigate in DDS	5 points scale
Var55	Navigate through URL	4 points scale (from always to never)
Var56	Navigate through map	4 points scale (from always to never)
Var57	Navigate through index	4 points scale (from always to never)
Var58	Navigate through walking around	4 points scale (from always to never)

Groupware, Community, and Meta-networks: The Collaborative Framework of EdNA (Education Network Australia)

Jon Mason

Education.Au Limited
178 Fullarton Road, Dulwich, SA 5065, Australia
jmason@educationau.edu.au

Abstract. This paper describes evolving notions and expressions of community and networks in the context of educational culture which is engaged in the process of discovering the opportunities and challenges presented by Communications and Information Technologies (CITs). Supporting this focus is a brief analysis of socio-cultural change providing a context for presenting a case-study overview of Education Network Australia (EdNA), a government-sponsored 'meta-network' formally launched in Australia in 1997 primarily as an online Information Directory Service. In its current stage of development EdNA has firmed as a framework geared toward fostering collaboration and co-operation throughout the various education and training systems and sectors. As such, it is an exemplar of 'Community Computing and Support Systems' which extend collaborative computing beyond the conventional limits of groupware. A key success factor in its development has been the convergence of the structural opportunity inherent within any growing network with the need for strengthening and developing identity within and among related communities.

1   Introduction

Communications and Information Technologies (CITs) provide both enacted and potential opportunities for human communication and interaction which have not hitherto been possible. However, despite this enabling potential, CITs are not intrinsically enabling and evidence exists which suggests the contrary. [2], [11] While this is an important perspective it is still true that CITs have been, and are, pivotal to the emergence and development of so-called 'electronic communities', 'virtual communities', online 'learning communities', and other associated collaborative and co-operative activities which occur in online environments (with 'online' being used here in its broad and common usage to include both synchronous and asynchronous computer networks). The communications cultures evolving with usage of these technologies are unprecedented and in educational settings pose transformative challenges (opportunities *and* threats) for the established pedagogical and organisational cultures. [5], [20] Conceived initially in 1995 as an initiative with a focus on connectivity and infrastructure, Education Network Australia (EdNA) now represents an exemplar of this new culture with collaboration and co-operation its guiding principles. In the history of education in Australia this collaborative endeavour is unprecedented, thus making EdNA an excellent case-study of Community Computing and Support Systems (CCSS).

2   Socio-Cultural Change

To be rigorous, any analysis of CCSS must be cognisant of the co-evolution of social institutions, organisational structures, and technology. It would be an error to conceive of CCSS as driven primarily by the enabling characteristics of communications technologies, though this terminology lends itself to this kind of association. At the same time, the emergence of the so-called Information Superhighway amidst the complexities of socio-cultural dynamics suggests that recognition of the current historically pivotal role of technology is not unreasonable. [1], [14] On this point, however, Castells concludes:

"the dilemma of technological determinism is probably a false problem, since technology is society, and society cannot be understood or represented without its technological tools." [1]

2.1   The Meaning of Community

In determining the semantic domain of 'community' it is worthwhile considering the mission statement of the Center for the Study of Online Community at UCLA:

"There are many ways to approach the social, technical, political, economic, and cultural explosion that surrounds computers and the networks that interconnect them. The Center for the Study of Online Community seeks to present and foster studies that focus on how computers and networks alter people's capacity to form groups, organizations, institutions, and how those social formations are able to serve the collective interests of their members. If you are willing to use the word loosely, all of these social formations can be thought of as some form of community." [16]

Indeed, the word 'community' can be laden with blurred meaning. For example, while one could loosely refer to the 'Internet community' or a specific 'Newsgroup community', any attempt at an analogous statement applied to telephone or television usage seems absurd. At the recent WWW7 conference held in Brisbane, Australia, there were plenty of examples of discourse adopting this common usage: such as, 'resource discovery communities', the 'Dublin Core community', the 'Australian community', etc. [21] In the bulk of these cases, the semantics indicate some descriptive identity of a particular group. In terminology recently coined by learning theorist Etienne Wenger, "communities of interest" also act as "communities of practice". [19] Perhaps, though, the wide semantic usage or 'looseness' of the word community also points to the fact that it is a term indicative of inclusiveness. It therefore seems that in identifying or defining the elements and drivers of effective CCSS we must proceed with caution. Furthermore, while the word 'community' is likely to conjure up 'civic' or 'neighbourly' connotations, more often than not there is evidence to suggest that the early adopters of communications technologies are from either the military or criminal elements of society! The most notable example of this is of course the origins of the Internet itself within a research unit of the USA military in the late 1960s as the world's first decentralised data communications system. Furthermore, with the (sensationalised) help of the mass media, the presence of 'unwholesome' activity and information on the Internet (such as hardcore pornography and all kinds of 'anti-community' violence) is what seeded the widespread and ongoing debate on censorship and privacy of recent years. It was indeed a significant win for 'free speech' in the USA in 1996 when a three-judge panel ruled to extend the individual's and community's rights under the USA First Amendment to cyberspace: they have been quoted as describing the Internet:

"as a never-ending worldwide conversation...[and]...the most participatory form of mass speech yet developed."[10]

2.2 CIT and CMC

Some CITs are geared primarily as 'groupware' or software applications designed specifically for enabling collaboration and enhancing workgroup productivity through application and data sharing within an organisation. With the popularisation of the Internet via the World Wide Web, the power of groupware solutions is challenged by the power of the network, though common to both is the lure of efficient communication and data exchange. In the corporate world this challenge has been recognised as a major opportunity – for example, *Sun's* 'the network is the computer' slogan is also descriptive of its organisational structure where groupware and geographically dispersed networks have merged. But, whether it is groupware supported or an expression of a less cohesive but nonetheless highly functional networked community, the significant cultural component of CIT usage is what is termed Computer Mediated Communication (CMC). Without CMC, groupware and CCSS are meaningless concepts. In many respects, CMC is a pivotal component in contemporary flexible education systems. [12]

2.3 Language, Communication, Education and CMC

It is a rather trite observation that (most) human beings are naturally gregarious. That they are disposed toward the process of 'networking' is a little less obvious to some as it is very clear that some individuals and social groups are more disposed to it than others! From an historical perspective, civilisation has been a story of the evolution of small tribal communities into large city-states and nations. Together with this other key historical foundations of civilisation are the evolution of language and technologies for interacting with the environment, and with fellow human beings. In the late twentieth century there is much talk of globalisation, communications revolutions and a new world order, though some commentators have referred to the latter as a new world 'disorder'. [1], [4] With all this change, however, language can be regarded as the primary vehicle for communication and in the new world of online learning communities it occupies a primary position. Or, as Castells expresses it:

"How specific is the language of CMC as a new medium? To some analysts, CMC, and particularly e-mail, represents the revenge of the written medium, the return to the typographic mind, and the recuperation of the constructed, rational discourse. For others, on the contrary, the informality, spontaneity, and anonymity of the medium stimulates what they call a new form of "orality," expressed by an electronic text." [1]

But, he adds, the significance of CMC does not overshadow other socio-political realities:

"Because access to CMC is culturally, educationally, and economically restrictive, and will be so for a long time, the most important cultural impact of CMC could be potentially the reinforcement of the culturally dominant social networks, as well as the increase of their cosmopolitanism and globalization." [1]

Castells' argument is somewhat more sober than Rheingold's earlier perspective although for Rheingold the primacy of language is also emphasized while pointing to the fundamentally disembodied character of virtual communities:

"People in virtual communities use words on screens to exchange pleasantries and argue, engage in intellectual discourse, conduct commerce, exchange knowledge, share emotional support, make plans, brainstorm, gossip, feud, fall in love, find friends and lose them, play games, flirt, create a little high art and a lot if idle talk. People in virtual communities do just about everything people do in real life, but we leave our bodies behind. You can't kiss anybody and nobody can punch you in the nose, but a lot can happen within those boundaries." [15]

From more of an educational perspective, Tiffin and Rajasingham provide a theoretical model applicable to online teaching and learning which identifies communication, rather than language, as primary. In developing this model they argue that:

"Education systems are communication systems and therefore they are networks which can exist at different fractal levels." [17]

These fractal levels are categorised as intrapersonal, interpersonal, group, organisational, mass, and global where communication is defined as having three key components: transmission, storage, and processing. [17] While 'community' as such is not discussed, their model of intermeshed networks may have application in the design and development of CCSS:

"Systems for organised learning are complex communications systems concerned with the transmission, storage and processing of information. Their purpose is to assist learners so that from being unable to deal with problems they become proficient problem solvers. This depends on communication networks that intermesh four related factors: learning, teaching, knowledge and problem. There appears to be a fractal dimension in that the network that intermeshes the four related factors can prove to be a node in a network at a higher level. Similarly, a processing node in a network can, at a lower level, prove to be a network. The existence of different levels in a communications system for learning allows learners to shift levels in the process of learning." [17]

2.4 Meta-Networks, Community and Identity

In a pilot study commissioned by UNESCO in 1997 addressing regulatory issues relating to content on the Internet, it is argued:

"It is widely recognised that if the Internet is to be used to its full potential, there is a need for enhanced community understanding of the Internet and the opportunities it offers." [18]

While such a comment is contextualised within a broad concern for community education it reveals that 'community' has a fundamental role for the Internet. After all, as an inter-network or meta-network, it also represents a 'community' of users. However, despite the awesome information resources and communications potential of the Internet it is still largely unregulated or uncontained and therefore this very lack of boundary tends to also limit the scope of community as it is conventionally understood. Do we speak of the Earth community?

With the Internet clearly established as the Meta-Network of all meta-networks it is *identification* with a particular community which can make an electronic network truly value-added and conducive toward collaboration. Thus the earlier reference to the profusion of diversely labeled communities at forums such as WWW7 – the 'Dublin Core community', for example, clearly identifies a common interest that brings together individuals and other groups. This identification helps build a network. Clearly, there is not much point to building a network from a collection of nodes without some reason that provides meaning.

Rheingold's (1993) exposition of 'virtual communities' was mainly concerned with such interest groups who are often organised or share a common purpose. In the case of EdNA (Education Network Australia), it is the education and training communities of Australia, and indeed the Australian focus, which serve to define the identity of the network – or more accurately, this *meta-network* since it brings together several other large regional networks. Castells lends theoretical weight to this argument in his important recent sociological analysis outlining the "rise of the Network Society":

"New information technologies are integrating the world in global networks of instrumentality. Computer-mediated communication begets a vast array of virtual communities. Yet the distinctive social and political trend of the 1990s is the construction of social action and politics around primary identities, either ascribed, rooted in history or geography, or newly built in an anxious search for meaning and spirituality. The first historical steps of informational societies seem to characterize them by the pre-eminence of identity as their organizing principle."[1]

3   The Framework of EdNA

Education Network Australia (EdNA) is an initiative of the Commonwealth, State and Territory governments together with key stakeholders from the Education and Training sector within Australia. It has been established to provide value-added online services to this community and as a means of optimizing the potential for communications and information technology in education and training. [6]

Since its original conception, in 1995, EdNA has undergone a number of significant changes. These changes demonstrate to some extent that the sustained response to technological development has been one concerned with facilitating collaboration and the development of professional networks and communities of users. Originally, EdNA was conceived as a physical network with emphasis being placed on infrastructure development and connectivity, particularly for the schools and Vocational Education and Training (VET) communities (AARNet, the Australian Academic and Research Network already being well-established for universities). As Internet usage in Australia has increased over the last few years, EdNA has developed to its current form as a national framework for collaboration between all sectors of the Australian education and training community, with a view to maximizing the benefits of CITs in education. A key component of this endeavour is the building of a value-added Directory Service that utilises metadata (customised from the Dublin Core) as a means for ensuring that information retrieval and resource discovery is effective, thereby maintaining quality of content. This is currently at an early stage of development but much progress has already been made.

In order to proceed along the path of collaboration (and, of necessity, co-operation) a number of consultative groups have been established, which in turn are geared toward facilitating further diffusion of collaboration in the applications of CITs as well as in the ongoing development of the EdNA Directory Service. Sectoral advisory groups have been established to provide input to the development of EdNA from each sector's perspective and to exchange information and ideas about the use of information and communications technologies in education.

It can be argued that this framework has an economic agenda in that significant cost savings will likely follow-on through the avoidance of excessive duplication and overlap. Perhaps this is more keenly observed by government stakeholders but it would be quite inaccurate to see this as the primary opportunity or unstated agenda. There is much more to networks than the economics of minimising costs, even though a new economics will also likely ensue in the broader marketplace. Yes, it may be true that the EdNA initiative can be viewed as having a strong economic appeal and it is also very true that there is a decline in public funding of higher education worldwide with governments scrutinizing university management more closely. But the opportunities that accompany the new so-called 'global' economy (what some commentators prefer to describe as a trend toward an 'Informational Economy' or a 'Network Economy') are shaping new economic 'rules'. [1], [9] A tightening of public funding in higher education may be the downside but as the networks develop so do the opportunities for new alliances and markets. In this scenario it is the connections and the potential for collaboration that will be a driving force for change. As Kelly puts it:

"The grand irony of our times is that the era of computers is over. All the major consequences of standalone computers have already taken place. Computers have speeded up our lives a bit, and that's it. In contrast, all the most promising technologies making their debut now are chiefly due to communication between computers - that is, to connections rather than computations. And since communication is the basis of culture, fiddling at this level is indeed momentous. Information's critical rearrangement is the widespread, relentless act of connecting everything to everything else. We are now engaged in a grand scheme to augment, amplify, enhance, and extend the relationships between all beings and all objects. That is why the Network Economy is a big deal." [9]

3.1 Organisational Framework

The sectoral groups and Ministerial nominees, both State and Commonwealth, come together in a common forum as the EdNA Reference Committee to provide advice on matters relating to the use of information technology in education and to the Ministers. The Reference Committee has representatives from each State and Territory school and VET system, from the Catholic school system and the Independent schools sector as well as from the higher education sector. It is currently chaired by the Commonwealth representative. Overall management of the process is effected by a small non-profit company, Education.Au Limited, based in Adelaide and jointly owned by the Ministers of education. Its Board meets regularly and makes policy recommendations to the Ministers.

Thus, it is clear that EdNA has established an organisational framework and vision for collaboration with respect to the utilisation and development of online services in educational contexts within Australia. However, while these foundations are in place, their durability and effectiveness in supporting value-added services for the education and training communities is yet to be tested over time. Some commentators warn that such networks may even be short-lived, reflecting the demise of 'goodwill' in cyberspace culture as e-commerce gains the ascendancy. [3]

The politics intrinsic to the EdNA process is also an important factor in making progress and it would be fair to say that most of those active stakeholders contributing to the process have a developing appreciation for the complexity of agendas and needs that must be considered. The bottom line would suggest that ongoing participation by a number of communities, which vary both in scope and scale, will be the measure of future success. Without doubt, the evolution of EdNA will provide a rich resource for research on determining critical success factors or impediments concerning online culture.

3.2 The EdNA Directory Service

Complementing and supporting the organisational framework is the EdNA Directory Service, an online 'first entry-point' (Website) for a wide range of information and resources relevant to education and training in Australia. One key feature of the Website is that the collaborative and co-operative framework is also reflected in its administration. In terms of scale of implementation, this is indeed a unique initiative insofar as CCSS is concerned. Of course, for many people the EdNA Directory Service may be experienced as just another fairly ordinary Website. This is certainly true of its various iterations of interface design to date. However, where content is concerned, both high quality catalogued online information resources are made easily accessible as are a wide range of discussion groups, or 'communities', also hosted.

The EdNA Directory Service was officially launched by the Commonwealth of Australia on November 28th, 1997. [6]

The following discussion provides an overview of the system, network configuration, software, and category structure for the storage and retrieval of resources.

3.2.1 System Overview

The EdNA Directory Service undergoes continued development and enhancement. It is guided by principles of *quality information retrieval* and *resource discovery* together with the provision of *networking opportunities* to its stakeholders. The first version of the Directory went online as a Website in early 1996, although at this time it was very much in a prototype phase. The architecture that was implemented at this time still persists and is based on an Oracle database Web Server, where the bulk of Web pages delivered to the user are dynamically constructed (see Fig. 1 at end of discussion). This is run in conjunction with the Netscape Enterprise and Collabra Servers together with Majordomo which combine to deliver general Web and messaging services. In this configuration, customised PL/SQL code is also implemented, particularly for specific functionality such as the administration of the site, which is based on a *distributed* model and, as such, mirrors the system and Web architecture itself. That is, all stakeholder groups have an opportunity to participate in the uploading of items into the database, the maintenance of collections relevant to their sector, and various other functions.

Users can access information stored on the EdNA Directory through browsing the extensive category tree of core items or through using the search function. Items are indexed and attached to specific categories, with core items having metadata attached to enable well-targeted resource discovery. The database also stores harvested (robotically-collected) 'non-core' or 'leaf-node' items which are indexed from specified levels referenced from the core items. The Search function allows for retrieval of these resources. Navigation cues on the homepage also provide users with a variety of other options including *Noticeboards*, a *'What's New'* list, a *Help* system, and an entry point into *Discussion Groups* hosted on the site.

Search functions on the Website are built around Harvest Gatherer software in conjunction with the Verity Topic search engine. Users can specify standard search requests based on keywords and 'freetext' matches. Resources searched include core items, harvested items that are collected with the Gatherer software, as well as archived discussion lists. There have been various iterations of the search function and in mid 1998 plans to enhance the functionality of search were underway. These include the likely replacement of Harvest with the Netscape Compass (Catalogue) Server and implementation of appropriate thesauri developed specifically for the education sector.

Redundancy is built into the system for security and backup purposes. Equipment used consists of 3 *Sun Microsystems* Sparcstations: one each for development, testing and production. Most users only interact with EdNA-prod though authorised stakeholders use EdNA-test prior to uploading (publishing) any static pages or for evaluating prototype enhancements.

3.2.2 Network Configuration

The EdNA Directory Service is currently connected to the Internet via a dedicated 2 megabit per second link. Network infrastructure, however, varies considerably across the various education and training sectors. Universities were the first to establish connectivity to the Internet (in 1989) through the establishment of AARNet (the Australian Academic and Research Network) under the direction of the Australian Vice-Chancellors' Committee. In 1997, much activity proceeded throughout the sector as a result of government legislation concerning de-regulation of telecommunications. Universities responded by collaborating in implementation of a number of high-speed ATM regional networks. These regional networks combine to form what is now known as AARNet2.

For schools and the vocational training sector the story of connectivity began a little later and in many respects has not been planned – certainly not in the way as it currently is in China! [21] This is not to say that State Governments have not provided resources but what makes this situation different to the universities is the number of institutions involved and the disparity in resources available. Unlike AARNet2, which purchases its bandwidth in bulk from one of the major carriers, schools and TAFE institutes enter into arrangements with local Internet Service Providers, and in some cases State governments have brokered deals. By and large progress on this front has been substantial in the last few years and the initial EdNA vision which was actually framed around addressing the disparities in connectivity is being realised although EdNA does not play a significant role in any roll-out of infrastructure these days.

3.2.3 Category Structure

The top level of the EdNA Directory Service category structure is as follows:

General References
Educational Organisations
Adult Community Education (ACE)
Higher Education
Schools
Vocational Education & Training (VET or TAFE)

The category tree branches several levels deep and there are over 1000 discrete categories on the Directory Service. While this number may seem large, about 30% of these occur as sub-categories (particularly where location is represented according to State or National coverage). Because of the current size of the category structure, discussions are now proceeding among stakeholders aimed at developing a more efficient architecture. While the Oracle database was important in the beginning process of building the present category structure, and while many iterations and revisions took place, it no longer makes a lot of sense to involve a database query at the level of the category tree itself. With the indexing capabilities of Netscape Compass Server there seems to be a straightforward solution at hand.

An example of branching in the category tree from the Higher Education Teaching and Learning category is as follows:

Discussion Forums and Email Lists
Educational Multimedia Development
Electronic Publications and Journals
Libraries and Archives
        Australian Archives
        Australian University Libraries
        International University Libraries
        Other Library Resources
Subject Gateways and Clearinghouses
Teaching and Learning Centres
Teaching and Learning Resources
        Administration, Business, Economics, Law
        Agriculture, Renewable Resources
        Biological Sciences
        Built Environment, Architecture
        Chemical Sciences
        Earth Sciences
        Education
        Engineering, Processing
        Health and Medical sciences
        Humanities
        Mathematics, Computing
        Physical Sciences
        Social Sciences
        Visual/Performing Arts

Linked to all these categories are currently around 7,000 core, or 'approved' items and a further 15,000 leaf-node items. Of the approved items, 63% represent Australian content.

3.3   Parallels of EdNA

There is an increasing number other developments around the globe which parallel the EdNA initiative to some extent: in the UK, the Department of Education and Employment launched in 1997 a discussion paper, 'Connecting the Learning Society: National Grid for Learning' as part of a consultation process concluded at the end of 1997. Implementation was planned to begin in early 1998. [13] In North America, EDUCOM has merged with CAUSE to become EDUCAUSE and released a metadata specification specifically for the education community. This metadata specification is more extensive than EdNA's but both specifications are based on the Dublin Core standard and aimed at developing quality online resources useful to education communities. [7] In Europe, the European SchoolNet Project (EUN) is established for the purposes of providing value-added services to the European K-12 community. Its espoused goals are very much framed in language that expresses collaboration and co-operation between key stakeholders. [8]

4 Conclusion

In the case-study outlined the EdNA Directory Service can be characterised as an exemplar of Community Computing and Support Systems (CCSS). However, it did not begin as such. The use of the terminology of CCSS here is intended to be indicative of computer systems which are both complex and dynamic as a direct result of a reflexive relationship with human communities engaged in a common pursuit of developing online support systems. Close analysis of the development of EdNA (and the EdNA Directory Service) reveals that the process is iterative. The EdNA Directory Service began as an online *information delivery* service but through ongoing and widespread collaboration, aimed at value-adding, it is broadening through developing interactive services and facilitating networking opportunities for its diverse stakeholders. As such, there is a congruence of culture on the one hand and technology on the other. That is, the collaborative and co-operative effort that is manifest in the development of EdNA – itself an expression of networking – maps well to the architecture of the Internet and cyberspace made possible by Communication and Information Technologies. This is a critical point, for without both a viable community and a robust technology expressed as CCSS cannot evolve.

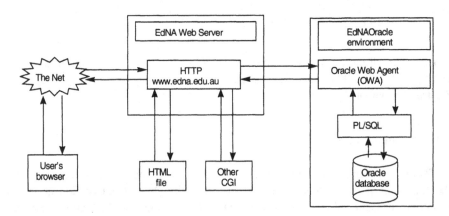

Fig. 1. Dynamic generation of Web pages on EdNA (source: DEETYA, Commonwealth of Australia, 1997)

References

1. Castells, M.: The Information Age: Economy, Society and Culture - Vol I - The Rise of the Network Society. Blackwell, Oxford, UK (1997a)
2. Castells, M.: The Information Age: Economy, Society and Culture - Vol II - The Power of Identity. Blackwell, Oxford, UK (1997b)
3. Clarke, R.: Encouraging Cyberculture. Presented at CAUSE 97, Melbourne (1997) http://www.anu.edu.au/people/Roger.Clarke/II/EncoCyberCulture.html
4. Dobbs-Higginson, M. S.: Asia Pacific: Its Role in the New World Disorder. Minerva/Mandarin, Port Melbourne (1996)
5. Dolence, M. & Norris, D.: Transforming Higher Education: A Vision for Learning in the 21st Century. Society for College and University Planning, Ann Arbor (1995)
6. Education Network Australia http://www.edna.edu.au/
7. EDUCOM http://www.educom.edu/
8. European SchoolNet http://www.eun.org/
9. Kelly, K.: New Rules for the New Economy – twelve dependable principles for thriving in a turbulent world. Wired, September (1997) 140-144, 186-197
10. Lipnack, J. & Stamps, J.: Virtual Teams - Reaching Across Space, Time and Organizations with Technology. John Wiley & Sons, New York (1997)
11. Mason, J. & Hart, G. Computer Mediated Communications: Alleviator or Alienator? presented at CAUSE in Australasia 97. Melbourne (1997a) 387-394
12. Mason, J. & Hart, G.: Effective Use of Asynchronous Virtual Learning Communities, Proceedings from Virtual Communities 97. The University of Sydney (1997b) http://www.arch.usyd.edu.au/kcdc/conferences/VC97/
13. National Grid for Learning (UK) http://www.open.gov.uk/dfee/grid/index.htm
14. Negroponte, N.: Being Digital. Knopf, New York (1995)
15. Rheingold, H.: The Virtual Community. Minerva (1993) Also online at: http://www.rheingold.com/vc/book/intro.html
16. The Center for the Study of Online Community http://www.sscnet.ucla.edu/soc/csoc/
17. Tiffin, J. & Rajasingham, L.: In Search of the Virtual Class. Routledge, London (1995)
18. UNESCO: The Internet and some international regulatory issues concerning content. Australian Broadcasting Authority, Sydney (1997)
19. Wenger, E.: Communities of Practice - Learning, Meaning and Identity (Learning in Doing: Social, Cognitive and Computational Perspectives) Cambridge University Press, Cambridge (1998)
20. West, R. & Review Committee: Learning for Life, final report – Review of Higher education Financing and Policy, Canberra: DEETYA, Commonwealth of Australia (1998)
21. WWW7 - Proceedings of the 7th International World Wide Web Conference, Brisbane, Australia. Computer Networks and ISDN Systems 30 ix-xi. Elsevier Science, Amsterdam (1998)

C-MAP: Building a Context-Aware Mobile Assistant for Exhibition Tours

Yasuyuki Sumi, Tameyuki Etani, Sidney Fels[†],
Nicolas Simonet[‡], Kaoru Kobayashi[§], and Kenji Mase

ATR Media Integration & Communications Research Laboratories,
Seika-cho, Soraku-gun, Kyoto 619-0288, Japan
sumi@mic.atr.co.jp

Abstract. This paper presents the objectives and progress of the Context-aware Mobile Assistant Project (C-MAP). The C-MAP is an attempt to build a personal mobile assistant that provides visitors touring exhibitions with information based on their locations and individual interests. We have prototyped the first version of the mobile assistant and used an open house exhibition held by our research laboratory for a testbed. A personal guide agent with a life-like animated character on a mobile computer guides users using exhibition maps which are personalized depending on their physical and mental contexts. This paper also describes services for facilitating new encounters and information sharing among visitors and exhibitors who have shared interests during/after the exhibition tours.

1 Introduction

This paper presents the objectives and progress of the Context-aware Mobile Assistant Project (C-MAP) [1–3]. The C-MAP is an attempt to build a tour guidance system that provides information to visitors at exhibitions based on their locations and individual interests.

Our long-term goal is to investigate future computer-augmented environments that enhance communications and information sharing between people and knowledgeable machines. The introduction of computer and network technologies into human communications is expected to enable us to go beyond temporal and spatial distributions. Stefik [4] has proposed the notion of a new knowledge medium, which is a kind of information network with semiautomatic services for the generation, distribution, and consumption of knowledge in our society. We believe that the consideration of computer networks that include humans as knowledge media will reveal the future form of Human-Computer Interaction (HCI). The knowledge media include environments for the collaboration of humans and machines, where software acts not as a passive tool but as an autonomous and active machine agent.

[†] Presently with The University of British Columbia.
[‡] Presently with TELECOM Paris.
[§] Also with The University of Tokyo.

In order to investigate how to create such a knowledge medium, we have chosen museums and open house exhibitions as our research laboratories. These are places where knowledge is accumulated and/or conveyed, and where specialist exhibitors provide knowledge to visitors with diverse interests and viewpoints[1]. Actual exhibitions, however, have many restrictions. For example, exhibitors are unable to display all of their collected material due to temporal and spatial restrictions, all visitors are unable to receive individual explanations from exhibitors, all visitors are provided with the same information prepared beforehand, and the one-way communication flow from the exhibitors to the visitor is often limiting. As a solution, recent computing technologies, such as mobile computing, are expected to remove many of the restrictions preventing natural two-way communications between exhibitors and visitors. At this time, we believe that the mediation of real objects in actual exhibitions is inevitable for knowledge sharing, even in the forthcoming digitized society.

The main goals of the C-MAP are as follows:

(1) To provide visitors touring exhibitions with information based on temporal and spatial conditions as well as individual interests, and

(2) To provide users with onsite and offsite services through the Internet (online exhibit information and communications support between exhibitors and visitors in combination with onsite services)[2].

The first goal will involve an approach to facilitating communications mediated by real objects by augmenting real environments with computing technologies [6]. The second goal will aim at implementing communications support between exhibitors and visitors in the long run.

Both goals are expected to enhance human communications distributed temporally and/or spatially. One characteristic of our approach is a mutual augmentation between two spaces, i.e., the information space and the real space. That is, the information space with guide services will reinforce tours in the exhibition (real space), and conversely, tours in the exhibition will provide users with motivation and focal points for communication beyond the existing temporal and spatial restrictions.

2 Related Work

The Cyberguide [7] is another attempt at providing a tour guide system. The authors of the Cyberguide proposed the concept of context-aware mobile applications, and prototyped a system that is able to provide users with location-sensitive information on exhibition site maps displayed on portable PCs. Although the technologies used in the Cyberguide and the C-MAP are similar,

---

[1] Kadobayashi [5] has discussed this in detail.

[2] In this paper, we call services provided at exhibitions "onsite services", and services provided through a network before and/or after exhibition visits "offsite services".

there are two big differences. First, the context-awareness achieved by the Cyberguide can only detect the user's location, i.e., physical (temporal and spatial) context. In contrast, we focus on capturing and utilizing the user's interests (mental context) as well. In the C-MAP system, two maps which visualize the geographical and semantic information of the exhibition space are used for showing exhibit information to the user, capturing his/her interests, and providing personalized information based on his/her individual context. Second, the C-MAP introduces an interface agent which mediates interactions between the system and the user. The interface agents have a life-like appearance, with animated characters. Residing in the mobile assistants, they draw the user's attention to information provided by the system, and show messages according to situations.

The Ubiquitous Talker [8], which consists of an LCD display and a CCD camera, allows users to view real objects (exhibits in our case) with related superimposed information by attaching color-bar ID codes to the objects. It also allows speech interaction, and hence, the users feel as if they are speaking with the objects themselves. The authors of the Ubiquitous Talker intend to demonstrate the augmentation of real space with information space, which we are also interested in. However, one of the goals of our system is to facilitate person-to-person interaction, e.g., new encounters based on shared interests and information exchange, as well as person-to-exhibit interaction. Our feeling is that the people behind each exhibit are knowledgeable and interested in this. The exhibit is a focal point for particular communities and guide agents should help visitors become part of them, if appropriate. In the C-MAP, we intend to increase mutual awareness among people having shared interests by providing them with information on exhibitors and visitors who share similar interests on the exhibit as well as information on the exhibit itself.

The ICMAS-96 Mobile Assistant Project [9] was an attempt to support communities that share certain interests by using mobile technologies. The project provided portable digital assistants with various services to assist conference attendees. The users could use e-mail and online-news services. They were also able to use the InfoCommon [10], which supports the exchange of information related to the conference, and the Community Viewer [11], which supports the formation of communities. The latter two applications were pioneering attempts at community support. Communities do not share clear goals and tasks like groups do, but often have wide interests. Therefore, community formation and communication hold the dynamics of a collaborative kind of creativity. Hence, community support research has been attracting many computer scientists recently [12]. In the ICMAS project, however, network communications was made possible by cellular phones, so the users themselves were responsible for connecting to the network to use services, and the servers could not provide spontaneous services. In contrast, the C-MAP system uses a wireless radio LAN to connect portable PCs. The constant, high-speed access allows servers to spontaneously provide information based on the current situation, and the users' portable PCs are able to communicate in real time. Moreover, for community support, providing only onsite services during the conference is insufficient. Accordingly, the C-MAP

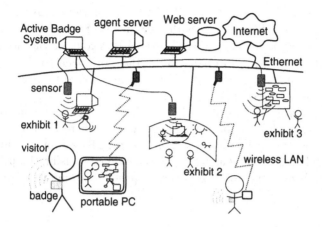

Fig. 1. Schematic diagram of C-MAP system

system uses the Web as an infrastructure for system development, enabling its services to offer offsite services.

3 C-MAP System

3.1 Hardware Architecture

We prototyped a mobile assistant at a two-day open house exhibition held by our research laboratory. **Fig. 1** illustrates the hardware architecture of the system. The system principally consists of servers providing exhibit-related information and guide information, and portable PCs connected with the servers by a wireless LAN.

We use Windows95 PCs with 32MB of RAM, i.e., fifteen Mitsubishi AMiTYs with pen-based interface and fifteen Toshiba Librettos with keyboards. To connect these PCs to the servers, we use a 1.2GHz radio wireless LAN (WaveLAN) that allows 1Mbit/sec communications.

The Web server is used as a server of Java applets for the mobile assistant, and as a server of Web pages related to the exhibits.

Olivetti's Active Badge System (ABS) [13] is used for user location detection. The ABS server has many sensors at the exhibit sites, to detect the locations of the users by infra-red linking to the badges that they wear. The server gathers the latest sensor data and updates the location data of all users. The sensors can detect badges within a 1 to 2 meter perimeter.

The agent server provides guidance, such as route planning and exhibit recommendation, by monitoring the ABS information and each user's interaction with the system on the portable PCs. The guide agent for each portable PC, which runs on the agent server, processes the personalized guide according to the user's context and displays the result on the portable PC. Therefore, thirty guide agents (equal to the number of PCs) at most run simultaneously on the agent server. We use SGI's Onyx with four processors and 128MB of RAM for the agent server. The servers and the portable PCs connect via the LAN, which further connects with the Internet, and is therefore open to the outside. This facilitates the collection of content and guidance material from the outside, and the provision of offsite services.

Note that since most exhibits demonstrated computer applications at our open house, the exhibit applications were able to share information with the mobile assistant servers by the LAN. Consequently, for example, exhibitors were able to provide highly personalized demonstrations by using the personal data (e.g., personal interests, touring histories, profiles) accumulated in the guide agent server.

3.2 Prototyping the Mobile Assistant

Overview of the Mobile Assistant Each portable PC runs the HotJava browser[3] for Java applets to guide the tour, show exhibit-related information, interact with the user, and display the animated characters of the guide agents.

Examples of a portable PC's display are shown in **Fig. 2** and **Fig. 3**. Both displays have a main window on the right and a frame on the left. The user obtains visual guidance of the exhibition space in the main window by alternatively viewing a physical map applet (**Fig. 2**), which displays the geographical layout of the sites, and a semantic map applet (**Fig. 3**), which visualizes the semantic relationships between the exhibits. The controlling frame displays links for viewing the two applets and the animated character and message box of the personal guide agent.

To provide the user with a personalized guide, we need to personalize the mobile assistant on the portable PC in some way. However, putting an individual's data into a portable PC just before he/she begins the tour is undesirable because the thirty portable PCs are used by many visitors. Instead, we install only the HotJava browser on each portable PC and put all of the information into the servers, e.g., the HTML file loaded by the browser, Java applets, guide agent server programs, and individual data dynamically obtained during the tour. First, data for identifying an individual PC and its user (badge ID) are written in the HTML file automatically generated at the reception. Second, the HTML file is loaded by the browser onto the PC, and finally, the agent applet started on the browser registers itself to the agent server.

We next explain the two guidance applets of the exhibition space and the personal guide agent provided on each portable PC.

Visualization of Exhibition Space: Physical Map and Semantic Map
The principal function of the mobile assistant is guidance based on the visualized

---

[3] Since we needed to use the latest JDK1.1 to utilize the facilities of network communication and Japanese processing, HotJava was the only web browser able to support the JDK1.1.

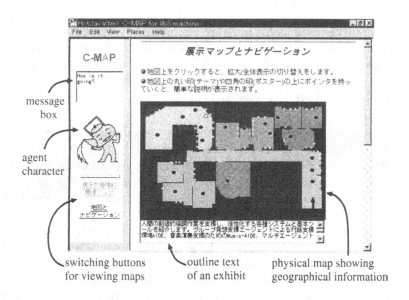

Fig. 2. Screenshot of the mobile assistant display showing a physical map

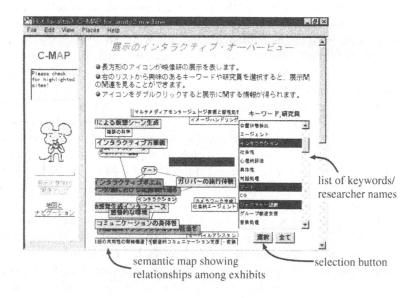

Fig. 3. Another screenshot showing a semantic map

exhibition space. This provides the user with the whole view of the exhibition space involving two aspects, i.e., a geographical map of the exhibition sites and a visualization of the semantic relationships between the exhibits. We believe this complementary guidance helps the understanding of the visitors during the tour because visitors tend to lose the overall view of the exhibition after visiting several of the individual exhibits, viewing demonstrations, and/or speaking with exhibitors (researchers).

The physical map shown in **Fig. 2** displays a two-dimensional view of the exhibition floor. This map provides the locations of exhibit sites (19 in our open house) and the posters (about 70) at the sites. A user can view short explanations by moving the mouse pointer to site/poster marks on the map. The map also shows the user his/her current location as another color mark by using the ABS data.

The semantic map shown in **Fig. 3** displays the graphical relationships between exhibits. The rectangular icons in the graph signify exhibits and the oval icons signify keywords and researchers (exhibitors). The keywords are technical terms characterizing the contents of the exhibits, which were previously extracted from outline texts prepared by the exhibitors. The semantic map provides the user with graphs having links between exhibit icons and keyword/researcher icons; this helps the user connect the fragments of knowledge.

However, because the keyword/researcher icon total is 75, a graph including all of these does not provide useful visualization. Therefore, we have adopted a display method with only the keyword/researcher icons selected by the user based on his/her interests. As a result, the graph of the semantic map can be structured based on the individual user's interests. For example, if the user selects the keyword "art", he/she can view a partial graph formed with only "art"-related exhibits. If the user selects other keywords, the semantic map restructures the graph based on the corresponding viewpoint.

What keywords the user selects affects the restructuring of the semantic map and the guide agent's recommendation of exhibits as well. Whenever the user pushes the keyword selection button, an interest vector[4] that quantifies the user's interests is sent to the agent server, and the personal guide agent calculates a new recommendation with the current interest vector of the user. In addition, this interest vector can be used to support meetings between visitors and exhibitors based on their current and previous interests.

The reason why we adopt this approach is due to our previous research [14, 15], which showed us that personalizing shared information based on individual viewpoints and exploiting the results can facilitate mutual understanding and information sharing between people with similar interests. To accomplish this task, we visualize the structure of the information space. In [14, 15], we visualize the information space structure of a set of texts by adopting a statistical method for quantifying the texts with weighted keywords as multivariate data, and we then compose two-dimensional metric spaces with two principal eigenvectors

---

[4] An interest vector is a multi-dimensional keyword vector, which is a sequence of 0 and 1.

of the data. However, with the mobile assistant used in tours, each and every user requires simple use and results that are easy to understand. Accordingly, we adopt another method to visualize the semantic structure of the exhibition space, by linking icons together and simulating dynamic behaviors with a simple spring model.

To provide the user with an overview of the exhibition, the semantic map displays all of the exhibit icons including those with a keyword not selected by the user. However, the semantic map displays exhibit icons having selected keywords with a larger size and more conspicuously, and in contrast, displays exhibit icons having non-selected keywords with a smaller size.

By double-clicking the exhibit icons, the user can view popup windows with a short explanation of the exhibits, and there are links to Web pages of research projects related to the exhibits.

Guide Agent: Recognition of User Situation, Exhibit Recommendation, Agent Character We have designed a personal guide agent that provides its user with personalized guidance in an exhibition. The guide agent calculates the user's mental context, processes the tour guidance by capturing his/her temporal and spatial context with the ABS information, and monitors the interaction between the user and the mobile assistant. The internal process of the guide agent is performed in the agent server and it is started for each portable PC, basically, for the user of the mobile assistant.

We prototyped the task of exhibit recommendations based on some user contexts, for spontaneous guidance by an agent. Several criteria were used for the recommendations, e.g., the similarity between the interest vector described in the previous section and each exhibit's keyword vector, the touring histories of users, the geographical distances between exhibit sites and user locations, the exhibit site attendance, and the exhibit demonstration schedule. The calculation of a recommendation responds to changes in the contexts, e.g., a user's selection of keywords on the semantic map and the user's movement to different exhibit sites. Recommended exhibits are indicated to the user by the highlighting of three icons (with higher scores) on both the physical and semantic maps.

The guide agent must interpret the primitive information obtained from the ABS to detect the user's movement through the exhibition sites and to generate individual touring records. The ABS server gathers badge IDs detected by the individual sensors every ten seconds or less. When the guide agent notices that a certain sensor successively detects the same badge, it interprets only one detection as "cruise", two detections as "enter", and more detections as "stay". Accordingly, when a user's badge is successively detected twice by a sensor located at a certain exhibit site, the guide agent decides the person has entered the exhibit site. When detected three or more times, the agent decides it is a visit and then records the time of the visit for the touring record.

One characteristic of our guide agent is the life-like character residing in the mobile assistant. It plays a role in the interaction between the user and the mobile

Table 1. Determination of agent motion and message according to internal state

Internal state	Action	Message
Recommendation	Suggesting	"Please check for highlighted sites!"
In calculation	Thinking	"Please wait. I'm thinking."
Urging to move	Hurrying	"Please hurry to the next sites!"
(No guide)	Idling	Random messages

Random messages: "How is it going?"
"I hope you are enjoying yourself!"
"Double click on the Semantic map for further information!"
"Click on the Map to zoom!"
"Move onto the site on the Map for a short overview!"

assistant and represents its internal state. The agent character is presented by an animated applet using GIFs with a text message box. Its roles are:

- To express the internal state of the guide agent with the animated character behaviors,
- To draw the user's attention to the results of the exhibit recommendations shown in the maps,
- To hurry the user to the next site if he/she appears to be using up too much of the tour time[5], and
- To inform the system usage by messages and encourage the use of the system.

Table 1 shows the correspondence of the guide agent's internal state with its behaviors and messages. We have prepared four actions for each animated character, i.e., suggesting, thinking, hurrying, and idling, and several corresponding messages. The guide agent switches these actions and messages according to its internal state. When it is idle, it displays messages for basic system usage in a random order.

4 Public Experiment and Evaluation

4.1 Outline of the Experiment

Using our annual open house held November 6th and 7th, 1997, we carried out a public experiment on the first version of the C-MAP system by setting up a reception booth for use of the mobile assistants at the entrance of the exhibition floor. The exhibition space consisted of five rooms. **Fig. 4** shows snapshots of the open house.

For a total of ten hours on the two days, approximately 170 users were registered for use of the mobile assistant. The static data of the users (names, affiliations, and so on) were recorded into a database at the time of user registration. After that, the host name of the portable PC, badge ID, and guide character[6] selected by the user were registered to generate the personal guide

---

[5] Because of the limitation of the portable PC's battery, we set a time limit of two hours for the guide service.
[6] We prepared eleven kinds of characters for the guide agent.

Portable PCs with
radio transceivers

An ABS sensor installed
on a wall of an exhibit site

ABS badges

Fig. 4. Snapshots of a public experiment

agent. For first-time users of the system, we prepared three model courses of the tour to determine the default values of their interest vectors. Moreover, we tried to lighten the burden imposed on the receptionists by preparing desktop PCs which would let each of the visitors do the user registration by himself/herself and preview the exhibition by using the semantic map. The exhibition floor held nineteen exhibit sites and approximately seventy posters. The scale was appropriate for a 1 to 2 hour tour. We set up thirty ABS sensors on the walls of the exhibition site.

4.2 Evaluation of the Mobile Assistant: What Worked and What Didn't

The prototyped mobile assistant runs with the cooperation of several distributed sub-systems. Below, we summarize the parts which worked properly and those that did not.

- The procedures for user registration, preparation of the mobile assistant, and battery replacement (for the portable PCs) at the reception booth went smoothly. Although these procedures were done by receptionists unrelated to the system development, there were no errors in initiating the use of the mobile assistants.
- Each of the applets, i.e., the semantic map, the physical map, and the animated character, performed well.
- The exhibit recommendations by the guide agent were simple yet functional. The interest vector from the semantic map was properly used for the calculation of each recommendation.
- The ABS did not work as advertised by Olivetti as it was incapable of monitoring more than six sensors. Due to this complication, we had to limit our experiment using the location data of users for six demonstration sites inside one room.

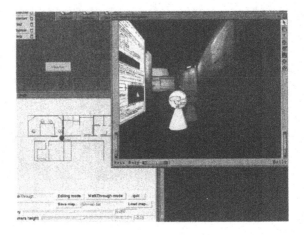

Fig. 5. Prototyping a virtual exhibition space including user avatars

- The guide agent did not use any location information for the exhibit recommendations because the ABS did not work properly.
- In the room with the ABS sensors, the location detection of the users was properly done. The location-aware services worked by displaying each user's current location on the physical map. However, badge detection by the sensors was unstable; sometimes a badge was not detected for a while after the user wearing it entered a new site.
- The animated character was able to display the different states of the agent with animation behaviors and text messages. However, the guide agent itself was not very complex so there were no states to display.

4.3 Combination with Exhibit Applications

As described at the end of Section 3.1, we can combine our mobile assistant with exhibit applications by allowing the applications to use the user information accumulated in the agent server. In this section, we show two examples.

Fig. 5 is an example of reproducing a virtual exhibition space with 3D graphics. This was accomplished by taking previous pictures of the exhibit sites and mapping these on the walls of the 3D space for texture. The 3D graphics were rapidly prototyped with an interpretive VR description language called InvenTcl [16] which is being developed at our laboratory. In the virtual exhibition space, there are avatar icons[7] of the current C-MAP users, which reflect the location information of these users by the C-MAP's agent server. By clicking on the avatar icons, one is able to view profile information of the users. Although this exhibit application was originally prototyped to lend appeal to the development

---

[7] Because we could not prepare users' portraits or illustrations, we mapped the illustrations of their agent characters on their avatar icons instead.

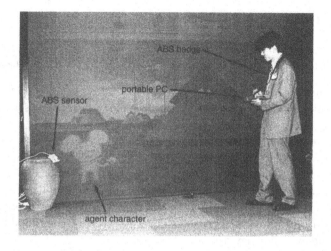

Fig. 6. Guide character appearing in an exhibit application

efficiency of the VR description language, the users could use it to determine whether remote exhibit sites were crowded or to obtain information for meeting other C-MAP users. At the beginning, we had thought of providing meeting support for the guide services, but we left its implementation out because of insufficiencies in the portable PCs to perform calculation and display. In fact, this application was accomplished by implementing and running a high-performance graphics computer, SGI's Indigo2. However, since we assume that such computer restrictions will be removed in the near future, we are continuing to examine how to provide such applications for mobile assistant services.

An attempt to personalize an exhibit demonstration according to personal user data obtained by the mobile assistant, is another combination example. **Fig. 6** shows an exhibit application where a user's personal guide agent character appears. This application is called VisTA-walk [17]. VisTA-walk is an experimental system being developed at our laboratory that will allow users to walk through and access information in 3D virtual spaces with gestures by using Computer Vision technology. Usually, the users of VisTA-walk explore virtual spaces alone. In this example, however, once a user's badge is detected by a sensor located in the demonstration area, the agent character residing in his/her mobile assistant automatically appears and leads the user in the virtual space of VisTA-walk. For a combination of exhibit applications with the mobile assistant, various directions are expected such as exhibit guidance personalization based on the individual interests and knowledge of the user, inferred by his/her previous touring records. This time, the user's frequency in using the mobile assistant was used to quantify the activity and (based on this value) to automatically switch the demonstration courses of VisTA-walk [18]. This personalization is simple but effective for increasing user satisfaction in experience-based demonstrations.

4.4 User Evaluation and Discussion

We asked the users to fill in a questionnaire about the usability of each function after use. In this section, we present a summary along with a discussion.

- The usability of visual guidance for the exhibition space with the semantic and physical maps was evaluated. The frequency of keyword selection on the semantic map, which can be regarded as a standard of user activity in our system, reached 3.7 times during the tour for an average of 84 users. More than 10% of the active users performed the keyword selection approximately ten times. Considering the inconvenience of the portable PC and the scale of the exhibition, this result seems to show the acceptability of the semantic map. We believe the semantic map is simple and easy to understand for all users; visitors, in fact, are generally eager to receive background information about the exhibits they attend.
- According to the evaluation, the users had a feeling of intimacy with the character of the guide agent. However, they did not think it was helpful for improving the agent's reliability and the representation of its internal state. If we consider the combination of the exhibit applications shown in the previous section, the appearance of the identifiable guide agent enhances the consistency of the entire guidance for the user.
- We received many comments that the portable PCs were heavy and hard to use. We therefore need to improve the portable devices, e.g., the separation of the user interface part from the computer itself, and the ubiquity of the interface devices in exhibition environments. This is an important future modification.
- We received many requests for voice guidance. Actually, it could be effective to use audio information together with visual information, especially when the guide agent provides spontaneous guidance.

5 Current Directions: Extending Offsite Services

5.1 Online View of Exhibit Information

In this section, we describe one of our current issues, i.e., enrichment of the services in the information space in order to facilitate deeper person-to-exhibit interaction and person-to-person interaction as well.

Although we had prepared links to Web homepages related to the exhibits on the semantic and physical maps, Web-surfing by users was rarely observed during the open house exhibition. This is understandable because, in general, users are not expected to search the Internet with such inconvenient PCs when the actual exhibits are in front of them. However, when we consider the provision of these applets as an offsite service, the semantic map is useful for providing homepages of projects in our research laboratory, and it is adaptive to restructuring according to the individual interests of users. Evaluation of such cases by publicly providing offsite services is our present focus.

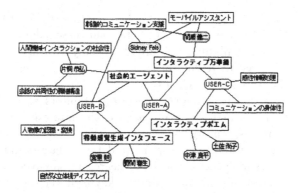

Fig. 7. Graphic view of a social network

Our mobile assistant can be used on Web browsers in remote sites because its user interface is built with Java applets. For example, although its development was not completed in time for the experiment, if we had released the semantic map before the open house it could have allowed potential visitors a preview of our research exhibition. This would have helped in the advance preparation of the personalized guide agents and in improving the exhibit.

Since the user data that can be obtained by the mobile assistant during a tour is limited, obtaining detailed user data such as user interests and areas of expertise by online services would be very beneficial. We are currently developing such an offsite service, i.e., an online viewing system based on question-and-answer interaction, which personally directs a user in exploring the information space of exhibitions [19].

5.2 Constructing Social Networks: Community Support

One of the main objectives of the C-MAP is to encourage human-to-human communications based on exhibitions. Namely, we aim to support communications among visitors/exhibitors sharing interests and knowledge concerning the exhibits.

Accordingly, we are planning to structure the records of mobile assistant users to provide them with social networks [20] that can be accessed by the Web. The social network's structure will be a graph whose nodes represent visitors, exhibitors, and exhibits and will have connections between people and exhibits according to their degree of attachment to exhibits[8].

Fig. 7 is a graphic view of the kind of social network which we are aiming for. We applied the semantic map applet to graph social networks by representing exhibits with rectangular icons and visitors/exhibitors with oval icons. The network in this example was constructed by placing a visitor, "USER-A", in the

---

[8] By *attachment to exhibits*, we mean exhibitors being involved in the exhibits and visitors being interested in them or spending much time to see them.

center. The exhibit icons which are directly connected to the "USER-A" icon are the exhibits in which he had deep interest. Beyond these exhibit icons, you can find other visitors and exhibitors, who are also deeply attached to the exhibits. Further beyond these visitor/exhibitor icons, you can find other exhibits, which other visitors/exhibitors are attached to.

The degree of attachment between visitors/exhibitors and exhibits might be determined by individual user data such as the interest vectors which we described before, profiles, touring histories, and so on. We expect offsite services, described in the last section, to capture more detailed data of individual users. In the example, we simply determined the degree by keyword co-occurrences between users' interest vectors and exhibits' keyword vectors, which were all of the quantified data we could capture during the open house exhibition. The selection of visitors to be shown in the network, which are related to "USER-A", was also determined by keyword co-occurrences between their individual interest vectors.

It is hoped that such a social network can be used to encourage new encounters between individuals and the formation of new communities based on their shared interests. For example, by viewing the social network, USER-A can easily notice the existence of exhibitors and other visitors, such as USER-B and USER-C, for exhibits which attract his interest.

Another expected effect of social networks is the social (collaborative) recommendation of exhibits. For example, the social network may encourage USER-A to visit exhibits which had not been noticed by him yet but had been deeply appreciated by USER-B, who shares many interests with USER-A.

The Thinking Tag [21] is well known as another effort to facilitate communication between humans sharing interests at places where many people gather. This is an electronic name tag that is capable of displaying the degree of agreement between the interests of two persons wearing the tags in a face-to-face encounter. Individual users' interests are quantified by means of questionnaires at the entrance to the party place. Compared with the Thinking Tag, the characteristics of our method are: The users do not have to face each other; the users can view shared information among them, which may be common ground for communication; and the social network can be dynamically reconstructed according to changes in the contexts of users and exhibition environments.

Practical issues for providing social networks are topics for future work, e.g., forms of provision, combination with other information resources, privacy protection against the public dispersal of individual information, and so on.

6 Conclusions

We have prototyped a mobile assistant that can personally guide visitors touring exhibitions based on their locations and individual interests. This mobile assistant was used as a testbed at our two-day open house. The usability of geographically/semantically visualized guidance was experimentally demonstrated. In addition, a personal guide agent that spontaneously recommends exhibits based on user context was demonstrated. We also proposed a novel style of exhibition, i.e., the personalization of exhibit demonstrations from user data obtained by the mobile assistant.

The characteristics of our project's targets can be summarized as follows:

(1) To extend the concept of context-awareness for exhibition guidance,

(2) To design a life-like agent that spontaneously guides a visitor,

(3) To facilitate communication in a community by the sharing of knowledge and interests related to the exhibition, and

(4) To extend the temporal and spatial view of exhibit-related services including offsite services.

Targets (1) and (2) were partially accomplished and offered material for the evaluation and discussion of such forms of HCI. Targets (3) and (4) have not been completed, but we have prepared an infrastructure for carrying them out.

Our system consists of many distributed sub-systems and users who work together cooperatively. In this system, communication and information sharing between people and knowledge-bases are mediated by machine agents that facilitate their knowledge conveyance and future association. This is an approach that shows one direction of the future HCI. Although the current version of the C-MAP system uses only a guide agent as a machine agent, we plan to design an agent that acts as an exhibitor, one that acts as an interface secretary for visitors, and one that acts as a mediating agent for all participants including these machine agents. This will involve human-to-agent communication as well as agent-to-agent communication and will have great relevance to recent multi-agent research.

Finally, we mention the distributed cooperation performed in the project. In this project, there were various collaborations among project members. For example, the system development involved the collaboration of approximately ten members. To collect content and combine the exhibit applications, we relied on the cooperation of close to fifty researchers in our laboratory. To carry out the public experiment, we relied on the cooperation of receptionists in the reception procedure. In order to achieve the above forms of cooperation, the infrastructure of the Web was indispensable. The Web facilitated the distributed development and flexible integration of sub-systems. The test results of the system integration showed the sharing of information as it was. This made it easy to manage the versions of the system. Moreover, we needed only to install a Web browser on each of thirty personal PCs, and hence, last minute changes could be easily integrated. We were able to use updated information provided by researchers to collect content involving exhibit-related information. All in all, this means our system of using the Web as an infrastructure consistently supports knowledge conveyance from specialists to visitors and, furthermore, it allows the communication form itself, of the people involved in an exhibition, to be changed.

Acknowledgments

Development of the system and accomplishment of the public experiment relied on the cooperation of the members of ATR MI&C research laboratories. Especially, their President Ryohei Nakatsu gave us the chance to perform the project, and Dr. Rieko Kadobayashi's Meta-Museum concept [5] gave us stimuli for starting the project. Dr. Katashi Nagao at Sony CSL, Prof. Toru Ishida at Kyoto University, and Prof. Toyoaki Nishida at NAIST offered valuable comments and encouragement throughout the project. Ms. Keiko Nakao took part in the design and illustration of the agent characters. We thank all of the above people.

References

1. Yasuyuki Sumi, Tameyuki Etani, and Kenji Mase. Context-aware mobile assistant. In *55th Annual Convention of Information Processing Society of Japan*, volume 4, pages 443–444. September 1997. in Japanese.
2. Kenji Mase, Yasuyuki Sumi, Tameyuki Etani, Kaoru Kobayashi, Sidney Fels, Nicolas Simonet, and Rieko Kadobayashi. Personal and mobile interface agents for exhibition guiding. In *Third Symposium on Intelligent Information Media*, pages 219–224. IEICE, December 1997. in Japanese.
3. Sidney Fels, Yasuyuki Sumi, Tameyuki Etani, Nicolas Simonet, Kaoru Kobayashi, and Kenji Mase. Progress of C-MAP: A context-aware mobile assistant. In *AAAI Spring Symposium on Intelligent Environments*, pages 60–67. March 1998.
4. Mark Stefik. The next knowledge medium. *AI Magazine*, 7(1):34–46, 1986.
5. Rieko Kadobayashi and Kenji Mase. MetaMuseum as a new communication environment. In *Multimedia Communication and Distributed Processing System Workshop*, pages 71–78. Information Processing Society of Japan, 1995. in Japanese.
6. Mark Weiser. Some computer science issues in ubiquitous computing. *Communications of the ACM*, 36(7):74–84, 1993.
7. Gregory D. Abowd, Christopher G. Atkeson, Jason Hong, Sue Long, Rob Kooper, and Mike Pinkerton. Cyberguide: A mobile context-aware tour guide. *Wireless Networks*, 3(5):421–433, 1997.
8. Katashi Nagao and Jun Rekimoto. Ubiquitous Talker: Spoken language interaction with real world objects. In *IJCAI-95*, pages 1284–1290, 1995.
9. Yoshiyasu Nishibe, Hiroaki Waki, Ichiro Morihara, and Fumio Hattori. Analyzing social interactions in massive mobile computing –Experiments of ICMAS'96 Mobile Assistant Project–. In *IJCAI-97 Workshop on Social Interaction and Communityware*, pages 19–24, 1997.
10. Harumi Maeda, Masao Kajihara, Hidekazu Adachi, Atsushi Sawada, Hideaki Takeda, and Toyoaki Nishida. Weak information structure for human information sharing. In *IJCAI-97 Workshop on Social Interaction and Communityware*, pages 7–12, 1997.
11. Toshikazu Nishimura, Hirofumi Yamaki, Takaaki Komura, Nobuyasu Itoh, Tadahiro Gotoh, and Toru Ishida. Community Viewer: Visualizing community formation on personal digital assistants. In *IJCAI-97 Workshop on Social Interaction and Communityware*, pages 25–30, 1997.
12. Toru Ishida, editor. *Community Computing: Collaboration over Global Information Networks*. John Wiley & Sons, 1998. in printing.

13. Roy Want, Andy Hopper, Veronica Falcão, and Jonathan Gibbons. The active badge location system. *ACM Transactions on Information Systems*, 10(1):91–102, 1992.
14. Yasuyuki Sumi, Kazushi Nishimoto, and Kenji Mase. Facilitating human communications in personalized information spaces. In *AAAI-96 Workshop on Internet-Based Information Systems*, pages 123–129. August 1996.
15. Yasuyuki Sumi, Kazushi Nishimoto, and Kenji Mase. Personalizing shared information in creative conversations. In *IJCAI-97 Workshop on Social Interaction and Communityware*, pages 31–36, 1997.
16. Sidney Fels, Silvio Esser, Armin Bruderlin, and Kenji Mase. Inventcl: Making open inventor interpretive with tcl/[incr tcl]. In *Visual Proceedings of SIGGRAPH'97*, page 191. ACM, August 1997.
17. Rieko Kadobayashi, Kazushi Nishimoto, and Kenji Mase. Design and evaluation of gesture interface for an immersive virtual walk-through application for exploring cyberspace. In *Proc. of Third IEEE International Conference on Automatic Face and Gesture Recognition (FG98)*, pages 534–539. April 1998.
18. Rieko Kadobayashi and Kenji Mase. Seamless guidance by personal agent in virtual space based on user interaction in real world. In *The Third International Conference and Exhibition on The Practical Application of Intelligent Agents and Multi-Agent Technology (PAAM98)*, pages 191–200. March 1998.
19. Kaoru Kobayashi, Yasuyuki Sumi, and Kenji Mase. Information presentation based on individual user interests. In *Second International Conference on Knowledge-based Intelligent Electronic Systems(KES-98)*, volume 1, pages 375–383. IEEE, April 1998.
20. Henry Kautz, Bart Selman, and Mehul Shah. Referral Web: Combining social networks and collaborative filtering. *Communications of the ACM*, 40(3):63–65, 1997.
21. Rick Borovoy, Michelle McDonald, Fred Martin, and Mitchel Resnick. Things that blink: Computationally augmented name tags. *IBM Systems Journal*, 35(3&4):488–495, 1996.

Managing Large Scale On-Line Discussions:
Secrets of the Open Meeting[*]

Roger Hurwitz and John Mallery

The Artificial Intelligence Laboratory
Massachusetts Institute of Technology

Abstract. The possibility of communities steering themselves by large scale, online meetings are limited by support system capabilities for managing their discourse. An asynchronous conferencing system the Open Meeting supported a meeting in which thousands of U.S. government workers discussed reengineering government services. It enabled users to learn and share opinions about proposed changes, because its design focused on decomposing the inflows of comments, structuring multi-lateral conversations and maintaining civility. Access was provided over SMTP and HTTP to a topically differentiated hypertext synthesized from an object database, which was extended by users' comments. The comments composed virtual conversations, structured by a discourse grammar that constrained what types of comments could be attached in specific contexts. Civility benefitted from use of moderators and from participants' having similar bureaucratic culture backgrounds. The results suggest that cultural diversity is a greater challenge than numbers to enabling effective on-line democratic action.

Can the Internet invigorate the democratic practices of large communities? Will it become a new public sphere[1], a space where people gather to rationally discuss issues in the hopes of reaching consensus and influencing policy makers? Expectations for that have been raised by a) the diffusion of on-line community forums and newsgroups, b) the power of the Internet to quickly and cheaply gather dispersed individuals around common interests, and c) its use by governments and political activists to distribute information. Parties, candidates and even rebellions now have web sites and email. As expressed in the ugly buzzword *disintermediation*, digital networks can create direct links between people and government, bypassing the mass media, interest groups and other gate keepers.

---

[*] The on-line meeting described herein was a collaboration of the Artificial Intelligence Laboratory, the National Performance Review, Lawrence Livermore National Laboratory and Mitre Corporation. Jonathan Gill, Thomas Kalil, Randy Katz and Howard Shrobe provided more support. Research was partly supported by the Defense Advanced Research Projects Agency of the Department of Defense under contract number MDA972-93-1-003N7.

[1] The term public sphere was brought to contemporary attention by Habermas [1], who links the decline of public spaces for political discussion to the rise of mass media.

Some argue that the Internet will not nurture a public sphere, which, in any case, is an inappropriate model for democratic practice. Its earlier manifestations in Berlin salons and American civic associations were unrepresentative and exclusivist; its rhetoric, abstractions and self-evident truths assume an underlying homogeneous society, steered by white, literate and propertied males[2]. On this critical view, characteristics of on-line communications as well as the growing diversity of voices on the Internet prevent the realization of a public sphere, even one accessible to all and where difference is acknowledged. These include a bias toward speedy, unreflected responses, the absence of social context cues and hyperlinking which, pointing a reader elsewhere, dissolves the authority of the text at hand. On-line political discussions will be situated, personal, and chaotic; more likely to immobilize a community than help form its collective will.

This paper joins the debate by examining how the Open Meeting an experimental network-based information system brought together many, dispersed people to discuss government policies, which affected their work lives. The system's architecture and its theory of knowledge representation have been described elsewhere[3]; the present focus is on how the system organized the large scale discussions, particularly with regard to managing inflows, structuring interactions and maintaining civility. The achievements and shortcomings of the experiment are examined for their relevance to issues of on-line governance. Clearly just broadening people's access to one another and to information does not generate participation, order discourse or produce group decisions. So it is important to show how it is possible to get some of these results.

1   Overview of the System

The Open Meeting system was initially designed and implemented in fall, 1994, to support an on-line meeting, in which several thousand United States government workers conducted virtual discussions of recommended changes in government operations and performance standards. At the system's core is a persistent object database, which coupled to a task engine, supports email and web servers. These present messages and pages, with content generated on-the-fly by the database, in response to users' inputs through queries, remote commands or interactive forms. Inputs can include users' comments which are added to the database and reconfigured as threaded conversations or annotation overlays. The recommendations for discussion had been prepared by the National Performance Review (NPR),[4] a unit in the Office of United States Vice-President Al Gore, with the mission of "reinventing government." It believed a large scale on-line meeting would

- Increase the visibility and support for these recommendations;
- Enhance their prestige through association with new technology;
- Gather reports on promising practices in line with them;
- Bypass organizational boundaries that keep employees in different organization from discussing common work problems;

- Overcome geographical barriers that confine discussions on government to the capital;
- Demonstrate the possibility of on-line/ electronic governance.

As the last point suggests, in the NPR view, government workers comprised a community whose opinion needed to be articulated and mobilized. The NPR project team[2] for the meeting was guided by the metaphor of a New England town meeting, where any member can of the community can speak to issues of common concern. It envisioned an on-line environment analogous to a town hall, that would include chat rooms for an assembly hall, committee rooms and water cooler.[3]

The trajectory toward a community activation system changed with the involvement of the Open Meeting developers, members of an MIT group, whose research concerned intelligent networks that route and enhance messages, based on understanding of their contents and the organizations through which they flow. At the time, the research group was planning a web based system that would manage public participation in government inquiries on proposed changes in regulations. The initial plan called for interested parties to attach their views as annotations to the proposals, differentiated according to the types of comments being made, e.g., question, statement of support. Officials could then retrieve these comments by target and type from a textbase of review documents, using the system, in effect, as an annotation server. Alternatively, the comments on a document could be routed directed to officials whose profiles indicated their in that document. By enabling the public and officials to receive and reply to each other's comments, the system would support virtual discussions composed of threads of typed comments. Through the prism of this plan, the federal workers appeared like individual stakeholders responding to inquiries on proposed changes in regulations affecting their individual interests, work rules and performance standards. They were primarily sources of information about the benefits, feasibility and acceptability of the proposals.

To encourage broad participation and knowledge sharing, regardless of organizational differences, we consequently advised that the meeting focus on eleven NPR reports, each of which concerned reinventing an operating system, like human program development or information management, found in all departments and agencies and subject to the same rules and standards. These could provide common grounds for discussions across organizational boundaries, but recommendations for a specific department were unlikely to draw workers from other departments into a discussion. We also advised dropping the town hall format for several reasons:

---

[2] Led by Larry Koskinen and Andy Campbell

[3] The Clinton-Gore team used face-to-face "townhall meetings" 1992 presidential campaign and later in the Clinton I administration to get public attention for its issues and positions, while bypassing the national mass media. This populist strategy was highly successful with citizens and voters, but soured the team's relationships with the journalists, editors and owners of the media.

- a reluctance to assume the participants already recognized themselves as a community;
- the desired dispersion of participants over time zones made asynchronous communications more feasible;
- chatrooms, MUDs and MOOs would not scale for the desired number of participants;
- email would not support the GUIs which could suggest a town hall setting, and email was mandatory because relatively few workers then had web browsers.

The group proposed instead a system similar to the public comment system sketched above, as an application layer for Comlink, an enhanced document distribution system, developed primarily by Mallery and used for the indexing, publication and retrieval of White House electronic releases on the Internet.[5]. The principal features and functionalities of the resulting system included

- *An extensible, persistent object database* whose instances include texts and users. The text instances include hypertext links and indices, and so support extension of an initial textbase configurable as hypertext; arbitrarily constrained, on-the-fly construction of local hypertext; and views of the hypertext, restricted by arbitrary indices, like quality ratings, security classifications, etc. The user objects can include slots for interests and preferences, enabling subscription to and routing of texts.
- *Dynamically generated web pages* which facilitate representation and navigation of the online discussions and collaborations. Regions of the resulting hypertext can be isolated; pointers to comments and annotations descending from an initial text can be displayed in an outline or tree, each with an icon for the type of the comment. This permits both overviews of the link structure and direct access to those comments which interest the user.
- *Interactive form processing* to support user queries and comments, hypertext traversal, and search interfaces for retrieval by indices.
- *Message threading* that constrains input according to conversation or discourse grammars. Grammar means a set of (context sensitive) rules that specify the types of texts or comments that can be linked to another text or comment, according to its type. By type, we mean remarks that constitute recognizable moves or roles in discourse or communicative interaction, e.g., remark types in a debate include claim, challenge, rebuttal, question, answer, etc. A grammar thus represents a procedural order, often with possible branching.
- *Subscription to arbitrary node:* A retrieved text was wrapped in a form which could be used to request emailing of comments that are later attached to the text or any of its descendants. Since the particular text as a database object is automatically identified in the form, subscription is transparent: The user does not have to specify the node.
- *Moderator tools* enabling submissions to be handled before being posted to public view. These include a) a moderator's view, b) virtual queues for routing submissions on a topic to its moderator, c) forms for attaching ratings

and view restrictions, c) form letters accepting and rejecting submissions. With these, the Open Meeting can support moderated as well as unmoderated online conferences.

2 Meeting the Challenges

This technology better met the NPR goals than chatrooms or list-serves, but it put more emphasis on the meeting as interactive knowledge building than the NPR team originally planned and had less regard for the meeting as community activation. Its deployment was shaped by our recognition of the major challenges that a large on-line meeting presented to the system's potential for organizing texts and building knowledge: Managing the fan-in of comments on the proposals, structuring the interactions of participants and maintaining civility among them.

2.1 Fan-in

In hierarchically structured communication flows, viz., 1-to-many/ many-to-one, a request for comments to a community can produce a stream of responses likely to overwhelm the source of the request, but miss other interested parties. Directing the response stream to all members of the community in a many-to-many pattern just compounds the problems of message volume (gain) and recipients' discrimination of messages that interest them. A strategy to meet this challenge is the decomposition of both the request and response streams, according to a taxonomy of the issue space. This was done for the on-line meeting by considering the NPR reports on the operating systems as subdomains and their respective proposals as categories in a reinventing government domain, and requiring that a comment be subsumed by a proposal. A comment either had to target a specific proposal or another comment descending from it. Instead of being asked "what are your views on reinventing government," a participant was in effect asked: "Should government offices be issued credit cards for making small purchases?" by the presentation of that proposal. Users could find proposals and later comments on them that interested them by drill down through the hypertext o rhrough a taxonomic listing. They could subscribe to receive comments added to such a proposal or, even more finely grained, to a node subsumed by it.

Decomposition of the domain was facilitated by NPR having prepared each of the reports according to the same strategic-plan like format: an Executive Summary described the problems in the respective system, a set of Recommendations proposed how to fix them, one or two Actions were described for effecting each Recommendation, and Appendices added some details of the implementations. These parts were easily reconfigured into a hypertext, using a standard node architecture, that replicated the structure across the main branches of the hypertext (the individual reports), simplifying implementation and providing a consistent user interface. Eleven such nodes, one for each operating system, were linked to a root document which presented the plan and procedures of the meeting. The standard node eventually had links to the parts of the report, including a link to each recommendation, and to other relevant documents, including a short Overview of the system problems, official examples of practices that satisfied a recommendation, and newsletters, which summarized the ongoing discussions of the proposals.

The decomposition is based on the idea that knowledge can be hierarchically localized in the sense that understanding in one branch or area of a domain requires knowledge of more general domain principles but not of fine grained propositions in other branches. The decomposition was intended to reduce the number of people in a conversation and the circulation of their comments, enhance their interest and focus and make the conversational threads easier to follow. The resulting topology was small circles of lateral communication, i.e., several dozen to several dozen, with isolation of conversations from one another being overcome in practice by users' visiting several conversations. Systematic, updated overviews of the discussions regarding an operating system were provided by the newsletters. These were hand-made summaries by the moderators, but automatic summarization or gisting which exploits the hypertext links is an important focus of work to extend the system.

2.2 Structuration

The challenge of devising an interaction structure for the meeting had two sides: First, the need to enable orderly, yet relatively unconstrained conversations, through which knowledge and information about the proposals could be built; second, the need to produce a coherent textbase which would index each comment according to its type of move in a conversation. The messages posted to the meeting were imagined as both pieces of ongoing conversations about particular proposals and parts of a self-extending, distributed hypertext, contributed by multiple sources, including NPR. However conventional messages threaders, such as subject, target ("in reply to"), submission time, were deemed insufficient to structure or represent a set of messages as a sequence of conversational or rhetorical.

Indexing the intentions of the moves is important: First, on the view that conversations are composed of interlocking moves or speech acts[6], on-line communications are problematic, because they have fewer inflection, non-verbal and setting cues which speakers in face-to-face communications exploit to make and recognize speech acts, their intentions, and the expected responses. When the move types of posted comments are indicated, a user can know what types are appropriate responses to a target she has chosen, and by identifying the type of her comment, she can indicate the type of response she expects. Second, when comments are threaded through their targets in hypertext display, the tagging clarifies the relationships between otherwise opaque texts (especially when the text itself is not displayed but only pointed at by a link), and provides an overview of the flow of intentions and expectations through the entire conversation. Finally indices are needed so for a given target, all replies of the same attitude, agreement for example, can be displayed together, retrieved together or more easily checked for redundancy.

The indices can be obtained by asking contributors to identify the types of moves they are making. This self-indexing is similar and not necessarily more inhibiting than the widespread practice of putting "smilies" and other cues into email messages to reduce their ambiguity.[4]. Self-indexing of utterances is also a standard linguistic practice, especially when there is a probability of misinterpretation or a particular type of move is privileged, in the sense of having a priority on getting attention, e.g., "I have a question?"[5]

We also imagined that the sequences of moves and the discussions they created would be constrained by a context sensitive discourse grammar, a set of moves and rules that restricts their possible combinations by specifying the moves that can be legally attached to each move. These rules abstract the notions of appropriateness and expectation that are associated with the move types in a sequence. Since they have institutional as well as logical bases, a grammar encapsulates a quasi normative order or a procedure employed for a social purpose, not just idealized linguistic phenomena[6] The sequences which we thought most likely to occur and best to support on-line were multi-lateral arguments for and against the proposals. Our model of argument was influenced by modern dialectical theories, which understand argument as an ordered, interactive process whose utterances are constrained to speech acts for making and supporting claims, challenges and rebuttal.[7, 9, 8]. The highly restricted move sets of the dialectical argument models were attractive because they barred the flames, digressions, emotional discharges and similar failings of newsgroups. However, we anticipated that discussions constrained by that grammar would be more conflictual and address fewer possibilities than if the grammar also permitted alternatives, examples, information seeking questions and answers. Because the Open Meeting was intended to stimulate interest and accumulate information about government reinvention, the teams selected moves that could lead to consensus while permitting differences of opinion: Agreement (reason for), Disagreement (reason against), Question, Answer, (propose an) Alternative, Qualification ("yes, but"), or (report a) Promising Practice. The root document explained these types, presented a distinctive icon for each, and asked users to frame comments according to them.

The grammar for the meeting was additionally shaped by pragmatic institutional as well as logical constraints. To avoid the scent of electronic plebiscite, polling, voting and simple endorsements were not implemented. Agreements and Disagreements had to provide reasons. Because the executive summaries, the

---

[4] Multi-media messages will not entirely eliminate the problem, especially when speakers do not know each other or are from different cultures.

[5] Self-indexing is often used in political discourse to emphasize the intention of certain utterances. One famous example is Zola's attack on the French government for its cover-up in the Dreyfus affair: *J'accuse.*

[6] People are often upset because discourse grammars work to mitigate the threats to face – people's power and dignity – that is inherent in social interactions. Violations of the grammar are consequently implicit attacks on face[10].

overviews based on them, the appendices and the example promising practices were approved by NPR leadership, they were in a sense above debate, at least by workers at the meeting and no comments could be attached to them. Finally, the attachment of alternatives to questions, answers or promising practices, and the attachment of anything but answer to question were considered illogical and excluded.

The discourse grammar is weakly enforced in the Open Meeting system by using it to drive the dynamic reconfiguration of input interfaces. Given the user's choice of target, the server presents an input interface which limits the choice of comment types to just those which can be "legally" attached to the target's type. Of course, this does not prevent a user from flouting the rules, by identifying a comment as a permitted move, but actually making one that is not. A common case of flouting in political meetings is the use of a turn in the question period to assert one's own position, sometimes eliciting the rebuke: "That's not a question?" In general, to prevent potentially disruptive flouting requires natural language processing capability that understands the intention of utterances – not just recognizes forms. Absent robust natural language processing technology for this, human moderators are needed to verify that the contributor has not flouted. As noted above, moderators for the meeting did verify that Agreements and Disagreements gave reasons, but verified no other move types, because of the low potential for disruptive flouting.

The resulting virtual discussions in the Open Meeting differed from face-to-face, multi-lateral discussions in not having an inherent linearity, that is, forward movement toward conclusions. In face-to-face conversations, discourse contexts or foci of attention are successively closed to further comments and are only reopened with difficulty[11]. A speaker might present a reason against a proposal, with the reason then becoming the context of subsequent debate among speakers. At some point, however, discussion returns from this stack to the top level and moves to another point, opening another context. There will be no backtracking to the first context, unless information or conclusions are premises that have been contradicted in the current context. In the virtual discussion on a proposal, all the contexts (and their contexts recursively) remained open to further comment, even if recent comments were in the same context. The discussion could therefore develop as a set of statement and reply sequences on different points, a long sequence elaborating one point (analogous to breadth versus depth search) or a mix of both approaches. This openness partly reflects the primary orientation of the meeting toward collecting information and building knowledge rather than moving a community toward a consensus.

Unfortunately, the outline form used on the web page to represent the links in the hypertext obscures the time dimension and possible focus or convergence in the discussion. This regime recursively indents the pointer to a comment with its move type icon under the pointer to its target, with comments at the same level listed in order of submission. As a result some comments at a deep level that were more recent than other comments at a more shallow level can higher on the page. Since all submissions are time stamped, it is trivial to present the

hypertext in ways that could encourage or represent convergence, such as hiding
or closing contexts that have received no comment for an arbitrary time and
color coding contexts according to how recent are the last comments in each.

2.3 Civility and Moderation

The design included several means of maintaining civility and the quality of interactions. Users were prodded to self-reflection and some restraint on impulsive
commenting by having to identify comment type and summarize the content in
the a subject line. A user was also unable to disguise her identity, because had
to submit the comment on a form that was mailed to her email address[7] In addition, moderators were used to minimize the posting of low quality, redundant
and inappropriate comments.

The moderators' tools included virtual queues to allocate work, review forms,
form letters to users, and a constraint-based view system. These were used to
overview all submissions to the meeting, access unreviewed and pending submissions on a topic, rate a submission's quality and decide its status. Options for
the last function included accepting the submission for exposure to users, rejecting it or returning it for revision with a form letter explaining the reason, and
deferring a decision to another moderator. The moderators in the on-line meeting, volunteers recruited by NPR and assigned to specific nodes, were trained to
reject submissions that were low quality, redundant, obscene, personal attacks,
whistleblowing or commercial solicitations. By checking on the review form the
reason for a rejection, a moderator automatically returned the submission to
the user with the appropriate letter of explanation. Much of this labor can be
further reduced by the development of rule and neural network based programs
that can automatically detect some prohibited content types.

Moderation exploits the database support of views, since accepting a comment merely included it in the public view. As implemented, moderators could
see all submitted documents with their review status and quality ratings, while
the general user saw or received only those that had been accepted for public display. More generally, views are displays generated by constraints that determine
what gets shown to whom, display of the textbase and can be apportioned by
arbitrary criteria, e.g., security classifications, organizational roles. A role, like
moderator, then can be defined as a capacity to make certain moves towards
others, based on the information the role holder gets or sees. Information is thus
the context for interactions and power relations in the group.

The discourse grammar and the moderator reviews were constraints on what
was said during the meeting, but there were factors that diminished their potential for arbitrary suppression of voices by the moderators. First the grammar
itself was fairly transparent and was consistent with the announced purpose of
the meeting as a discussion. Second, the moderators for the meeting were peers of
the users, shared an interest in a meaningful discussion of the recommendations,
and had to give reasons for rejecting a submission. Nevertheless, it is worthwhile

---

[7] This method is no longer useful, due to the proliferation of free mail services.

comparing the risks that having rules of order and moderator authority poses for democratic practice with other means of control in on-line forums.

- *Unmoderated forums*, bulletin boards, mailing lists, etc., depend on the civility and common sense of their users. They are plagued by digressions and flame wars which drive away users, effectively suppressing diverse opinions. Efforts by some users as self-appointed "thread police" may be counterproductive. An option to improve control is collective moderation in which all participants rate the value, relevance and civility of the posted comments, with users receiving low scores being automatically barred. Certified registration could foil attempts by exiles to post under assumed names and also determine who is a participant.
- *Moderated forums* involve posted guidelines and moderators who usually preview (sometimes review) submissions to block (remove) from posting those violating the guidelines. The costs are a) possible abridgment of free speech rights[14], b) moderators seeing themselves as proprietors of the forum, c) moderators' interpretations of the guidelines are opaque regarding how and what they judge are violations. Users, after all, do not see what is not posted. The use of content analytic as filters on submissions would reduce the need for moderators and enable collective reviews of rules or examples of violations more fine-grained than the initial guidelines. This leaves open the questions of who writes the rules or chooses the egregious examples and how intelligent do the filters need be.
- *Adding Roles to Discourse Grammars* is a means to reduce the potential for aberrant, disruptive interpretations of the situation, that can be enacted within the constraints of the grammar. A cheap implementation of this idea is providing more directions to users in the introduction to the meeting, including the roles they might imagine themselves playing and there motivations in these roles. A more complete fix would be the support, similar to that given moderators, of roles that are either help the group pursue the discussion or manage itself. For example, a resident expert with access to specialized sources may be able to settle questions of facts that arise in the discussions. In contrast, a mediator could handle the problem of two participants using the forum as a private battleground by opening a back channel to them with suggestions to resolve their differences, or just remove their exchanges from the view of other participants. Increasing the organization of the meeting also increases disparities in power and social relations, since these are based on the information and moves available to the respective users.

3 Discussion

3.1 Use Patterns

Announced over specialized mailing lists and bulletin boards for government workers, the meeting attracted the interest and participation of workers from a wide and geographically dispersed range of federal government offices and military installations. By its beginning in early December, 1994, over 4200 people had returned an on-line registration survey. 90% were government workers, with over 60% located outside the Washington, DC area, including in all fifty states and twenty countries besides the United States. They represented 40 executive branch agencies and departments, with the large and more technically oriented organizations, viz., Defense, NASA, Interior, tending to have the most representatives. They were typical of government workers with respect to age (average in early 40s) and experience, but significantly more senior, educated, and technically oriented (60% vs. 25% in supervisory capacities; 47% vs. 15% with MA or more; 66% vs. 11% in information systems or engineering). Women were under-represented (30% vs. 42%), but their rate of registration was double the estimate percent female of Internet users at the time (15%). These distributions indicated that interest and network access were key factors for participation. The registration rate of women, despite their lower levels of employment in technical positions, and the large registration at Housing and Urban Development were due to special outreach efforts by NPR personnel to these groups. In contrast, few Treasury and National Security Agency personnel registered because these offices had firewalls blocking access to outside networks.

Over 3000 users accessed the meeting during its two week, but only about 2000 went beyond the introductory page and welcoming pages to a standard node and only 1000 attended the discussion threads. Several factors accounted for the attrition: End-of-the-year and holiday chores left workers little time for the meeting; they found email traversal of the hypertext too cumbersome and the texts themselves overwhelming, and may user were interested only in information and not discussions.

The distribution of web accesses by file types shows two patterns among users accessing a standard system node. About two-thirds of these users surfed the meeting material in several reinvention topics, looking primarily at the overviews and newsletters when available. Users in the second group tracked online discussions on several proposals apiece, in one or two reinvention topics, through both retrieval from the hypertext interface (16 comments read on average), and subscription to mailings of comments posted to the thread (as indicated by the concentration of subscriptions on those topics and proposals which were most accessed). Those who commented were necessarily in this group and similarly focused in their comments; with few exceptions, they posted to just one or two discussions. There was relatively little use of the tools in the meeting environment for search directly by reinvention topic, comment type, government agency referenced and other indices. On the whole, these patterns suggest an orientation toward the meeting as a source of general, rather than specific information, and an interest on the part of the in-depth users in what their peers had to say on a few specific issues.

290 different individuals contributed 1013 comments that were accepted for posting. The ratio of one contributor for five actual lurkers at the discussions is much higher than the 1 to 10 or 20 ratio variously estimated for newsgroups.

Half the comments were identified as Agreement and 15% were Disagreements. The relatively large number of Questions (167), Alternatives (106) and Promising Practices (72) indicates the contributors' willingness to seek and share new information at the meeting. The near absence of the cognitively complex Qualification (3) supports the contention that cyberspace does not nurture the reflection desired in a public sphere, although a sampling of comments found that some qualifications were misidentified as agreements. Possibly these users did not want their comments to be construed as unsupportive. As a group, the commenters were positive toward the proposals and tried to present constructive ideas, some of which NPR leadership culled for further examination.

Web users were generally satisfied with the system, email users complained about its clumsiness for traversing hypertext, and both groups complained about an overwhelming amount of text to read. These responses, particularly the last, were anticipated. We believed that, consistent with their bureaucratic training, people attending the meeting would want to read the "manual" (the reports) before commenting on the proposals, so we wanted to reduce the texts to much shorter pieces. Because, the NPR team lacked the authority and personnel to do the editing, the overviews were produced as a means for users to get acquainted quickly with reinvention topics.

3.2 Discourse Management

The on-line meeting demonstrated that virtual discussions localized to specific topics in a domain could attract people across organizational boundaries, remain coherent and produce possibly valuable ideas. What factors account for the success? Can they be replicated in other venues and with other groups?

The meeting provided individual self-esteem incentives for access and participation, felicitous levels of discussion and effective discourse management. Users knew they could acquire, share and be seen to have information or ideas. Any positive motivation which they as information workers had toward these activities was strengthened by the salience of the discussion domain and the opportunity to investigate a new information technology. "Reinventing government" was frequently mentioned by the media at the time in the context of downsizing and hence a possible threat to their employment, but fewer than half the registered reported knowing much about it or even having seen an NPR report. The meeting also offered concerned workers possibly their only opportunity to influence the implementation of the recommendations. This incentive was strengthened for some workers by their belief the Vice-President would personally review the discussions[8]. More group oriented motivations, like helping to form a group or speaking with one's peers, may have motivated some users to revisit or track discussions. In informal, post-meeting evaluations, these users reported having a "we" feeling when they discovered people from other organizations who were contending with the same problems.

---

[8] In addition to contributing a letter of welcome to the meeting, the Vice-President Gore did post two questions.

The focus on individual recommendations for common operating systems placed the discussions at a level close to that of concrete operations, without requiring users to know terminology or conditions of a particular organization. It was consequently easy for users to draw on their own experiences in reading and responding to the recommendations and comments. Because the focus also limited the attraction and participation for any particular discussion, potential contributors could have realistic expectations that their opinions would be noticed and could influence the discussion. This sense of being critical encourage some users to expend the intellectual energy and time to comment, rather than just lurking. Note the meeting was arranged to reduce other costs of participation by enabling attendance from their desktops and at any time convenient for them during work hours – with the blessings of the Vice-President. Indeed the potential for the Internet to decrease the transaction costs of participation is a major reason to imagine it can help revive a public sphere.

The presentation format for the recommendations and the structure provided by the discourse grammar were sufficient cues for participants to recreate the collective policy or program reviews, that many were practiced in their work. This result could be expected, given their background organizational cultures and bureaucratic roles, but was not inevitable. Since roles were under-specified, and the discourse moves were general, the situation was open to interpretations. One participant, a line worker and union steward, submitted scores of questions, agreements and disagreements, which emphasized the need for the government as employer to improve working conditions. He seemed to be following a script or personal role of questioning authority and only stopped, when a moderator suggested by private email communication that he could get more attention by posting fewer comments. The incident highlights that discourse grammars do not constitute a universal pragmatics, that is sets of moves (speech acts) and rules which are understood similarly by all and which construct processes that are transparent to everyone.

As implied above, the second source of success was the people who attended the meeting. Most had training that made them ideal participants: They were information workers, socialized to a culture of meetings, with a professional or managerial interest in what was being said and pre-existing familiarity with how to say it. Such attributes can also be found among the information workers, who have some experience of collaboration over networks. But while their rapidly increasing numbers make them politically significant in the United States[12] these workers hardly constitute the universe, and newsgroups demonstrate that discussions of political and social issues among networked information workers are no more rational and orderly than those of the general population[13]. Online public spheres open to politically and culturally heterogeneous participants are consequently likely to have problems of governability, beyond the capacities of current types of controls.

3.3 The Open Meeting as a Public Sphere

How well did the Open Meeting realize the ideal of a public sphere? How good a model is it for an on-line democratic institution? One answer is that the participatory process through which a community becomes an active agent on an issue requires members' access to relevant information, their deliberation, decision, privacy, commitment to the decision and time. Privacy here refers to protection of participants from intimidation, insult, defamation or similar means intended to chill participation in public discussions. Time refers to the examination of a significant issue and the expression of all interested parties' views on it taking a considerable amount of time – weeks or months. By these standards, the Open Meeting does half the job; it successfully provides a platform for accessing information and participating in orderly discussions.

As implemented for the meeting, the major shortcomings of the system appear in regard to decision and developing a community spirit that would facilitate commitment by participants to a decision. As noted, there were reasons for not implementing a decision mechanism, and such a mechanism, arguably, might not be needed, since argument grammars have an implicit decision mechanism. They terminate when challenges to a claim are exhausted, a challenge cannot be countered or the opposing sides agree to disagree. These endings are more in keeping with a consensus seeking process based on force of reason alone. Nevertheless, few communities really have the time for exhaustive arguments and few scenarios allow decisions to wait for them. Realistic, effective support of on-line processes in which communities clarify issues and take stands has to include event-creating moves like cloture and voting procedures. These moves are event creating; they change the phase of a deliberative process by ruling out some previously permitted moves and activating other ones. More generally, an effective Open Meeting system will need a library of tested procedures, represented by discourse grammars, with projected outcomes and identified risks, against which conveners of community meetings or collaborations can measure their needs.

As noted earlier, the strategy of decomposing large meetings into small discussions has the potential to isolate users and block their sight of the large community. A low cost means of meeting this problem is an interface display of the distribution of interests over the various topics and proposals, as measured by user visits or comments. Users would be able to gauge where their own discussions fit in the distribution of the community's attention and to directly access popular or other spots, if they so wanted. Slightly more expensive is the automatic generation of cross-links, based on statistical information retrieval methods and patterns of semantic links, that point users to other discussions with themes or information similar to their own. As well as discovering cross cutting themes or issues to integrate the knowledge produced in the discussions, this technique can also be used to discover construct wider circles of participants with similar problems.[9]

---

[9] The second idea follows from [15], an implemented application of agent technology, using cluster analysis of email to find individuals with similar interests. Inversely,

By showing under certain condition, suitable mechanisms can produce a successful, widely-attended discussion of issues, the Open Meeting was a useful step toward building democratic practices in networked communities. However, because of the importance of shared organizational/ cultural backgrounds for the success of these discussions, it is more realistic to think about multiple public spheres, each serving a different subcommunity. Each group could develop its own discourse grammar, and agents in each sphere would seek cross-links to other groups by similarities in issues discussed. While that procedure does not create consensus, it might promote mutual awareness.

References

1. Habermas, J.: The Structural Transformation of the Public Sphere. M.I.T., Cambridge, MA (1989), first published as Strukturwandel der Offentlichkeit. Luchterhand, Berlin (1962).
2. Knapp, J.: Essayistic Messages: Internet Newsgroups as an Electronic Public Sphere. In: Porter, D. (ed.): Internet Culture. Routledge. New York London (1997).
3. Hurwitz, R., Mallery, J.: The Open Meeting: A Web-Based System for Conferencing and Collaboration. Proceedings of The Fourth International Conference on The World Wide Web. Boston (1996) 19-36 http://www.w3j.com/1/ hurwitz.349/paper/349.html
4. http://www.npr.gov
5. http://www.whitehouse.gov/WH/publications/html/Publications.html
6. Searle, P.G., Searle, J.: Speech Acts. Cambridge U. Press, Cambridge (1970).
7. Toulmin, S.: Uses of Argument. Cambridge U. Press, Cambridge (1958).
8. Rescher, N.: Dialectics: A Controversy-oriented Approach to the Theory of Knowledge. State U. of New York Press, Albany (1978)
9. Eemeren, F. v., Grootendorst, R.: Speech Acts in Argumentative Discussions. Foris Publishers, Dordrecht, Holland (1984).
10. Brown, P., Levinson, S.: Politeness : Some Universals in Language Usage. Casmbridge University Press, Cambridge (1987).
11. Grosz, B., Sidner, C.: Attention, Intentions and the Structure of Discourse. Computational Linguistics 12 (1986) 175-204.
12. Winograd, M., Buffa, D.: Taking Control: Politics in the Information Age. Holt, New York (1996).
13. Schneider, S.: Expanding the Public Sphere through Computer-mediated Communication: Political Discussion about Abortion in a Usenet Newsgroup. Ph.D. dissertation, Political Science Dept., M.I.T. (1997)
14. Docter, S., Dutton, W.: The First Amendment Online: Santa Monica's Public Electronic Network. In Tsagarousianou, R., Tambini, D., Bryan, C. (eds.): Cyberdeomocracy: Technology, Cities and Civic Networks (1998).
15. Foner, L.: Yenta: A Multi-Agent, Referral Based Matchmaking System. The First International Conference on Autonomous Agents Marina del Rey, California (1997).

---

cluster analysis of the distribution of participants over the discussions may suggest cross links that are not apparent at the text level.

Social Pattern Development Analysis: A Case Study in a Regional Community Network

Toshihiko Yamakami[1] and Gen-ichi Nishio[1]

NTT Multimedia Networks Laboratories, 1-1 Hikarino-Oka JAPAN 239-0837

Abstract. Community development is a dynamic process in which a group of users show their own communication style and culture. Communication development patterns are different from ones from the common diffusion theory since it has a wide variety of use development patterns. This variety comes from the richness of the community communication contents and variety of time spans of transitions. We learned some lessons from two-year experience of a regional community network trial based on a fiber network. To observe the social pattern development, we analyze a social network development patterns in our system. We propose the adaptive time span analysis. In this method, multiple time spans are compared until the stable communication patterns are obtained. This analysis lead to the estimation of context duration time and social pattern development time to understand the dynamics of the community evolution. The case studies in done in NTT-Hayashi trial e-mail communication log data to obtain the time span of persistent bilateral e-mail communication relationship.

1 Introduction

As the computers are widely spread in homes and communities, it is important to understand the community electronic behaviors. Behaviors reflect the community culture, community adoption patterns, community social structures, and community power balance. Community's embedded culture deeply affect the use of computer communication systems, and the same time, the computer communication systems influence exposure of the community culture in multiple aspects. Over a span of time, this bilateral interactions take place. The formation of stable community communication takes long time, so it is important to capture the transitions of communication structures. Community in computer communication has a virtual and dynamic nature. In particular, the group formation process catches a special attention during the adoption period because the understanding of the process deeply influence the design of the community support systems.

There are several types of community network such as

---

[2] Toshihiko Yamakami's current affiliation is NTT Data, Advanced Information Network Services Sector, Toyosu Tokyo JAPAN 135-6033

- home network The network is used by home users. The interaction among home users are the main purpose of the network.
- local business network The network is uses by the local business such as commerce or industries. The business transactions among local business offices are mainly covered by this type of network.
- regional public network The network is used by regional public organizations. Information for the public is shared in this network.

Each network is characterized by the main interactions and forms a different pattern of communities. In this paper, a methodology to explore home networks is considered. Home users are mainly weak-tied and informally structured. The roles of users and power balance among users are often implicit.

In these three types of networks, the driving force of the home network is the most difficult to capture. The interactions among home users are usually driven by the local relationship which is difficult to identify. The role development heavily depends on the local power balance in the home users. Also, this balance is naive and changeable. Unlike the business structures, the information flow in home networks heavily depends on the temporary contexts among users. The information flow includes various message exchanges in e-mail and bulletin boards systems. In the local business networks, the information flow depends on the business flow. In the regional public network, the information flow is from the public organizations to the general public users.

Our research group is involved in the Hayashi NTT-Company House field trial using fiber optic network [5]. Hayashi is a regonal location name in Yokosuka City in Japan. The fiber optic network and a bridging system provides a regional area network to offer TCP/IP-based application services. The trial started in October 1995 with about 80 families, provided a personal computer and LAN-access at their homes. It provides a regional closed network with e-mail and a bulletin boards system. The trial will continue until March 1999.

During our trial, we became aware of the dynamism of home user behaviors. The dynamism means that the activeness and social structures of computer communication vary over a span of time. At the same time, it was recognized that it is important to develop a methodology to identify the dynamic process of the accept ion and rejections of naive home users. Especially, such a methodology is required to support adoption of the naive home users at the early adoption stage [6].

2 Requirements

At the Hayashi NTT-Company house field trial, we did not have any specific methodologies to observe the community network behaviors. NTT-Company house is the place where NTT employees are provided the housing facilities by NTT. Such a condo-type of housing facilities are popular among many Japanese companies. Such an environment is quite different from the office ones. In this paper, we call such an environment, community communication environment.

The applications based on the regional LAN is not yet well developed. One of the reasons of this lack is the shortage of community communication experience. People think they don't need communication in a regional network since they can talk in a face-to-face manner if they need. Also, it should be noted that there is few methodologies to observe the fits between the community communication culture and the applications in order to identify the special needs of regional networks.

The past research focused on the usability, and white-collar productivity in academic and business domains. In the community communication environment, the users themselves are not aware of the communication patterns. The stability of the communication is also assumed to be weak, because the driving force of communication is vague and implicit in the home user environment. There is little requirement to communicate online to exchange scheduling information or organizational decisions, or to exchange the paper work in the home environment.

For the first step to understand the community communication patterns, we take the first step in the social structural analysis. Social network is one of major research areas in sociology [9]. We would like understand the electronic communications' effects on social networks. The social network is one of the indicators of culture, an important dimension of communication behaviors [13] [11]. Social dynamics is one of the key issues in group support systems [3].

In the home user networks, it is important to capture the time span of the transitions. In addition, it is important to capture the communication culture. To cope with these requirements, a methodology to capture the social dynamics can be used to understand the dynamics of the home community user behaviors.

The requirements about the methodologies of identifying social dynamics are as follows.

- identifying community communication culture It is important to identify the community communication patterns to support stable adoption and smooth transitions from the non-electronic social interactions to the electronic social ones.
- identifying transition stages It is important to identify how many stages the communication patterns are categorized into.

The authors became aware that the activeness in user communication is unstable during the formation of a group. This time period is important to understand the early adoption in community support systems, however, the lack of stability makes the analysis work difficult and misleading. It leads to the fact that the first exploratory analysis needs some consistent disciplines to cope with the instability of a group in the early stage.

3 Evolution and Networked Development

3.1 Evolution in Community

Social network is a network in which a social structure is represented. The social structure evolved over a time. In the office systems, the formed network depends on the job structure [10]. Community networks are electronic networks implemented in a regional community. In this type of network, the main users are home users, in which the social structure is driven by the more implicit human relationship than in the business networks.

Before we were involved in this home user research project, the author was engaged in the office system research project. In the project, the target group was a research group with about 20 research members. The target group's communication behaviors in e-mail, bulletin boards system, and a know-how sharing research prototype system were observed [10]. From this experience, the author learned that the social structure of information flow and the dynamics of flow depended one the communication systems. E-mail flow is most variable, especially depending upon the task group dynamics. Bulletin boards system flow dynamics is the most stable in that group, partly because the bulletin boards communication takes place in the public. Know-how system flow started from the core active group, in which a small number of active users started to use the system, then the satellite group grew. The satellite group is the users who had one or two flows to the core group. The members in a satellite group heavily depended on one or two specific active users.

Compared to the past research in office systems, regional community networks needs methodologies for the earlier stages of group formation. Especially because the community user behavior found in the Hayashi trial is the housewife behavior which is driven by the different motivation from the office worker's ones.

The home user behavior is very easy to change because there is no special norm in the home user community. The relations are based on the informal relationship. In addition, such a relation can be easily replaced by the real world communications. To observe such a community, it is important to visualize the communication patterns using a wide range of parameters to explore the implicit structure of the home user network.

For this purpose, the authors implemented a tool for on-demand visualization of social network. The tool is named as Visualization of Electronic Network User Social processes, VENUS [12]. The user interface built on the WWW browser is shown in Fig. 4. The user interface part is build using PHP/FI [8]. In order to draw a graph, GD1.15 [2] is used.

VENUS is developed to identify the characteristics in community culture. To explore the culture, a wide range of parameters are tested using VENUS to identify the community-specific parameters to understand the social network and its dynamics.

We developed a visualization tool named VENUS using Spiral Visualization method.

In the past research, Eades's spring model is famous in graph visualization [1]. The author's approach is different from the general drawing algorithm since the approach focuses on the core-satellite social structure. Krackplot is a publicly available social network software. The author's approach is different from Krackplot since Krackplot does not provide the automatic node allocation [4].

The Hayashi trial started on October 1995. In this case study, we analyze the e-mail communication data from August 1996 to January 1998. During this period, 121 users exchanged 7062 messages. When an message has multiple recipients, each recipient is counted as a different message flow. These data are used to analyze e-mail communication flow. The Hayashi trial is a closed network, so the originators and recipients were all Hayashi Trial users.

The output example of VENUS is shown in Fig. 1, which depicts the user interaction patterns using threshold message value 25. Interactions less frequently than 25 message exchanges in 80 weeks are ignored to highlight the communication patterns.

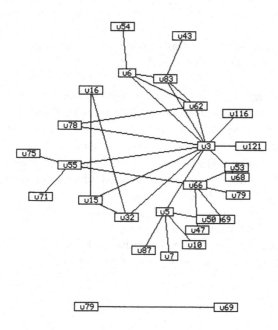

Fig. 1. Social Network Example from Aug 1996 to Jan 1998 in the Hayashi Trial (email exchange) using VENUS

3.2 Three Phases in Network Cognition

In the network evolution, the users gradually form the common understanding of a network. It should be noted that the users implicitly assume that the electronic social structure reflects the real world social structures. Since it is not common to have the same social structure in the electronic network and in the real world, the users adjust the cognitive image of the electronic social network over a span of time.

How can we model the cognitive phases about the stages of this cognitive development? In order to capture the dynamics, it is important to capture the development psychological facets of the early adoptions. In the early stages, the naive users encounter a lot of confusions about the social interactions in networks. Some of the confusions come from the user's mistakes or misunderstanding of the system. It should be noted that the users cannot distinguish the uncommon temporary failures from the permanent facts in the networks. Some of the events and failures from the mistakes confuse the users. In addition, the feedback from the systems or other users are often late or recognized as confusing. The late feedback from the system, such as deferred notice of delivery failure can confuse the naive users. The late feedback can come from the irregularity of the other naive users. In many cases, the naive users' responses are unpredictable.

From our observation in the Hayashi trial, we became aware of the following three different viewpoints depicted in Fig. 2.

- system understanding The naive users assumed that the network interactions reflects the real world interactions. However, the immature system understandings was the main obstacle to the smooth transitions from the real world interactions to the networked interactions.
- importance of content The naive users want the direct benefits from the networked communication. Community-related information such as local events, medical care captured the distinguished attention from the users.
- understanding and interpreting others' behaviors The electronic social interactions will be formed according to the basic system and content understandings. After the established cognitive understandings, the users start to form images about the social feedback expectation.

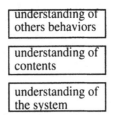

Fig. 2. 3 Layer Model of Cognitive Development

The last stage in which the electronic interactions are interpreted by a user can be split into several stages of group formation.

From this model, it is important to identify steps toward the higher cognitive stages. To capture the stage changes, we use the social network dynamics to identify the group formation stages.

Social network based on communication logs is a rich source of information about how user behavior evolves over a span of time.

4 Adaptive Time Span Analysis

Adaptive time span analysis is an exploratory heuristic method to identify the transitional user behavior evolution. The method is outline in Fig. 3. The basic idea of this approach is to split the communication log data into a small unit time span log. Next, the whole time span is equally split into some pieces, and the social dynamics during each span is examined.

For example, when we have a 64-week log, we can set up 2-week for the unit time. Then we can compare multiples of 2, such as 2-week log, 4-week log, 8-week log, 16-week log, 32-week log to adaptively compare the user behavior evolution. The time span division will stop when the meaningful social patterns disappear.

We learned from the past experience in office communication analysis. When the trial continues, the communication log incrementally increases. The analysis takes time, so we needed some improvement in the process to incorporate the dynamics of the communication log into analysis. In this situation, it is important to dynamically set up time span boundaries. From this point, the communication log is split into weekly units in order to flexibly manipulate the time span length in the analysis.

It is a powerful strategy when the group formation or social patterns are unknown. This is usually true in the early adoption stages. In addition, during the early stages of understanding open home communities, we can use this methodology because the social dynamics are unknown.

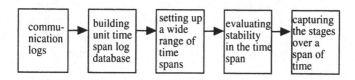

Fig. 3. Processing Flow in Adaptive Time Span Analysis

The purpose of the adaptive time span analysis is to identify the stages in the long-term community user behavior evolution. The final stage identification image is outlined in Fig. 4. In this example, the five different stages are identified using the metrics which are variable.

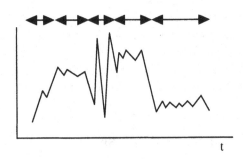

Fig. 4. Identifying Stages using Adaptive Time Span Analysis

5 A Case Study

5.1 Overview

In order to evaluate the adaptive time span analysis approach, the authors try to capture the reciprocity in the e-mail exchange in the Hayashi trial. 7062 messages were exchanged by 121 users during the time period from August 1996 to January 1998. The time span is 80 weeks long.

In this analysis, reciprocity is defined when a pair of users exchange messages both directions. It means that user A sent a message to user B and that user B sent a message to user A during a specified time span. This metrics is an indicator of the reciprocity in the community network.

There are two questions. One is how stable the metrics are in a real community network. The other is how can we specify the appropriate time span in the analysis. How long the message exchange context is maintained in a community?

We have a 80-week e-mail communication log. So we try to capture the reciprocity in 40-week span, 20-week span, 10-week span, 5 week span, 4-week span, 2-week span and 1-week span.

To evaluate this process, we implement a Perl5 program to store weekly unit time span database and to manipulate extraction of collective communication log with an arbitrary time span using the unit time span database.

Reciprocity ratio is defined in the two method. One is to calculate the reciprocity relation ratio compared to the total messages. The other is to calculate the reciprocity relation counts compared to the total number of originators.

5.2 Results

The reciprocity relation ratios in 40-week, 20-week, 10-week and 5-week are shown in Fig. 5. The same ratios in 4-week, 2-week, and 1-week is shown in Fig. 6.

From Fig. 5, the 40-week time span is inappropriate because it is not aligned to 5-week, 10-week, and 20-week results. 5-week time span is quite stable and

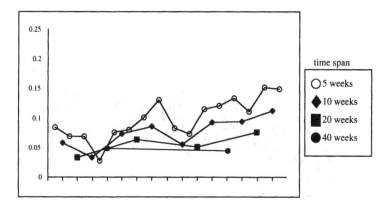

Fig. 5. Reciprocity per Messages using 40,20,10 and 5-week time spans

shows the increasing trend. This is remarkable because it shows that the reciprocity in home users are defined in a longer time span compared to the ones in office systems. This comes from the weak-tie nature of community networks. In addition, it shows that the adoption of regular e-mail exchange is quite limited to a certain small number of users. From this sense, it should be noted that this sample group needs more support for regular e-mail exchange to form strong-tied group.s

From Fig. 6, 1-week and 2-week span are considered to be too short to observe e-mail reciprocity in this group. It depicts that the first one-third of time (August 1996 to January 1997), the reciprocal relations among users were very unstable even though the field trial started in October 1995. Considering these Figures, the appropriate time span in this reciprocity per messages can be 4-6 weeks in this group.

It should be noted that the reciprocity per messages number decreases as the time span is extended because the strength of the each pair's reciprocity over time is ignored in this analysis. This is not related to the essential point of the adaptive time span analysis. However, usually, when the time span is extended more than the appropriate context duration time, the pair-wise bidirectional relationship gets strong, however, the number of reciprocal pairs stays. It means the value divided by the total number of messages decreases.

The reciprocity relation ratios in 40-week, 20-week, 10-week and 5-week to the total number of originators are shown in Fig. 7. The same ratios in 4-week, 2-week, and 1-week is shown in Fig. 8.

From Fig. 7, the time span of 40 and 20 weeks are inappropriate compared to the context duration in this community network. The number of reciprocity per originators seems saturate in the middle of the observation. It is understood that the average number of regular reciprocal relations are from 1 to 2, which means the regular e-mail exchange partners do not grow in a monotone manner.

From Fig. 8, it can be concluded that the 2 weeks and 1 week time span is

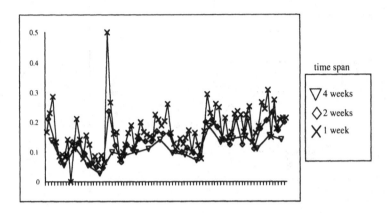

Fig. 6. Reciprocity per Messages using 4,2 and 1-week time spans

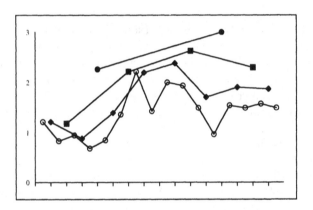

Fig. 7. Reciprocity per Originators using 40,20,10 and 5-week time spans

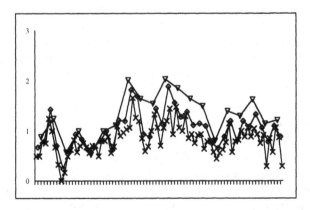

Fig. 8. Reciprocity per Originators using 4,2 and 1-week time spans

unstable. The 4-week time span and 5-week time span has the similar results. The reciprocity per originator is stable in the last quarter of the observation period, which is Oct 1997 to Jan 1998. In this stable stage, the reciprocity per originator is 1.2 (4-week time span) to 1.5(5-week time span).

It should be noted that the messages with multiple recipients are not so common even in Jan 1998.

6 Discussion

The dynamic time span analysis gives the heuristic methods to identify the time scale factor in the group formation process. This give a hint for the context duration time in community support systems, which is an important key to support early stage adoption process. The arguments about the reciprocity dynamics in this Hayashi trial group is for further studies.

Time is an important factor to understand the community behaviors. It is also important to understand the interactions between the community and the technology used in the community. The context duration time is influenced by the life time of the information shared in the community. In addition, the life time of the community information can influence the context duration time observed in the community communication.

The term reciprocity in this study means the persistent bidirectional relationship observed in computer communication. The reciprocity embedded in the community communication from the semantics viewpoints is for further studies. In this e-mail analysis, it is significant whether the community develops active mailing list or not. In our study, the users did not frequently use mail with multiple recipients. It is partly because the major part of users are naive users in early adoption stages.

The message exchange numbers per week varies from week to week, however, 4-week to 6-week time span gives a consistent view about the slowly developed social process in the target group.

It should be noted that the Hayashi trial's special factors are different from those in usual home communities. This does not influence the validity of the time span analysis. However, the results should be carefully treated. The trial is intentionally isolated from the internet environment, therefore the trial environment is a closed regional network. The main users are wives and children because the business people would like to use the open internet environment. The intention of the original trial design was to focus the regional community network environment, not the internet environment. In addition, NTT-Company house's community culture can be deeply influence by the NTT company culture. The major parts of NTT employees in NTT-Company houses are basically engineers, which can be influence the community culture in an implicit manner. The user behaviors can be influence by the seasonal factors in NTT-Company houses. One of the examples are the major family changes are in February due to annual organizational structuring. New trial members are usually added in this time of the year.

In this study, we present the methodology to identify the time scale of the social structure dynamics using exploratory visualization. In order to capture the social structure development, it is important to establish the methodology to identify the time scale factor in the social development. The proposed adaptive time span analysis is general and applicable to a wide range of applications with social interaction patterns. This type of methodology gives an important clue to compare the different communities based on different communication systems because the time span of the group formation dynamics can be compared. The communication log is not the single source of community understanding. However, such a inter-community study based on communication log can provide the starting points to form assumptions for the in-depth questionnaires and interviews.

7 Conclusions

In order to analyze the variety of community network users, it is important to capture the dynamics of social network. Especially, home user network is flexible. In this paper, the community structure transitions are studied from the information flow log. It is difficult to capture the communication patterns in a home user community because the information flow among home users are unstable. It is necessary to analyze the dynamics of the communication pattern changes to validate any assumptions from long-term communication log.

The communication patterns in home users varies from time to time. It is important to identify how stable the communication patterns are over a span of time. To cope with this issue, the authors propose the adaptive time span analysis method. In this method, multiple time spans are compared until the stable communication patterns are obtained. This analysis lead to the estimation of context duration time and social pattern development time to understand the dynamics of the community evolution. The case studies in done in NTT-Hayashi trial e-mail communication log data to obtain the time span of persistent bilateral e-mail communication relationship.

The time span analysis provides important clues for social process visualization done by our tool VENUS which depicts the social network in a community in a WWW browser.

The adaptive time span analysis can be applicable to a wide range of long-term behavioral studies in electronic communication which has consistent communication logs. These studies can provide the starting points for the in-depth interviews and questionnaires to explore the theories to understand the interactions among community users and community support systems.

References

1. Eades and Tamassia, "Algorithms for Drawing Graphs: An Annotated Bibliography," Tech Rep CS-89-09, Dept. of CS, Brown Univ (Feb. 1989) (ftp://wilma.cs.brown.edu/ pub/papers/compgeo/gdbiblio.tex.Z)

2. GD.pm, version 1.15, http://www.genome.wi.mit.edu/ftp/pub/software/WWW/GD.html

3. Grudin, J.: Groupware and Social Dynamics: Eight Challenges for Developers, *CACM* (January 1994) 92–105

4. KrackPlot 3.0 User Manual, ftp://bikini.heinz.cmu.edu/ dist/krack/kp3man.ps (1995).

5. Morisaki, Nishio, Mori, Tsuji: The Field Trial of Regional Community Network in Hayashi Company Houses, Fourth International Workshop on Community Networking, IEEE Communications Society, (Sep 1997).

6. Nishio, Yamakami: "Issues on User Behavior Modeling in Regional Community Network" (in Japanese), IPSJ, DPS&GW workshop (Jan 1998).

7. Perl 5.004, http://language.perl.com/ info/documentation.html

8. PHS/FI Version 2.0, http://php.iquest.net/ phpfi/doc/doc.html

9. Scott, J., Social Network Analysis. Newbury Park CA: Sage (1992).

10. Yamakami, T.: Information Flow Analysis: An Approach to Evaluate Groupware Adoption Patterns, *Trans. IPSJ* , **36,10** (October 1995) 2511–2519

11. Yamakami, T.: An Approach Toward Fits Evaluation Between Organizational Culture and Groupware , Proc. of WWCA'97 (also in the Lecture Notes in Computer Science in Springer-Verlag), Tsukuba, Japan (March 1997)

12. Yamakami, T.:Social Process Visualization in Regional Community Network Users, APCHI'98, IEEE Computer Society Press (July 1998) (to be published).

13. Watson R., Ho, T., and Raman, K.: Culture: A Fourth Dimension of Group Support Systems, *CACM* , **37, 10** (October 1994) 45–55

CoMeMo-Community: A System for Supporting Community Knowledge Evolution

Toyoaki Nishida[1], Takashi Hirata[2], and Harumi Maeda[3]

[1] Nara Institute of Science and Technology, Nara, Japan,
Kansai Advanced Research Center, Communications Research Laboratory, Japan
nishida@is.aist-nara.ac.jp,
WWW home page: http://ai-www.aist-nara.ac.jp/doc/people/nishida/
[2] Nara Institute of Science and Technology, Nara, Japan
[3] Osaka City University, Osaka, Japan

Abstract. CoMeMo-Community is a system that is designed to support knowledge evolution in a community. It is based on two ideas. One is associative representation for facilitating externalization of both personal and community knowledge. The other is visualization of knowledge interaction based on the talking-alter-egos metaphor.

In this paper, we present how these ideas are incorporated into the CoMeMo-Community system and report preliminary experimentation with it. We also discuss how CoMeMo-Community helps us to understand community.

1 Introduction

A community, as is characterized in this research, is a group of persons with common interests. Unlike an association, a community imposes few explicit conventions to tie its members together. People may join a community if they find it interesting and attractive, while they may leave it without much difficulty if they do not like it. What causes a community to attract people?

Accumulation of shared knowledge is considered to be one of the key factors that intrigue people. The more common knowledge is accumulated, the more attractive is a community. Rich knowledge provides community members with a feeling of a rich ground that will produce a fruitful harvest.

A community would be much more fascinating if it brings about a feeling of continuous evolution. It would be particularly the case in academic communities. In evolving communities, members continually witness explosive outcome of new knowledge, often caught by a temptation of making contribution to the activity by getting involved.

Nonaka and Takeuchi analyzed the structure of knowledge creation in corporations and proposed a model of knowledge evolution [15]. According to their model, knowledge is created in what is called a knowledge spiral consisting of four stages: externalization, combination, internalization, and socialization (Fig. 1). Knowledge is classified into two types, explicit knowledge and tacit knowledge. Externalization is a stage on which explicit knowledge is created by representing

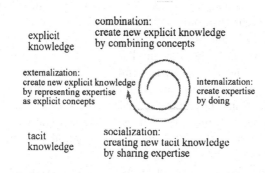

Fig. 1. Nonaka and Takeuchi's knowledge spiral model

expertise as explicit concepts. On the combination stage, new explicit knowledge will be created by combining existing explicit knowledge. On the internalization stage, expertise is created by executing explicit knowledge in an interpretive fashion. Such tacit knowledge will diffuse into a group of people and new tacit knowledge will be created by sharing expertise on the socialization stage.

Although their model was originally intended to analyze the knowledge process in associations, we consider it also constitutes an adequate basis of modeling knowledge evolution in communities. The role of knowledge spiral in communities would be more critical than that in associations. In communities, knowledge spiral might be a direct cause of attracting participants, while it might be rather tacitly embedded in a long tradition.

We have been working on the Knowledgeable Community project, an endeavor to develop a computational framework for facilitating the knowledge process by humans and computers [13]. In this project, we explore a new way of investigating intelligence. Rather than building autonomous agents that are intelligent by themselves, we explore a new methodology in which a synthetic approach of designing tools for augmenting people's intellectual process and an analytic approach of modeling people's intelligence by observation are closely tied together.

In this paper, we apply our methodology to the community knowledge process and present a system called CoMeMo-Community for facilitating the knowledge spiral. We claim that through the use of CoMeMo-Community, we can actually facilitate the community knowledge process and learn the community knowledge process at the same time. It was based on two ideas. CoMeMo-Community was designed based on a couple of ideas.

One is associative representation for facilitating externalization of both personal and community knowledge [12]. Our associative representation allows for representing information without forcing rigid semantics. At a first glance, such a design principle may seem considerably limit the utility of the knowledge base because the precise meaning of stored data may not be recovered later. However, enforcement of monopoly in semantics also result in blocking out useful information that might turn out useful at hindsight.

We use informal semantics to allow any information to be incorporated into the memory without much elaboration. The first reason for that is because any inspiration or insight may be so subtle and fragile that they may easily disappear as soon as rigid verbalization is required. The second reason is because we would like to accommodate heterogeneous information coming from different community members with incompatible perspectives. The CoMeMo subsystem allows the user to create, organize, and recall external personal memory with associative representation.

The other idea is visualization of knowledge interaction by introducing the talking-alter-egos metaphor. The MysticSalon subsystem mimics a salon in which alter-egos representing each community member interact with each others, thereby the user can see how their own or others' knowledge interact. By observing such virtual conversations, one can learn lots of things about the community, including who knows what, and what are common interests, and so forth.

We have implemented a prototype of CoMeMo-Community based on these ideas, and have carried out preliminary experiments. Among others, we investigated how far people can exchange ideas with associative representation and how people react the talking-alter-egos metaphor.

In section 2, we overview CoMeMo-Community. In section 3, we describe associative representation, its implementation CoMeMo and a psychological experiments with it. In section 4, we describe MysticSalon, a virtual conversation system with talking alter-egos and report preliminary experimentation with it. In section 5, we discuss the contribution of this research to the study of community.

2 Overview of CoMeMo-Community

CoMeMo-Community is a system designed to support the knowledge spiral underlying community knowledge evolution by enhancing awareness of a community. In CoMeMo-Community, the talking-alter-egos metaphor is employed. The user can initiate and observe virtual conversation among alter egos of herself/himself or/and others.

CoMeMo-Community consists of two major components, shown in Fig. 2. One is an alter-ego that retains the externalized memory of a person. Associative representation is used to represent personal memory. The other is a conversation place where alter-egos make utterances in turn according to the rules of conversation.

In each session of conversation, alter-egos participating in the conversation place collaborate with each other to generate a story by alternately reproducing memory fragments from the personal memory embedded in each elter-ego. A typical example of conversation is shown in Fig. 3. Each alter-ego is represented by an image. In this case, five images of alter-egos are put of the left end of the conversation place. The situation in Fig. 3 is the one obtained after a handful of such cycles are repeated. The original keyword was "Internet", which reminds

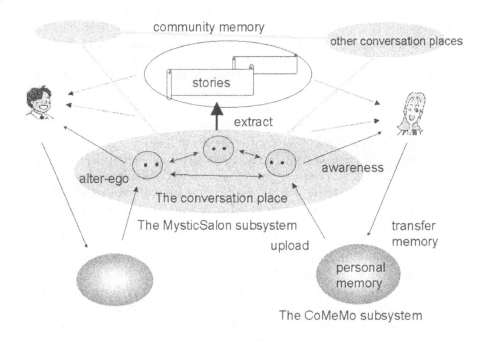

Fig. 2. The framework of CoMeMo-Community

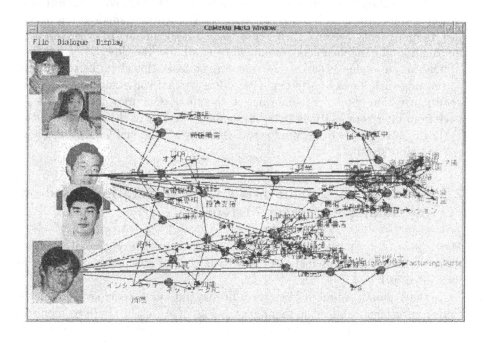

Fig. 3. Example screen image of CoMeMo-Community

"AI", which in turn reminds "a workshop", resulting in "Nara", the site of that workshop.

The users may play two roles. One is to enter information into one's own alter-ego. The other is to initiate and observe the conversation among alter-egos. The user can control the subject and focus in the conversation place and see what happens. Unlike net surf, the user need not click the mouse all the time. Instead, s/he can sit back in the couch and control the conversation from time to time. In that sense, the system is mixed initiative.

One may run the virtual conversation as many times as s/he likes, and see what happens. One may see different story at each time even if the same set of keywords is given, for a certain degree of randomness is employed in each phase of generation, e.g., to select a small set of items from a large set of potential items. Five images in the left represented represents alter-egos of five persons. When a keyword "Internet" was given, "AI" was reminded by one of the alter-egos, which in turn caused "a workshop" to be reminded. After a handful of such cycles are repeated, the topic shifted to Nara, for one alter-ego had a memory of a AI-related workshop held in Nara, Japan.

From the exercises with virtual conversation, one may learn a lot about the community. For example, one may see that who is interested in what. In addition, a large cluster of nodes may mean that the amount of information is large; a tangled interconnection of nodes from different persons may mean the existence of shared interest in the subject and it is likely for them to enjoy a good conversation about it; an inconsistent set of keywords may mean disparity in the characterization of the world, and so on. Even in a small group of, say just around twenty persons, there tends to be a large amount of otherwise tacit information, for the members are not chatting all over the time.

One may also play an active role by entering information about herself/himself or the subject s/he has much experience. The virtual conversation may give a good motivation about what information to expose. One may get a good feed-back from later conversations either in the real world or in the virtual worlds.

In the next two sections, we describe the MysticSalon and CoMeMo subsystems in more detail.

3   MysticSalon: Collaborative Story Generation based on the Talking Alter-egos Metaphor

MysticSalon is a subsystem that pursues collaborative story generation based on the talking alter-egos metaphor. Its basic control mechanism is simple, as illustrated in Fig. 4.

In the beginning of the session, the user may put one or more keyword on the conversation place and make them active (Fig. 4(a)). Each alter-ego monitors the conversation and see if there is active keywords to which it can add some information. If any, the alter-ego will actually add the information by copying one or more new keywords from its memory. These new keywords are put to the right of the original keywords and a little circle representing associative representation is created in-between (Fig. 4(b)). Then, the original keywords are deactivated, the new keywords will be activated, and the entire activation cycle will recur (Fig. 4(c)). The temporal behavior goes from the left to the right on the screen.

(a) Keywords are given　(b) Related memory items are　(c) Memory recall is repeated
recalled　for new keywords

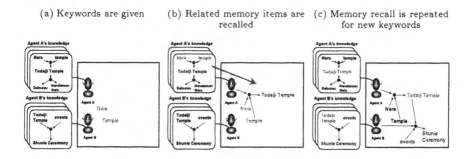

Fig. 4. Story generation with MysticSalon

Example of story generation process is shown in Fig. 5. There are many factors that affect story generation: principles for choosing alter-egos for story generation (e.g., round-robin, some competition, or random), principles for each alter-ego to throwing back memory items for a given keywords in the conversation place, the maximal number of keywords activated in the conversation place, the order of extending the story (e.g., breadth-first or depth first), and so on. The current version of MysticSalon employs a simple control regime: bread-first expansion of stories, round-robin for invoking alter-egos, and no upper-limit of reproduction of memory fragments at a time, and direct reminding in which personal memory fragments are put to the conversation place only when they are limited to those directly related to the active subject.

(a) A keyword is given　(b) Reaction by alter-egos　(c) Story grows as more
memory items are recalled

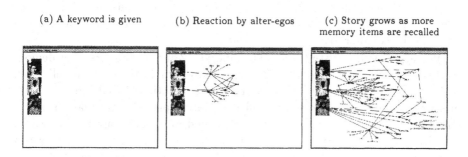

Fig. 5. Example of actual story generation with MysticSalon

Even with a mechanism of that simple, lots of interesting phenomenon are observed. Conversation among alter-egos bears some similarity with conversations by humans. A typical example is shown in Fig. 6 where the conversation is initiated by the keyword representing the name of the laboratory project. The alter-ego representing the leader talks about the global picture of the re-

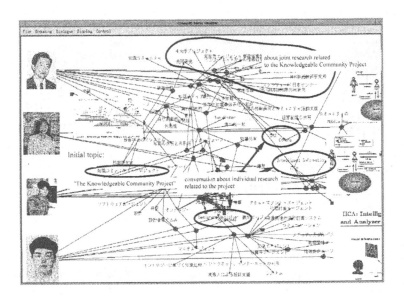

Fig. 6. Conversation about the laboratory project

search, while those representing laboratory members talk about their systems and relevance with the common research subject.

The topic may shift during a conversation, as in Fig. 7. In the conversation in Fig. 7, the original topic "international conference" was overridden by "ruins" with the topic "Mexico" as a turning point.

Although the control issues are considered critical to high quality story generation, our claim is that even with a simple mechanism, the user can learn a lot from the collaborative stories generated.

We interviewed five students in our laboratory and ten visitors after demonstration of CoMeMo- Community. The reaction was all favorable. Generally they understand what is meant by associative representation. People from companies were talking about possible applications to implement corporate memory. One (a newspaper reporter) said that this kind of virtual conversation would significantly enhance the real conversations, for the opportunities of real-world meetings are quite limited due to temporal and spatial constraints, while such limitation is highly relaxed in virtual conversation places. One was interested in coincidence of experience in everyday life and how it might lead to an invaluable discovery. Students were interested to see their colleagues' interest and knowledge. They all said that they would publish their own knowledge if it contributes to their community. On the other hand, some of them are concerned with privacy issues. At least, it is evident that CoMeMo- Community significantly contributed to invoke various concern with community.

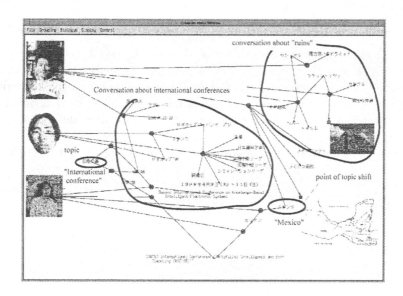

Fig. 7. Example of topic shift

In addition, we find that the use of the facial images of the alter-egos is effective in demonstration, in particular when the observer is acquainted with the person herself/himself each alter-ego represents.

It is considered to be the virtue of the background knowledge shared with community members that have the output make sense to the observer. As is described in the next section, it is shown that the more background knowledge is shared, the less complete representation is accepted to communicate information.

Although we feel that the effectiveness of the CoMeMo-Community as a community communication facilitator is empirically validated by discussions with about other twenty people who have seen the demonstration of the system, a comprehensive evaluation is necessary to gain detailed insights.

4 CoMeMo: Maintaining Personal Memory with Associative Representation

CoMeMo is a subsystem for maintaining personal memory. CoMeMo employs associative representation [12] for integrating information representation with different degrees of formality. The semantics of associative representation itself is left open to permit raw information materials to be accumulated with minimal overhead. In preliminary evaluation, we are convinced that the original meaning of associative representation can be mostly recovered in an intimate community of people and the recovering ratio gradually degenerates as the intimacy of the community decreases.

4.1 Associative Representation as Memory Organization Principle

Associative representation provides many-to- many hyperlink associating one or more key unit with one or more value unit. An associative representation may be informally interpreted as an associative relation in which the key units normally remind one of the value units. In graphical notations, each associative representation is denoted as a large dot connecting one or more unit called keys and those called values.

Example of associative representation is shown in Fig. 8. A collection of

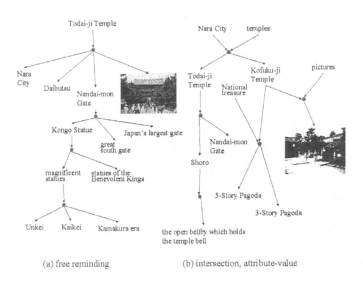

(a) free reminding   (b) intersection, attribute-value

Fig. 8. Example of associative representations

associative representations in Fig. 8(a) typically results from free reminding. Associations in this collection are rather incoherent in the sense that various semantic relations, such as part-whole, the value of some attribute, and so on may be mixed up in one associative representation. Fig. 8(b) shows a more articulated and homogeneous collection of associative representations, which would reflect certain efforts of articulation.

We leave the semantics of units and the two structure making operators open to the user. The user can give them her/his own interpretation or develop

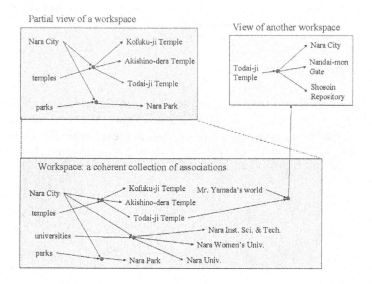

Fig. 9. Workspaces

software agents that manipulates associative representation based on tacit semantics. This does not mean that we insist on neglecting the semantics. Quite the opposite. We envision that the user will continually revise and refine the information base and come to grant relatively well-defined semantics to her/his representation in a long run. In addition, we anticipate consensus on the semantics of associative representation will be eventually reached by a group of users after a certain amount of mutual transactions of associative representation. We prefer the semantics resulting from the process of natural selection to the one defined in a top-down fashion. Convergence to the better semantics will be accelerated by software agents, which credit better articulation and intelligent tools which help the user refine information representation.

4.2 CoMeMo Information Base

The CoMeMo information base is a collection of units. Each unit represents an atomic memory unit which is not articulated any further in the CoMeMo system. Any data items handled by the platform of the CoMeMo system, e.g., character strings, bitmaps, video clips, audio streams, text files, URL addresses and so on, are eligible as a unit.

There are only two kinds of structure making operators. One is associative representation described in the above. The other operator is a workspace making operator which abstracts a collection of units and associations as a workspace unit. The user is encouraged to make workspace coherent but it is not a constraint from the system. Example of workspaces is shown in Fig. 9. A workspace is shown which contains information about the Nara city, Japan. The user can define her/his own view of the workspace for convenience. A workspace can be referred to as a unit from another workspace.

4.3   The CoMeMo Workbench

The CoMeMo workbench provides the user with a workplace for aggregating and articulating information by incorporating new insights. Apparent incompleteness and inconsistency may become evident in the knowledge cycle. In a more global picture, the CoMeMo workbench is characterized as an engine that thrusts a personal knowledge cycle, as shown in Fig. 10.

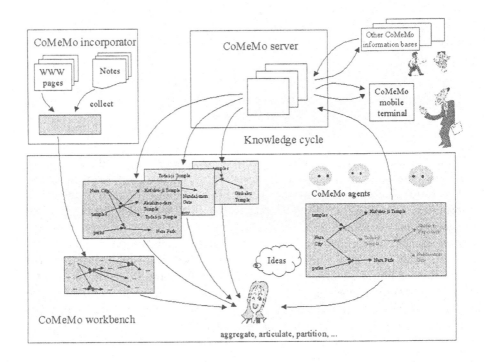

Fig. 10. The CoMeMo architecture

The CoMeMo workbench provides the user with the following functions for exploring a given CoMeMo workspace.

(a) focus: displays only units in a neighborhood a given set of units.

(b) neighborhood search: uncovers those units in a neighborhood that are not on the screen.

(c) path search: displays all paths connecting a given set of units.

The user may add her/his own interpretation and insights and save the result in the information base for later use.

4.4 How much people can generate and understand associative representation?

In this section, we overview three experiments that we have conducted to investigate how people generate associative representations, and how people understand their semantics.

Experiment 1

The purpose of this experiment was to investigate how much people can understand the meaning of associative representation. For this experiment, we used the following five test screens.
- Test 1: shop information around the authors' institute;
- Test 2: description of the Peru Case generated from an newspaper article;
- Test 3: information of CFPs(Call For Papers) redistributed in our laboratory;
- Test 4: research memoranda about agents drawn by one of the authors;
- Test 5: research memoranda on knowledge media drawn by one of the authors.

Two of them are shown in Fig. 11 and Fig. 12. Original tests were given in Japanese except Test 5; their translations are shown here for the readers. The subjects were graduate students in our laboratory, including three Ph.D. students (hereafter D), five 2nd-year M.Eng. students (hereafter, M2), and four 1st-year M.Eng. students (hereafter M1). They were all newcomers at the experiment.

We showed the subjects the five test screens (from Test 1 to 5) and asked the following two questions for each test: "Do you understand the outline of the screen?", and "Can you say the meaning of each circles?"

We didn't explain what associative representation and just used terms circle.

As a result, we found that:

(1) all subjects answered the outline in Test 1 without being explained the meaning of associative representation and

(2) the restoration rate was 78% on average, as shown in Table 1.

Table 1. Restoration Rate in Experiment 1

subjects	Test 1	Test 2	Test 3	Test 4	Test 5	Average
D	100%	66%	100%	100%	97%	93%
M2	100%	56%	80%	100%	56%	78%
M1	60%	70%	40%	93%	44%	61%
Average	87%	64%	73%	98%	66%	78%

Restoration rate: $\dfrac{\text{(Number of correctly interpreted associations)}}{\text{(Number of associations)}}$

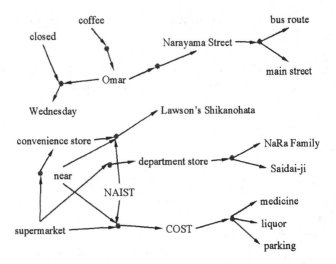

"COST (a supermarket) is reminded by NAIST, the authors' institute because it is located near NAIST and is a popular shop for the NAIST community. Medicines and liquors are sold at COST. COST has a parking. Convenience stores are reminded by supermarkets. The nearest convenience store from NAIST is Lawson's at Shikahata. Supermarkets also reind me of department stores. Department stores remind me of NaRa Family, a department store at Saidai-ji. I often buy coffee beans at a shop called Omar. Omar closes every Wednesday. Omar is along with Narayama Street, which is the main street on a bus route."

Fig. 11. Test Screen 1 (Shop information around the authors' institute)

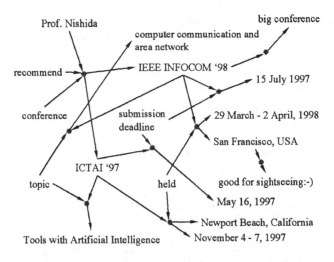

Fig. 12. Test Screen 3 (Information of CFP distributed in our laboratory)

From the results, we concluded that associative representation is comprehensible to adults who have computing skills.

It is interesting to see that the restoration rate was better in D(93%) > M2(78%) > M1(61%) suggest the more human background knowledge people have, the more people understand associative representation. The subjects restored the meaning of associations by referring units they can understand when they didn't understand the unit's labels. This tendency was apparent in Test 3 in which the structure of associative representations were coherent (e.g. conference names, venue, period and so on). We suggest that the context helps human understanding of associative representation.

Experiment 2

The purpose of Experiment 2 was to investigate how people generate associative representations from ideas and how people understand those generated by others. We chose as subjects one Ph.D. students, four 2nd-year M.Eng. students, and one staff in our laboratory.

We pursued the following procedure:

(1) The subjects were trained how to generate associative representations (students only).

(2) They generated associative representations reminded by a keyword "agent" on the CoMeMo Workbench (students only).

(3) They were shown associative representations generated by other subjects and asked the following questions: "Do you understand what are written?", "Do you identify who wrote this screen ?", "If you identify who, why ?", and "Say anything you felt in this experiment" (students only).

(4) The same as (3) (the staff subject only).

An example screen generated by the Subject A is shown in Fig. 13. All subjects were able to generate associative representations within 30 minutes. From these result, we concluded that adults who have computing skills can generate associative representation without difficulty.

On the other hand, all subjects were able to understand the meaning of associative representations generated by others. Concerning a screen generated by the subject C, all other subjects identified that it was made by him. We concluded that ideas can be transmitted using associative representation among people who share knowledge. All subjects except for the subject C laughed when they saw screens drawn by the subject C. 80% (4 out of 5 student subjects) said that they had some fun during the experiment. The staff subject said that "I can guess the student's knowledge level concerning research topics", "I will be interested to read a report by this student", "I want to talk to this student, because he/she may have an interesting idea", and so on. We think that transmitting ideas using associative representation between groups leads to know people and therefore facilitates for human communication.

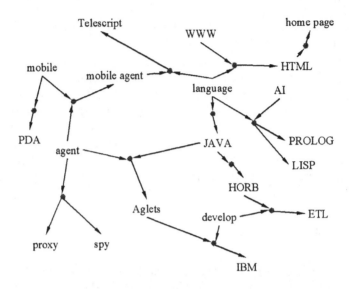

Fig. 13. Associative Representation generated by subject A in Experiment 2

Experiment 3

We investigated the difference of understanding between natural language texts and information extracted from them using associative representation. We chose as subjects three 2nd-year M.Eng students in our laboratory. We pursued a couple of exercises:

- Test 1: Each subjects was shown Test Screen 2 of Experiment 1 and original articles, and was asked some comments.

- Test 2: Each subjects was shown Test Screen 3 of Experiment 1 and three CFPs of international conferences (each CFP was written in a physical A4 paper), and was asked for comments.

In both tests, subjects were not explained the meaning of associative representation.

As a result of exercises, we obtained a collection of comments, such as: "An index like the test screen is helpful for browsing an newspaper article", "I thought I understood the meaning of information in the test screen first but I found that I misunderstood the article after reading it" for Test 1, and "The test screen is helpful because I can pick up important information quickly although it took me for a while to know how to understand the associative representations", and "I prefer seeing the test screen to reading a collection of CFPs" for Test 2.

We conjecture that it is useful to extract information from information sources using associative representation.

Summary of the insights obtained in experiments

Insights obtained from the above-mentioned experiments can be summarized as follows.

(a) Adults who have computing skills can generate associative representation without difficulty.

(b) Ideas can be transmitted using weak information structures among people who share knowledge.

(c) Associative representation is comprehensible to adults who have computing skills.

(d) The more human background knowledge people have, the more people understand associative representation.

5 Discussion

Communityware [7] can be characterized as a system that help people establish valuable human relationships. Research in that direction involves Yenta that finds people who share similar interests [2]; Contact Finder [9] and IKNOW [1] that suggest whom to contact in order to draw an answer to a given question; Community Viewer [14] and Community Organizer [4] that visualize interactions among participants and provides a view of community activities; and Referral Web that extract human relations from published documents [8]. A common characteristic of these systems is that they explicitly show potential social relations to the users. It would be interesting to see how those suggestions are accepted by the users, what kind of effect they have for people to make social relations, and so on.

In contrast, CoMeMo-Community does not directly show the user potential social relations. Instead, it aims at more knowledge-centric supports. It mainly visualizes the contents and the structure of common knowledge and interests shared among the community members, which may be used to explore potential human relations. CoMeMo-Community provides the community with an indirect means of establishing new human relations.

The more knowledge people share and the more people are aware of it, the more sympathy will result. The more mutual knowledge they have, the more they understand with each other and the more motivated will they be to externalize their information. That is the major contribution that we expect for the MysticSalon subsystem to make on facilitation of the knowledge spiral in community. In effect, we suspect that the feeling of collaborative construction of shared knowledge will eventually enhance the coherency of a community.

The role of CoMeMo is to feed the knowledge spiral with a sufficient amount of "raw materials." Work on accumulating and utilizing personal memory in everyday life is also in progress in elsewhere, including Active notebook [18], Lifestreams [3], Remembrance agent [16], and Forget-me-not [10].

Some systems are dedicated to visualize the structure of shared interest and discussions. AIDE [17] and CommunityBoard [4] are for small groups, while The

Open Meeting System [6] has been applied to large scale discussions over the Internet.

The originality of CoMeMo consists in the use of associative representation with informal semantics and structure. It is a little more structured than hypertexts in the sense that it allows for many-to-many links. It grants a powerful means of structural representation. On the other hand, its semantics is not rigorously defined. It both relaxes an overhead on information acquisition and encourages moderate imagination in interpretation, giving rise to large freedom both in the authors and readers.

So far, we have only obtained weak evidences on the effect of CoMeMo-Community as a community support. We would like to undergo more thorough evaluation in search for strong evidences. We consider small scale laboratory tests are inadequate particularly when they are controlled. Instead, we think evaluation through large and open field trials is necessary to gain deeper understanding of CoMeMo-Community and community itself.

There are many interesting issues open for future research. Among others, it might be interesting to investigate more detailed analysis of how much associative representation facilitates externalization, how much people are willing to expose their personal information, what kind of information they reserve, how much we can guess the structure of the community from the reactions from people, and how much the CoMeMo-Community facilitates the knowledge process.

All of these study are only feasible once a system like CoMeMo-Community is put into practical use.

6 Conclusion

In this paper, we explored two ideas for community knowledge sharing and evolution. One is associative representation for facilitating externalization of both personal and community knowledge. The other is visualization of knowledge interaction based on the talking-alter-egos metaphor. The idea has been implemented as CoMeMo-Community. We have reported preliminary experimentation and discussed issues in community support from the viewpoint of knowledge spiral in community.

References

1. Contractor, N.S., Zink, D., and Chan, M.: IKNOW: A tool to assist and study the creation, maintenance, and dissolution of knowledge networks, presented at the First Kyoto Meeting on Social Interaction and Communityware, June 8-10, Kyoto, Japan (1998)
2. Foner, L.: Yenta: A Multi-Agent, Referral Based Matchmaking System, The First International Conference on Autonomous Agents (Agents '97) (1997)
3. Freeman E., and Fertig S.: Lifestreams: Organizing your electronic life. In 1995 AAAI Fall Symposium on AI Applications in Knowledge Navigation and Retrieval (1995) 38–44

4. Hattori, F., Ohguro, T., Yokoo, M., Matsubara, S., and Toshida, S.: Supporting Network Communities with Multiagent Systems, presented at the First Kyoto Meeting on Social Interaction and Communityware, June 8-10, Kyoto, Japan (1998)

5. Hirata, T., Maeda, H., and Nishida, T.: Facilitating Community Awareness with Associative Representation, in Proc. Second International Conference on Knowledge-based Intelligent Electronic Systems (KES '98) (1998) 411–416

6. Hurwitz, R.: Who speaks and when: ordering discourse communities, presented at the First Kyoto Meeting on Social Interaction and Communityware, June 8-10, Kyoto, Japan (1998)

7. Ishida, T.: Towards Communityware, New Generation Computing, Vol. 16, No. 1 (1998) 5–22

8. Kautz, H.A., Selman B., and Shah M.: The Hidden Web. AI Magazine, 18(2) (1997) 27–36

9. Krulwich, B. and Burkey, C.: The ContactFinder agent: Answering bulletin board questions with referrals. In Proceedings AAAI-96 (1996)

10. Lamming, M. and Flynn, M.: "Forget-me-not:" Intimate Computing in Support of Human Memory. In Proceedings of FRIEND21, '94 International Symposium on Next Generation Human Interface, Meguro Gajoen, Japan (1994)

11. Maeda, H. and Nishida, T.: Generating and Understanding of Weak Information Structures by Humans, in Proc. IASTED International Conference Artificial Intelligence and Soft Computing (ASC'98) (1998) 74–78, 1998

12. Nishida, T., Takeda, H., Iino, K., and Nishiki, M., A knowledge media approach to ontology development. In N.J.I. Mars (ed.): Towards Very Large Knowledge Bases: Knowledge Building & Knowledge Sharing 1995, IOS Press (1995) 84–94

13. Nishida, T., Takeda, H., Iwazume, M., Maeda, H., and Takaai, M.: The Knowledgeable Community: Facilitating Human Knowledge Sharing, in Ishida, T. (ed.): Community Computing: Collaboration over Global Information Networks, Chapter 5, London: John Wiley and Sons (1998)

14. Nishimura, T., Yamaki, H., Komura, T., Itoh, N., Gotoh, T., and Ishida, T.: Community Viewer: Visualizing Community Formation on Personal Digital Assistants, 1998 ACM Symposium on Applied Computing (ACM ASC '98), Mobile Computing Track (1998)

15. Nonaka, I. and Takeuchi H.: The Knowledge-Creating Company: How Japanese Companies Create the Dynamics of Innovation. Oxford University Press (1995)

16. Rhodes, B.: Remembrance Agent - A Continuously Running Automated Information Retrieval System, in the Proceedings of the First International Conference on the Practical Application of Intelligent Agents and Multi Agent Technology (PAAM '96) (1996) 487–495

17. Sumi, Y., Nishimoto, K., and Mase, K.: Personalizing shared information in creative conversations, in Proc. of IJCAI-97 Workshop on Social Interaction and Communityware (1997) 31–36

18. Torrance. M. C.: Active Notebook: A personal and group productivity tool for managing information. In 1995 AAAI Fall Symposium on AI Applications in Knowledge Navigation and Retrieval (1995) 131–135

IKNOW: A Tool to Assist and Study the Creation, Maintenance, and Dissolution of Knowledge Networks[1]

Noshir S. Contractor, Daniel Zink, Michael Chan
244 Lincoln Hall, 702 South Wright Street
University of Illinois at Urbana Champaign
Urbana IL 61801
USA
nosh@uiuc.edu, zink@uiuc.edu, m-chan@uiuc.edu

Abstract

The introduction of new communication and information technologies in work communities has primarily been used to create new channels of communication and/or reduce the cost of communication among members in the workplace. Ironically, the pervasiveness of electronic communication media in virtual work communities make it increasingly difficult for individuals to discern social structures. Fortunately, information technologies that are responsible for triggering this problem can also be used to overcome these obstacles. Because information transacted over electronic media such as the Web can be stored in digital form, a new generation of software called "collaborative filters" or "communityware" (Contractor, O'Keefe, & Jones, 1997; Kautz, Selman, & Shah, 1997) can be used to make visible the work communities' virtual social structure. One such tool, IKNOW (Inquiring Knowledge Networks On the Web; http://iknow.spcomm.uiuc.edu/), has been designed by a team of UIUC researchers to assist individuals to search the organization's databases to automatically answer questions about the organization's knowledge network, that is, "Who knows what?" as well as questions about the organization's cognitive knowledge networks, that is, "Who knows who knows what?" within the organization. Unlike traditional web search engines that help an individual search for content on the web, tools such as IKNOW search for content and contacts (direct and indirect). In addition to being instantly beneficial to users, they also provide the researcher with an opportunity to unobtrusively and reliably study the influence of communityware on the co-evolution of knowledge networks.

Introduction

More than at any other time in human history, advances in the 21st century will be based on knowledge networks. What it is, how it is represented, how it is distributed and to whom, are all pressing questions with significant economic, social, and political impact. Communities that generate and control the distribution of knowledge will have considerable competitive economic advantage over those who do not. Communityware is a new generation of tools that can help these human advances occur. This paper seeks to examine the role of communityware tools to identify the factors that lead to the creation, maintenance and dissolution of dynamically linked knowledge networks. The core research question is: How does communityware

---

[1] The conceptual development of IKNOW was conducted as part of a research project funded by the National Science Foundation (ECS-9422730).

influence the co-evolution of social networks, cognitive social networks, knowledge networks and cognitive knowledge networks?

Conceptual Frameworks for Representing Knowledge and Knowledge Networks

Definitions of Knowledge

A number of definitions exist for the concepts of knowledge and intelligence, each reflecting the disciplinary context in which they are used. A common hierarchy offered in computer science is that data (bits, bytes, pixels, voxels) when combined with content (e.g. metadata, often implicit) leads to information. The integration, analysis, and synthesis of information leads to knowledge. In artificial intelligence, the knowledge level is one in a hierarchy of many representational schemes. These formalisms imply that knowledge can only be defined and understood within a network of other knowledge concepts (Carley & Newell, 1994). In organizational and management theory, knowledge is also defined in reference to networks. However, in this case the links are between "actors," a term that will be used throughout this paper to refer to individuals, groups, or organizations.

Definitions of Knowledge Networks

From the standpoint of studying work communities, it is valuable to define knowledge networks that map on to the network of actors. The location of knowledge within this network of actors can vary along a continuum from centralized, where knowledge resides with only one actor, to distributed, where knowledge exists among many actors (Farace, Monge, & Russell, 1977). Further, distributed knowledge may refer to the flow or diffusion of knowledge, which increases the level of knowledge among all actors. Alternatively, it may refer to the parts of a larger knowledge base, each possessed by separate actors within the network. In this form of distributed knowledge, actors bring relatively unique, non-redundant knowledge which enable a collective to accomplish complex tasks (Gore, 1996). Distributed knowledge occurs at many levels in the empirical world, including work groups, large scale project teams, and interorganizational strategic alliances, to name but a few. The figure below represents a knowledge network. The nodes in this network are individuals; included (in parenthesis) within the nodes are the knowledge items each individual reports possessing. The links between the nodes represent knowledge items shared by individuals.

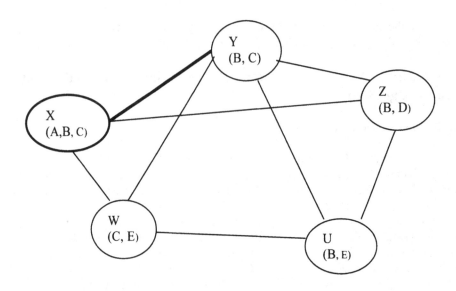

Figure 1. Knowledge network among members in a work community

In addition to these characteristics of the observable knowledge networks, actors have their own "cognitive" perceptions of the knowledge network -- that is, their perceptions of the knowledge possessed by each actor in the network. An idealized analogy often used is that of a set of networked computers, in which knowledge about a given domain is available on one of the hard disks (i.e. one of the actors), while the directory of information on all of the other hard disks (i.e., the entire knowledge network) is available to all actors (Wegner, 1995). In reality, the directory of information possessed by each of the actors (i.e., each actor's perception of "who knows what?") may be incomplete and/or inaccurate. Hence, all actors within an observable knowledge network, have their own <u>cognitive knowledge networks</u> describing their (potentially incomplete and/or inaccurate) perceptions of the overall observable knowledge network. The set of cognitive knowledge networks among the actors collectively constitute a transactive memory system. A transactive memory system begins when actors learn something about one another's domains of knowledge (Hollingshead, 1998; Wegner, 1987). Through self-disclosure and shared experiences, actors learn who is the expert across knowledge domains.

The accuracy of actors' cognitive knowledge networks (i.e., the extent to which their perceptions accurately reflect the observable knowledge network) reduces the amount of knowledge for which each actor is responsible, while providing each actor access to a larger pool of knowledge across domains. For instance, consider a work community as a knowledge network. The cognitive knowledge networks of individual participants within this knowledge network may be incomplete or inaccurate. That is, individual participants may not know about the areas of expertise of their colleagues. However, the cognitive knowledge network of a manager may be more accurate. That is, she is more likely to have a better understanding of the various areas of expertise represented within the work community. In responding to new information received by the group, the accuracy in her cognitive knowledge network gives her the ability to identify participants who could lead new projects and/or offer expert analysis of ongoing projects. The figure below represents Individual X's cognitive knowledge network. The nodes in this network are individuals; included (in parenthesis) within the node are the knowledge items that X perceives are possessed by each of the individuals in the network. The links between the nodes represent X's perceptions of common knowledge items shared by individuals. Note that according to the knowledge network defined above (Fiure 1), individuals Z and U share knowledge item B in common. However, X is unaware of this shared knowledge and hence X's cognitive knowledge network has no link between individuals Z and U.

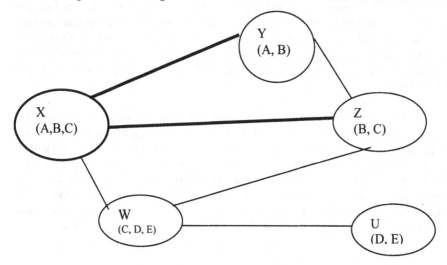

Figure 2. Individual X's cognitive knowledge network of the work community

To summarize, the work community can be represented in terms of two types of networks. Knowledge networks represent the extent to which the same or disparate knowledge is distributed among the various members of the group. Cognitive knowledge networks represent individuals' cognitive perceptions of "who knows what" within the group.

A final defining characteristic of knowledge networks is their fluidity, both in terms of actors and linkages. The actors join or leave a knowledge network on the basis of tasks to be accomplished, and their levels of interests, resources, and commitments. The links within the knowledge network are also likely to change on the basis of evolving tasks, the distribution of knowledge within the network, or changes in the actors' cognitive knowledge networks. Next we turn to the field of network analysis to provide a framework to analyze the state and co-evolution of knowledge networks

Knowledge Network Analysis

The conceptualizations of knowledge networks discussed in the previous section can be represented and analyzed exceptionally well using techniques developed within the field of social network analysis (Wasserman & Faust, 1994). Network analysis consists of applying a set of relations to an identified set of entities.

The growing interest in social network analysis can be attributed to its focus on relationships among social entities, and on the patterns and implications of these relationships. It is based on an assumption of the importance of relationship among interacting units (Wasserman & Faust, 1994). This focus stands in sharp contrast to other areas of the social sciences, which have tended to study "attributes," the characteristics of people, groups, and organizations rather than the relations between them (Monge & Contractor, 1988, in press). Hence, "(T)o an extent perhaps unequalled in most other social science disciplines, social network methods have developed over the past fifty years as an integral part of advances in social theory, empirical research, and formal mathematics and statistics" (Wasserman & Faust, 1994, p. 3).

The three major network mathematical foundations of network analysis have been graph theory, statistical and probability theory, and algebraic models. These foundations have been used to develop a suite of metrics that capture network properties of individual actors (e.g., actor connectedness, range, prominence, betweenness, isolation, popularity, and centrality), dyads (e.g., reciprocity, symmetry), triads (e.g., transitivity) as well as the global characteristics of the overall network (e.g., network density, heterogeneity, and centralization). The substantive interpretations of these metrics depend on the types of actors and relations being analyzed.

In the context of knowledge networks, the entities are actors (individuals, groups, organizations, etc.) and the relations between the entities represent the knowledge they share in common. The metrics developed in network analysis can easily be extended to the study of knowledge networks. For instance, an actor with high "betweenness" is defined as one who shares knowledge with several other actors in the network who do not share knowledge with one another. As such, this actor serves as a "knowledge broker" in the network. Likewise, the density of the knowledge network would index the extent to which the knowledge is distributed in the network. Network analysis can also be used to measure cognitive knowledge networks. For instance, an actor whose cognitive knowledge network accurately maps on to the observable knowledge network is more likely to be identified as the one "who knows who knows what." In general, network analysis offers the ability to measure the evolving characteristics of knowledge networks with a degree of precision that might otherwise be defined only in metaphorical terms.

While developing formal metrics of knowledge networks is an important contribution, it is only a means towards the substantively more challenging goal of understanding the theoretical processes by which these networks co-evolve across the various levels and over time. Before examining these theoretical mechanisms it is helpful to overview the technological infrastructures that are enabling knowledge networks in twenty-first century organizational forms.

Technical Infrastructure for Knowledge Networks in Work Communities

The diffusion of Internet-based networking technologies has accelerated the emergence of novel forms of work communities. The resulting Intranets, Extranets, and communityware support the co-evolution of knowledge networks. First, <u>Intranets</u> allow work communities to implement on a unified network platform a wide set of knowledge distribution activities that support teams and networks of teams within work communities. Second, because the underlying Internet standards are open and public, organizations can seamlessly interconnect their Intranet with those of clients, partners, suppliers or sub-contractors, via secure "<u>Extranets</u>". Third, while the pervasiveness of Internet technologies has enabled the creation of network work communities, they also make it increasingly difficult for actors to discern the scope and range of their "virtual" knowledge networks. <u>Communityware</u> technologies are especially beneficial for actors assembling cross-skills teams to address specific tasks or projects by helping them accurately determine: "Who knows who?" "Who knows who knows who?" "Who knows what?" and "Who knows who knows what?" IKNOW (Inquiring Knowledge Networks On the Web), is one example of "communityware" (Contractor, O'Keefe, & Jones, 1997).

Intervention of Infrastructure Technologies on the Co-evolution of Knowledge Networks

An important research focus is to explore the relation between knowledge networks and the technological infrastructures that work communities use to support them. Network analysis, described earlier, offers a framework to conceptualize and measure the various co-evolving networks. Communityware technologies described in the previous section influence how these networks co-evolve. The current deployment of Intranets, Extranets, and communityware provides an excellent opportunity to explore this recursive relationship. The evolving configurations of these technologies shape, and are in turn shaped by, the evolving knowledge networks (Contractor & Eisenberg, 1990).

Based on a review of the extant empirical literature on organizational networks, Monge and Contractor (in press) explicate several theoretical perspectives that describe various aspects of network evolution, including their formation, maintenance, transformation, and dissolution. These include: (a) theories of self-interest (social capital theory and transaction cost economics), (b) theories of mutual self-interest and collective action, (c) exchange and dependency theories (social exchange, resource dependency, and network organizational forms), (d) contagion theories, (social information processing, social cognitive theory, institutional theory, structural theory of action), (e) cognitive theories (semantic networks, knowledge structures, cognitive social structures, cognitive consistency), (f) theories of homophily (social comparison theory, social identity theory), (g) theories of proximity (physical and electronic propinquity), (h) uncertainty reduction and contingency theories, (i) social support theories, and (j) evolutionary theories. Some of these perspectives are particularly relevant because they focus on co-evolution across multiple levels, including individual cognitions, dyads, groups, and organizations. We are therefore interested in making theoretical predictions about the impacts of communityware technologies on the co-evolution of knowledge networks in general and, more specifically, the social capital of actors within this network (Burt, 1997).

Unlike knowledge capital, which refers to the knowledge possessed by an actor (i.e. who knows what?), social capital refers to an actor's knowledge about the knowledge possessed by other actors (i.e., who knows who knows what?). Enhancing social capital is an especially important resource for actors in work communities because communityware makes it possible to broaden actors' knowledge networks, thereby increasing their ability to exercise their social capital for a competitive advantage. However, the "virtuality" of this knowledge network sometimes makes it more difficult to identify the appropriate network links within this extended network. To the extent that communityware tools make the knowledge networks more visible to the actors, they can enhance the social capital of all the actors in the network by making their cognitive knowledge networks more accurate. A key research question here is the extent to which the introduction of communityware tools increases or reduces the gap between the social capital "haves" and the social capital "have-nots." Examining the influence of communityware on social and knowledge capital, encompasses the following set of research questions:

1. What effect does communityware, such as IKNOW, have on the community's power structures? Does it undermine the perceived centrality of those individuals in the community who are viewed as important resources about the community's social and knowledge networks.

2. What configurations of knowledge networks are more appropriate to specific types of tasks (such as brainstorming, design, buying-selling, execution, etc.) To what extent are knowledge networks reconfigurable to accommodate the team's changing tasks?

3. How can the use of Communitware such as IKNOW (Inquiring Knowledge Networks On the Web) alter the structures and growth of Knowledge Networks by making the virtual network more visible to the members?

4. What theoretical mechanisms are most influential in "growing" a Knowledge Network (in terms of its size as well as the density of connections)? To what extent does the initial configuration of the network influence the speed and characteristics of its growth patterns?

5. How do exchange and trust mechanisms explain the likelihood that individuals will remain members (or drop out) of a knowledge network?

6. How can credentialling (where knowledge network members anonymously rate the quality of contributions by fellow network members) serve as communityware, while not violating an individual's privacy.

This section has described research questions that can be addressed by studying the co-evolution of communication, knowledge, and cognitive knowledge networks. The schematic in the following figure describes a comprehensive analytic methodology to computationally model, empirically assess, and statistically validate the effect of communityware on the co-evolution of knowledge networks.

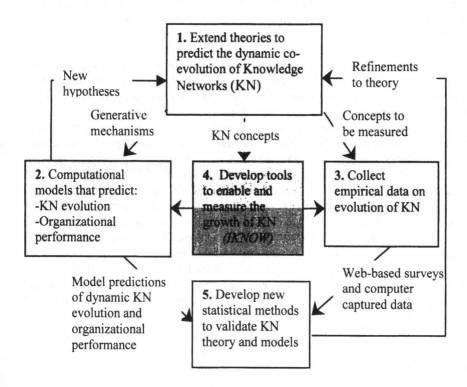

Figure 3. Methodology to study the influence of communityware on co-evolution of knowledge networks.

It shows the relationship among the key elements of the research approach: (1) theory building/hypothesis formulation about mechanisms of KN co-evolution; (2) computational modeling/simulation of those mechanisms and how they produce emergent behavior; (3) collection and analysis of empirical data, (4) development and deployment of "community-ware" tools to enable and study knowledge networks, and (5) statistical techniques for modeling, validating, and analyzing dynamic knowledge network data (Contractor et al., 1998). The next two sections describe how modeling and empirical field studies can be used to better understand the effect of communityware on the co-evolution of knowledge networks.

Modeling

Computational models offer a "virtual test-bed" to articulate and examine the theoretical effects of communityware on the co-evolution of knowledge networks. Previous research has led to an increasing number of computational models that can be used to theorize about networks within and among work communities. Recently there has been a surge of interest in the creation of computational models (Carley, 1990; Carley, 1991; Carley & Prietula, 1994; Young, 1998) that can be used to capture and examine the dynamics of knowledge networks. These models serve as computational aids for theory construction by generating non-linear, empirically testable, dynamic hypotheses.

Blanche is one such object-oriented environment for computationally modeling network systems. It models networks as a set of <u>actors</u> characterized by some collection of <u>attributes</u> and related by one or more network <u>links</u> (Hyatt, Contractor, & Jones, 1997). In addition, it requires specification of a set of theoretical mechanisms to examine the evolution of networks. A discrete set of theoretical mechanisms provides flexibility and expressiveness such that dependencies among actors' attributes and links over time are modeled as a function of values at previous time steps. The theoretical mechanisms are implemented as nonlinear difference equations. The suite of mathematical and logical operators implemented within Blanche make it a general purpose computational modeling environment for a variety of network theories. For instance, the dynamic theoretical mechanisms among the actors' attributes (e.g., their levels of resources, interests, skills) and actors' networks (e.g., density, heterogeneity of observable and cognitive knowledge networks) proposed by various theories can be specified and executed using *Blanche*. The dynamic hypotheses generated by computational modeling provide theoretical predictions about the co-evolution of knowledge networks. These predictions must then be empirically validated in test-beds.

Test-beds

Versions of IKNOW are currently being designed for use in the (i) National Computational Science Alliance (NCSA) at the University of Illinois at Urbana-Champaign, (ii) Faculty Summer Institute on Collaborative Learning, (iii) a ten-week Summer Workshop at the Engineering Research Center for Collaborative Manufacturing at Purdue University, (iv) the Public Works Division of a U.S. military installation, (v) the Global Information Systems Project at the Office of International Programs at Purdue University (IPPU), (vi) a PrairieNet Community Networking project in Champaign-Urbana,. (vii) and several graduate and undergraduate courses taught at the University of Illinois at Urbana-Champaign.

These work communities represent diverse characteristics in terms of (i) their size (30-300), (ii) unit of analysis (individuals versus organizations) (iii) geographical dispersion of members (co-located to world-wide), (iv) content of social interaction (e.g., computational science, voluntary non-profit communities, manufacturing, education), (v) current use of Intranet-based technologies (no prior use to high performance computing environments), (vi) past history as a community (start up communities to 10 years old), and (vi) life cycle of the community (1 week to projected five year life cycles).

Data Collected from Testbeds

In addition to serving the user community, IKNOW also serves as an effective data collection instrument for researchers. Unlike most network based research in work communities, the data provided by users are generated as part of their ongoing use of communityware. Since users have a vested interest in the information provided being accurate and current, the large corpus of longitudinal data has a greater likelihood of being reliable.

Five types of network data are captured by IKNOW: (i) a communication network of actors based on existing task and projects links between them; (ii) a knowledge network based on actors providing an inventory of their skills and expertise, (iii) a knowledge network of actors based on the links between their web sites, (iv) a knowledge network of actors based on common links from their web sites to third party web-sites and (v) a knowledge network based on similarity in content (vocabulary) between different actors' web sites. The data from these networks are automatically captured longitudinally and serves as empirical data to validate the networks generated from computational modeling tools such as *Blanche*.

Benefits to the Community

As discussed in this paper, IKNOW serves as a Communitware tool that has benefits for the researcher as well as for the community. It is this synergy that makes it a particularly useful tool to study the co-evolution of knowledge networks.

There are at least three ways in which IKNOW can assist user communities create, sustain, and grow their knowledge networks:

1. First, it provides all members of the community the ability to efficiently and effectively identify others within the community who share common and complementary interests, and how they may be directly or indirectly connected to them. This is especially beneficial for members assembling ad-hoc cross-skills teams to address specific project concerns.
2. Second, it provides members with a set of visual tools to inspect, identify, and critically analyze the existing and potential collaborations (both in terms of membership and topics) among the members of the community.
3. Third, it offers members the ability to track over time the growth characteristics of the knowledge network (in terms of the size of the network, the density of inter-connections, and the content areas).

Below are four current examples of he use of communityware:

I. PrairieNet Communityware

The PrairieNet communityware (http://iknow.spcomm.uiuc.edu/prairienet login/password: guest/guest) consists of 285 organizations in Central Illinois with public web pages. Each organization's set of web pages were scanned to create a list of links on those pages and a list of words that occurred on those pages. From this information we can view networks of web page links between these organizations, how many outside links these organizations have in common, as well as similarity in the content of their web site. For instance, the Danville Public Library shares a tie with the Urbana Free Library, and the Urbana Free Library shares a tie with the Friends of the Urbana Free Library. Boy scout troops, religious organizations, bands, clubs, and political groups all share similar ties. Thus IKNOW communityware is especially useful to community organizations that are trying to use their resources efficiently and effectively to mobilize for joint collective action.

II. NCSA Alliance Communityware

The NCSA Alliance communityware (secured web site) consists of 291 members in over 200 organizations. As part of their registration on the Alliance Intranet they were required to enter information about their interests by choosing items from a list. The similarity of these lists are used to create network visualizations similar to the ones described for Prairienet. Thus IKNOW communityware is especially useful to members in the Alliance who want to identify others within the distributed community who share common and/or complementary interests.

III. Faculty Summer Institute Communityware

The Faculty Summer Institute on Collaborative Learning communityware (http://iknow.spcomm.uiuc.edu/fsi login/password: guest/guest) was used by twelve faculty members from state universities in Illinois participating in a week long workshop on the use of technologies to support collaborative learning. Communityware was used by the group as a quick and effective "ice-breaker" to identify common and complementary interests among the participants, as well as to choose partners to work on group projects during and after the workshop.

IV. Communityware for a course on Communication Technologies in the Workplace

During Spring 1998, IKNOW communityware (http://iknow.spcomm.uiuc.edu/class login/password: guest/guest)was used by 36 students in an undergraduate course on "Communication Technologies in the Workplace" at the University of Illinois. The students used IKNOW to form their own teams for semester projects. They were required to assemble teams that included individuals with some common skills (such as interest in aviation, advertising, etc.) and some complementary skills (such as at least one member with web-authoring skills).

V. Communityware for participants in the Kyoto meeting

A version of IKNOW (http://iknow.spcomm.uiuc.edu/kyoto/ login, password: guest, guest) was developed to examine the knowledge networks among participants of the Kyoto meeting. After logging in, participants viewed the screen shown in Figure 4:

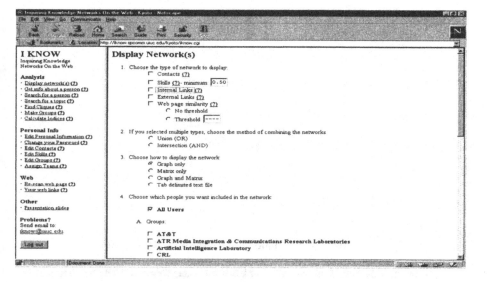

Figure 4. User interface for IKNOW

Figure 5 shows the knowledge network as indicated by web links between participants' web sites. For instance, Yoko Kubota (the node colored white) has links pointing to his web site from Yasuyuki Sumi and Toru Ishida (the nodes colored blue). Kubota has links from his web site pointing to the individuals whose nodes are colored green.

Figure 6 shows the knowledge network as indicated by participants whose web sites point to the same external web sites. Unlike Figure 5, where the nodes were arranged in a circle, here the network was annealed so that similar nodes appear clustered closer to one another. As a result several of the Japanese participants in the meeting were clustered together. Figure 7 shows the output of clicking on the link between Leonard Foner and Keiki Takadema. The two each have links from their web sites pointing to web pages at NASA and EFF.

Figure 8 shows the knowledge network as indicated by common vocabulary appearing on the participants' web sites. This annealed network indicates that many of the Japanese participants not only have similar vocabulary on their web pages. Further, they appear to share common terms with more of the non-Japanese participants than the latter do with one another. Finally, Figure 9, shows a listing of the common terms found between the web sites of Geoffrey Bowker and Vijay Saraswat. The words are listed in descending order, so that words that are more

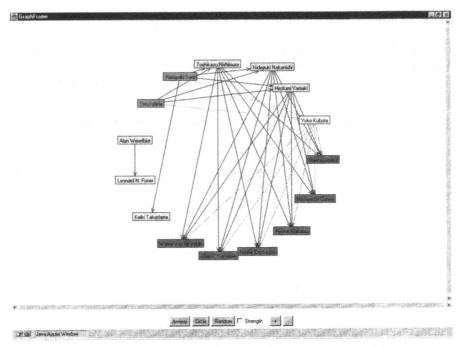

Figure 5. Network of web links between the web sites of participants

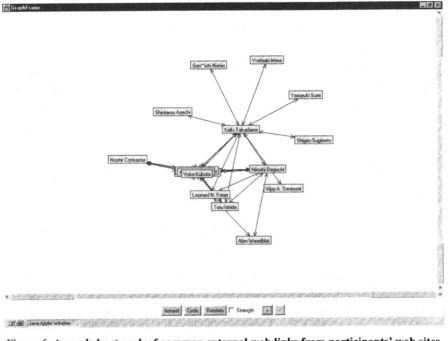

Figure 6. Annealed network of common external web links from participants' web sites

frequently used by the two participants, and less frequently used by any other participants are weighted higher. A quick inspection of the list indicates that Vijay and Geoffrey both indicate an interest on their web sites in the following terms: computer science, John Seely Brown, teachers, participatory design, videotaping, and etiquette.

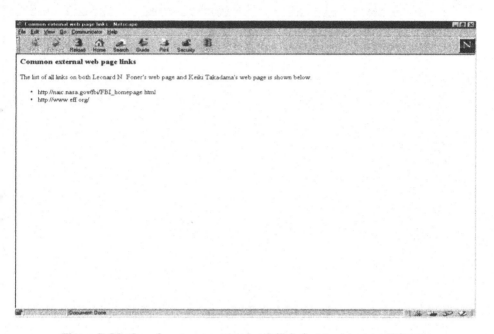

Figure 7. Display of common external web links between two participants

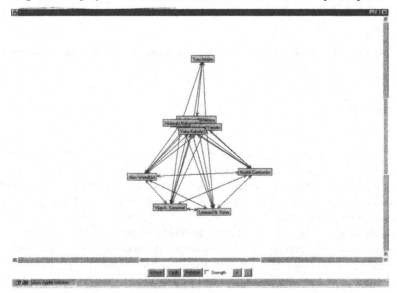

Figure 8. Annealed network of common vocabulary between participants' web sites

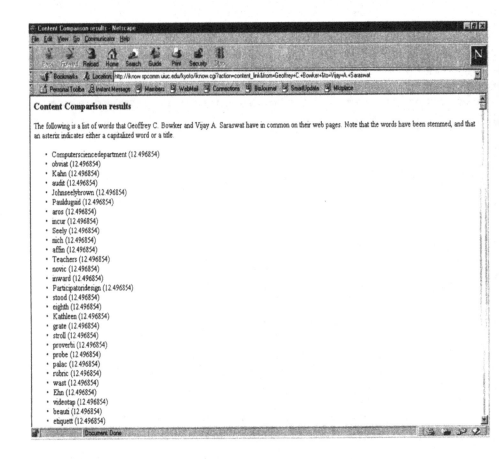

Figure 9. Display of common vocabulary between two participants' web sites

Conclusion

This paper has argued for the potentially important role of communityware in assisting the creation, maintenance, and dissolution of knowledge networks. Network analytic techniques offer an appropriate methodology to represent and analyze the evolution of knowledge networks and cognitive knowledge networks. Communityware tools, such as IKNOW, have the potential to assist in the evolution of these networks by making the virtual networks more visible to the actors and by adding contacts to the content of the knowledge network. The paper identified several theoretical mechanisms that can be used to study the effect of introducing communityware on the evolution of these networks. Computational models offer researchers the ability to simulate the long term non-linear implications of these theoretical mechanisms. The results of these simulations must be validated using the type of test-beds described in this paper.

References

Burt, R. S. (1997). The contingent value of social capital. *Administrative Science Quarterly, 42,* 339-365.

Carley, K. M. (1990). Group stability: A socio-cognitive approach. In Lawler E., Markovsky B., Ridgeway C., & Walker H. (Eds.). *Advances in group processes: Theory & research . Vol. VII* (pp. 1-44). Greenwich, CN: JAI Press.

Carley, K. M. (1991). A theory of group stability. *American Sociological Review 56,* 331-354.

Carley, K. M., & Newell, A. (1994). The nature of the social agent. *Journal of Mathematical Sociology , 19*(4): 221-262.

Carley, K., & Prietula, M. J. (Eds.) (1994). *Computational Organizational Theory.* Hillsdale, NJ: Lawrence Erlbaum.

Contractor, N. S., Carley, K, Levitt, R., Monge, P. R., Wasserman, S., Bar, F., Fulk, J, Hollingshead, A., Kunz, J. (1998). *Co-evolution of Knowledge Networks and Twenty-first Century Organizational Forms: Computational Modeling and Empirical Testing.* Working Paper.

Contractor, N. S. & Eisenberg, E. M. (1990) Communication networks and new media in organizations. In J. Fulk & C. Steinfield (Eds.) *Organizations and Communication Technology* (pp. 143-172), Newbury Park: Sage.

Contractor, N. S., O'Keefe, B. J., & Jones, P. M. (1997). *IKNOW: Inquiring Knowledge Networks On the Web.* Computer software. University of Illinois. (http://iknow.spcomm.uiuc.edu/.

Contractor, N. S. (1997). *Inquiring Knowledge Networks on the Web. Conceptual overview.* http://www.tec.spcomm.uiuc.edu/nosh/IKNOW/sld001.htm

Farace, R.V., Monge, P. R., & Russell, H. M. (1977). *Communicating and organizing.* Reading, MA: Addison Wesley.

Gore, A., Jr. (1996). The metaphor of distributed intelligence. *Science, 272,* 177.

Hollingshead, A. B. (1998b). Retrieval processes in transactive memory systems. *Journal of Personality and Social Psychology, 74,* 659-671.

Hyatt, A., Contractor, N., & Jones, P. M. (1997). Computational organizational network modeling: Strategies and an example. *Computational and Mathematical Organizational Theory, 4,* 285-300.

Kautz, H., Selman, B., & Shah, M. (1997). Combining social networks and collaborative filtering. *Communications of the ACM, 40,* 63-65.

Monge, P. R., & Contractor, N. S. (1988). Communication networks: Measurement techniques. In C. H. Tardy (Ed.), *A handbook for the study of human communication: Methods and instruments for observing, measuring, and assessing communication processes .* (pp. 107-138). Norwood, NJ: Ablex.

Monge, P.R., & Contractor, N. (in press). Emergence of communication networks. In F.M. Jablin & L.L. Putnam (Eds.), *Handbook of organizational communication* (2nd ed.). Thousand Oaks, CA: Sage Publications.

Wasserman, S., & Faust, K. (1994). *Social network analysis: Methods and applications.* New York: Cambridge University Press.

Wegner, D. M. (1987). Transactive memory: A contemporary analysis of the group mind. In B. Mullen & G. R. Goethals (Eds.) *Theories of group behavior* (pp. 185-208). New York: Springer-Verlag.

Wegner, D. M. (1995). A computer network model of human transactive memory. *Social Cognition, 13*:3, 319-339.

Young, J. (July 24, 1998). Using computer models to study the complexities of human society. *Chronicle of Higher Education, 44,* 46, A17.

Building Agent Community toward Business Knowledge Base Generation

Toshiaki Miyashita, Yosuke Takashima, Yoshihide Ishiguro,

Takayoshi Asakura and Koji Kida

Human Media Research Laboratories
NEC Corporation
8416-47 Takayama, Ikoma-city, Nara 630-0101
{miyasita, yosuke, ishiguro, asakura, kida}@hml.cl.nec.co.jp

Abstract. Messages exchanged among agents are useful in building business knowledge base, because of its descriptive formality and of human's decision contents included. Based on this idea, we are trying to build multi agents community. More agents exist, more useful knowledge base we can build. An arrangement technique will be used to generate knowledge information including event causality from those messages. For example, we have developed a multi agent system, named WorkWeb, for workflow coordination, which consists of personal schedule agents and a workflow management agent. In this system, the workflow management agent generates an appropriate workflow communicating with personal schedule agents to keep the job deadline. Messages gathered from this agent communication tell us that who is boss, what coordination strategy he frequently uses, and workflow (or job procedures) itself, also persons' names in charge. We, office workers and various agents also require many views of business knowledge base. Therefore, we need many and wide variety of business agents. Our research aim of building agent community is to automatically build knowledge base in business domain. In this paper, we introduce our multi agent system and clarify the possibility of what information we get through our multi agent system communication messages, and the possibility of its usage as knowledge.

1. Introduction

This paper considers the possibility of knowledge base construction from messages exchanged among software agents. Messages exchanged among agents are useful in building business knowledge base, because of its descriptive formality and of human's decision contents included. Our starting point was to realize multi agent community on world wide computer network. The reason why we hope multi agent community is that it will be potential energy to give us readable knowledge on our society. Assume that my shopping agent goes to virtual shopping mole with my order of buying a bicycle. It will talk with several bicycle shop agents and messages exchanged among them may include that a certain shop does not treat the credit card "AMEX" and sells it at 10% off price in cash. Once my agent knows this fact, it can tell other people's agents about it when it is asked. This is the one of daily but social knowledge around us, and also implies knowledge reuse.

We want to develop the above discussion in the office business domain. For example, we have developed a multi agent system, named WorkWeb [1], for workflow coordination, which consists of personal schedule agents and a workflow management agent. In this system, the workflow management agent generates an appropriate workflow communicating with personal schedule agents to keep the job dead-line. Messages gathered from this agent communication tell us that who is boss, what coordination strategy he frequently uses, and workflow (or job procedures) itself, also persons' names in charge. We, office workers and various agents also require many views of business knowledge base. Therefore, we need many and wide variety of business agents. Our research aim of building agent community is to automatically build knowledge base in business domain.

In this paper, we first introduce our multi agent system and secondly clarify the possibility of what information we get through our multi agent system communication messages, and the possibility of its usage as knowledge.

2. Multi Agent Office Work System

2.1 Layered Architecture

To provide two different views to the system, a two-layered architecture is introduced. Figure 1 shows this layered architecture. The first layer is a group work support layer. This layer provides a communication channel among groupware agents and personal agents. The groupware agents, for example, are workflow management and office resource management, etc. This communication capability among personal and group agents realizes the group view, that is, a manager can quickly collect information on other workers, the reservation status of meeting rooms, etc.

The second layer, called personal work support layer, exists inside the personal agent. This layer provides a communication channel among sub-agents. These agents act as software tools for the individual worker, and together give the personal view to the worker.

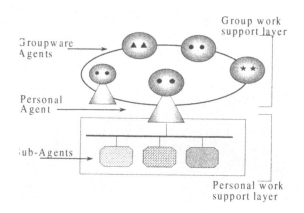

Group work
support layer

Groupware
Agents

Personal
Agent

Sub-Agents

Personal work
support layer

2.2 Agents to Support Group Work

Figure2 shows the global agents in our system, called the "WorkWeb system"[2]. Four types of agents, including the personal agent, are defined to support both personal and group work: resource agents, data management agents, workflow agents, and personal agents. The first three types of agents are concerned with group work support and are called groupware agents.

(1) Resource agent

Manages non-human resources: budget allocations, meeting rooms, shared tools or facilities, etc.

(2) Data management agent

Does not manage any resources, but collects group sharable data from the agents according to some given theme s and gives back the collected information to the agents per their requests. This agent is called the "Group Information Management (GIM) agent" in our system.

(3) Workflow agent

Manages each workflow process instance and tries to complete it within the deadline or as early as possible.

(4) Personal agent

Mainly supports personal work, for example, schedule management, e-mail filtering, electric memorandum management.

Fig.2 Agents in the WorkWeb system

2.3 Communication Protocol

In our layered architecture, there are two communication protocols for personal and group work support layers described before.

2.3.1 Global Communication

A global communication protocol is used for peer-to-peer communication among global agents. Each global agent is given a unique address represented by a Uniform Resource Locators (URL) format. For example, the personal agent for Mr. Tanaka has the following URL address.

Inalip://hml.cl.nec.co.jp/people/tanaka

, where "inalip" is the original protocol name, "hml.cl.nec.co.jp" is the domain name, and "people" is a keyword that indicates the address of a personal agent. All personal agents belonging to this domain are collected into this "people" directory and have a unique name that corresponds to a certain user's name such as "tanaka."

A workflow agent has the following URL address.

Inalip://hml.cl.nec.co.jp/bpt/1

This kind of URL format is used for a dynamically generated address. "bpt" is the subdirectory with workflow agents and "1" is a serial number generated by the agent management process. This process generates an agent address by applying a predefined generation rule and registers it to the agent table or erases it when the agent finishes execution.

These mechanisms are implemented with OMG (Object Management Group)'s Common Object Request Broker Architecture (COLBA)[3]. The global communication message format is defined based on the KQML [4] format. Two types of performatives are used from the KQML: "evaluate" and "reply." Global messages are always used with a pair of "evaluate" and "reply."

2.3.2 Local Communication

The local communication protocol is used for sub-agent communications. Unlike the global communication, all local communication messages are processed by one main process: the local communication channel. Each sub-agent is always connected to the local communication channel and exchanges massages through this channel. Each sub-agent's address is represented by its name because of communication limitation within the same machine.

In this local communication protocol, there are three kinds of messages and two types of addressing methods. The three message types are "Request," "Answer," and "Order." "Request" and "Answer" form a pair of messages for synchronous communication. These messages correspond to the global messages' "evaluate" and "reply." "Order" is a message type for asynchronous communication without ACK ("Acknowledgment"). The two addressing method types are "Private" and "Broadcast." "Private" addressing is normally used to send a message to one sub-agent. "Broadcast" addressing is used to send a message to all sub-agents currently connected to the local communication channel. It is useful for collecting different solutions from different agents at the same time.

2.4 Example of the WorkWeb Usage

Some agents based on our architecture and communication protocols have been developed. They are part of the WorkWeb system and work together to support personal and group work in the business office. We briefly describe how these agents work in cooperation.

Figure 3 shows a screen image of each worker's terminal. On this screen, there are several personal agents' windows including his /her own personal one. A worker interacts with the other agents through this window.

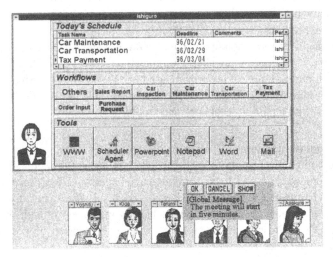

Fig. 3 A screen image of a personal agent

The workflow management agent is automatically generated when a workflow is invoked, that is, when a certain manager executes a workflow. This agent starts negotiating with workers scheduler sub-agents included this workflow member and access GIM, which collects data from other agents. GIM collects data on the workflow achievement and holds a target value which represents how many workflows should be completed in a certain term. The workflow management agent, by getting the target number and completed number from GIM, calculates the priority for the workflow. If the difference between target and completed number of workflows is large, the priority for incomplete workflows are rated high. Then the workflow management agent makes a plan to finish incomplete workflows due to priority, and distributes the plan to the appropriate personal agents.

The scheduler sub-agent, that exists inside the personal agent, receives this plan and decides if the worker can achieve this task by the given deadline. If all answers from scheduler sub-agents possessed by workers ,who are included in the workflow, are "Yes," the workflow management agent starts executing workflow and proceeds tasks imposed on each worker step by step. If some answers from scheduler sub-agents are "No," the workflow management agent re-plans the workflow.

This is a dynamic workflow control function, or a workflow simulation function. With the cooperation of the workflow management agent, GIM agent, the scheduler sub-agents, group work represented by workflow is achieved.

3. Knowledge from Massage Exchange

Our WorkWeb system is small size, having only four kinds of agents, one resource agent, one GIM agent, some workflow management agents, and ten scheduler sub-agents. Experimental usage of the system told us that agent message exchange histories have a possibility of habits on office works with statistic calculations.

3.1 Overview of Knowledge Generation from Exchanged Messages

Figure 4 shows the simple arrangement of messages exchanged by agents in the case of the workflow coordination. Between the workflow agent and the schedule sub-agent, and also between the workflow agent and the GIM agent, these messages are exchanged.

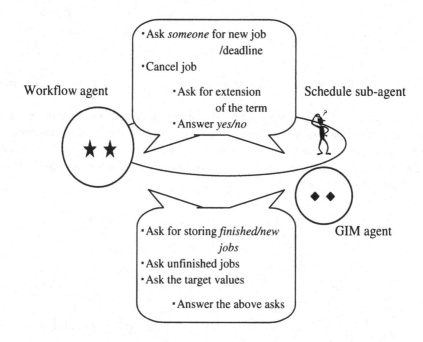

Fig.4 Messages exchanged among agents in the case of the workflow coordination

Figure 5 shows the case of meeting coordination. In this case, the meeting coordination agent and the schedule sub-agent exchange upper messages and also the meeting coordination agent and the resource management agent exchange the lower messages.

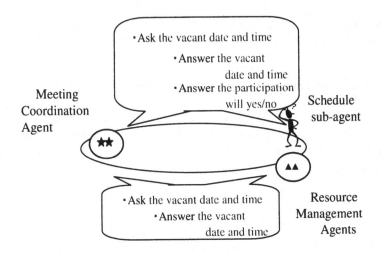

Fig.5 Messages exchanged among agents in the case of the meeting coordination

What things business managers and workers want to know on daily work ? We cannot make that kind of sweeping generalization. Our experiences, however, tell us that these questions depicted in figure 6 happen frequently. Especially, considering the kind of our agents, it seems that four questions with underlines have appropriate difficulties to be answered.

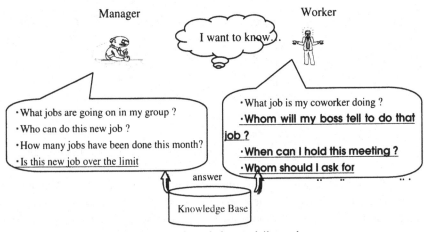

Fig.6 Business knowledge on daily work

3.2 Business Knowledge on Daily Work

Similar to our system architecture, business knowledge seems to be classified into two levels. One is macro scope knowledge concerning group activities. Another is micro scope knowledge concerning individual worker. Questions mentioned before are also classified according to knowledge level needed to be answered. Figure 7 depicts this classification.

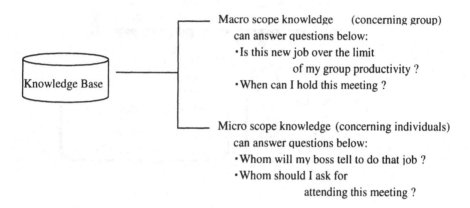

Fig.7 Arrangement of business knowledge on daily work

Figure 8 shows the way to derive knowledge from the history of exchanged messages in the case of the workflow coordination. First two data surrounded by the quadrilateral, the number of finished jobs and the number of accepted new jobs, can be derived straightforward manner such as a counting up. The last one is derived by arranging worker's name and yes/no answer together with job name as primary key.

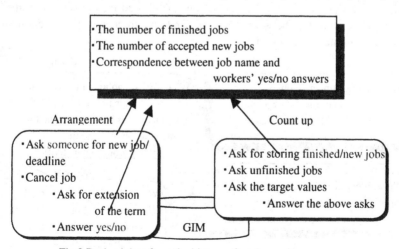

Fig.8 Derived data from the history of exchanged messages
in the case of the workflow coordination

In the case of meeting coordination, we get these knowledge depicted in figure 9 by the same way above mentioned. In this case, arrangement is done by a day of week and meeting subject as primary keys.

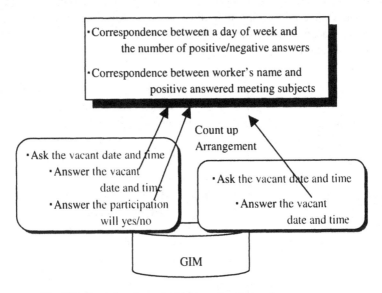

Fig. 9 Derived data from the history of exchanged messages
in the case of the meeting coordination

Correspondence between questions and knowledge to be answered them is shown in figure 10. The left sided quadrilaterals are knowledge and the right side shows questions. For example, to answer the question "Is this new job over the limit of my group productivity ?," we observe the ratio of the number of both finished jobs and new added jobs per a month, and the number of rejected jobs during the same time period. The relationship between the ratio and the frequency of rejection makes judgement of limitation of productivity.

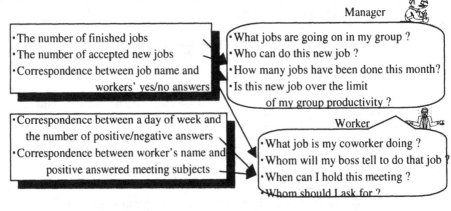

Fig.10 Usage of the derived data as business knowledge

3.3 Macro Scope Knowledge

(1) Case 1: limit of office productivity

GIM agent knows both current workflows and finished ones. Assume that GIM agent can calculate the numbers of both finished workflows and new added workflows per month, say α and β, respectively. If we get the number of rejected workflows per a month from exchanged messages among the workflow management agent and scheduler sub-agents, say γ, we may suppose that the ratio α/β is proportional to $1/\gamma$. Then the limit of our office productivity is prospected by knowing the value α/β.

(2) Case 2: maximum meeting chance

The scheduler sub-agent can coordinate a meeting schedule communicating with other scheduler sub-agents and resource agent (in this case, meeting rooms reservation management). Dialog among scheduler sub-agents and resource agent is vacant date, time and room number. If we calculate times of failure of holding a meeting according to date and time, then we might take a notice of better date and time to hold a meeting.

3.2 Micro Scope Knowledge

(1) Case 1: the reason of substitute for a job

The workflow management agent uses some strategies for job assignment when a worker, say Mr. Tanaka, put in a workflow refuses a job or cannot keep the job deadline. That agent substitutes another worker, say Mr. Suzuki for him. The history of this message exchange among the workflow management agent, Mr. Tanaka's scheduler agent and Mr. Suzuki's one represents the reason why Mr. Suzuki does that job. Also it will be seen that a boss tends to use somebody as a substitute.

(2) Case 2: frequently meeting absence

Among scheduler sub-agents message exchanges are done to set a meeting. From these messages we can read that a worker frequently excuses from attending some kind of meetings. Also we may read the reason ,that is, He/she might have no vacant time or he/she had any other reason. Conversely, in the case that almost always he/she attends a certain meeting, he/she possibly is interested in a theme or he/she deeply related to the job concerning that meeting.

4. Discussion

What kind of knowledge can be extracted from agent massage exchanges depends on the ways of combination of application agents. Perhaps messages themselves are not so valuable. Once we statistically calculate them, we will obtain the possibility both macro scope (concerning group) and micro scope (concerning personal) knowledge above mentioned.

What effect will this knowledge base give for us ? We think that it is the tendency of the group productivity and individual worker activity. That will be the most important effect. If the office work agents, moreover, can be used this knowledge base, they will show us more intelligent behavior.

To do this, we have several problems to be solved. At first, we must have many kinds of agents. It is, however, difficult to find what kind of agent we should develop. So we need to study what kind of knowledge are we, office workers, getting from histories of cooperative activities with others, namely cooperative office work model.

Secondly, we had better consider both sides of agent function and of message utilization as knowledge when we design an agent. For example, our schedule sub-agent does not exchange the message of the meeting absent reason beside the reason on schedule data. We can only guess the actual reason why he/she refused a meeting. Of course, users should not be charged with unnecessary interactions with agents. Therefore, we have to carefully design an agent and exchanged messages balancing between generation of useful knowledge and charge of user's load.

Thirdly, it is to keep office workers' and group's privacy. We have to sufficiently pay attention to knowledge utilization purposes. Possibly the history of agent message exchanges should not be opened and we might be able to only access the knowledge base. Figure 11 depicts the summary of the discussion.

Problems to be solved
(From exercises to practical uses)

■ A lot of cooperative agents are needed
leads   to generate useful knowledge.
⟹ **Building an Agent Community**

■ An agent design method should be considered from
both sides of its functions and message utilization as knowledge.
leads
⟹ **Building a Cooperative Office Work Model**

■ Absolutely keep privacy of individuals and group.

Fig.11 Summary of discussion

5. Conclusion

In this paper, we look for a meaning of developing agent community in generating knowledge base. We introduced our multi agent system, called WorkWeb, which supports office works in the sense of both group and personal works. Then, we showed that contents of agent message exchange history in this system has the possibility of generating both macro and micro scope knowledge, where macro scope and micro scope knowledge mean group level and personal level knowledge, respectively. Also we depicted four examples as both scope knowledge. Toward business knowledge base generation, we discussed that we should make a cooperative office work model and pay attention to the agent design both functions and utilization of knowledge keeping privacy in order to build agent community.

Acknowledgements

The authors would like to thank Mr. Masao Managaki , Kenji Yoshifu and Hiroyuki Tarumi for their helpful comments and discussions.

References

1. Y. Ishiguro, et al., "An Agent Architecture for Personal and Group Work Support," Proc. 2nd Int. Conf. on Multi-Agent Systems, pp. 134-141, 1996.
2. H. Tarumi, et al., " An Implementation of the WorkWeb System" (in Japanese), IPSJ SIG Notes, SIG-GW-15-22, 1996.
3. Object Management Group, The Common Object Request Broker: Architecture and Specification, 1993.
4. T. Finin and J. Weber, DRAFT Specification of the KQML Agent Communication Language, 1993.

Building Information Infrastructures for Social Worlds – The Role of Classifications and Standards

Geoffrey C. Bowker

Susan Leigh Star

Graduate School of Library and Information Science
University of Illinois at Urbana-Champaign
bowker@uiuc.edu

Abstract.   Through an analysis of information systems in medical communities – notably the development of the International Classification of Diseases and the design of a Nursing Interventions Classification scheme – we argue that community systems designers necessarily build for multiple social worlds simultaneously. So doing, we argue, they make a series of significant social and political choices. We draw some design implications from this observation: notably arguing for a sensitivity to the nature of the work of representing a community to itself.

Introduction

"A classified and hierarchically ordered set of pluralities, of variants, has none of the sting of the miscellaneous and uncoordinated plurals of our actual world." (Dewey, 1989: 49)

In the call for papers for this conference, it was noted that:
> … communityware is intended to support more diverse and amorphous groups of people. We think that communityware will become important with the advance of public communication systems such as the Internet and mobile communications. Communityware typically supports the process of organizing people who are willing to reach some mutual understanding. In other words, compared to groupware, communityware focuses on an earlier stage of collaboration: group formation from a wide variety of people.

In line with this observation, we seek to draw attention to the importance of classifications and standards as sites for mediation between the technical requirements of the systems developer and social and political requirements of the community. We argue that both designers and users need to be aware of the choices being made at this level; especially at the community level – since as more and more social worlds are drawn into a computing web ever more standards and classification schemes will be implemented. In the following paper lay a theoretical basis for such choices by asking:

* What work do classifications and standards do? We want to look at what goes into making things work like magic: making them fit together so that we can buy a radio built by someone we have never met in Japan, plug it into a wall in Champaign and hear the world news from the BBC.

* Who does that work? We want to explore the fact that all this magic involves much work: there is a lot of hard labor in effortless ease. Such invisible work is often not only underpaid - it is severely underrepresented in theoretical literature (Star and Strauss, in press). We will discuss where all the 'missing work' that makes things look magical goes.

* What happens to the cases that don't fit? We want to draw attention to cases that don't fit easily into our created world of standards and classifications: the left handers in the world of right-handed magic, chronic disease sufferers in the world of allopathic acute medicine, the onion-hater in MacDonald's (Star, 1991b) and so forth.

Through looking at classification systems and standards, we will move towards an understanding of the stuff which makes up the networks of actor network theory – a theory from the field of the sociology of knowledge which has been highly influential in describing work practices in scientific communities. Latour, Callon and others within the actor-network approach have developed an array of concepts in order to describe the development and operation of technoscience. Their valuable concepts include: regimes of delegation; the centrality of mediation; and the position that nature and society are not causes but consequences of human scientific and technical work. The position that a fact may be seen as a consequence, and not as an antecedent, is axiomatic to the American pragmatist approach as well, particularly in the work of John Dewey (e.g., Dewey, 1929).

We draw attention here to the places where the work gets done of assuring that delegation and mediation will work: to the places where human and non-human are constructed to be operationally and analytically equivalent. And following both Dewey and Latour, we also question the indifference -- of nature, and of machines. So doing, we explore the political and ethical dimensions of actor-network theory as a theory of the ways that communities (scientists, business organizations) work, restoring the interlinked and webbed relationships between people, things, and infrastructure.

Two Definitions

We will take a 'classification' to be a spatial, temporal or spatio-temporal segmentation of the world. A 'classification system' is a set of boxes, metaphorical or not, into which things can be put in order to then do some kind of work - bureaucratic or knowledge production. We will not demand of a classification system that it has properties such as:

- the operation of consistent classificatory principles (for example being solely a *genetic* classification (Tort, 1989) classifying things by their origin);
- mutual exclusivity of categories;
- completeness (total coverage of the world being described).

No working classification system that we have looked at meets these 'simple' requirements and we doubt that any ever could (Desrosieres and Thevenot, 1988).

With a broad definition we can look at the work that is involved in building and maintaining a family of entities that people call classification systems - rather than attempt the Herculean, Sisyphian task of purifying the (un)stable systems in place. Howard Becker makes the point here: "Epistemology has been a ... negative discipline, mostly devoted to saying what you shouldn't do if you want your activity to merit the title of science, and to keeping unworthy pretenders from successfully appropriating it. The sociology of science, the empirical descendant of epistemology, gives up trying to decide what should and shouldn't count as science, and tells what people who claim to be doing science do..." (1996: 54-55).

We will take a 'standard' to be any set of agreed-upon rules for the production of (textual or material) objects. There are a number of histories of standards which point to the development and maintenance of standards as being a key to industrial production. Thus, as David Turnbull points out, it was possible to build a cathedral like Chartres without standard representations (blueprints) and standard building materials (regular sizes for stones, tools etc.) (1993). However it is not possible to build a modern housing development without them: too much needs to come together - electricity, gas, sewer, timber sizes, screws, nails and so on. The control of standards is a central, often underanalyzed (but see the work of Paul David - for example David and Rothwell, 1994 - for a rich treatment) feature of economic life. They are key to knowledge production as well - Latour (1987) speculates that far more economic resources are spent creating and maintaining standards than in producing `pure' science. Key dimensions of standards are:

- They are often deployed in the context of making things work together - computer protocols for Internet communication involve a cascade of standards (cf. Abbate and Kahin, 1995) which need to work together well in order for the average user to gain seamless access to the web of information. There are standards for the components to link from your computer to the phone network, for coding and decoding binary streams as sound, for sending messages from one network to another, for attaching documents to messages and so forth;
- They are often enforced by legal bodies - be these professional organizations; manufacturers' organizations or the State. We can say

tomorrow that volapük (a universal language that boasted some 23 journals in 1889[2]) or its successor Esperanto shall henceforth be the standard language for international diplomacy; without a mechanism of enforcement we shall probably fail.

- There is no natural law that the best (technically superior) standard shall win - the QWERTY keyboard, Lotus 123, DOS and VHS are often cited in this context. Standards have significant inertia, and can be very difficult to change.

Classifications and standards are two sides of the same coin. The distinction between them (as we are defining them) is that classifications are containers for the descriptions of events - they are an aspect of organizational, social and personal memory - whereas standards are procedures for how to do things - they are an aspect of acting in the world. Every successful standard imposes a classification system.

Understanding Classifying and Standardizing

This paper will offer four major themes for understanding classifying, standardizing (and the related processes of formalizing) and their politics and histories. Each theme operates as a gestalt switch - it comes in the form of an infrastructural inversion (Bowker, 1994). Inverting our commonsense notion of infrastructure means taking what have often been seen as behind the scenes, boring, background processes to the real work of politics and knowledge production[3] and bringing their contribution to the foreground. The first two, ubiquity and material texture, speak to the *space* of actor-networks; the second two, the indeterminate past and the practical politics, speak to their *time*. Taken together, they sketch out features of the historically creation of the infrastructure which (ever partially, ever incompletely) orders the world in such a way that actor-network theory becomes a reasonable description.

The first major theme is seeing the **ubiquity** of classifying and standardizing. Classification schemes and standards literally saturate the worlds we live in. This saturation is furthermore intertwined, or webbed together. While it is possible to pull out a single classification scheme or standard for reference purposes, in reality none of them stand alone. So a subproperty of ubiquity is interdependence, if not smooth integration.

The second major theme is to see classifications and standards as **materially textured.** Under the sway of cognitivism, it is easy to see classifications as properties of mind and standards as ideal numbers or settings. But both have material force in the world, and are built into and embedded in every feature of the built environment (and many of the borderlands, such as with engineered genetic organisms). When we think of classifications and standards as material, we can afford ourselves of what we know about material structures, such as structural integrity, enclosures and confinements, permeability, and durability, among many others. We see people doing this all the time in describing organizational settings, and a common way to hear people's experience of this materiality is through metaphors. So the generation of metaphors is closely linked with the shift to texture.

The third major theme is to see **the past as indeterminate**[4]. This is not a new idea to historiography, but is important in understanding the evolution of ubiquitous classification/standardization and the multiple voices that are represented in any scheme. No one classification orders reality for everyone -- e.g. the red light-green light-yellow light categories don't work for blind people or those who are red-green color blind. In looking to classification schemes as ways of ordering the past, it is easy to forget those who are overlooked in this way. Thus, the indeterminacy of the past implies recovering multi-vocality; it also means understanding how standard narratives that seem universal have been constructed (Star, 1991a).

The fourth major theme is uncovering **the practical politics of classifying and standardizing**. There are two aspects of these politics: arriving at categories and standards, and, in the process, deciding what will be visible within the system (and of course what will thus then be invisible). The negotiated nature of standards and classifications follows from indeterminacy and multiplicity that whatever appears as universal or, indeed, standard, is the result of negotiations or conflict. How do these negotiations take place? Who determines the final outcome in preparing a formal classification? Visibility issues arise as one decides where to make the cuts in the system, for example, down to what level of detail one specifies a description of work, of an illness, of a setting. Because there are always advantages and disadvantages to being visible, this becomes crucial in the workability of the schema.

Ubiquity

In the built world we inhabit, thousands and thousands of standards are used everywhere, from setting up the plumbing in a house to assembling a car engine to transferring a file from one computer to another. Consider the canonically simple act of writing a letter longhand, putting it in an envelope and mailing it. There are standards for (inter alia): paper size, the distance that lines are apart if it is lined paper, envelope size, the glue on the envelope, the size of stamps, their glue, the ink in the pen that you wrote with, the sharpness of its nib, the composition of the paper (which in turn can be broken down to the nature of the watermark, if any; the degree of recycled material used in its production, the definition of what counts as recycling). And so forth.

A systems approach would see the proliferation of both standards and classifications as a matter of integration -- almost like a gigantic web of interoperability. Yet the sheer density of these phenomena go beyond questions of interoperability. They are layered, tangled, textured; they interact to form an ecology as well as a flat set of compatibilities. There ARE spaces between (unclassified, non-standard areas), of course, and these are equally important to the analysis. A question: it seems that increasingly these spaces are marked as unclassified and non-standard. How does that change their qualities?

It is a struggle to step back from this complexity and think about the issue of ubiquity broadly, rather than try to trace the myriad connections in any one case. We need concepts for understanding movements, textures, shifts that will grasp larger patterns in this. For instance, the distribution of residual categories ("not elsewhere classified" or "other"), is one such concept. In communities, "others" are everywhere. The analysis of any one instance of a residual category might yield information about biases or what is valued in any given circumstance; seeing that residual categories are ubiquitous offers a much more general sweep on the categorizing tendencies of most modern cultures. Another class of concepts which are found ubiquitously, and which speak to the general pervasiveness of standards and classification schemes, concern those which describe tangles or mismatches between subsystems. For instance, what Strauss calls a "cumulative mess trajectory" is a useful notion (Strauss, et al., 1985). In medicine, this occurs when one has an illness, is given a medicine to cure the illness, but incurs a serious side effect, which then needs to be treated with another medicine, etc. If the trajectory becomes so tangled that you can't return and the interactions multiply, cumulative mess results. We see this phenomenon in the interaction of categories and standards all the time -- ecological examples are particularly rich places to look.

In terms of designing community computing systems, this ubiquity underlines the fact that such systems necessarily radically interpenetrate the community that they are designed for – and so change the very nature of that community in the process of their implementation.

Texturing Classification and Standardization

How do we 'see' this densely saturated classified world which constitutes and is constituted by communties? We are commonly used to casually black-boxing this behind-the-scenes machinery, even to the point, as we noted above, of ascribing a casual magic to it. All classification and standardization schemes are a mixture of physical entities such as paper forms, plugs, or software instructions encoded in silicon and conventional arrangements such as speed and rhythm, dimension, and how specifications are implemented. Perhaps because of this mixture, the web of intertwined schemes can be difficult to 'see.' In general, the trick is to question every apparently natural easiness in the world around us and look for the work involved in making it easy. Within a project or on a desktop, the seeing consists in seamlessly moving between the physical and the conventional. So when a computer programmer writes some lines of Java code, she moves within conventional constraints and makes innovations based on them; at the same time, she strikes plastic keys, shifts notes around on a desktop, and consults manuals for various standards and other information. If we were to try to list out all the classifications and standards involved in writing a program, the list could run to pages. Classifications include types of objects, types of hardware, matches between requirements categories and code categories, and meta-categories such as the goodness of fit of the piece of code with the larger system under development. Standards range from the precise integration of the underlying hardware to the 60Hz power coming out of the wall through a standard size plug.

Merely reducing the description to the physical aspect such as the plugs does not get us anywhere interesting in terms of the actual mixture of physical and conventional. A good operations researcher could describe how and whether things would work together, often purposefully blurring the physical/conventional boundaries in making the analysis. But what is missing there is a sense of the landscape of work as experienced by those within it. It gives no sense of something as important as the texture of an organization: it is smooth or rough? Bare or knotty? What is needed is a sense of the topography of all of the arrangements -- are they colliding? co-extensive? gappy? orthogonal? One way to begin to get at these questions is to begin to take quite literally the kinds of metaphors that people use when describing their experience of organizations, bureaucracies, and information systems (Star, in press). As Schon pointed out in his seminal book, *Displacement of Concepts,* a metaphor is an import, meant to illuminate aspects of a current situation via juxtaposition (1963). It is also a rich and often unmined source of knowledge about people's experience of the densely classified world. Designers of community systems need to be able to draw on and elaborate the metaphor systems employed by the communities they are designing for.

The Indeterminacy of the Past

There is no way of ever getting access to the past except through classification systems of one sort or another - formal or informal, hierarchical or not ... . Take the unproblematic statement: "In 1640, the English Revolution occurred; this led to a twenty year period in which the English had no monarchy". The classifications involved here include:

- The current segmentation of time into days, months and years. Accounts of the English revolution generally use the Gregorian calendar, which was adopted some hundred years later - so causing translation problems with contemporary documents;
- The classification of peoples into English, Irish, Scots, French and so on. These designations were by no means so clear at the time - the whole discourse of national genius really only arose in the nineteenth century;
- The classification of events into revolutions, reforms, revolts, rebellions and so forth (cf. Furet, 1978 on thinking the French revolution). There really was no concept of `revolution' at the time; our current conception is marked by the historiographical work of Karl Marx.
- And then, what do we classify as being a monarchy? There is a strong historiographical tradition which says that Oliver Cromwell was a monarch - he walked, talked and acted like one after all. Under this view, there is no hiatus at all in this English institution; rather a usurper took the throne.

There are two major schools of thought with respect to using classification systems on the past - one saying that we should only use classifications available to actors at the time (authors in this tradition warn against the dangers of anachronism - Hacking (1995) on child abuse is a sophisticated version) and the other that we should use the real classifications that progress in the arts and sciences has uncovered (typically history informed by current sociology will take this path - for example Tort's (1989) work on 'genetic' classification systems, which were not so called at the time, but which are of vital interest to the Foucaldian problematic). Whichever we choose, it is clear that we should always understand classification systems according to the work that they are doing -the network within which they are embedded. For practical purposes in the design of community support systems, it means that new members of social worlds entering a community computing space will often find it extremely difficult to represent their own past and developing traditions within that space: they will feel pressure to reinterpret their own pasts according to the schemas available, or will exert pressure to change those schemas.

Practical Politics

Someone, somewhere, often a body of people in the proverbial gray suits and smoke-filled rooms, must decide and argue over the minutiae of classifying and standardizing without which community computing would be impossible. The negotiations themselves form the basis for a fascinating practical ontology -- our favorite example within the medical community is when is someone really alive? Is it breathing, attempts at breathing, movement ....? And how long must each of those last? Whose voice will determine the outcome is sometimes an exercise of pure power: we, the holders of Western medicine and of colonialism, will decide what a disease is, and simply obviate systems such as acupuncture or Ayruvedic medicine. Sometimes the negotiations are more subtle, involving questions such as the disparate viewpoints of an immunologist and a surgeon, or a public health official (interested in even ONE case of the plague) and a statistician (for whom one case is not relevant) (Neumann and Star, 1996).

Once a system is in place, the practical politics of these decisions are often forgotten, literally buried in archives (when records are kept at all) or built into software or the sizes and compositions of things. In addition to our archaeological expeditions into the records of such negotiations, we provide here some observations of the negotiations in action. Finally, even where everyone agrees on the way the classifications or standards should be established, there are often practical difficulties about how to craft their architecture. For example, a classification system with 20,000 "bins" on every form is practically unusable. (The original International Classification of Diseases had some 200 diseases not because of the nature of the human body and its problems but because this was the maximum number that would fit the large census sheets then in use). Sometimes the decision about how fine-grained to make the system has political consequences as well. For instance, in describing and recording the tasks someone does, as in the case of nursing work, may mean controlling or surveilling their work as well, and may imply an attempt to take away discretion. After all, the loosest classification of work is accorded to those with the most power and discretion, who are able to set their own terms.

These ubiquitous, textured classifications and standards help frame our representation of the past and the sequencing of events in the present. They can best be understood as doing the ever-local, ever-partial work of making it appear that science describes nature (and nature alone) and that politics is about social power (and social power alone). Consider the case discussed at length by Young (1995) and Kirk and Kutchins (1992) of psychoanalysts who in order to receive reimbursement for this procedures need to couch them in a biomedical language (the DSM) that is anathema to them, but is the lingua franca of the medical insurance companies. There are local translation mechanisms that allow the DSM to continue to operate and to provide the sole legal, recognized representation of mental disorder. A 'reverse engineering' of the DSM or the ICD reveals the multitude of local political and social struggles and compromises which go into the constitution of a 'universal' classification.

Community support systems designers make a series of relatively irreversible decisions when they are forced to decide between conflicting representational structures (espoused by conflicting social worlds). These decisions need to be made in full recognition of this fact – and so to be made both as open and as reversible as possible.

Infrastructure Actor Network Theory, and Community Systems

We have, then, looked briefly at the space and time of the infrastructures that subtend community support systems. Our position is that through due attention to these infrastructures, we can achieve an understanding of how it is that actor network theory comes to be a useful way of describing the nature of knowledge work on the one hand and the (increasing) convergence of human and non-human on the other.

The converging sameness of humans and non-humans, and in general the construction of a world in which actor-network theory is true, is a political and ethical question. Work by scholars such as Joan Fujimura (1991), Valerie Singleton and Mike Michael (1993) and Leigh Star (1991b; 1995) has pointed to the fact that actor-network theory can be read as an uncritical *celebration* of the power of modern science and technology. There are certainly readings of Latour's *Science in Action* or *The Pasteurization of France* which could support such an assertion. Through our concentration on the work of standardization and classification - a concentration fully consonant with the analysis of Latour and Callon - we are pointing to a place where actor-network theory can be further developed; and to a place where its political side meets its philosophical underpinnings.

In order to clarify our position here, let us take an analogy. In the early nineteenth century in England there were a huge number of capital crimes - starting from stealing a loaf of bread and going up.... . However, precisely because the penalties were so draconian, few juries would ever impose the maximum sentence; and indeed there was actually a drastic reduction in the number of executions even as the penal code was progressively strengthened. There are two ways of writing this history - one can either concentrate on the creation of the law; or one can concentrate on the way things worked out in practice. This is very similar to the position taken in Latour's *We have never been modern*: where he says we can either look at what scientists say that they are doing (working within a purified realm of knowledge) or at what they actually are doing (manufacturing hybrids). Actor network theory has looked in detail at the role of relatively black-boxed hybrids in creating the discourse of pure science as endpoint; we are advocating a development of the theory that pays more attention to the classification and standardization work that allows for hybrids to be manufactured and so explores the terrain of the politics of science in action. Further, we are arguing that we need to look at precisely this level of analysis in order to build effective community support systems.

The point for us is that both of these are valid kinds of account. Early actor-network theory concentrated on the ways in which it comes to seem that science gives an objective account of natural order: trials of strength, enrolling of allies, cascades of inscriptions and the operation of immutable mobiles. It drew attention to the importance of the development of standards (though not to the linked development of classification systems); but did not look at these in detail. We were invited to look at the process of producing something which looked like what the positivists alleged science to be. We got to see the 'Janus face' of science. In so doing we `followed the actors'. We shared their insights (allies must be enrolled, translation mechanisms must be set in train so that, in the canonical case, Pasteur's laboratory work can be seen as a direct translation of the quest for French honor after defeat in the battlefield).

However, by the very nature of the method, we also shared their blindness. The actors being followed did not *see* what was excluded: they constructed a world in which that exclusion could occur. Thus if we just follow the doctors who create the International Classification of Diseases at the World Health Organization in Geneva, we will not see the variety of representation systems that other cultures have for classifying diseases of the body and spirit; and we will not see the fragile networks these classification systems subtend. Rather, we will see only those actants who are strong enough, and shaped in the right way, to impact the fragile actor-networks of allopathic medicine. We will see the blind leading the blind.

We ascribe to Latour's (1987) definition of reality as 'that which resists' (again, a concept with strong American pragmatist resonances, se e.g. Dewey, 1916). The actor-network will be changed by the resistances that it encounters. We have suggested that the work of dealing with resistance is twofold:

- Changing the world such that the actor-network's description of reality becomes true. Thus if all diseases (of the mind and body) are classified purely physiologically and systems of medical observation and treatment are set up such the physical manifestations are the only manifestations recorded and physical treatments are the only treatments available then it is of course possible that the world will be such that schizophrenia, say, results purely and simply from a chemical imbalance in the brain. It will be impossible to think or act otherwise. We have called this the principle of *convergence* (Star and Bowker, 1994; Neumann, Bowker and Star, in press). Thus the community's view works, through the community support system, to change the world such that its vision is accurate.

* Distributing the resistance in such a way that it becomes marginalized and can be overlooked. Here the community though its community support system works to mark dissenting views as non-significant.

A good example of responses to resistances comes from the nursing administrators we are studying at present. We will see how they are producing a classification of nursing work whose political edge is in the technical work of meshing this classification system with those already operating within the sociotechnical framework of the hospital. There is a play of resistances around this political of representation.

The Iowa Intervention Team are producing a classification of all nursing work - a nursing interventions classification (NIC) (McCloskey and Bulechek, 1996). NIC itself is a fascinating system. Those of us studying it see it as an ethnomethodological nirvana. Some categories, like *bleeding reduction - nasal*, are on the surface relatively obvious and codable into discrete units of work practice to be carried out on specific occasions. But what about the equally important categories of hope installation and humor? Hope installation includes the subcategory of 'Avoid masking the truth.' This is not so much something that nurses do on a regular basis, as something that they should not do constantly. It also includes: 'Help the patient expand spiritual self.' Here the contribution that the nurse is making is to an implicit lifelong program of spiritual development. With respect to humor, the very definition of the category suggests the operation of a paradigm shift: "Facilitating the patient to perceive, appreciate, and express what is funny, amusing, or ludicrous in order to establish relationships"; and it is unclear how this could ever be attached to a time line: it is something the nurse should always do while doing other things. Further, contained within the nursing classification is an anatomy of what it is to be humorous, and a theory of what humor does. The recommended procedures break humor down into subelements. One should determine the types of humor appreciated by the patient; determine the patient's typical response to humor (e.g. laughter or smiles); select humorous materials that create moderate arousal for the individual (for example 'picture a forbidding authority figure dressed only in underwear'); encourage silliness and playfulness and so on to make a total of fifteen sub-activities: any one of which might be scientifically relevant. A feature traditionally attached to the personality of the nurse (being a cheerful and supportive person) is now attached through the classification to the job description as an intervention which can be accounted for.

Within the context of the hospital's sociotechnical system, nursing work has been deemed irrelevant to any possible future reconstruction; it has been canonically invisible, in Star's (1991a) term. The logic of NIC's advocators is that what has been excluded from the representational space of medical practice should be included. The Iowa group, the kernel of whom were teachers of nursing administration, made essentially three arguments for the creation of a nursing classification. First, it was argued that without a standard language to describe nursing interventions, there would be no way of producing a scientific body of knowledge about nursing. NIC in theory would be articulated with two other classification systems: NOC (the nursing sensitive patient outcomes classification scheme) and NANDA (the nursing diagnosis scheme). The three could work together thusly. One could perform studies over a set of hospitals employing the three schemes in order to check if a given category of patient responded well to a given category of nursing intervention. Rather than this comparative work being done anecdotally as in the past through the accumulation of experience, it could be done scientifically through the conduct of experiments. The Iowa Intervention project made up a jingle: NANDA, NIC and NOC to the tune of Hickory, Dickory, Dock to stress this interrelationship of the three schemes. The second argument for classifying nursing interventions was that it was a key strategy for defending the professional autonomy of nursing. The Iowa nurses are very aware of the literature on professionalization - notably Schon (1983) - and are aware of the force of having an accepted body of scientific knowledge as their domain. (Indeed Andrew Abbott, taking as his central case the professionalization of medicine, makes this one of his key attributes of a profession [1988].) The third argument was that nursing, alongside other medical professions, was moving into the new world of computers. As the representational medium changed, it was important to be able to talk about nursing in a language that computers could understand - else nursing work would not be represented at all in the future, and would risk being even further marginalized than it was at present.

However, there is also a danger in representing. It is more difficult to hive off aspects of nursing duties and give them to lower paid adjuncts, if nursing work is relatively opaque. The test sites that are implementing NIC have provided some degree of resistance here, arguing that activities should be specified - so that, within a soft decision support model a given diagnosis can trigger a nursing intervention constituted of a single, well-defined set of activities. As Marc Berg (1996) has noted in his study of medical expert systems, such decision support can only work universally if local practices are rendered fully standard. A key professional strategy for nursing - particularly in the face of the ubiquitous process re-engineer - is realized by deliberate non-representation in the information infrastructure. What is remembered in the formal information systems resulting is attuned to professional strategy and to the information requisites of the nurses' take on what nursing science is.

Further, there is a brick wall that they come up against when dealing with nurses on the spot: if they overspecify an intervention (that is break it down into too many constituent parts), then it gets called, in the field, an NSS classification - where NSS stands for 'No shit, Sherlock' and is not used (Bowker, Star and Timmermans, 1996). It is assumed that any reasonable education in nursing or medicine should lead to a common language wherein things do not need spelling out to the ultimate degree. The information space will be sufficiently well pre-structured that some details can be assumed. Attention to the finer-grained details is delegated to the educational system, where it is overdetermined.

These NIC-related strategies of dealing with overspecification and the political drive to relative autonomy by dropping things out of the representational space - are essential for the development of a successful actor-network system that includes nursing. These two forms of erasure of local context are needed in order to create the very infrastructure in which nursing can both appear as a science like any other and yet nursing as a profession can continue to develop as a rich, local practice. The ongoing erasure is guaranteed by the classification system: only information about nursing practice recognized by NIC can be coded on the forms fed into a hospital's computers or stored in a file cabinet.

Nursing informaticians agree as a body that in order for proper health care to be given and for nurses to be recognized as a profession, hospitals as organizations should code for nursing within the framework of their memory systems: nursing work should be classified and forms should be generated which utilize these classifications. However, there has been disagreement with respect to strategy. To understand the difference that has emerged, recall one of those forms you have filled in (we have all experienced one) which do not allow you to say what you think. You may, in a standard case, have been offered a choice of several racial origins; but may not believe in any such categorization. There is no room on the form to write an essay on race identity politics. So you either you make an uncomfortable choice in order to get counted, and hope that enough of your complexity will be preserved by your set of answers to the form; or you don't answer the question and perhaps decide to devote some time to lobbying the producers of the offending form to reconsider their categorization of people. The NIC group has wrestled with the same strategic choice: fitting their classification system into the Procrustean bed of all the other classification systems that they have to articulate with in any given medical setting in order to form part a given organization's potential memory; or rejecting the ways in which memory is structured in the organizations that they are dealing with. We will now look in turn at each of these strategies.

Let us look first at the argument for including NIC within the information infrastructural framework of the hospital's sociotechnical system. They argue that NIC has to respond to multiple important agendas simultaneously. The development of a new information infrastructure for nursing, heralded, will make nursing more `memorable'. It will also lead to a clearance of past nursing knowledge - henceforth prescientific - from the textbooks; it will lead to changes in the practice of nursing (a redefinition of disciplinary boundaries) - a shaping of nursing so that future practice converges on its representation.

Many nurses and nursing informaticians are concerned that the profession itself may have to change too much in order to meet the requirements of the information infrastructure. We murder, they note, to dissect. In her study of nursing information systems in France, Ina Wagner (1993) speaks as follows of the gamble of computerizing nursing records:

Nurses might gain greater recognition for their work and more control over the definition of patients' problems while finding out that their practice is increasingly shaped by the necessity to comply with regulators' and employers' definitions of 'billable categories.'

Indeed, a specific feature of this 'thought world' into which nurses are gradually socialized through the use of computer systems is the integration of management criteria into the practice of nursing. She continues: "Working with a patient classification system with time units associated with each care activity enforces a specific time discipline on nurses. They learn to assess patients' needs in terms of working time." This analytic perspective is shared by the Iowa nurses. They argue that documentation is centrally important; it not only provides a record of nursing activity but structures same:

> While nurses do complain about paperwork, they structure their care so that the required forms get filled out. If the forms reflect a philosophy of the nurse as a dependent assistant to the doctor who delivers technical care in a functional manner, this is to some extent the way the nurse will act. If the forms reflect a philosophy of the nurse as a professional member of the health team with a unique independent function, the nurse will act accordingly. (Bulechek and McCloskey, 1985: 406).

As the NIC classification has developed, observes Joanne McCloskey, the traditional category of 'nursing process' has been replaced by 'clinical decision making plus knowledge classification'. And in a representation of NIC that she produced both the patient and the nurse had dropped entirely out of the picture (both were, she said, located within the 'clinical decision making box' on her diagram) (Iowa Intervention Project meeting, 6/8/95). A recent book about the next generation nursing information system argued that the new system:

> A dominant feature of the new system is its focus on the acquisition, management, processing, and presentation of 'atomic-level' data that can be used across multiple settings for multiple purposes. The paradigm shift to a data-driven system represents a new generation of information technology; it provides strategic resources for clinical nursing practice, rather than just support for various nursing tasks. (Zielstorff et al., 1993, 1).

This speaks to the progressive denial of process and continuity through the segmentation of nursing practice into activity units. Many argue that in order to `speak with' databases at a national and international level just such segmentation is needed. The fear is that unless nurses can describe their process this way (at the risk of losing the essence of that process in the description), then it will not be described at all. They can only have there own actions remembered at the price of having others forget, and possibly forgetting themselves, precisely what it is that they do.

Some nursing informaticians have chosen instead to challenge the informational framework existing in the medical organizations they deal with. They have adopted a Batesonian strategy of responding to the threat of the new information infrastructure by moving the whole argument up one level of generality and trying to supplant 'data-driven' categories with categories that recognize process on their own terms. They draw from their secret (because unrepresented) reservoir of knowledge about process in order to challenge the data-driven models from within.

Within this strategy, the choice of allies is by no means obvious. Since with the development of NIC we are dealing with the creation of an information infrastructure, the whole question of how and what to challenge becomes very difficult. Scientists can only, willy nilly, deal with data as presented to them by their information base, just as historians of previous centuries must, alas, rely on written traces. When creating a new information infrastructure for an old activity, questions have a habit of running away from one: a technical issue about how to code process can become a challenge to organizational theory (and its database). A defense of process can become an attack on the scientific world view. One of the chief attacks on the NIC scheme has been made by a nursing informatician, Susan Grobe, who believes that rather than standardize nursing language computer scientists should develop natural language processing tools so that nurse narratives can be interpreted. Grobe argues for the abandonment of any goal of producing: "A single coherent account of the pattern of action and beliefs in science" (1992, 92); she goes on to say that: "philosophers of science have long acknowledged the value of a multiplicity of scientific views" (92). She excoriates Bulechek and McCloskey, architects of NIC, for having produced work: "derived from the natural science view with its hierarchical structures and mutually exclusive and distinct categories." (93). She on the other hand is drawing from cognitive science, library science and social science (94). When the infrastructure is not in place to provide a 'natural' hierarchy of levels, then discourses can and do make strange connections between themselves.

If they want to prove a case within a given hospital for the opening-up of a new nursing position, they need to demonstrate that nursing is cost-effective according to the dominant accountancy paradigm. Now they in fact disagree with this paradigm (arguing, for example, that 'quality of care' is not quantifiable but is still significant); and yet they feel that they must act *as if* they accept it - or else their voice will not be heard at all. In order to not be continually erased from the record, nursing informaticians are risking either modifying their own practice (making it more data driven) or waging a Quixotic war on database designers. The corresponding gain is great, however. If the infrastructure itself is designed in such a way that nursing information has to be present as an independent, well defined category, then nursing itself as a profession will have a much better chance of surviving through rounds of process re-engineering and nursing science as a discipline will have a firm foundation. The infrastructure assumes the position of Bishop Berkeley's God: as long as it pays attention to nurses, they will continue to exist. Having ensured that all nursing acts are potentially remembered by any medical organization, the NIC team will have gone a long way to ensuring the future of nursing. Standards and classifications – crucial to the development of community support systems - however dry and formal on the surface are suffused with traces of political and social work.

Conclusion

We have argued that community systems are of necessity social and political systems as well as technical infrastructures. We have developed the position that where the rubber hits the road in terms of the enfolding of community values into community information systems is at the point of the development of classifications and standards. This incursion of the political and social into computer science is not a negative feature to be eschewed: it is a necessary feature of moving between multiple social worlds – which we must do if our systems are ever to scale up outside of particular interest groups.

The design task is a difficult but one but bears great promise. As we build computing infrastructures for communities we enter into and transform the life of those communities. So doing, we need to understand not only 'information needs' in a superficial sense – we need a deep understanding of the structure and nature of the community we are building for, and of the ways it represents itself, others, and the past. The magic of modern technoscience is a lot of hard work.

References

Abbate, J. and Kahin, B. (eds). 1995. *Standards Policy for Information Infrastructure.* Cambridge, Ma : MIT Press.

Abbott, A. 1988.*The System of Professions: An Essay on the Division of Expert Labor.* Chicago: University of Chicago Press.

Baudrillard, Jean. 1990. *Cool Memories .* New York: Verso.

Becker, H.S. 1996. `The epistemology of qualitative research' in R. Jessor, A. Colby and R. A. Shweder, eds*., Ethnography and human development; Context and meaning in social inquiry,* Chicago: University of Chicago. pp. 53-71.

Berg, M. 1996. *Rationalizing medical work - decision support techniques and medical problems.* Cambridge, MA: MIT Press.

Bowker, Geoffrey C. 1994. *Science on the run: Information management and industrial geophysics at Schlumberger, 1920-1940.* Cambridge, MA: MIT Press.

Bowker, Geoffrey C. and Star, Susan Leigh. (1994). Knowledge and Infrastructure in international information management: Problems of classification and coding. In L. Bud-Frierman (ed), *Information acumen: The understanding and use of knowledge in modern business* (Pp.187-216). London: Routledge.

Bowker, G., Star, SUSAN LEIGH. and Timmermans, S. 1996. "Infrastructure and Organizational Transformation: Classifying Nurses' Work." In W. Orlikowski, G. Walsham, M. Jones and J. DeGross, eds. *Information technology and changes in organizational work.* (*Proceedings* IFIP WG8.2 Conference, Cambridge, England.) (Pp. 344-370) London: Chapman and Hall.

Bulechek, G. and McCloskey, J. 1985. "Future Directions." In Gloria M. Bulechek, Joanne C. McCloskey, *Nursing Interventions: Treatments for Nursing Diagnoses* (Pp.401-408). Philadelphia, PA: Saunders.

Callon, M. 1986. "Some elements of a sociology of translation." In John Law (ed.), *Power, Action, and Belief: A New Sociology of Knowledge?* (Pp. 196-233). London: Routledge and Kegan Paul.

Castles, M.R. 1981. "Nursing Diagnosis: Standardization of Nomenclature." In H. H. Werley and M. R. Grier (eds), *Nursing information systems* (Pp. 36-44), New York: Springer.

David, P. and Rothwell, G. S. 1994. *Standardization, Diversity and Learning: Strategies for the Coevolution of Technology and Industrial Capacity.* Stanford, CA: Center for Economic Policy Research, Stanford University.

Desrosieres, A. and Thevenot, L. 1988. *Les Categories Socio-professionnelles*. Paris: Decouverte.

Dewey, John. 1916. *Logic: The theory of Inquiry*. New York: Holt, Rinehart and Winston.

Dewey, John. 1929. *The Quest for Certainty*. NY: Open Court.

Dewey, John. 1989. [Originally published in 1925). *Experience and Nature*. La Salle, IL: Open Court Press.

Cody, W. 1995. "Letter from William K. Cody." *Nursing outlook* (Pp.93-94), 43 (2).

Fujimura, Joan. 1991. "On Methods, Ontologies, and Representation in the Sociology of Science: Where do we stand?" In David Maines (ed.) *Social Organization and Social Process: Essays in Honor of Anselm L. Strauss*. Hawthorne, NY: Aldine de Gruyter.

Furet, Francois. 1978. *Penser la Revolution Francaise*. Paris: Gallimard.

Grobe, S. 1992. "Response to J.C. McCloskey's and G.M. Bulechek's Paper on Nursing Intervention Scheme." In The Canadian Nurses Association, *Papers from the Nursing Minimum Data Set Conference, October 27-29, 1992*, Edmonton, Alberta: The Canadian Nurses Association.

Hacking, Ian. 1995. *Rewriting the Soul: Multiple Personality and the Sciences of Memory*. Princeton, N.J.: Princeton University Press.

Huffman, E. 1990. *Medical Record Management*. Berwyn, IL: Physicians' Record Company.

Hutchins, E. 1995. *Cognition in the Wild*. Cambridge, MA: MIT Press.

ICD-10. 1992. *ICD-10. International Statistical Classification of Diseases and Related Health Problems, tenth revision*, Volume 1. Geneva: World Health Organization.

Jenkins, T. 1988. "New Roles for Nursing Professionals." In M.J.Ball, K.J. Hannah, U. Gerdin Jelger, H. Peterson (eds), *Nursing Informatics: Here caring and technology meet* (Pp.88-95). NY: Springer.

Kirk, S. A. and Kutchins, H. 1992. *The Selling of DSM: The Rhetoric of Science in Psychiatry* . New York: A. de Gruyter.

Latour, Bruno. 1987. *Science in Action: How to Follow Scientists and Engineers through Society*. Milton Keynes: Open University Press.

Latour, Bruno. 1993. *We Have Never Been Modern*. Cambridge, Mass. : Harvard University Press.

Latour, B. 1996a. *Aramis or the Love of Technology*. Cambridge, MA: Harvard University Press.

Latour, B. 1996b. *Petite Reflexion sur le Culte Moderne des Dieux Faitiches*. Paris: Les Empecheurs de Penser en Rond.

Latour, B. forthcoming. "Did Ramses II die of tuberculosis? On the partial existence of existing *and* non-existing objects." Typescript from author.

McCloskey, J. and Bulechek, G. 1996. *Iowa Intervention Project - Nursing Interventions Classification*. NIC Second Edition. St Louis, MO: Mosby.

MacKenzie, Donald A. 1990. *Inventing accuracy: an historical sociology of nuclear missile guidance* . Cambridge, MA : MIT Press.

Neumann, L. J. and Star, S. L. 1996. "Making Infrastructure: The Dream of a Common Language." *Proceedings of PDC `96 (Participatory Design Conference)*, Eds. J. Blomberg, F. Kensing and E. Dykstra-Erickson. Palo Alto, CA: Computer Professionals for Social Responsibility, pp. pp. 231-240.

Neumann, L., Star, Susan Leigh., and Bowker, Geoffrey C. In press. "Information convergence." Submitted to *Journal of the American Society for Information Science (JASIS)*.

Proust, Marcel. 1989 *A la recherche du Temps Perdu, tome iv*, Paris: Pleiade.

Schon, D. 1983. *The Reflective Practitioner: How Professionals Think in Action.* New York: Basic Books.

Schon, D. 1963. Displacement of concepts. London: Tavistock Publications.

Serres, Michel. 1993. *Les Origines de la Geometrie.* Paris: Flammarion.

Singleton, V. and M. Michael. 1993. "Actor-networks and ambivalence: General practitioners in the UK Cervical Screening Programme." *Social Studies of Science* 23: 227-64.

Star, Susan Leigh. 1989. *Regions of the Mind: Brain Research and the Quest for Scientific Certainty.* Stanford, CA: Stanford University Press.

Star, Susan Leigh. 1991a. The Sociology of the invisible: The primacy of work in the writings of Anselm Strauss. In David Maines (Ed.), *Social Organization and Social Process: Essays in Honor of Anselm Strauss* (Pp.265-283). Hawthorne, NY: Aldine de Gruyter.

Star, Susan Leigh. 1991b. "Power, technologies and the phenomenology of standards: On being allergic to onions." In *A Sociology of Monsters? Power, Technology and the Modern World,* John Law (ed.), Sociological Review Monograph. (Pp. 27-57). No. 38, 1991. Oxford: Basil Blackwell.

Star, Susan Leigh. 1995a Introduction. In Susan Leigh Star (ed.) *Ecologies of knowledge: Work and politics in science and technology.* Albany, NY: SUNY Press.

Star, Susan Leigh. 1995b. "The Politics of Formal Representations: Wizards, Gurus and Organizational Complexity." Pp. 88-118 in Susan Leigh Star (ed.). *Ecologies of knowledge: Work and politics in science and technology.* Albany, NY: SUNY Press.

Star, Susan Leigh. In press. "Leaks of Experience: The Link between Science and Knowledge." To appear in Shelley Goldman and James Greeno (eds). *Thinking Practices.* Hillsdale, NJ: Lawrence Erlbaum Associates.

Star, Susan Leigh and Geoffrey C. Bowker. 1997. "Of Lungs and Lungers: The Classified Story of Tuberculosis." *Mind, Culture and Activity.*

Star, Susan Leigh and Anselm L. Strauss. In press. Layers of Silence, Arenas of Voice: The dialogues between visible and invisible work. In B. Nardi and Y. Engeström (eds.). *A Web on the Wind: The Structure of Invisible Work.*

Strauss, Anselm, S. Fagerhaugh, B. Suczek and C. Wiener. 1985. *Social Organization of Medical Work.* Chicago: University of Chicago Press.

Tort, Patrick. 1989. *La Raison Classificatoire: les Complexes Discursifs: Quinze Etudes* Paris: Aubier.

Turnbull, David. 1993. "The Ad Hoc Collective Work of Building Gothic Cathedrals with Templates, String, and Geometry." In *Science, Technology, & Human Values.* (Pp. 315-343). Vol. 18(3).

Wagner, I., 1993. "Women's voice: The Case of Nursing Information Systems." In *AI and society.* Vol. 7(4).

Weick, K.E. and Roberts, K.H., 1993. "Collective Mind in Organizations: Heedful interrelating on flight decks. In *Administrative science quarterly* (Pp.357-381). Vol. 38.

Young, A. *The Harmony of Illusions: Inventing Post-traumatic Stress Disorder .* Princeton, N.J. : Princeton University Press.

Zielstorff, R.D., Hudgings, C.I., Grobe, S. J.and The National Commission on Nursing Implementation Project (NCNIP) Task Force on Nursing Information Systems. 1993. *Next-Generation Nursing Information Systems: Essential Characteristics For Professional Practice.* Washington, DC: American Nurses Publishing.

Interactional Resources for the Support of Collaborative Activities: Common Problems in the Design of Technologies to Support Groups and Communities

Paul Luff and Marina Jirotka

King's College, London and University of Oxford, UK.

Abstract

A typical challenge for designers of technologies to support groups and communities is how to support the early stages of interaction and collaboration. Whether the system is for individuals in an organisational setting or for more 'diverse and amorphous groups of people', a common problem is for the technology to facilitate individuals getting together to accomplish more focused collaborative activities. In this paper we will explore how in work settings, individuals use various resources including talk and visual conduct to move into participation with others around an artefact. Explicating these interactional resources offers some useful insights into the requirements of technologies to support emergent interactions. It also reveals that in everyday work settings participation and interaction can be amorphous and diverse.

1.   Introduction

Although it may appear one of the more straightforward features for a collaborative system to support, providing a suitable environment in which groups of participants can collaborate and interact is deeply problematic. Even simple video links, such as those explored within CSCW, transform the domain in which interactions take place (Heath and Luff, 1992b). In technologies such as media spaces, participants are no longer able to rely on the interactional resources, such as the design and receipt of gestures or the production of a glance, they utilise in everyday co-present interaction. This has been one of the motivations for researchers to explore more radical technological possibilities for providing spaces in which distributed individuals can work and interact. In CSCW, and the emerging body of work in community support systems, system designers have been developing Collaborative Virtual Environments (or CVEs) in which spaces are developed where representations of the participants (so-called 'avatars' or 'embodiments') come together to interact and collaborate (e.g. Benford and Fahlén, 1993). However, rather than circumventing the everyday interactional resources of participants, these developments appear to require an understanding of such resources. The representations on the screen have to move in particular ways, be positioned in various orientations and be tied to the talk of the participants and their other activities. Even if developers wish to devise spaces in which innovative forms of interaction can take place, preliminary observations appear to show that participants in these virtual spaces are attempting to make use of everyday resources to both make sense of and produce conduct in these domains (Bowers, et al., 1995).

In this paper we wish to explore the nature of the resources that individuals rely on in everyday interactions. Taking a few instances of naturally-occurring activities drawn from ordinary work settings, we consider whether recent approaches to the study of social interactions could provide some resources for designers of technologies, such as CSCW and community support systems. To provide a focus for this consideration we examine the resources utilised by participants when they move into work on and around a common artefact: the kind of occasion when individuals come together to discuss a common issue or problem. For example, this could be when journalists begin to discuss an emerging story in a newsroom, engineers consider some technical problem on some equipment in a maintenance centre or individuals in an office try to cope with some difficulty which appears on a computer screen. Although this domain of concern may appear rather arbitrary, we hope it suggests the nature of the resources, their talk, body orientations and other visual conduct that participants utilise in social interaction. This could, at least, imply some possibilities when considering the features which could be available in technologies to support communities, how these might be interrelated and the ways in which virtual environments could allow for dynamic and flexible interactions.

Even if less sophisticated technologies are considered, exploring the details of everyday social interaction may be of interest. Indeed, given the focus of many in this volume on supporting the formation of communities rather than on supporting the activities in those communities once they have been formed, it might be useful to explore the resources individuals utilise to move into co-participation. It may be that even when exploring enhancements to text-based computer-mediated communication, developers could consider the ways the technology could allow users to delicately move into an interaction and provide them with different ways of being able to participate (cf. Jirotka et al. 1991). Moreover, when designing agents which need to 'interact' with users it may be useful to consider how these could be made sensitive to the users' concerns, particularly when these systems can be used by individuals who may also be interacting, in quite different ways, with co-present colleagues (cf. Nagao and Katsuno this volume, Van de Velde this volume).

For our analysis, we draw on a growing body of work which has used audio-visual recordings of everyday activities in order to reveal how social interactions emerge. Using activities taken from three quite distinct settings, architectural practices, financial dealing rooms and control rooms, we outline the resources used for the moment-to-moment production of collaborative activities. In particular, we consider the details of how talk, glances and changes in body orientation, and activities surrounding artefacts are interrelated. From these initial investigations it may be possible to draw out some requirements for developers of new technologies and we briefly suggest some resources that might be of relevance to designers of community support systems. Of course, this is not to suggest that the aim of such technologies should be merely to reproduce or replicate resources utilised in social interactions. It is hard to conceive of a technology that could allow for, let alone simulate, the richness and delicacy of social interaction. More importantly, it may lead to a reconsideration of the types of capabilities that such technologies are aiming to support and to a rethinking of the conceptions that underpin the developments not only of systems to support communities but of other areas where support for collaboration and interaction is a concern.

To provide a background, we will first briefly review some of the motivations behind our approach and why it may be relevant to developers of systems to support communities. There are numerous orientations that can be taken to the analysis of social conduct, and particularly to social interaction. We outline some of the critical features of the orientation which has underpinned a growing body of work in CSCW, and show some of the relevancies of this to community support systems.

2. Background

In some ways, developers of collaborative technologies, such as CVEs, have already been drawing upon understandings of social interaction in their recent designs. For example, the representations of users on the screen often can be moved and oriented to, to give the sense of features of social interaction. Indeed, several systems have been augmented by several rather crude devices to assist users overcoming various communicative problems that occur in the virtual space (Benford and Fahlén, 1993). Images of faces have been provided with representations of mouths which move when a user is talking. These can give a sense of who is speaking and some assistance when trying to take turns of talk. It is hoped that such capabilities will enable the technologies to not only support focused collaborative activities and interactions between distributed users, but also provide ways for such individuals to come together and participate in communal events in virtual space (e.g. Benford et al. 1996).

These preliminary efforts at developing virtual spaces for interaction between remote participants appear to have certain resonances with studies of visual conduct in the social sciences. Indeed, both the orientations of the representations that users are expected to adopt and those they seem to utilise appear to have certain similarities to the formations and spaces discussed by Kendon (1990) in his analysis of human behaviour in social interaction. More generally, CVEs and other collaborative environments have sought to provide for more than just spaces where particular individuals can interact, but for users to adopt a range of ways of participating with each other. Particular attention has been given to providing ways of allowing users to participate peripherally in activities and interaction, providing them with different kinds of awareness of activities happening in the virtual environment. Here, a set of distinctions drawn originally by Goffman seem relevant (Goffman, 1963; 1974), particularly with the various ways of contributing to the production of an activity ('the production format') and of participating in an interaction ('the participation status'). This work has, with more recent studies of workplace interaction (e.g. Goodwin and Goodwin, 1996; Heath and Luff, 1992a), given a warrant for providing users not just with capabilities for interacting with ratified others but also giving them a general awareness of colleagues and activities in remote domains (e.g. Borning and Travers, 1991; Dourish and Bellotti, 1992). Typical examples, provide users with different kinds of spaces on their screen so that they can carry out some focused task whilst peripherally monitoring the activities of others.

Admittedly, these attempts to develop virtual spaces for social interaction are somewhat crude. It is difficult to allow accessibility to a remote space whilst providing details that can be attended to in the 'periphery' without this becoming too intrusive. It is also hard to give users the capabilities that allow for the delicate ways in which individuals both need to move into and maintain a sense of participation in a collaborative activity or group interaction. It appears particularly problematic either to provide the resources for, or get a sense of, how a colleague is participating in an activity or the interaction. Hence, various extensions have been proposed. Users have been given choices about the different kinds of access into another domain they require and the capabilities of the representations on the screen have been extended. For example, developers have considered allowing the representations on the screen to point to others and artefacts in various ways and augmented the representations with video images of their participants (Benford, et al., 1996; Nakanishi, et al., 1996). Such extensions should allow different kinds of participation in activities particularly in relation to other artefacts like documents, and also provide some resources for users to get a sense of how a colleague is participating in an activity. However, such capabilities appear to require more than a static conception of the possible spatial configurations of participants. It would also appear necessary to understand how participants manage such mundane accomplishments as pointing to an artefact or movement into closer, more focused, collaboration. Indeed, although writers such as Kendon do explore the various positions individuals adopt relative to each other in social settings, they also pay attention to how these emerge through time within interaction between participants.

Needless to say, given the stage in their development, the capabilities of current prototypes developed for virtual social interactions are necessarily crude. It may be that recent approaches that are endeavouring to mimic or simulate particular features of co-present interactions may be the precursors of more radical developments. However, even for collaborative environments that do not necessitate the representation of individual users on the screen, an understanding of certain rather mundane, yet robust, resources utilised by participants in interaction may be useful (cf. Heath, et al., 1995). Hence, given the capabilities being explored at this time, it would appear worthwhile to consider the resources that such systems currently need to support.

The attempts at developing systems to support social interaction not only suggest the current limitations of the technology, but also the paucity of understanding of even the most mundane of activities in social interaction. Over the last thirty years a growing body of research has emerged which has analysed recordings of everyday interaction in order to reveal the details of the practices through which these are achieved (Atkinson and Heritage, 1984; Goodwin, 1981; Heath, 1986; Sacks, 1992; Sacks, et al., 1974). Although these studies have developed a corpus of findings concerning the organisation of talk and visual conduct, we still have little understanding concerning how individuals collaborate with respect to objects and artefacts in the local environment. Recently, in concert and collaboration with various other researchers, we have begun to explore these issues, analysing both the use of mundane artefacts, like documents, and electronic systems, like computer technologies, in everyday settings (Goodwin, 1993; Greatbatch, et al., 1993; Heath and Hindmarsh, 1995; Whalen, 1992). These have focused on such matters as how turns-at-talk are coordinated with those of co-participants, the commitments and demands placed by participants through the production and placement of different kinds of turns and how visual conduct, body orientation and gestures, is interrelated with talk. This work has revealed the sequential nature of conduct, and how it emerges turn-by-turn, each being produced with respect to a prior and shaping the context for the next. Although the findings emerging from this research may be preliminary, this work attends to the details of the ongoing production of activities-in-interaction, and may be of some relevance to developers of technologies that aim to support participation and collaboration.

In the following sections of this paper we explore the ways individuals come together in everyday settings to accomplish activities with artefacts. In these settings, which include an architectural practice, a financial dealing room and a control room of an urban transportation system, participants come together to engage in some activity. The participants may be co-located or dispersed; connected merely through a telephone system. Nevertheless, in the single instances considered, we hope to give some sense of the complexity of the activities in which the participants engage and how they are sensitive to the moment-to-moment conduct of their colleagues. Consideration of these issues raises some possibilities for the development of technologies for collaboration. Although, it appears at first that these findings are constrained to circumscribed work settings, in more 'open' and 'flexible' systems, these rather simple problems of initiating interaction and collaboration may be even more acute (cf. Hindmarsh et al. 1998). Moreover, the studies outline some problems in considering the support for groups, not only for what is known as groupware intended to support collaborative work, but also for the support necessary for collaboration between more diverse collections of individuals. It may be that holding onto too static a conception of group or community may unduly constrain the potential of such technologies.

3.   Establishing a Common Orientation to an Artefact

Initially, we consider a straightforward example. Two architects come together to discuss a problem with the set of drawings they are currently working on. Whilst Pete (P) works on his computer, another architect, Richard (R) comes up to the paper plans to Pete's left and asks him about a particular feature on the plans.

(1) Transcript 1

Pete   Richard

R: are you sure you're flipping the right one
     around Pete.   ➜
     (0.2)
P: yeah

254

(2.5) →

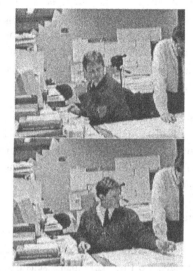

P: I'm flipping (0.5) look on level one →
(1.1)
R: you you just told me that you have
flip flipped that one around
(0.6)

In the course of major changes to the design of the building, the directions of all the main staircases have to be changed ('flipped around'). Richard's question concerns some of these changes. Although his 'are you sure you're flipping the right one around Pete' secures a reply from his colleague, Pete's 'yeah' does not seem adequate. Richard remains oriented to the plans. After over 2 seconds Pete turns towards the paper plans and begins to discuss the changes he is making – 'I'm flipping (0.5) look on level one'. From this moment a long discussion of over five minutes ensues concerning the changes Richard is making and the various alterations Pete has marked up on the paper plans and made on his computer. It is worth considering therefore, some of the details through which this interaction comes about.

Although, whilst he utters his initial question Richard glances towards Pete, his body remains oriented to the paper plans. He then returns back to look at the paper plans. Pete, on the other hand, remains oriented to the drawings he is working on displayed on his computer screen, uttering only 'yeah' to Richard's question. The pause in the talk and Richard's continued orientation to the paper plans, appears to mark a juncture in the activity, drawing Pete away from his computer system and into a collaborative activity. Indeed, following this Pete not only turns towards the paper plans, but begins to remark about a particular feature on them, pointing to the staircase he is changing on his and Richard's far left. The timing of the talk and its delay produced with respect to a particular body orientation appears to draw a colleague into a joint, focused activity.

In some ways, Pete and Richard's conduct is utterly ordinary and unremarkable. Richard, using conventional devices like the design of a question, a pause in talk, a particular body orientation and changes to that orientation, secures an alignment of a colleague to an object of common concern (cf. Goodwin, 1981; Jefferson, 1989). However, these devices are used with some sensitivity and rely on the resources available to Pete. As can be seen from the images above, Richard is standing to the left and some way behind Pete – he is just on the periphery of Pete's regard. Although Pete is hunched over his computer, Richard takes it as unproblematic to ask him a question. It may be that Pete is also sensitive to Richard's changing orientation, through the changes in the direction of talk as Richard first glances towards and then away from Pete. In any case, maintaining one's regard at an object accompanied by the potential withholding of a turn-at-talk, appears to place demands on a colleague to upgrade their participation.

This simple movement into a collaborative activity over an artefact is accomplished quite unproblematically through the participants' coordinated use of a range of resources: the design and pacing of talk, shifts in glances towards colleagues and artefacts and changes in body orientation. These are both designed for a co-participant and place demands on a colleague's participation. Hence, the movement into a focused collaborative activity is itself achieved collaboratively by the participants, from moment-to-moment the nature of the participation is gradually upgraded, emerging from the coordinated use of talk and visual conduct. It comes off as unremarkable and unproblematic through the skilled practices of the participants.

Obviously this is only a simple and momentary instance of the emergence of a collaborative activity between two participants. However, in numerous instances of everyday interactions, in various settings we find such delicate use of interactional resources for moving between different kinds of co-participation. Here, and elsewhere in our materials, we find participants sensitive to changes in the orientation of colleagues often discriminating between the various demands placed by shifts in glances and body orientations within the course of the emerging conduct. In this they frequently make use of what appears to be happening in the periphery of their regard with respect to the current moment in the interaction, and particularly in relation to the artefact of concern. However, the movement into what could be called 'focused collaboration' is not simply a coordination between different individual's behaviours, it is thoroughly interwoven with the talk of the participants. The participants not only make use of features of the talk, the direction and shifts of direction of its production, but on the very demands talk places on them. For this, the design of a question or the timing of a pause, at a particular moment, can be *critical* to the ways in which the emerging commitments of colleagues are seen and understood.

4.   Multiple Participation and Involvement

Of course, movement into a collaborative activity may not always appear so delicate. In many settings, focused interactions appear to follow from explicit requests to collaborate in specific activities. Further, more extreme examples can be seen in settings where someone is shouting out something, for example an 'outloud', which can be picked up by one of a range of colleagues, and that initiates some kind of collaborative group activity. Perhaps the most well-known example of such a setting is the financial dealing room where, on some markets, prices of stocks and names of buyers and sellers are regularly shouted out across the floor with the possibility of initiating a trade. In the following instance, Derek, a salesman in stocks and shares, shouts across the desk for the current prices on 'Bats' (the abbreviation for British American Tobacco shares).

(2)   **Transcript 1**

Derek: What are Bats
          (1.0)
Paul: ⌈ Thats us
Tim: ⌊ Bats
          (0.6)
Derek: Bats
          (0.4)
Paul: Thats us
          (5.3) *((Derek comes round and looks at the screens))*
Tim: What have you got in mind sir
          (1.0)
Derek: I want to sell a hundred
          (0.7)
         I want to sell fifty Orange D'you do Orange?

Derek does not get a direct response to his question about the price of Bats. Instead, two traders Tim and Paul reply simultaneously with 'That's us' and 'Bats'. This response identifies them as the traders in the share, whilst also withholding actually giving a price. After his initial request Derek comes around to stand behind Tim and Paul whilst repeating the name of the share, to which Paul replies again: 'that's us'. When Derek is stationery behind Tim, Tim turns around to briefly glance at him and then turns back to his screen.

Tim   Paul   Derek

Tim: What have you got in mind sir

Derek stands behind Tim for over four seconds before Tim asks 'what have you got in mind sir'. Only then does Derek say the amount he wants to sell, a hundred (thousand) shares, and adds that he wants to sell fifty (thousand) 'Orange' (a telecommunications company) stock as well.

Through various interactional devices, Tim, Paul and Derek come together to trade in some shares. Indeed, one could consider this as an instance of a 'group' of individuals emerging to accomplish some activity. Whether or not Derek wants a price, there and then, Tim and Paul's minimal responses to his initial shouted question at least selects for him potential co-participants in a trade. This provides him with the resources to move into a more focused interaction with Tim and Paul. However, his repetition of his query only gets the same self-selection from Tim and Paul. Indeed, Tim actually turns towards Derek and then asks him directly what he 'has in mind'. Derek's initial query is particularly vague, neither stating whether he wants to buy or sell nor the amount he wants to trade – critical matters when dealing in shares. Tim and Paul's responses may then reflect this vagueness. Indeed, it takes an explicit query from Tim for Derek to give more details of the trade he is proposing.

From the initial shouted query, Derek, Tim and Paul come to be oriented towards the screens in front of them. These screens, which give the current prices of various stocks and shares become a resource in the subsequent trading.

(2)   Transcript 2

Derek:	I want to sell fifty Orange D'you do Orange?
	(0.3)
Paul:	Yeah
	(2.0)
Tim:	I can do them both on the prices Derek I (wouldn't)
	(5.0)
Derek:	(Give) me a half penny in one of them
	(0.3)
Tim:	No (i ⌜ ts)
Paul:	⌞ I'll give you three and a half for the Orange *((To Derek))*
	(0.4)
Derek:	That's fair enough
	(0.3)
Derek:	Three and a half for the Orange
	(0.3)
Derek:	Three and a half for the Bats
	((Tim turns to look at Paul, Paul looks at Tim))
Derek:	Thank you

Derek Tim Paul

Paul: I'll give you three and a half for the Orange

After Paul's confirmation that they deal in Orange shares, Tim says he can only buy at the prices on the screens, turning to Derek as he mentions his name. Tim relies on Derek's orientation towards the screen to make sense of his utterance. Derek appears to do this, however he does not seem happy with that price. Instead, he requests a higher price – '(give) me a half penny in one of them', which Tim rejects. As Tim begins to give an account of his rejection, Paul turns towards Derek and agrees to the proposal. Derek confirms, in full, the prices on both shares and the trade is done.

Although Tim and Paul deal in a common list of shares, they each keep individual accounts, or 'books'. So, despite collaborating over many deals, they also can trade separately. Hence, there is an ambivalence to whom Derek's request to sell is being made. It could be to Tim or Paul, or to both of them. It is only after Tim's rejection of Derek's suggestion that Paul discriminates himself as an alternative buyer. Indeed, up to this moment Paul's participation appears to emphasise the joint nature of his dealing with Tim, repeating 'thats us' in reply to Derek's initial request.

So, although what could be considered a group quickly and delicately emerges to engage in a deal, each maintains an orientation to their individual responsibilities. Paul's offer, at that moment, in the light of Tim's rejection, discriminates that activity potentially on his own behalf, from the foregoing talk by Tim. In doing this, it is interesting to note that he not only glances towards Derek, but also at Tim. Indeed, after the deal has been accomplished Paul asks which deal Tim will record as his own.

So, even after the deal there is some ambivalence to the ways in which activities are tied to the individuals in question; it is still open who will buy which share. Although the traders have individual responsibilities and can engage in individual tasks and activities, the distinctions between them and between these and 'collaborative' activities are produced in the ongoing interaction. The participants can delicately shift between an individual activity and a joint venture and can even let which orientation they are engaged in remain open. It is thus hard to identify a stable characterisation of the 'group' in such an instance, even between the two traders Tim and Paul. Although the participants in 'the deal' could be discriminated between seller and buyers, or between salespeople and market-makers, when the three participants come together jointly to accomplish the deal, they can, in a moment and through their talk and activities, delicately shift their orientations to these activities and responsibilities. It can be ambivalent whether participants are collaborating in a 'group' or engaged in a collaborative activity, or even how they are at any moment in time discriminating their participation from those of their colleagues: even a participant's demarcation of an activity as his own can be sensitively produced with regard to the concerns of others.

In this instance, we see through the talk and visual conduct participants gradually coming together to accomplish an activity focused on the artefacts in front of them: the computer screens. Although the initial query is shouted, this does not mean that it is necessarily insensitive to the conduct of colleagues. Indeed, as has been mentioned elsewhere (Heath, et al., 1993) the design of outlouds and other shouted utterances can be tailored to the demands of the local setting; they can be heard by a range of participants and in their very design they do not demand particular responses. In the instance considered here, the shouted question is not only answered, but is a resource for a more focused collaborative activity. As in the previous instance in the architecture practice, the movement into collaboration is accomplished through the delicate production of talk and visual conduct of the participants. It may be noted, however, that though they momentarily turn to each other, the critical resources for the activity are the computer screens. The contents of these are utilised not only to accomplish particular activities, for example, to refer to a specific price for a trade, but are essential in the production of activities. Through the screens, sense is made of the deals and of the ongoing interaction. Though a face-to-face orientation is important, and in some ways used in critical junctures in the activity, it is by orienting towards the artefact that collaborative activities are accomplished.

5. Disparate Participation in an Activity

The examples we have considered reveal some ways in which two or more people can come together to deal with a problem or issue over some common domain; a paper plan or a computer screen. In many cases it may be that the common domain or the common problem cannot be so well circumscribed. The following instance is drawn from the activities which take place in the control room of an urban train system in London. The day-to-day running of this system is coordinated by several personnel in the control room. Also situated in the control room and at the same console are staff responsible for announcements and staffing arrangements (CRAs). With the various managers and engineers located in the control room and visiting staff, executives, trainees, trainers and train drivers, it is not uncommon for the control room to become quite overcrowded and noisy. In the following instance, one controller (Ci) is talking with a visiting engineer (E) about the trains required for a future test, whilst the other (Cii) is talking with one of the CRAs (CRAi), who is simultaneously dealing with a phone conversation.

(3)   Transcript 1

Ci   Cii   CRA

(Ci turns from talking to engineer to answer phone))	CRA: how long are you keeping that A Tee Pee train there
Ci: train base (to) train seven <u>one</u> (0.1) go ahead <u>o</u>ver?	(0.2)
	Cii: there is a train (leaving) (0.2) all the ones
	(0.2)
(0.1)	CRA: (oh there is one)
Op: (Stratford	(0.5)
West India Quay over)	CRA: ((*on phone*)): ( ) leaving Stratford now
(0.4)	
Ci: Select emergency shun<u>t</u> proceed <u>for</u>ward in that mode dock at Poplar routeboard tw<u>o</u> zero seven	
(0.2)	

Whilst she (Cii) is talking to the CRA concerning a train which needs to be brought into the maintenance centre to be repaired ('the ATP train' or train numbered 111), the principal controller (Ci) finishes the conversation with the engineer, answering a radio phone call that has been ringing. This radio phone conversation is with a train operator (Op) who needs to change the mode of his train out of automatic operation. This takes some time to handle. In the meantime the second controller deals with the query from the CRA; the CRA passing on the message to the remote caller that the problem train is 'leaving Stratford now'. Cii then enters several commands into the computer system, whilst Ci continues to talk to the train operator, two of which are concerned with taking the problematic train out of action. She goes on to deal with other trains out on the track. When Ci finishes his phone conversation, looking at the screen in front of him, he says to her: 'ehhm (0.2) I was go̱ing to sa̱y let the one (one one) go̱'.

Although the multifarious happenings in this instance are complex and may seem confusing, Ci's utterance to Cii at the end of his phone conversation with a train operator concerns the train Cii had been discussing with the CRA at the beginning of the call; a train Cii has just set to go into the sidings.[1] After Ci's utterance Cii changes its setting back. For a brief moment both Ci and Cii are focused on the computer system in front of them and concerned with a common problem. They then go onto other more distinct tasks.

So, although he has been engaged with the engineer and then the call, Ci is also sensitive to the activities of Cii and the CRA. He is both aware of the previous conversation of his colleagues and its consequences. Indeed, he even seems to be sensitive to the fact that the commands Cii has entered into the system have been with respect to this train. Nevertheless, when he does suggest 'letting the 111 go', Cii immediately goes on to type the command. Despite all the activities that have been underway in the control room, not only has Ci been aware of the details of what has been happening, but Cii does not find it problematic that he has done so.

As has been revealed in workplace studies of other settings (Goodwin and Goodwin, 1996; Heath, et al., 1993; Heath and Luff, 1992a), participants can, whilst being engaged in one activity, remain acutely aware of other activities underway in the local environment. In this case, and many others we have observed, this is not just some casual awareness of happenings in the periphery of vision, it is a situated practice accomplished by being immersed in the ongoing activities occurring in the domain. Here, Ci attends to a co-interactant - the engineer - whilst making sense of the talk between two colleagues alongside him on his desk. Later he makes sense of the typing of his colleague whilst talking on the phone with a remote caller. But these accomplishments are not distinct. Cii's typing is made sense of in the light of the foregoing talk between her and the CRA, just as Cii understands Ci's utterance in the light of these activities and the conduct of her co-participant. The activities are continually being understood in the light of the ongoing interactional activities of one's co-participants. The context is being continually reshaped and renewed by the contributions of the participants in the setting.

In (3), from early in the call Ci adopts an orientation where he can see both system displays and the consequences of Cii's typing. Hence, whilst he is engaged in one activity, the call, he can observe what is visible and public in another, Cii's typing. However, making sense of the typing depends on it being recognised as part of a situated activity, specifically with regard to a particular train and course of action. With respect to the case at hand, making sense of the course of the activity which Cii is engaged in relies on seeing her typing in relation to the happenings on the screen, to the state of the service and in the light of prior activities with others. Although adopting a bodily orientation where multiple activities may be visible is critical for the accomplishment of such activities, these activities can only be made sense of through the inherent skills of the participants. The production of these activities relies on the participants' skills in the domain, in this case in operating a transportation service, revealed and made intelligible through the everyday interactional competencies of the participants.

In this instance, several individuals with a range of disparate interests and concerns come together in a variety of ways to accomplish various tasks and activities. It involves participants who have been working together for several hours in the same control room

---

[1] Further background is given in Luff (1997) and Heath and Luff (forthcoming)

and have worked together before, and other participants, engineers and callers who have more temporary relationships with the personnel in the control room. These participants are both co-presently located in the control room and in various, perhaps even unknown locations, outside. The collaboration between them can appear to be straightforward, as when one colleague talks to another about a particular train or happening on a computer screen, or more diffuse, as when one is found to be attending to the details of another's conduct. Hence, it would be hard either to circumscribe relevant 'groups' involved in the various activities or the collaborative activities being undertaken. Both the participation in any particular activity and the nature of the participation appear to be continually in flux. For a moment individuals can come together to focus on a common object and artefact, and yet the resources they rely on to achieve this make use of prior understandings of the activities of colleagues in the domain. Similarly, whilst they may be collaborating over some activity with a colleague they may also be attending to other ongoing events in the local domain. As with the dealing room and other settings we have considered, individuals and 'groups' then not only participate in different ways with each other, for example, overhearing, overseeing or monitoring the activities of others, but can also participate in multiple ways in different activities.

6.   Implications for Requirements

Common to both the aims of developers of groupware and community support systems is the requirement to support groups of individuals in some form of collaboration. Although it may be considered useful to focus on the kinds of support necessary for more 'diverse and amorphous groups' of people, the instances considered in this paper reveal just how diverse and amorphous collaborative activities can be in circumscribed work settings. Remote individuals can call up on the phone and engender a range of types of participation from various individuals within a local environment. The talk can be overheard by others and it may require some explicit involvement from another colleague which may, in turn, necessitate some focused collaboration over an artefact. For a brief moment, several individuals can come together, deal with a problem and then disperse to engage in other activities. This coming together being accomplished by the collaborative production of talk, shifts in orientation and other visual and vocal conduct. Moreover, even when engaged in apparently individual tasks, they can be sensitive to the involvements of others; their talk, visual conduct and activities with artefacts. Such collaboration can appear disparate and amorphous; it emerges through the ongoing interactions of participants. Hence, it may be that the requirements of groupware, systems to support communities and CSCW may not be that distinct.

It may, of course, not be appropriate to replicate the ways in which individuals collaborate and participate with each other in co-present interactions; though many of the recent technological solutions currently have a flavour of this. 'Embodiments' are provided with the ability to 'point' within the local environments, to turn and move towards other embodiments and in closer proximity 'hear' and 'speak' to each other. It is difficult, even with the inclusion of video images, for such solutions to provide the kinds of resources available and utilised by participants in co-present interactions. It may be that more novel developments are possible. However, despite the many proposals for new 'spaces' for work and interaction and the oft-cited hopes of radically transforming the ways in which we currently participate in activities, it is hard to conceive the resources individuals will utilise in such envisionments. Indeed, in both the proposals for new collaborative and interactional technologies and in those systems currently being developed, the actual resources provided to individuals can appear remarkably crude, relying on participants engaging in explicit activities at the interface in order to accomplish quite simple activities. Nevertheless, before proposing a radical transformation in the way we interact and collaborate it would seem prudent to consider the nature of the activity one wishes to transform.

In trying to outline some requirements for technologies to support interaction and collaboration it is worth reviewing some of the interactional resources utilised by the participants in the settings considered so far. Even if a technology was developed that aimed to support resources of this kind, it would no doubt transform the interactional practices of the users in some way. Moreover, identifying requirements from such studies is problematic. The demands on an analyst in trying to warrant a particular analyses of interaction are quite different to those of a designer or requirement engineer aiming to develop some novel technology (Jirotka and Wallen, forthcoming). Indeed, it is uncertain whether strong warrants can be given for developed requirements, or whether such a commitment is appropriate. Any requirements identified would better be considered as provisional, being part of an iterative design process, needing testing, prototyping and experimentation with various options and trade-offs identified by the analysis. Nevertheless, it is useful to outline the interactional resources that are apparent from the three settings considered above and from recent workplace studies undertaken by ourselves and others.

- *Talk.* Critical to the accomplishment of collaborative activities is the production and intelligibility of talk. Participants are sensitive to the timing of talk, its pacing, pauses in its delivery and even changes to the pitch and contour in its production. From such resources participants can make sense of and draw inferences concerning the speaker's conduct. Particular features in talk, positioned at relevant moments, can draw a participant into an interaction, demand a response or a particular kind of response and maintain alignments to an ongoing activity.
- *Body Movement and Orientation.* Participants can produce and make sense of delicate changes to body orientation, subtle shifts of glances and movements towards particular domains. An individual can remain oriented to an object whilst glancing to another domain or co-participant. Co-participants not only discriminate these, but make use of them in the production of appropriate next activities.
- *Gestures and Pointing.* These can be delicately designed and mark out critical features and aspects in a collaboration, for example, in the development of an 'iconic' gesture, where a certain matter is illustrated through the hand and body movement. Critical, however, to their intelligibility is their production with respect to the ongoing talk. Their initiation, shaping and development is both tied to the talk, and also to the participation of the recipient.
- *Engagement in Multiple Activities.* Individuals can be engaged in more than one activity with different co-participants. Their participation in these may be of different kinds, and their footing to each may be marked or discriminated for their colleagues. For example, participants whilst taking a phone call may break away from it to engage

in a conversation with a colleague, marking this juncture not only for the remote caller, but for the co-present co-participant.

- *Double Duty Activities.* Apparently simple activities and utterances can be produced simultaneously for different participants. A shouted question or remark may not only select a particular recipient in a local domain but also make others in the setting aware of an ongoing activity. Similarly a reply can self-select a respondent and display to others that the matter is being dealt with.

- *Peripheral Participation.* Participants frequently adopt orientations which allow them to monitor, oversee and overhear the conduct of others. When they are engaged in seemingly individual activities, participants may be sensitive to the conduct of others, even designing those activities with respect to the activities of colleagues.

- *Use of Artefacts.* Critical to the accomplishment of collaborative activities is the use of artefacts. Artefacts and features of artefacts are not only a key resource utilised within interaction, but also emerging talk and visual conduct may only be made sense of with respect to the details of the current state of the objects. Hence, having access to the artefact and a colleague's orientation to that artefact is critical to the accomplishment of collaborative activities. Objects may be brought into the interaction only momentarily, and their sense and relevance understood with regard to the ongoing talk and to the emergent natural history of events.

These are merely some of the more straightforward interactional resources which participants rely on in collaborative work. It would be hard, even with the sophisticated video and distributed computer systems currently available, to support the delicacy and sensitivity of such practices. Nevertheless, they may point to some rather straightforward requirements for technologies to support real-time interaction and collaboration. No doubt, in choosing amongst the following there are trade-offs which have to be made, and in developing particular solutions developers may undermine critical resources on which participants depend. Pointing out some of these critical resources may thus be useful when considering the transformations that are likely to be required of potential users.

It may be worthwhile re-emphasising the need to consider the activities of users even in systems that are designed to be open to adaptation. However, it appears curious that the activities that community support systems are intended to support are so unclear. This may be because developers of community support systems wish to deploy technologies that transform the way in which individuals communicate or just let new forms of communication emerge through the use of these systems. However, in such cases it may be more important to ensure that the technology does offer support for the activities that these systems do offer - that is for the establishment and maintenance of forms of communication. In this light, though the following requirements may seem more pertinent to sophisticated developments in groupware and community support systems, for example CVEs and other virtual interaction spaces, they may also be a starting point for considering the support that more conventional technologies could give to collaborative activities and interaction.

- First, it should be noted that talk frequented is related to some object or artefact. Hence, resources are required that allow individuals to commonly refer within interaction to objects and the details of these objects;

- talk should be available synchronously with the resources for performing activities, whether these are for altering the orientations of individuals or for manipulating objects.
- the sequential organisation of talk should be preserved. The ordering, and if possible, the pacing of turns of talk by participants needs to be maintained.
- the technology should afford a flexibility in the movements of the participants. Users may need easily to adjust their orientation with respect to others and objects. They should not only be able to adopt different orientations with respect to an object (cf. maintaining a body orientation whilst glancing elsewhere), but these must be apparent to co-participants.
- if the technology is to support the delicate movement into focused collaboration between participants this movement should itself be achieved collaboratively through the technology. A participant should be able to make use of the previous conduct of a colleague as a resource to produce an appropriate next sequential activity.
- the technology should allow for subtle discriminations to be made in the talk. Participants are sensitive to pauses and delays in talk. They also can be sensitive to changes in the tone and direction of speech.
- the technology should allow for different formats in the production of talk, for example, allowing for broadcasts, selected audiences, overhearers etc.
- the technology should allow for a range of gestures to be made with respect to artefacts. Note, that the impact of these may not be so much in their design but how they can be made visible to co-participants.

Together these suggest that developers at least consider, if not focus on, the resources that are produced through talk and the activities that surround artefacts. This may appear strange given the attention that has recently been devoted to developing video support for collaborative work, supplements to text-mediated communication or for those systems that make use of sophisticated graphics, for example those that provide embodiments of individuals. As can be seen from the instances above, talk provides a delicate range of resources for establishing, maintaining and differentiating distinct forms of participation. Therefore, talk or more accurately interaction, is itself a collaborative activity which developers of community support systems may need to consider, either to support through the technology or as a resource for novel designs and enhancements. Of particular interest are those through which interactions about and around artefacts are accomplished. What appears to be required, both for video-related technologies and for other collaborative virtual environments, is a focus on the ways of supporting artefact-centred activities.

7. Summary

Novel forms of technology suggest the possibility of new interaction where geographically distributed groups of individuals can interact together. However, such technology has also raised questions of exactly how people come together in those spaces to participate in various activities. It appears that even when the aims of the technology are to transform the very ways in which individuals work and interact, the resources used in the design still rely on some model, either implicit or explicit, of ordinary social interaction. We hope to have revealed, through just a few instances of everyday interaction, how complex and subtle ordinary participants' resources are for accomplishing collaborative activities.

In order to illustrate the type of detail that may be of interest to designers, we have reviewed studies that reveal the mundane, yet precise details of how people collaborate in these settings; details that are concerned with the timing and coordination of activities. The findings reveal how participation in activities emerges through the use of co-present interactional resources, for example, through talk and visual conduct, and by access to artefacts such as paper and electronic documents. On occasions when two or more people come together, each individual can draw upon various forms of talk, outlouds, questions oriented to another, and various body orientations, to move into focused interaction. However, and more importantly, collaboration emerges through the sequential nature of activities; the delicate and sensitive ways in which one activity is made sense of in relation to a prior and is utilised and provides a foundation for the next.

The studies suggest that even in simple work settings, participants with different rights and responsibilities come together momentarily, from a range of standpoints and collaborate in some activity. This collaboration may appear momentary, bringing together participants with a variety of skills and concerns. However, even a momentary point at a document or a glance at a screen is immersed within the ongoing interaction, made sense of with respect to the talk and visual conduct of colleagues. If just some of this sensitivity and delicacy, and if some common-sense skills and practices can be supported by a novel technology, then that technology would be a radical and innovative contribution to the development of tools to support collaborative work.

Acknowledgments

The authors would like to thank friends and colleagues for their helpful discussions concerning the various issues commented on in this paper including Christian Heath, Lincoln Wallen, Jon Hindmarsh, Steve Benford, Richard Tolcher and Mike Cummins-Fraser. We would also like to express our gratitude for the patience and understanding of the participants in the architecture practice, the financial dealing rooms and the Docklands Light Railway. The research informing the paper is supported by the EU ACTS Project MEMO (AC054), the EPSRC, the ESRC and the DTI.

References

Atkinson, J. M. and Heritage, J. C. (1984). (eds.) *Structures of Social Action: Studies in Conversation Analysis.* Cambridge: Cambridge University Press.

Benford, S., Brown, C., Reynard, G. and Greenhalgh, C. (1996). 'Shared Spaces: Transportation, Artificiality, and Spatiality', in *Proceedings of CSCW '96,* Boston, MA, pp. 77-86.

Benford, S. and Fahlén, L. (1993). 'A Spatial Model of Interaction In Large Visual Environments', in *Proceedings of ECSCW 1993,* Milan, September 13th -17th, pp. 109-124.

Borning, A. and Travers, M. (1991). 'Two Approaches to Casual Interaction over Computer and Video Networks', in *Proceedings of CHI '91,* New Orleans, Louisiana, April-May, pp. 13-19.

Bowers, J., Pycock, J. and O'Brien, J. (1995). 'Talk and Embodiment in Collaborative Writing Environments. in *Proceedings of CHI'96,* Boston, MA. pp. 380-389.

Dourish, P. and Bellotti, V. (1992). 'Awareness and Coordination in Shared Workspaces', in *Proceedings of CSCW '92*, Toronto, Canada, Oct 31 - Nov 4, pp. 107-114.

Goffman, E. (1963). *Behaviour in Public Places: Notes on the Social Organization of Gatherings*. New York: Free Press.

Goffman, E. (1974). *Frame Analysis: An Essay on the Organisation of Experience*. North Eastern University Press.

Goodwin, C. (1981). Conversational Organisation: Interaction between Speakers and Hearers. London: Academic Press.

Goodwin, C. and Goodwin, M. H. (1996). Seeing as a Situated Activity: Formulating Planes, in *Cognition and Communication at Work*, Engeström, Y. and Middleton, D. (eds.), pp 61-95. Cambridge: Cambridge University Press.

Greatbatch, D., Luff, P., Heath, C. C. and Campion, P. (1993). Interpersonal Communication and Human-Computer Interaction: an examination of the use of computers in medical consultations, *Interacting With Computers*. 5: (2), 193-216.

Heath, C. C. (1986). *Body movement and speech in medical interaction*. Cambridge University Press.

Heath, C. C. and Hindmarsh, J. (1995). 'Constituting Objects and Mutual Experience', in *Proceedings of 90th Annual Meeting American Sociological Association*, Washington, DC.

Heath, C. C., Jirotka, M., Luff, P. and Hindmarsh, J. (1993). 'Unpacking Collaboration: the Interactional Organisation of Trading in a City Dealing Room', in *Proceedings of ECSCW 1993*, Milan, September 13th -17th, pp. 155-170.

Heath, C. C. and Luff, P. (1992a). Collaboration and control: Crisis Management and Multimedia Technology in London Underground Line Control Rooms, *CSCW Journal*. 1: (1-2), 69-94.

Heath, C. C. and Luff, P. (1992b). Media Space and Communicative Asymmetries: Preliminary Observations of Video Mediated Interaction, *Human-Computer Interaction*. 7: 315-346.

Heath, C. C. and Luff, P. (forthcoming). *Technology-in-Action*. Cambridge: Cambridge University Press.

Heath, C. C., Luff, P. and Sellen, A. (1995). 'Reconsidering the Virtual Workplace: Flexible Support for Collaborative Activity', in *Proceedings of ECSCW'95*, Stockholm, Sweden. pp. 83-100.

Hindmarsh, J., Fraser, M., Heath, C. C., Benford, S. and Greenhalgh, C. (1998 forthcoming). 'Fragmented Interaction: Establishing mutual orientation in virtual environments', in *Proceedings of CSCW'98*.

Jefferson, G. (1989). Preliminary Notes on a Possible Metric which Provides for a 'Standard Maximum' Silence of Approximately One Second, in *Conversation: An Interdisciplinary Perspective*, Roger, D. and Bull, P. (eds.), pp 166-196. Clevedon and Philadelphia: Multilingual Matters.

Jirotka, M., Luff, P. and Gilbert, G. N. (1991). 'Participant Frameworks for Computer Mediated Communication', in *Proceedings of ECSCW 91*, Amsterdam, Netherlands. pp. 279-291.

Jirotka, M. and Wallen, L. (forthcoming). Analysing the Workplace and User Requirements: Challenges for the Development of Methods for Requirements Engineering, in *Workplace Studies*, Heath, C., Luff, P. and Hindmarsh, J. (eds.). Cambridge: Cambridge University Press.

Kendon, A. (1990). *Conducting interaction: Studies in the Behaviour of Social Interaction*. Cambridge University Press.

Luff, P. (1997). *Computers and Interaction: The Social Organisation of Human-Computer Interaction in the Workplace*. Ph. D. University of Surrey.

Nakanishi, H., Yoshida, C., Nishimura, T. and Ishida, T. (1996). 'FreeWalk: Supporting Casual Meetings in a Network', in *Proceedings of CSCW '96*, Boston, MA, pp. 77-86.

Sacks, H. (1992). *Lectures in Conversation: Volumes I and II*. Oxford: Blackwell.

Sacks, H., Schegloff, E. A. and Jefferson, G. (1974). A simplest systematics for the organisation of turn-taking for conversation, *Language*. 50: (4), 696-735.

Whalen, J. (1992). 'Technology and the Coordination of Human Activity: Computer-Aided Dispatch in Public Safety Communications', in *Proceedings of Discourse and the Professions*, Uppsala, March.

Interactive Consultation System
with Asymmetrical Communication Between People
in Different Electronic Communities

Hiroshi Yajima, Tadashi Tanaka, Hiroshi Tsuji,
Hirotaka Mizuno, Norifumi Nishikawa

Systems Development Laboratory
Hitachi, Ltd.
3-45 Nankouhigashi 8-Chome, Suminoe-Ku, Osaka 559, Japan
{yajima,ta-tana,tsuji,nishikawa}@sdl.hitachi.co.jp

Abstract. Recently, in electronic community, information retrieval and communication have bcome popular among people with different cultures, variety of circumstances and organization in electronic communities. However, it is sometimes difficult to find suitable information and services in a short enough time for real use, because quality of information on internet is not unified and quantity of information is enormous on internet.

In this paper, we discuss communication issues in electronic communities, especially asymmetrical communication between experienced experts and residents with less information. These are two view points: 1) Retrieving Heterogeneous Information Sources, and 2) Integrating Heterogeneous Information Sources.

Moreover, we propose an effective communication method that combines synchronous communication and synchronous communication to perform N:M communication. The proposed

1. Introduction

Recently, in a variety of electronic communities, many types of information sources and services specific for the community have become available. These communities extend beyond countries and languages, and information exchange among people with different cultures, circumstances and organizational ways is popular.

It is sometimes difficult for residents in such a community to find suitable information sources and services in a short time for realistic use. This is mainly because vast information is stored in a non-structured form on networks and there are poor retrieval tools for finding heterogeneous information. Moreover, most people have little experience with information retrieval on networks, and information on networks changes frequently.

There are two approaches to finding a solution for this problem. One is to edit information. Most network information is not structured, and sometimes it is not edited properly for retrieval.

In the other approach, it is reasonable to find a suitable retrieval expert and acquire the satisfactory information by communication with the expert. There are two types of communication with an expert, synchronous and asynchronous communication. Synchronous communication tends to restrict the expert's time, so when there are few experts, it is necessary to alternately use these two types of communication.

In this paper, we discuss issues of electronic community from the view point of communication between members who have different amounts of knowledge and experience, that is the expert and the resident with less knowledge. We mainly discuss the following points:

1) Retrieving Heterogeneous information Sources, and

2) Integrating Heterogeneous Information Sources.

Moreover, we propose a consultation method that enables smooth communication between members who have different amounts of knowledge and experience with both combination of synchronous and asynchronous communication. The proposed method can properly utilize the expert's time and satisfy the user.

2. Problem of Gathering Information from Heterogeneous Sources in an Electronic Community

A vast volume of information is stored in networks these days, but it is difficult for the typical person to search for proper information on a network. There is a big information gap in quality and quantity between people who provide information and people who search for information. There are three reasons.

1) Unstructured information storage on network

This is mainly because vast of information is stored in a non-structured form and there are poor retrieval tools for finding heterogeneous information. People provide information from their own view point on a network, and sometimes people with less experience edit information so the information is provided with poor structure. It is difficult not only to search for the proper information but also to understand the information.

2) Instability and Diversity of Information Source

The quality and quantity of information sent to a network is quite different from the environment and the intention of the sender. Deciding the preciseness or quality of the information should fully depend on the people who provide the information.

However, key factors about the information are usually not clear for the people who search for the information, so it is difficult for the user to make use of the difference. If key factors about the information, such as the date of publication, preciseness and presentation format, are not clear to the user, the information is of no use for the user because people can not use information without knowing these key factors. The information may be formed with some special viewpoint or may have quite relevance to the user. Information on networks also changes every day. Many homepages disappear without any notice, and do not reappear.

3) Heterogeneous Characters in Community

It is difficult to understand information stored in a network from a different culture and circumstance so the user must determine the exact information for his use. The user must check the domain, ontology, and re-structuring of the information. It is necessary for the user to combine asynchronous communication for the retrieval of information of stored information with synchronous communication.

4) Difficulty in Communication

It is also difficult for expert and resident to communjicate because of the following two reasons.

a) Difference of Task Features

The information retrieval task may be non-structued for the resident but not for the expert. The expert has a specialized dictionary and can access exact information from the given information using the dictionary.

b) Multitask Situation

It is sometimes necessary to use knowledge of multiple expert to find exact information. In addition, to save the time of expert, it is desirable for the expert to correspond with many questioners at one time. However, we don't have sufficient information search tools for the expert to conduct multi-conversations as he wishes.

3. Concept and Structure of Interactive Consultation for Gathering Information

Here, we discuss the issues mentioned above for the proposal of a remote consultation system as an example of a communication system among members in a community.

3.1 Purpose of Interactive Consultation

An interactive remote services system provides a wide range of public services to residents from expert staffs in a variety of fields.(Fig. 1)

Three types of services are provided in the system;

    a) Information services by remote servers

    b) Transaction services by remote servers

    c) Consultation service by expert staff at distant locations

Usually, residents receive unmanned service through a special terminal or PC at home, but the resident contacts with the expert in a central office at distant locations connected through the network when he can not find out what he needs. Through the communication with the expert, the resident finds the needed information and knowledge of using the information.

In the example of an insurance company, information such as catalog, procedure, location, etc. is provided. During the operation, the customer has procedures for acceptance and processing, and then uses tele-consultation by an expert clerk if the self operation service is not satisfactory (Fig. 2).

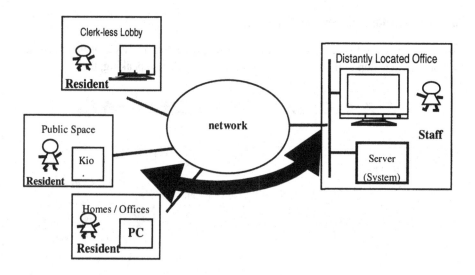

Fig.1   Structure of Consultation System
(Financial Application)

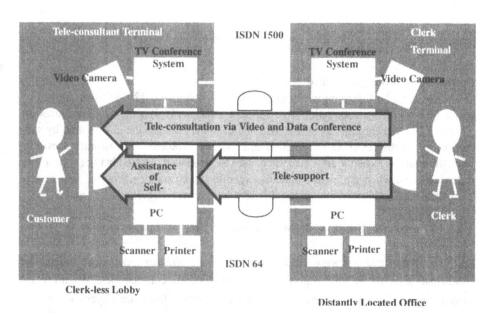

Fig. 2   Example of Consulting System (Life Insurance Company)

3.2 Strategy for Tele-Service Providing

We try to extend this group-ware system to support a community. For this purpose, we analyze each step in the process of consultation. Roughly speaking, the

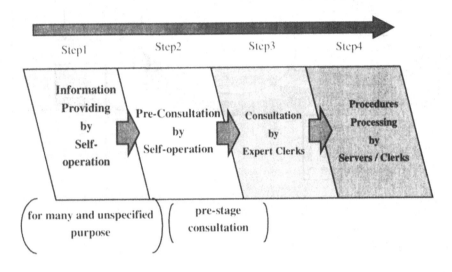

Fig. 3   Strategy for Providing Tele-Serv.

consultation process consists of four steps.

They are (1) Information Provided by Self-operation, (2) Self-operation Pre-Consultation, (3) Consultation by Expert Clerks,   (4) Processing Procedures by Servers / Clerks (Fig.3). In the first step, the customer searchs the information by self-operation at the customer terminal. If there is any problem, the customer uses tele-consultation by expert staff. Our system sets the intermediate step between these two steps, that is, when the expert staff intervene in the customer operation. Our system supports a smooth transition among different tele-service stages.

3.3 Information Exchange between people in heterogeneous community

In the first step, we suppose a situation of information exchange where the information is transferred between two heterogeneous communities. We think the exchange and sharing information is not easy directly from our experience with a consultation system, and also because of the reasons mentioned before.(Fig. 4) This is partially because of the heterogeneous character, i.e., different knowledge domain, ontology and procedural structure. In addition, the information source in a community is diverse, dispersive and dynamically changing.

To overcome this problem, we propose a two phase edit method, post-edit and pre-edit (Fig. 5). In a conventional media, information is edited by a professional editor, so the user easily and safely use the information because the editor guarantees the quality and preciseness of the information with a standard degree. However, a variety of people send information on a network,, and there is no editor between the

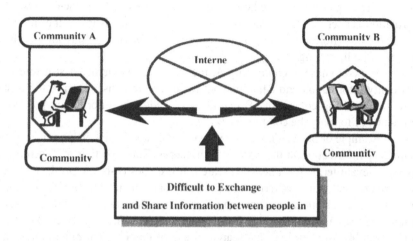

Fig. 4   Communication between People in Heterogeneous community

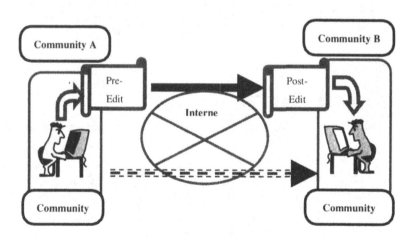

Fig.5   Communication between People in Heterogeneous community

information sender and information user.

We propose to set editors between the information sender and information user, and we believe there should be two types of editor for information exchange on a network because it may be difficult for one editor to know everything about the information sender and information user.

In the two phase edit method, one editor learns the characteristics of the information sender and the other editor learns the characteristics of the information user. Thus, the information of community A is transferred to community B through two types of editing (Fig. 5).

In the pre-edit phase in community A, the editor in community A structures of the community information and edits the content for common use. Then in the post-edit phase, the editor in community B classifies and edits the information processed in community A for only the community B user.

As an example of pre-editing, we developed "Theater" which helps people pre-edit community information in the style of a thesaurus. The objective of "Theater" is to provide relevant terms for a network search. It provides co-occurrent data as well as usual broader and narrower terms and provides maintenance function for community users as well as customization function for each user. An example of the "Theater" for an internet search is shown Fig. 6. In this example, "Theater" helps the user for finding suitable key words in his search in use of co-occurrent relation among key words as well as standard thesaurus.

By using "Theater", people are able to dynamically create thesaurus. The main point of our method is that this co-occurrent relation is community-specific. The key

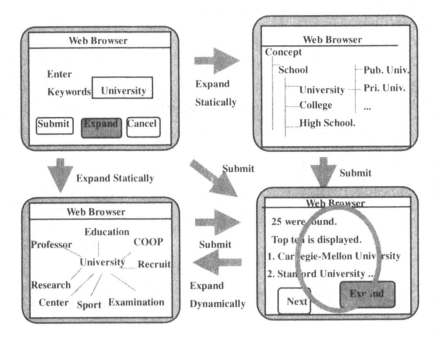

Fig. 6   User Interface by Theater

features of the community will be reflected on the co-occurrence relation, so people outside of the community will able to predict the key words concerning what they want to know.

In addition to the change in a community, that is, when a new document is added or created, this relation should be maintained. Looking at the history of change in a community may give some insight of the community change to the people outside the community.

As an example of post-editing, we also developed extended version of "Zooworks", which helps people post-edit the community information. Zooworks organizes and shares community information in a style that automatically records and indexes all sites and text visited with a Web browser (Fig.7). It uses a folder paradigm to categorize URLs and also allows the sharing of URLs. It allows for user to execute searches by keyword, dates, and search process. Extended version of ZooWorks helps users find, categorize and characterize the "previously visited URLs".

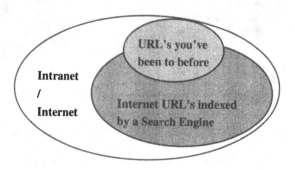

Fig. 7   Basic Idea of "Zooworks"

3.4   Cooperation between Human expert and System for service

Cooperation between expert and system is very important in the consultation system,, because the time of the expert is usually restricted and the service ability and flexibility of the system is also limited. When residents ask all questions to experts and experts provide all services, it is difficult for resident to contact the expert at any time.

There are three patterns of communication in the consultation system (Fig. 8):

  a) communication between heterogeneous group,
  b) N:1 communication, and
  c) succession of communication.

In our system, the communication between expert and resident is that between a heterogeneous group. A staff member sometimes corresponds to multiple (N) residents at a time. Also, a resident can not get all the information needed from one staff member, so a succession of communication is necessary.

Here, we propose a concept for coordination in the consultation system, that is, the expert and system give service in one body. Conventional cooperation between human and system is where the computer performs simple exercises and fixes the form of consultation, and experts share flexible and complicated consultation. The time of the human expert is expensive, so human expert only responds to flexible and complicated questions of many residents (Fig. 9).

In addition to the behavior of the human expert and the system in a conventional concept, our concept has the following,

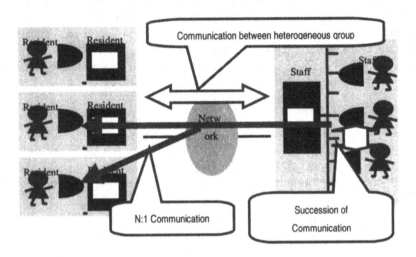

Fig. 8   Communication Patterns in Consultation System

1) Human expert assists communication between resident and system.

2) System assists communication between resident and human expert.

3) Human expert and system communicate with resident in turns to save the time of the human expert .(Fig. 10)

To achieve function 3), the expert and system respond to one resident in turns, but they must not let the resident find any difficulty in consultation, so smooth succession of communication with the resident. To perform this function, the expert and system share ongoing information on the consultation.

3.5   Three Characteristics of Communication

Here, the three communication functions mentioned before are described.

1) Communication between Heterogeneous Group (human expert and residents)

The objective of this function is to construct a satisfactory solution for the resident and save the time of the expert. To perform this function, we adopt a non-symmetric display and let the computer control the input, that is, the system has a consultation scenario.

2) N:1 Communication (Expert and N Residents)

The objective of this function is to provide just in time service, that is, necessary

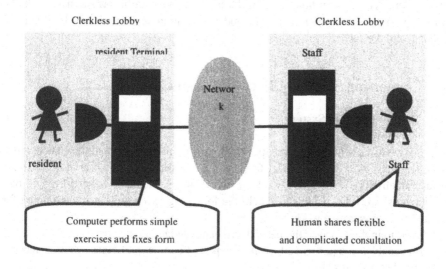

Fig. 9 Typical Cooperation between Human and System in service

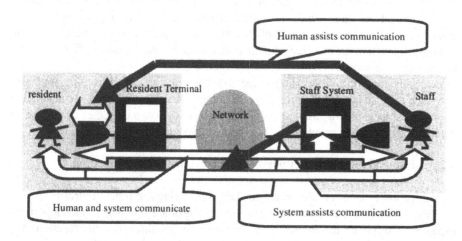

Fig. 10 Our Cooperation between Human and System for service

timing, necessary consultation, and an appropriate expert. To perform this function, we adopt a real time observation of the resident's behavior and their operation log.

3) Succession of Communication between Homogeneous Group (M Experts)

The objective of this function is to save the time of the experts and not to satisfy the resident. To perform this function, human experts share information such as the consultation log. their memorandum, and the communication history between the resident and the system.

4. Supporting System of Remote Consultation

4.1 Requirements of System

Here, we discuss the requirements, which the communication features stated above need to satisfy in order to support trouble-free consultation. We observe an example of asymmetrically cooperative work, in which the participants have differing roles in Hutchins' work [2]. In this research, the following two requirements are noted for trouble-free cooperative work:

(1) Overlap in the scope of the participants' knowledge

This enables one participant to take the part of another participant when   needed.

(2) The observation scope:

This means that each participant is within the scope of another's participant's observation. This enables one participant to be aware of the need to help another.

In remote consultation, the consulting staff have a specialist's knowledge and ontology in the field related to the consultation. They also have knowledge on how to use the remote consultation system. In other words, the consulting staff's knowledge is inclusive of the customers' knowledge. Therefore, it is the responsibility of the consulting staff to be appreciative of the other side's (customer's) role. The remote consultation system needs to have functionality to enable the support staff to take over a customer's operation.

Let us examine the observation scope. As stated above, the consulting staff also need to be able to take on the role of the customer. Therefore, the remote consultation system must have functionality to enable the staff to observe a customer's situation so that the staff can be aware of the need to help the customer.

4.2 Additional Functions Supporting Asymmetrical Communication

(1) Additional functions (Tele-operation, Tele-monitoring and Input-control)

Tele-monitoring, Tele-operating, and Input-control are functions, that support the expert staff in taking the initiative during a remote consultation. This functions are designed to aid customers who are having problems in completing a remote consultation.

We propose that the consulting staff take the initiative during a consultation. The tele-monitoring function would permit the consulting staff to monitor a customer's terminal without the customer's request. Furthermore, a tele-operating function would enable the expert staff to guide the customer through the various procedures by remotely operating the customer's terminal.

If a customer is confused by the procedures directed by the terminal, the remote consultation system enables staff to rapidly respond to the situation. One approach to enable one person to remotely monitor the situation of the other person involves the techniques to provide not only a detailed view (such as a standard videophone link) but also a "global view" [3]. This technique enables staff to comprehend the situation around the customer but does not provide information on the customer's terminal. However, the tele-monitoring function can provide the expert staff such information so that they can fully understand the stage of the operation where the customer is having difficulty. The staff would not need to explain the procedures to the customer, as the tele-operation function would enable the staff to remotely complete the operations as the customer wishes.

In the TV Conference system, it is difficult to see the reaction of other side, and this feature makes it difficult to intervene during the other side's. This feature sometimes causes redundant communication because both sides feel difficulty intervening the speech of the other side.

To overcome this problem, we developed a switching function that includes a control for the right to speak. The system detects the operation of a customer or staff, and it switches the right to speak according to the consultation scenario. It also it notices both customer and staff when they go to the next step after switching the right to speak, so the customer has to stop speaking.

(2) Overview of the remote consultation system

We designed a prototype remote consultation system as shown in Figure 1. It is composed of a single customer terminal and a single consultation staff terminal for use in financial services. Each terminal has a video-conferencing subsystem as videophone for remote conversation. The system provides the following services.

(a) Information service: customers can obtain information directly from the terminal.

(b) Consultation service: customers can consult with consulting staff via videophone.

Customers can simultaneously use these services. The consulting staff only participate in the remote consultation service.

4.3 Evaluation

This remote consultation system is now in practical use in the financial services field. We have investigated how the tele-operating function is being used. The finding of which are as follows:

(1) Changing the page displayed on a customer's terminal to that needed by the customer.

This need was observed when a customer called the support staff because of confusion on how to use the terminal in order to see a particular page. The customer explained the service he wanted to the support staff who changed the page displayed on the customer's terminal for the customer. The customer could then continue to use the information services as before.

(2) Displaying explanations on the customer's terminal

This case arose when the staff needed to explain information to a customer using the pages contained in the information service. The support staff, who had already initiated dialog with the customer, could also take control of the customer's terminal to aid in explanation by using information displayed on the customer's terminal.

We analyzed the consultation process into four phases: preparation phase, issues explanation phase, consultation phase and termination phase. This made it clear that the proposed function is most effective at the consultation phase because in the consultation process there often is a step where the staff directs the operation to the customer, and this step is greatly improved by the proposed function.

5. Conclusion

In this paper, we have proposed a method for information exchange between residents with an information gap in quality and quantity. We have discussed the characteristics of information exchange in an electronic community and clarified the issues. We then proposed a remote consultation system to facilitate the smooth operation of the system. The functions have been implemented in a system for the financial services field, and we have evaluated the effectiveness of the functions in practical everyday use. It has been suggested that an effective means of supporting remote consultation would enables the consulting staff to take control of the customer's terminal so the staff can initiate the consultation.

In our experiment, the characteristics of a TV conference were made clear. We find many usable features in it despite the lack of information compared with face-to-face communication and the lack of direct manipulation with articles on the other side. Examples include changing the viewpoint giving an intensive impression, changing the background, voice and image, and being able to record the communication log

By using a teleconference system, we can change our view, and this means we can get the viewpoint of the person we are talking to and take the view of an outsider who watches the conversation. This means a new possibility of "avata", for example, if your avata wears clothes specific to your community, how do people feel about the difference of characteristics in your community.

I would like to clarify these points clear in future work. Also, the social and psychological effects of our system should be made clear from the view point of human –agent collaboration

References

1. T. Tanaka, H. Mizuno, H. Tsuji, H. Yajima et al., "Tele-consultation System supporting Asymmetrical Communications between Customers and Expert Staff in a Distributed Environment," *Proc. On HCI'97* (1997)
2. H. Mizuno T. Tanaka, H. Tsuji, and H. Yajima, "Remote Consultation System for Participants with Different Roles and Skills," *Proc. of the 1997 IEEE International Conference on Systems, Man, and Cybernetics* (SMC *97), pp. 3728-3731 (1997)

3. Norifumi Nishikawa, and Hiroshi Tsuji, Allowing Multiple Experts to Revise a Thesaurus Database, HCI International '97 (21B Design of Computing Systems: Social and Ergonomic Considerations, pp.371-374), 1997

4. Tamayo Tokuda, Hisao Mase, Hiroshi Tsuji, and Yoshiki Niwa, Experimental Evaluation for Associate Keyword Reminder by Thesaurus, 7 th IFCA/IFIP/IFORS/IEA Symposium on Analysis, Design and Evaluation of Man-Machine Systems, 1998

5. Norifumi Nishikawa, Takao Shimada, and Hiroshi Tsuji, Proxy Server Technology for controlling the Information Traffic on the Internet, System / Control / Information Vol.42, No.3, pp.163-168, 1998

6. E. Hutchins: "The Technology of Team Navigation," in J. Galegher, R. Kraut, and C. Egido (Eds.), *Intellectual Teamwork: Social and Technical Bases of Cooperative Work*, Lawrence Erlbaum Associates.

7. K. Yamaashi et al., "Beating the Limitations of Camera-Monitor Mediated Telepresence with Extra Eyes," *Proc. on CHI'96 Conference*, ACM Press, 1996, pp. 50-57.

8. Watts, L., *et al.*, Remote assistance: a view of the work and a view of the face?, in *Conference   Companion CHI 96* (Vancouver Canada, April 1996), ACM Press, 101-102.

Communities through Time:
Using History for Social Navigation

Alan Wexelblat

MIT Media Lab, Software Agents Group
20 Ames St., Cambridge, MA 02139 USA
wex@media.mit.edu

Abstract. Communities distributed in time cannot interact directly. I propose that they can form and interact through histories recorded with digital information. The field of interaction history is defined and examples of tools built to help a communal process (social navigation) are shown. Ways in which these tools can aid the formation of certain kinds of communities are described.

1 Introduction

Communities are, for the purposes of this paper, groups of people with shared interests or similar problems who interact for reasons of mutual benefit. This interaction can be as simple as friendly support or as detailed as patients in a community of disease-survivors who relate entire treatment regimes to each other.

Digital communities are widely acknowledged to be less stable and more fluid than physical communities [16]. People enter and exit more easily, and communities form and dissolve with much greater rapidity than in the physical world. If one's goal is a long-lived and stable virtual counterpart to the physical community, this is a problem. However, we are interested in a different sort of community, one which is formed around a specific set of problems or set of similar interests. If the problems are solved or the members' interests change and they choose to move on that is not a problem.

We also consider our community members to be distributed in time as well as in space; as such they may never communicate directly. The usual CSCW 2x2 diagram is shown in Figure 1 with some example tools that fit three of the four combinations. In the fourth, unlabeled combination — different time, same place — we find an opportunity to use interaction history tools for problem-oriented communities.

	same time	different time
same place	meeting rooms	✳
different place	tele conf	email

Figure 1 — Distribution of community tools

Interaction history is the record of people and objects involved together in an effort. Interaction histories may contain many different kinds of information, as described in the next two sections. Digital information lacks history. It lacks the texture and depth and richness that comes from being used by many hands over much time. Where the physical world is rich with cues and montages that we take advantage of constantly, our data remains sterile. When we open a word processing document or visit a web site it is as though we were the first and only people ever to handle this data. Contrast this with a borrowed book or a lived-in house; both are rich with the markers of previous use and these markers (the dog-eared pages, the padded arch of a low doorway) serve as pointers and help us make better use of the information and the space.

I am investigating how interaction history can be used in digital information. My chosen domain is social navigation — the process of using cues from other people to help you find information and potentially to more fully understand what it is that you have found. Social navigation is a prototypical same-place/different-time problem. People leaving a record of their past interactions become guides for newcomers to the community space.

2 Interaction History

The histories of interaction with objects are the accumulated records of past actions, with emphasis on sequences of actions, relationships of elements on which the user has acted, and the resulting structures. History modifies an object's state, but not just any accumulation of state modifications are interesting history.

The modifications or additions that make up interaction history affect not just the object but our perceptions of, and uses for, the object. For example, near the end of 1997 news stories began appearing indicating that certain artworks in American museum collections had been plundered by the Nazis [19]. This bit of history did not change the objects themselves; instead it changed our perceptions of them. What had been done in the past changed our ideas on how to treat the objects in the present.

We use interaction history information daily in the physical world. Objects often carry their histories with them, as in the examples of the dog-eared book and padded doorframe above. Physical objects often change in response to use: brass shows a patina where human sweat and friction have been applied, stone stair treads show curvatures worn by thousands of shoes passing over them, etc. We make use of these traces, often without conscious thought, as when we let a book fall open to a particular page because it has been opened to this page often in the past.

The goal of our project is to find ways to make interaction history information as easily and naturally available in the digital world as it is in the physical. This effort is inspired by original work done by Hill and Hollan in the early 90s [4][6].

3 Dimensions of History

The first part of the problem is to characterize the problem space. We use six dimensions to describe the area we mean by "interaction history." These dimensions describe a large set of possible forms of history and many possible systems which could be built. In the real world, objects typically show several forms of history at the same time; it is an open question at this point which forms of history will be most beneficial to communities.

3.1 Dimension 1 — Visibility of Purpose

Purpose relates to why something was done. Some forms of history show only what was done but give no reasons. A later user must infer the reasons, if they are important. At the other end of the spectrum, some forms of history show "why it was done" so that we understand motivation, but not what happened.

In the physical world, we might see that the pages of a book have been selectively dog-eared, but not understand why. Alternatively, we might know that our colleague uses this technique to mark pages from which he wants to draw quotations, but not see which quotes had been extracted. In the digital realm, we could imagine a collaborative editing tool which would allow users to see what text had been removed by others, but not why. A different interface could allow authors to attach rules explaining why they made changes so that co-authors could see the notes.

3.2 Dimension 2 — Rate/Form of Change

History moves forward, building as more interactions take place. However, there are also two other processes occurring at the same time. One is "fading," the other is "obscuring." In a fading process, history-rich objects are replaced, people move on taking organizational memory with them, and history is discarded because it is no longer important or lost because people forget and there is no longer a record to remind them. In an obscuring process, records of new interactions cover up old ones. History is often layered and while this layering often gives a richness, it also covers up.

Fading can be characterized as a decay function, much as we talk about decay functions for signals. Both the accretion and decay functions will vary in any history-rich interface. A key benefit of modeling interaction history explicitly in digital systems will be to help users distinguish discarding from forgetting.

3.3 Dimension 3 — Degree of Permeation

Permeation is the degree to which interaction history is a part of history-rich objects. History may be inseparable from the object, as in the worn-stairs example, or it may be completely separate, as in the stolen-art example. In a history-rich interface, we must decide how closely to link the objects of interaction and the history information.

In most cases, the history information must be kept peripheral, as it should be an enhancement to the user's task environment. If interacting with the history information becomes a central focus, we have probably changed the task too much. An appropriate analogy here is to a painting: the painting may be appreciated for what it is alone, or it may be framed. A good frame will enhance our interaction with the picture; it complements our looking. Interaction history is like the frame; the picture is the information to which the history relates.

3.4 Dimension 4 — Personal versus Social

History can be intimate to a person — what have I done? Or it can be social — what has been done here? Many tools focus on personal histories; for example, the facilities within web browsers that allow users to see and revisit sites they have been to in the recent past. Group histories are more rare but, we believe, more valuable because most problem-solving tasks are collaborative in nature. One of the primary benefits of interaction history is to give new users the benefit of seeing what was tried in the past.

The other value of group history is that it promotes organizational learning. While it is true that organizations cannot learn unless individuals within the organization learn, it is also true that if the learning is confined to individuals then it cannot benefit the group as a whole.

3.5 Dimension 5 — Active versus Passive

Most interaction history is passive; it is recorded and made available without conscious effort. When we prop open a cookbook so that we can read the recipe while our hands are busy, we do not think of ourselves as recording our favorite recipes. But that is, passively, what we are doing. We could actively record the same information and we often do, but this takes additional thought and effort. Unfortunately, the "good stuff" may be in the active history. Just as we may make many editing changes to a document (passive history) before committing a new version to a repository (active history) we often find that people take the time to record history because they feel it is important. The challenge for history-rich interfaces is to find a good balance, allowing history to be passively collected while still capturing enough of the right data.

3.6 Dimension 6 — Kind of Information

There are an infinite variety of kinds of interaction history information that can be captured. What kinds of information are available are, to a large degree, dependent on the purpose of the observer. For example, a doorknob may show a particular pattern of wear accumulated over time, which may be important to someone interested in affordances (that is, how people have handled the knob). Alternatively, someone interested in the history of the building might take note of whether the knob was made of expensive brass or cheap aluminum.

One of the key distinctions in kind of history information is accumulation versus sequence. Some forms of history accrete, and are represented as changes in the state of an object; some forms are sequential and make the sequence longer as more history is added. Think of the difference between the accumulated wear on a road versus the added position fixes on a navigational chart.

Since we cannot possibly characterize all the kinds of information available, we use the following framework to organize this dimension. It focuses on the uses to which interaction history might be put. The framework is intended to be usable in two directions. The first takes the approach of looking at the kind of information available (grouped loosely into "who," "what," "how," and "why") and asserts tasks or problems for which that kind of interaction history information would be valuable. Conversely, one could start with a particular problem in mind and see what kind(s) of interaction history should be captured to help with that problem.

- Knowing "what"
  - search for value
  - reassurance
  - guidance
  - reduction of clutter

That is, we identify four distinct uses for "what" information. Knowing what was done can be useful if users are searching for value, particularly among clutter. The underlying assumption is that users will converge on solutions which satisfice; that is, which are good enough given the constraints of time, knowledge and resources. Interaction history provides the kinds of guidelines that are so valuable in satisficing.

Reassurance is a common concept. Simply put, if I want to be reassured about what I am doing, a record showing that someone has done it before can be reassuring in that it tells me I am not alone.

Guidance is the process of directing someone in a task or journey. Written directions can be guidance, and a record of what people have done before is also a form of guidance.

Reduction of clutter is a way of referring to history's organizing function. What was done provides structure and allows us to make sense of a mass of possibilities. I will argue (below) that history provides an extermalization of peoples' mental models and while any given user's model may not precisely match with any others, it is still an organizing framework to which one can react or relate.

- Knowing "who"
  - companionability
  - re-creation
  - sociability
  - authority

Knowing who has done something, or who is involved in the interaction history can be important as well. Companionability refers to our natural desire to do things with our friends. If I know what my friends have done I may be more likely to do it; conversely, I may avoid doing what my enemies have done, unless I want to know how they see the world.

This is related to sociability, our human tendency to do things in groups and to identify with groups even if no specific members of the group are present or known. For example, a Jew such as myself might have a greater interest in doing things if I know they have been done by other Jews in the past, even if I don't know the specific Jews involved.

This is similar to re-creation, the desire to do again what someone famous has done in the past. People in the Boston area often follow the path of Paul Revere's Ride because they are seeking to recreate a famous historical event. Americans might similarly seek to sleep in a bed once slept in by George Washington.

Knowing who has done something is also important for establishing authority and possibly authenticity. A margin note written in the author's own handwriting may be considered more relevant or authoritative than one written by an unknown reader. In some cases, authenticity and authority may be the same thing; for example, a baseball can have a scrawl on it which looks like Babe Ruth's signature, but unless the scrawl was actually produced by Ruth it is probably worthless.

- Knowing "why"
    - similarity of purpose
    - goal discovery

Knowing why something was done can be important for two related reasons. The first and most common one is similarity of purpose. That is, I may care a great deal about something that was done by people with a goal similar to mine. For example, knowing that the pages in a reference book were dog-eared by someone writing a paper similar to my current writing would be potentially important knowledge.

A rarer, but potentially more valuable, reason for knowing why interaction history occurred is goal discovery, a form of serendipity. I may be in the process of making an addition to my house and knowing that the previous owner built up the flooring to avoid rot from poor drainage could be very important.

- Knowing "how"
    - naturalness

Finally, knowing how some bit of interaction history was done can be important for issues of naturalness. Objects afford certain ways of interaction; that is, they make some interactions easier and some harder. Doorknobs afford turning; door plates afford pushing. Knowing how someone used an object in the past can make it easier to use in the present

4 Problem Domain

In order to investigate the possible forms of interaction history, we have chosen to focus on the domain of social navigation. That is, literally, using information from others to help you find what you want. I argue that social navigation leads to the formation of problem-oriented communities, as described above. These communities are people trying to solve similar problems (in this case, find and understand similar things) and looking to other community members for help. This assistance is provided in the form of records, or traces, of past actions.

Probably the most common form of social navigation is information recommendation, sometimes referred to as social filtering [14]. Information, usually in the form of ratings, from other users is applied to help the current user. This is done either by selecting one or a few items from a large database of potentially recommendable items, or by ordering, rating or filtering information items based on past ratings data. Systems which fall into this category include the Bellcore video recommender [5], the MIT Media Lab's HOMR music-recommendation system [13], the Do-I-Care Agent (DICA) for Web pages [15], and the Usenet news rating system GroupLens [11].

Although this sort of recommendation is "navigation" in a sense, we are more interested in the literal problems of finding one's way around. We believe this task is an appropriate one because it is an increasing problem in large information spaces such as the World Wide Web and because it is a task which normally makes use of traces and history information. Hutchins' book *Cognition in the Wild* [8] gives an elaborate description both of the artifacts used in modern ship navigation and the particularly social nature of the task.

To help in our Web-based social navigation task, we were inspired by three artifacts common to many forms of navigation in the real world: maps, trails (or paths), and signposts. We are investigating how these tools can be made history-rich or used in a history-rich interface.

5 Tools Built

As part of this project we have been developing prototypes associated with helping us understand the issues around interaction history. We have built several tools to use history in the display of navigation information. Each of the tools represents a point in the multidimensional space sketched out above. The project, called Footprints — by analogy with the footprints we leave in the physical world, involves deploying and testing these tools in controlled situations and users' normal browsing environments.

Footprints uses information from web server logs to see where users have gone, and then processes that information into various displays. Thus, all the prototypes so far are "passive," in that the user leaves history traces without any extra effort. The next version of the system, which should be deployed early in the spring, will allow users to create signposts, an active form of history. Signposts will also give users the chance to leave more purposive information, such as why they navigated where they did and should enable community members to communicate more directly with each other.

The kind of information gathered is a series of A->B transitions, where A and B are World Wide Web documents and the transition is any navigation technique used by people to get from document A to document B. This is often clicking in their web browser on a link embedded in the HTML of page A which takes them to page B, but can also be typing in a URL or selecting a bookmark. The system combines these simple transition pairs into more complex structures, such as:

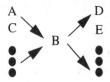

That is, the document B and all documents used to reach it as well as all documents reached from B. The system also assembles linear sequences of transitions into trails, as described below.

The first version of the system [17] used maps, as shown in Figure 2. These maps take the information about which pages at a Web site the user has visited and construct a directed graph representation: nodes are pages, and edges are traversals used to get from one web page to another.

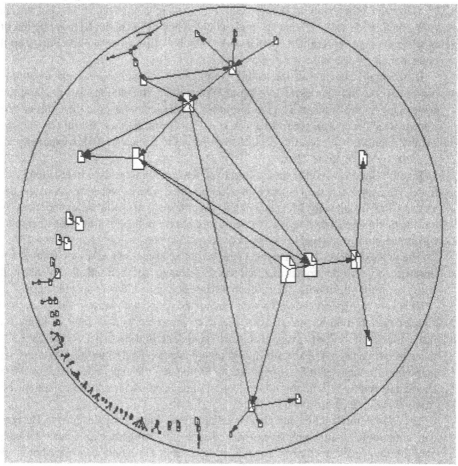

Figure 2 — Use Map of Agents Web Site

The map in Footprints is displayed using a hyperbolic geometry, in the style of Lamping et al's work at Xerox PARC [9]. Users can drag and rotate the objects in the map to improve their view of any given part of it. Links are color-coded to show the relative flow of traffic. The most heavily-used links are in red, the least heavily used are in blue and intermediate levels of use are in shades of purple.

Not all pages at a site are represented in a Footprints map; only those actually visited by users. Edges, as noted above, may be created by users clicking on URLs within the page, or by any other means, such as the user selecting a bookmark or typing in a new URL. In some ways, these "other" links are more interesting, in that they show transitions between pages which do not exist in the HTML but which users feel are appropriate for one reason or another. This is an insight into users' cognitive models of how information should be related, a point which is addressed in more detail below.

It is also one method by which community members can shape the information space to be more to their liking.

Maps and other tools in this project are not merely representations, but are also active navigation aids. Users can single-click on any of the nodes to bring up the title of the document represented by that node. Double-clicking on a node brings up the corresponding page in the user's web browser.

Usage maps provide an interesting complement to the conventional quantitative (hit-count) based methods of looking at Web traffic. Interaction history maps show sequence, obviously, but at a higher level they can be seen to expose the kinds of experiences which users can get from a web site. This information is useful for new community members who want to be able to see quickly and clearly what experiences an information space has to offer.

Figure 3 shows two different kinds of experience within the same interaction history map. This particular map is taken from about three weeks' worth of use of the Software Agents Group web site. The circled sets of node visits show the experiences. We have named these experiences for ease of reference, but have not developed an ontology or taxonomy of possible experiences.

The first experience (upper right) I call "narrative" because it takes the form of a traditional story: tell me something, tell me something else, then tell me another thing, with only minor diversions off the main thread for explanations of specific points.

This sort of experience works well for novice users, who want a slower-paced or simpler introduction to material. A user who preferred to dive right in might look instead for a "storefront" experience, such as the one in the lower left of Figure 3. In this experience (as in the aisles of a store) there is a rich interconnection of items, with no obvious natural sequence among them. By making the experiences explicit we can encourage people to join appropriate communities and to enter these communities at places which are comfortable for them.

Experience information can also be valuable for community designers. Designers can both look at an ongoing experience and can compare experiences based on changes they make to the information presentation. Designers can and should give thought to the kinds of experiences they want to provide for the community members they seek to attract. Any given presentation of a set of information will favor some experiences and discourage others.

In many ways maps (and the trails discussed below) are a vast oversimplification of the information used to create them. An edge in a map shows which documents it connects, the direction of travel, and the use of that transition path relative to other transitions in the map. It is possible to extract a wide variety of other history information from the data and to show this additional information in the map representation or in another form. For example, mean and standard deviation numbers could be generated for each link. Links could be filtered and shown or not shown based on a number of factors, such as similarity of purpose of past community members to the present user. Additional uses such as these are presently being investigated. We will return to this issue in the Status section.

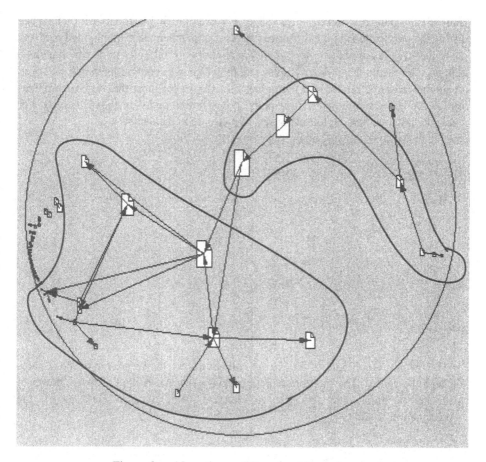

Figure 3 — Narrative and Storefront Experiences

5.1 Version 2 — Trails and Annotations

Experiences in Web browsing are rarely confined to one site. Therefore, our latest version allows users to be followed across multiple web sites as they browse. The result is a set of trails of pages which are connected both directly (by links on the pages) and indirectly (by other actions the user takes). These trails are then compared to show relative levels of use. The levels are also color-coded for ease of recognition. As with maps, shades from blue (lightly used) to red (heavily used) are intended to be suggestive. Nodes are again Web documents, and edges are transitions between them.

In order to help users identify which are the most and least-used trails, color-coded words are placed next to the end nodes of trails based on their level of use. Users can single-click on nodes to see their titles (thus the stair-step representation, which leaves room for text display). Double-clicking on a node brings it up in the corresponding browser window.

However, the trails representation does not stay static as the map does. When the user moves to a new page, either by clicking on a node in the trails view, clicking on a URL in the Web page, or typing in a URL, the trails view adjusts. It always shows all and only the trails relevant to a given page. For example, in [4], the user is on the page listing the publications of the Software Agents group; this node is highlighted in black.

In this case (as in many others) there are a number of different trails which include this page on them. The system displays all that it knows about all the paths; however, to minimize visual clutter and help give a sense of decisions, the system combines trails which have a common starting point so that similar paths are shown merged. For example, imagine that the following sets of paths are in the database.

A->B->C->D
A->B->C->E
A->B->D->F

Then if the user was looking at page B, the representation would be:

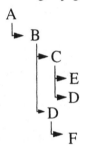

The two representations of 'D' are not collapsed since they represent different paths through the space. The multiple representations of A and B are collapsed, however, since their positions in the path space are identical. If the user now selects page C, the representation would change to:

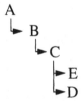

The A->B->D->F path is removed because it is no longer relevant. Other paths containing page C (which do not also contain page B) would be shown if they were in the database.

If we think of the map representation as the highest level in the sense that it over-views a set of history information from a great virtual altitude point of view, then the trails representation is slightly lower level. The same interaction history information as was shown on a map can also be shown in the trails; however, the trails separate out the sequences. In this sense, maps are a merged set of trails. Annotations, presented below, are a level below trails.

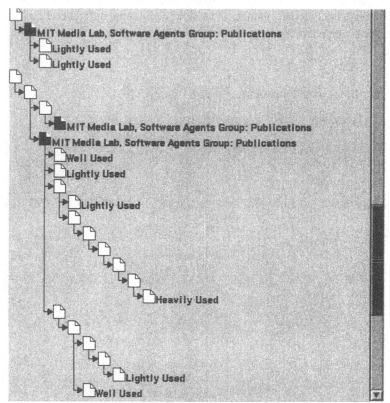

Figure 4 — Trails showing degrees of use

The next example, Figure 5, shows an interesting dichotomy in how people make and use Web pages. It shows two paths which include the home page of Pattie Maes, who heads the Software Agents group. In the more often used path (the bottom of Figure 5), people start at the "PowerGrid Journal" page. This journal has reprinted an article written by Maes [10], and in the Web version of the article, each page is given its own Web page. People who make it through the article are curious, and follow a link from there to Maes' home page. Since their interest is in software agents, they then go on to read about the Software Agents Group by visiting our group home page.

A different group of people start off searching for sites about software agents and for some reason find themselves interested in the people who make such agents. They then follow a link to a page on our Web server which describes the people in our group, including Maes. These people, once they have gotten to her page, continue to be interested in her personally and visit her page of family pictures.

One of the hardest problems in classical information retrieval [12] is the question of deciding what a document is "about." Various solutions, such as keywords, abstracts, and machine-generated summaries have been tried, each with varying degrees of success. The more homogeneous a document is, the more likely these methods are to succeed. Home pages on the Web are an uniquely bad data set for this kind of technique, because they are so diverse and so heterogeneous. Even within a single person's home page there are likely to be a number of sections about quite different things. Finding a single thing which a home page (or even most Web pages) are "about" is a recipe for failure.

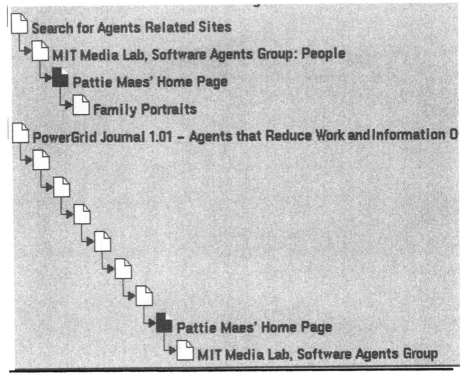

Figure 5 — Who is Pattie Maes?

Interaction history solves this problem by allowing multiple senses of "about" to co-exist. In Figure 5, we see that Maes' home page is in some sense about Maes-the-researcher and also in some sense about Maes-the-family-person. This multiplicity is natural in our everyday lives where we all play multiple roles, sometimes simulta-neously. Objects may have multiple uses: books can be doorstops or window props or even hammers in the right situations.

In addition, these multiple senses can aid our understanding. Earlier, I argued that interaction history was valuable in part because it helped to provide context for infor-mation to which users can navigate. Figure 5 provides an example of this: we under-stand much better who Maes is if we can see her not only as the leader of the Software Agents Group, but also as a person.

5.2 On-board information: annotated pages

As noted above, one of the major aspects of interaction history is the degree to which it is connected to the object itself. The tools discussed so far — maps, lists and trails — all use windows separate from the user's browser window. We are also beginning to experiment with on-board information, in the form of annotations placed within the Web pages themselves.

Figure 6 shows a Web page with the annotations turned on. The annotations appear in the form of percentages attached to each link which can be detected in the HTML of the page. They represent the percentage of people visiting this page who followed each of the links off the page. This is, essentially, the same information as is present in the trails discussed above, but shown from a still "lower" point of view, in comparison to the view given by maps and by trails.

Figure 6 — Annotated page

There are, however, some important differences. First off, the annotations are in numerical terms rather than the categorical (*lightly used... heavily used*) terms used to describe trails. Second, the annotations do not represent all the data that is available. Any links which exist but are not represented in the HTML of the document (for example in imagemaps or cgi-bin generated links) cannot be annotated.

In addition, the Web presents a number of difficulties for displaying on-board — that is, highly connected — interaction history information. The display parameters which one might manipulate in a traditional user interface, such as color, font type and size, and location of the displayed information, are all under the control of the page designer. An interaction history system which attempted to use any of these parameters for history display would risk obscuring or even destroying the very information which it was trying to augment.

This augmentation is key; we must remember that interaction history is not the point of the user doing the browsing and may in many cases not even be relevant to her accomplishing her task. If dealing with history information becomes the task, then we have done something wrong, much as someone who cuts pages out of a book may make impossible the later use of that book for its original intended purpose.

Even with these limitations, however, annotations may yet prove to be useful. They show very directly which options are of most interest to users; for example, in Figure 6 most people who visit the page are clearly interested in learning in about Programming by Example. Far fewer are repeat visitors (who likely clicked on "What's new here?"). In addition, the sum total of all the links followed is about one third of all the visitors. That is, two thirds of people who visited this page went somewhere other than to a page linked to this one. That indicates that either many people came to this page in error (which may be a problem with pages that link to this one), that this page answered their question or satisfied their curiosity, or that this page is simply not enticing enough. Separating out these reasons — and probably identifying the different communities they represent — requires a different sort of history information, which is discussed in the Future Work section.

5.3 Behind the Scenes

The first version of the Footprints tools used a Java applet to create and control the maps. However, we wanted more flexibility and the ability to work with more browsers, so we changed our design for the current version. The present design is represented in Figure 7.

In this design we use a proxy server, which is a Java program. This server handles communication with Web servers out on the net, but also includes a communication path to get data from the Footprints database. The proxy handles displaying the map and trail windows as well as inserting annotations into the Web pages, if the user requests them.

The use of a central database is an obvious drawback. In an ideal world, interaction history information would be present and kept with every digital object. However, until we reach that sort of world, we are using a central database for convenience and simplicity, even though this slows down the interaction by approximately a factor of two.

This architecture is primarily useful because it frees us from the constraint of depending on the browser manufacturers to support the latest versions of Java, which we may need and which may not be supported by the user's chosen browser. In most ways our proxy server is like any other, but it allows us to modularly control the HTTP stream into and out of the browser. This is convenient for us, as we wish to continue adding and testing different interaction history tools.

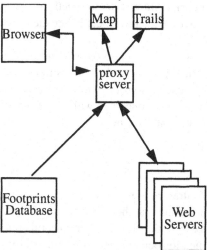

Figure 7 — Footprints Architecture

The proxy also has a simple control panel which allows users to individually turn on and off the various history tools. In addition, if users do not want to use the system, it is a simple button press to turn off the proxy in their browser's preferences.

There is also a Footprints Web site (footprints.media.mit.edu) which allows users to download the latest versions of the software and to search the database for trails of interest, based on simple keyword matching.

6 Status and Future Work

The Footprints tools are presently being given to beta-test users. In addition, we are beginning a series of experiments to determine the effectiveness of interaction history information for a social navigation task. We are building an artificial time-distributed community (of volunteers) to participate in a problem-solving task to see if the presence of interaction history information is helpful.

One of the key unanswered questions in this project is exactly what information should be shown in each of the tools. As noted in the discussion of maps, we are in fact showing very few of the possible bits of information that could be displayed. To some extent, this is based on advice and early experience [7] and a concern that showing too much history information would distract people from their primary tasks.

We are also considering ways in which various factors could be systematically applied as filters against the basic history information. So, for example, users might want to filter which paths they see based on how recently the paths have been used, or based on some measure of how "hot" the information is.

As noted above, the tools we have built so far concentrate on the passive side of Dimension 6. Version 3 of Footprints, which will deployed in summer 1998, will contain tools to allow users to input a more active form of history. Currently under consideration are tools which will accept comments on pages and trails that the user has seen or followed, and a mechanism to allow users to specify why they have visited a particular page. This should help users identify "people like me" which is important in community formation.

Similarity of purpose may turn out to be a useful filter, as noted above. However, we want to make sure that this project does not simply become another "guides" project in which people are encouraged to follow paths laid down by some authority [3] [18]. Footprints is much more concerned with the ability of communities of users to allow their own uses of the objects to be seen.

7 Conclusion

It is early in the project to draw any grand conclusions. At this point, our efforts are primarily aimed at demonstrating that the idea of interaction history is a valid one and that we can indeed transfer from the physical world useful notions of navigation which can be appropriately applied to social navigation in an information space. The examples in this paper are intended to show that not only is this possible, but that even simple tools can be extremely effective in helping users accomplish tasks which are difficult or impossible without interaction history information. We believe we have demonstrated usefulness in three areas in this paper:
- discerning what kind(s) of experiences an information space might offer;
- understanding different, orthogonal senses of a complex document;
- increasing understanding by providing multiple ways to reach the same information.

More tools need to be created, and more testing needs to be done, but I believe that the examples shown here hold promise for convincing others that interaction history can have useful and even surprisingly good effects on the problem of social navigation.

8 References

1. Brand, Stuart. *How Buildings Learn: What happens after they're built*, Penguin Books (1994)

2. Foner, Leonard. "Entertaining Agents: a sociological case study," *Proceedings of the First International Conference on Autonomous Agents*, ACM Press (1997)

3. Furuta et al. "Hypertext Paths and the World Wide Web: Experiences with Walden's Paths," *Proceedings of Hypertext'97*, ACM Press (1997)

4. Hill, Hollan, Wroblewski & McCandles. "Edit Wear and Read Wear," *Proceedings of CHI'92 Conference on Human Factors in Computing Systems*, ACM Press (1992)

5. Hill, Stead, Rosenstein & Furnas. "Recommending and Evaluating Choices in a Virtual Community of Use," *Proceedings of CHI'95*, ACM Press (1995)

6. Hill, Will and Jim Hollan. "History-Enriched Digital Objects," Proceedings of Computers, Freedom, and Privacy (CFP'93), available from http://www.cpsr.org/dox/conferences/cfp93/hill-hollan.html

7. Hill, Will. personal communication with the author.

8. Hutchins, Edwin. *Cognition in the Wild*, MIT Press (1995)

9. Lamping, Rao & Pirolli. "A Focus+Context Technique Based on Hyperbolic Geometry for Visualizing Large Hierarchies," *Proceedings of ACM CHI'95 Conference on Human Factors in Computing Systems*, ACM Press (1995)

10. Maes, Pattie. "Agents that Reduce Work and Information Overload," *Communications of the ACM*, Vol 37#7, ACM Press, 1994.

11. Miller, Riedl, & Konstan. "Experiences with GroupLens: Making Usenet useful again," *Proceedings of the 1997 Usenix Winter Technical Conference* (1997)

12. Salton, Gerard. *The SMART System — Experiments in Automatic Document Processing*, Prentice Hall (1971)

13. Shardanand, Upendra. *Social Information Filtering for Music Recommendation*, S.M. Thesis, Program in Media Arts and Sciences, Massachusetts Institute of Technology (1994)

14. Shardanand, Upendra & Pattie Maes. "Social Information Filtering: Algorithms for Automating `Word of Mouth'," *Proceedings of CHI'95 Conference on Human Factors in Computing Systems*, ACM Press (1995)

15. Starr, Ackerman & Pazzani. "Do-I-Care: A Collaborative Web Agent," *Proceedings of CHI'96 Conference on Human Factors in Computing Systems*, ACM Press (1996)

16. Turkle, Sherry. *Life on the Screen: Identity in the Age of the Internet*, Simon & Schuster (1995)

17. Wexelblat, Alan & Pattie Maes. "Visualizing Histories for Web Browsing," *RIAO'97: Computer-Assisted Information Retrieval on the Internet*, Montreal (1997)

18. Zellweger, Polly. "Scripted Documents: A hypertext path mechanism," *Proceedings of Hypertext'89*, ACM Press (1997)

19. see http://cnn.com/US/9712/25/lost.museum/ for one such article.

Reflections of Communities in Virtual Environments: The Mirror

Charanjit K Sidhu[1]

[1] BT Labs, Human Factors Unit, Martlesham Heath, Ipswich, Suffolk. IP5 3RE, UK
charanjit.sidhu@bt-sys.bt.co.uk

Abstract. Virtual Reality (VR) provides a powerful technology that will dramatically change the way we communicate in the near future. In BT, we have been collaborating with Sony and the BBC in researching VR technology by developing and delivering collaborative virtual environments (VEs) to support communities. This paper presents The Mirror, a ground breaking experiment in VR technology over the Internet, which provided a vehicle for exploring key questions like: How can we support evolving communities and enhance communication using this technology? What are the key components that constitute compelling, stimulating and easy to use VEs? We modified existing tools and techniques used for usability assessment to introduce concepts of 'trial by Internet' and 'cyberfocus groups'.

1 Introduction

"A rapidly expanding system of networks, collectively known as the Internet, links millions of people in new spaces that are changing the way we think, the nature of our sexuality, the form of our communities, our very identities."

(Sherry Turkle 'Life in the Screen', 1995 [1])

Advances in technology over the past decade have led to geographical boundaries coming down as we move towards an age of networked communities. The concepts of telepresence, teleoperation, virtual conferencing and shared environments are becoming a reality in supporting and creating these communities.

The explosion of the Internet[1], coupled with the emergence of Virtual Reality (VR) provides a powerful and easily accessible delivery mechanism that is dramatically changing the way we communicate. It is re-defining the role of computers and telephony to provide compelling virtual environments (VEs) that help mediate collaboration, conversation and social interaction between people.

Preliminary research has generated a wealth of information and insight into this area [3, 4, 5,]. However, many researchers are still unsure of the benefits VR technol-

---

[1] More than 4.5 million people have used the Internet during the past year in the UK [2].

technology brings to its users. Indeed, Pederson notes that, "After a decade of experience with emerging media space technology, we are still at odds as to how they benefit their users" [6]. Others feel it is a major design challenge to create a system that allows subgroups with widely differing needs and norms to form and re-form and to socially negotiate access control among the subgroups. This is achievable through virtual environments and our research aim was to understand some of the potential benefits.

In his plenary speech at CHI 97, Johnson [7] reported on some of the potential consequences and side effects of the Internet for society. He reported that although academics and educators stress information access, and business people stress commerce and entertainment as the primary uses of the Internet, what people really want from the net are new ways to communicate with each other.

It is essential for researchers to establish a sound understanding of user perceptions and behavior as they inhabit and progress through virtual spaces over time in the real context of use. We describe the background to the Mirror and the framework for establishing this knowledge. We outline our methodology for understanding the impact of this medium on users. Qualitative and quantitative results are presented with a summary of the implications of the findings for developers of Internet based VR community tools. We present the relative merits of the assessment tools and techniques used and end with a discussion of further research areas that need to be addressed in order to understand VEs from the user perspective.

2 Researching the Human Element

> "You [the user] not only give your avatar[2] life, but you give other avatars life via your presence. Pixels do not matter unless you have people behind them."

(Randy Farmer, Electric Communities, E2A '96)

> "It seems like the people really make the worlds."

(User comment from The Mirror Trial)

People are the main content of CVEs (Collaborative Virtual Environments). It is through their actions and experiences that the environment comes to life. As a result, technology must be harnessed to support the user experience and must not be the sole driver.

With collaborative VEs, we are moving into a new domain where the user becomes an integral part of the technology. Researching the human element requires a modification of the more traditional approaches to cater for the fact that unlike most other technologies, with VR, we are dealing with a dynamic medium where the environment is generated in real time in response to user actions and experiences. User

---

[2] Individuals are represented in virtual environments through their Avatars; a body image generated by the computer and controlled by the user.

User experiences vary depending on how they decide to interact with objects in the VE and who else is sharing the space at the time. Therefore, user trials need to involve real people in real time to make sure people are responding as they would in a real environment.

2.1 Assessing Virtual Environments over the Internet

At its core, the Internet brings together people who can be located absolutely any-where across the world. The traditional laboratory based trials therefore needs to be modified to investigate acceptability and usability issues when using controlled experiments.

In addition to researching specific aspects of VEs, it is essential for developers and designers to learn about the whole process of delivering virtual environments to end users i.e. the customer experience. This involves consideration of the technology, system performance, and content design, together with user interface issues.

The Mirror project provided an ideal opportunity to investigate these areas. The following sections describe our approach to assessing VEs to effectively capture collaboration between remote Internet users.

3 The Mirror virtual environment

The Mirror [9] was a research project created by BT Labs, Sony Corporation, the BBC and Illuminations. The project brought together key disciplines of 3D design, media, engineering and human factors with the aim of producing a compelling, stimulating 3D virtual interactive environment to support a community brought together through television. The Mirror comprised six multi-user on-line worlds which were made available to over 2000 viewers of the BBC2 technology programme, The Net.

3.1 Designing for collaboration, contribution and community

The worlds of The Mirror reflected the themes of six broadcast TV programmes of The Net in their overall settings and individual audio-visual interactive elements. Moreover, they were designed to experiment with specific aspects of VR content, to explore which would be most appealing to both new and experienced participants. The worlds were linked by an entry portal, (Figure 1) which highlighted a "World of the Week" corresponding with the broadcast TV programme.

The six virtual worlds were built around the following themes: Space, Power, Play, Identity, Memory, and Creation. Each world had a specific 'personality' which participants could experience with others. These are described below:

Fig. 1. The Mirror entry Portal presenting the 6 worlds to users

Space: Based on aspects of navigation and space on a lunar terrain, the environment included alien creatures, some of whom responded to users' presence. "Teleports" were used to produce unexpected transitions between different points in the world, there were a number of visual illusions, and a cage encouraged cooperation between visitors, since a trapped avatar could only be released by a friend on the outside.

Fig. 2. Interactive objects bring people together by encouraging collaboration

Power: Animated figures from the past and present of computing were included in a hall of fame, which led visitors into a debating arena. The arena could be customized, with an option to modify the image at the rear of the stage and to include celebrity "super-avatars", able to broadcast their chat to all of the audience. Additional

Additional functionality allowed the audience to record their votes, which were then visible on a scoreboard above the stage.

Identity: This world involved experimentation with notions of identity and the influence of the environment on people and places. The world changed between day and night, as did the characters and their surroundings. An X-ray machine identified new arrivals to those already in the world, a guided tour was available, and a garden with musical sculptures hinted at future instrumental possibilities.

Memory: Significant events from the last few decades were brought alive along memory lane, which wound through an open landscape. There were snippets of technological, political and cultural history designed to prompt comment and discussion: President Kennedy's motorcade would drive along the lane, and Elvis made fleeting appearances. Audio clips and image flick-books suggested scope for streaming of broadcast audio-visual content within a shared space.

Play: An over-sized playroom filled with games and tricks, designed to promote co-operation and rivalry between visitors. Features included a rocket that required three people to launch, a shuffleboard with persistent scoreboard to foster competition, and a bouncy castle which shook the avatars.

Fig. 3. Bouncy castle in "Play" - a popular meeting place!

Creation: Vibrant flora and fauna brought life to a world which provided visitors with a chance of "fifteen Megabytes of fame". Creatures included frogs, a dragon and a turtle. User authoring will be an important element of shared spaces, promoting a greater sense of community involvement and ownership. A simple VRML2.0 authoring package was supplied to citizens of The Mirror, and an art exhibition was held with exhibits downloaded into Creation world by users.

The Mirror worlds were launched in parallel with the broadcast of the first programme, and closed after seven weeks with an "End of the World" party.

When designing the worlds, one of the goals was to develop a self sustaining environment in which users could contribute to the content of the VE not only through communication with others, but through involvement in the special events. They

They could provide material for the art show in the Creation world, take part in debates and game shows in Power world, leave memories in Memory world, and interact with the application objects present across all the worlds. The assessment looked at the success of these features.

The assessment of the Mirror consisted of two phases:

- **Beta usability trial:** This comprised a controlled user trial which ran over a two week period, prior to the TV programme. The overall aim was to test the process for designing and delivering a virtual environment to end users in preparation for the 'live' trial with the BBC. The main trial consisted of four one hour sessions in which the participants were asked to complete a task.

    Participants did not meet each other outside the virtual environment until after the controlled sessions were complete and they attended a face to face focus group at BT Laboratories. All correspondence during the trial between the research team and the participants was conducted through WWW (World Wide Web) pages, a procedure we call, 'trial by Internet'.

- **The Mirror field trial:** This was the main trial which ran for 7 weeks. The main aim was to investigate and understand the technology and usability requirements for delivering interactive 3D environments to support communities over the Internet. The extended trial allowed us to look for changes in usage over time. We were also able to find out what users had expected from the technology.

The following sections describe the Mirror field trial.

3.2 Measuring usage and usability in The Mirror field trial

The key advantage a field trial has over a user trial is that it allows researchers to investigate usage over time and in the real context of use. Analysis of the content of the interaction between users helps to understand how communication and behaviour develops over time, the impact of and relationship between the different components that make up the user experience and the additional functionality required to support users over time.

Field trials of VEs pose new challenges for researchers. With the Mirror, there was little opportunity to control who went into the world and at what time. As a result, the complete suite of techniques used compensated for weaknesses present in individual techniques. A comparison of actual (objective) behaviour and perceived (subjective) feedback helped provide an overall assessment of The Mirror (Figure 4).

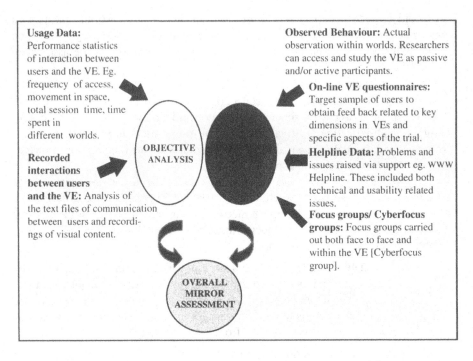

Fig.4. Usability framework for understanding VEs in real context of use

3.3 Findings from the Mirror Experiment

3.3.1 Overall results

The Mirror proved successful in providing an environment where people from across the world were able to meet, communicate and interact within the shared virtual environment.

Visitors to the Mirror: Over 2300 people registered to become citizens of the Mirror spending a total of 4408 hours logged onto the server. Of the total who registered, it was estimated that approximately 1,600 individuals connected to the Mirror server over the course of the experiment.

During the trial period, users spent between a few minutes to a few hours in any one session. In terms of the overall time spent in the world, a total of 1147 user hours were recorded in Play (Figure 5). Play appeared to be the most popular world. The hours spent in Power corresponded to the timing of the special events.

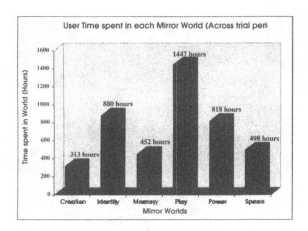

Fig. 5. User time spent in each Mirror World

Initial attraction: The link to the TV programme formed the initial incentive to visit. Once there, the graphics and the interactive applications provided the initial focus of interest which was essential in attracting people and ensuring return visits. Identity clocked up 880 hours of user time, most of which occurred early on in the trial. Users highlighted the design of Identity world as an initial incentive to remain and explore.

Special events: The special events played a key role in bringing together new people. Attendance at these events totaled over 500 hours across all the worlds. Such events contributed to an evolving 3D space where users' experiences and interactions change the environment. There were consistent increases in usage on the dates of the special events.

Communities in VEs: Users who became regular visitors to The Mirror developed a real sense of community over the trial period and feedback indicated a genuine emotional involvement rarely associated with new technologies.

The main reasons for return visits were to meet new people, look around the worlds, and interact with objects . Over time, communication between users became the most important reason.

User feedback was captured by the comments during the 'end of the World' party (figure 6) in the Mirror at the end of the trial:

> *"It wasn't until I was left standing on my own, in front of Elvis, that it really hit me what had happened. Thanks a lot for a month of fun and great community spirit...please pass a last farewell on to everyone.."*
> *"I very much enjoyed the experience, had a lot of fun and met some wonderful people"*

Fig. 6. Avatars at the end of the world party

Communication over time: The nature of communication within the worlds changed over time. Some described this change as positive, as relationships became more personal. Users enjoy the ability to communicate with others, first anonymously and then, if they feel comfortable, more socially. Conversations in the early days of the worlds often concerned topics such as where people were from and what they did for a living. As people became more familiar with other regulars inhabitants within the worlds, the conversation moved away from this general chit chat.

> *"With people that I trust, it [the conversation] has changed because of the fact that, OK they now know me, they know the kids, they ask about the kids."*

Others perceived the change in communication in a negative light. They reported that people became unfriendly and less open to outsiders as time progressed.

> *"At the beginning you'd go in and type 'Hi' and someone would immediately come back and say hello to you. Later on you'd go in and type 'Hi' and it was ignored."*

One disadvantage of this was that new visitors found it difficult to get to know existing users and feel at ease. Often existing groups would be huddle closely together, indicating a 'closed private chat'. Just as in real life, it is often difficult to join an existing chat, and subtle body movements and gestures are used (often unconsciously) to signal the intent.

The use of text also changed over time. Users reported that they became less concerned with the number of typos during a text chat. Users also made more use of e-mail short cuts to emote, e.g. :-), : -<. These findings support the evolution of text based communities [1]. Users were also aware of their position in the space, tending to stand in groups facing the people they were talking with.

Others ways of enhancing the use of text included the use of "....." at the end of sentences to indicate that other users should wait for the next sentence before replying. This was a way of overcoming the limited size of the text input window and also informed others that the content was still being constructed.

This development of "group etiquette" and conventions is evidence of community formation - it develops out of necessity but becomes the defining feature of the community, part of its "culture".

Impact of design of VEs on user behaviour: The Mirror also highlighted ways in which the design of the environments can influence behaviour. Below is an extract from the Mirror chat logs.

Rich: I'm much more aggressive in real life, compared to here.
Candy: So are you trying harder here?
Rich: no.
Candy: So why the difference?
Rich: It's not an aggressive environment.

Explanations for what constitutes aggression in VEs. Included, content of language, appearance of avatars, name of avatars, look of the environment, and positioning (e.g. invasion of personal space)

Avatars: In order for users to feel 'a part of the environment', contributing to the formation of a community, it is important to provide a degree of personalisation, so they can identify with their embodiment. Participants were given a choice of 4 distinctive avatars which were customizable through the Avatar changing room. (Fig. 7)

Fig. 7. The Mirror avatar changing room

Avatars were perceived as essential in allowing individuals to project their own personalities. Users highlighted the need to include additional functionality e.g. gestures, ability to signal emotions, functionality to enhance self-awareness in the VE.

"If you are interacting with other avatars, it is important that they perceive you as a unique presence."
"I would like to import my own VRML handbag?"
"I want to project more of myself into here. To be more expressive...."

Sense of presence and use of space: questionnaire feedback showed that users perceived sense of presence to be important regardless of which world they were in. This

is supported by comments given in other sources of feedback.

"The purpose of these type of places (virtual worlds) is to give you the feeling of being there. If they don't achieve that then it is only really a fancy IRC [Internet Relay Chat] type programme."

"You need to be part of it to get the most out of the experience."

"The more you feel you belong to ANY society, the more relaxing and enjoyable it becomes."

" I think I treat the VR world much the same as the real world."

".... but the interaction and emotions are v real"

From observation of interaction within The Mirror worlds, it was noticeable that users tended to stand in groups facing the people they were talking to and move around according to the changes in the conversation (fig. 8). This indicates that users were aware of their position within the worlds as well as their position in relation to others in that world.

Fig. 8. Users tend to gather in groups to communicate

Users themselves reported finding the sense of presence within the worlds convincing and encapsulating.

"After a while I found that my sense of presence improved and started to think of myself as an avatar rather than a person in The Mirror."

This quote not only shows the sense of immersion but also reveals the mechanism by which this sense of immersion occurs. This demonstrates identification with the avatar and a beginning of feeling "embodied".

More indirectly, some of the conversations users were having in the worlds suggested that they were feeling immersed within their surroundings.

Candy: "Can I stand next to you Saucy, I feel more comfortable."
Saucy: Some people like to face the person they talk to
Saucy: I hate people getting too close
Candy: Invading your space
Saucy: ..but others don't mind standing on top of someone

Having established the importance of feeling a part of the environment, participants noted that this was influenced by other factors such as system reliability, ease of navigation and experiences when trying to communicate [8]. In response to the question, "did you feel part of the environment?", one participant commented:

"Yes, right up until something went wrong. And it doesn't matter how big the window is. Once you are in there, you ignore the rest of the screen."

Virtual environments over the Internet on small screens are providing compelling, real life experiences. There is an analogy here with TV, film and computer games - a compelling film can be compelling on a small screen, a boring film can be boring on a big screen. Gameboys with tiny screens seem to be good at getting people totally involved.

The trial also highlighted some critical issues:

- *Initial contact with the Mirror:* The early contacts with customers: initial advertising, registration, delivery of CD and installation are key to providing a positive first impression. These are essential to the user's decision to buy (or reject!), or in the case of the Mirror, to use and continue using the product.

- *Speed of loading worlds/interaction speed:* Long loading/response times resulted in some users abandoning the trial at the onset. As one user commented:

"..there is no point in making this difficult as I thought the goal was to experience the worlds, not have problems getting through doorways!"

Speed was a major concern to all participants as it detracted from the sense of immersion in the 3D scene.

- *Restrictions caused by aura[3]:* The existence of a personal aura was seen as a major barrier to communication. For small numbers of users, this does not cause too much confusion, but when large numbers are gathered in a small space, restrictions arising from the aura mean users may not be able to see other people they are expecting to see. So, for example, if the aura size is ten, it may be that the

---

[3] The aura is specified by software algorithum which determines the field of interaction for users. Only those objects, information, and avatars that fall within the users aura are detected and made visible to the user.

eleventh person expecting to meet friends may seem to be alone or with complete strangers!

- *Achieving a critical mass of people within the worlds:* The primary motivator for visiting or returning to a particular world was the number of people in it. Users reported that many worlds were empty thus reducing motivation to return there in future.

4   Supporting communities in VEs: Conclusions from the Mirror

The Mirror was a pioneering experiment in interactive, multi-user VRML worlds and events such as debates, game shows and art exhibitions were world firsts in the field. Some of the key conclusions are now provided:

- **Users need clear incentives for visiting:** It is not as simple as putting people in a VE and letting them get on with it. Users seem to need some guidance or someone else to bring them together and get them talking. In the case of the Mirror the incentive was the broadcast programme. Once there, interactive objects and special events (figure 9) provided the incentive [10]. However, in the real world, people can move to new places if they get bored. As researchers and developers, we need to explore how to overcome these barriers to sustain interest over time, eg. providing users with the tools and authority to set up events themselves.

Fig. 9. Users participating in a real-time debate in the Mirror Power world

- **Cater for the impact of aura restrictions.** Auras pose problems for application developers and users [3]. These cause problems for large populations and will impact on communication, and hence development of persistent communities.

- **Experiment with influencing behaviour in VEs.** The Mirror findings have implications for service providers. Developers of VEs which assist the formation of communities need to take account of the potential negative aspects of communications, e.g. exclusion of individuals, ganging up on people [11, 12] as much as the positive community behaviours like looking out for each other.

- **Provide users with more flexibility to express themselves:** Even the 'low' pixel avatars in the Mirror contributed to the sense of identification and embodiment experienced by users. The ability to customise avatars is a key requirement for users. This can also influence behaviour. Findings from social psychology have shown that when people are made self-aware, they are more likely to act in accordance with prevailing standards. When self-awareness is reduced, people are less likely to act in accordance with the prevailing values [13].

5 What did/did not work from a usability evaluation standpoint

One of the aims of the Mirror trial was to understand how successful or problematic existing techniques are for understanding VEs. During the planning phase we made some modifications to the techniques we used.

5.1 Using the WWW: Trial by Internet

The Beta trial was successful in eliciting key improvements prior to the main field trial. Our user trial was conducted over the Internet via WWW pages and e-mails. This approach worked well, allowing users to access the environments from a real world setting as opposed to a laboratory.

Administration over the Internet also overcomes the potential problem of 'experimenter bias' and can reach users located remotely.

Although we are not advocating that all trials to be run over the Internet, we have shown that they can produce useful data. The approach has to be modified if the experimenter is interested in what actually happens outside the VE in the context of use.

5.2 Collecting subjective data

Cyberfocus groups: The Beta trial used face to face focus groups. With the main Mirror field trial, we conducted cyberfocus groups which proved useful and allowed us to reach a remotely located user base cost effectively. An extract from a cyberfocus group is now provided:

CK: ..what type of help should there be?
Treacle Pud: "..a guide would be good."
Dave: "..guides, signs and pointers."
Rich: "An assistant."

Candy: "Virtual of course."

A word of warning through. At this stage in our research we are not recommending moving over completely to cybergroups! It is important to further compare the output of face to face versus cyberfocus groups to fully understand the benefits.

On a similar thread, our research has shown that conducting one-to-one interviews in VEs can work well. The key challenge is to ensure that the interviewer establishes trust with the interviewee. Although this is true of any interview, the 'you can be what and who you like' ethos of virtual worlds may interfere with this.

5.3 Platform statistics

It is essential to obtain objective data for understanding usage and technical issues related to worlds. A wealth of insight can be achieved from data about movement in the worlds, the way in which groups form and behave in VEs, or the use of the content in the environment .

6 Future Direction

VR has the potential to help create, and sustain communities where individuals can come together to meet others, develop relationships and share experiences. This paper has provided an overview of some of the findings from the trial of a VE providing more than just a chat space.

With the Mirror, the look and feel of the themed worlds, the link to the TV programme, the interactive objects and the special events takes the VE beyond existing text and graphical chat spaces. It provides users with more choice and opportunities to meet others, express themselves and build relationships and communities.

The Mirror was an early experiment in using VR as a tool for supporting a community by bringing the Internet closer to TV. We are also exploring the possibility of supporting communities brought together under the education domain, and the use of VR to support collaborative working. In terms of assessment metrics, detailed statistical analysis of the questionnaire data will allow us to identify correlations between key dimensions of VEs (Figure 10) with a view to help benchmark future services and predict the combinations required for different application domains, eg. in business applications, ease of navigation may be less important than easy communication and avatar representation.

In parallel to the development of VEs which are effective and well received by their users, we are continuing our research focusing on specific aspects of VEs. We need to establish a better understanding of the following issues:

- Design of content for compelling VEs to sustain communities. What are the tools and functionality required to allow users to contribute to content of VEs?

- Social and ethical implications of VE technology. Do VEs break down cultural barriers or are they duplicating real life?

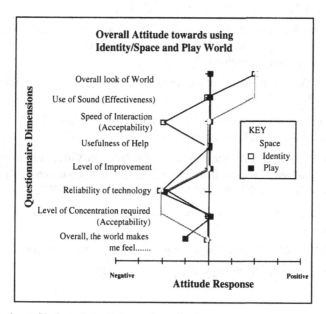

Fig. 10. Attitude profile from Beta trial questionnaire data

Acknowledgments

The author would like to acknowledge the excellent work of the Shared Spaces team which worked so effectively to create such an engaging and stimulating VE.

References

1. Turkle S.: Life on the Screen: Identity in the Age of the Internet. Pub. Simon and Schuster, (1995)

2. http://www.cyberatlas.com Geographics Aug 97

3. Benford, S., Bowers, J., Fahlen L, Greenhalgh, C., Mariani, J. and Rodden, T.: Networked Virtual Reality and co-operative work', Presence: Teleoperators and virtual environments. MIT Press. 1995

4. Crossley M, Davies N. J, Taylor-Hendry, R. J, McGrath, A.J.: Three-dimensional Internet developments', British Telecommunications Technical Journal. Vol. 15 No.2 July 1997

5. Myatt E., Alder A., Ito M., O'Day, V.: Design for networked communities. Proceedings of CHI '97(1997)

6. Pederson E. R. and Sokoler T. AROMA: Abstract representation of presence supporting mutual awareness. Proceedings of CHI 97 (1997)

7. Johnson J. Universal Access to the Net: Requirements and Social Impact http://www.acm.org/sigchi/chi97/ proceedings/invited/jj.htm Chi 97 electronic publications: plenary speech. (1997)

8. Boyd, C.: Does Immersion make virtual environments more usable? CHI 97, (1977) p325.

9. Walker G. The Mirror- Reflections on inhabited TV. British Telecommunications Engineering Journal Vol. 16, April 1997

10. Anderson B., McGrath A., Strategies for Mutability in Virtual Environments. Published in: Proceedings of British Computing Society Conference: "Virtual Environments on Internet, WWW, and Networks". 14-17 April 1997.

11. Baron R. S., Kerr N.: Miller Group process, group decision, group action. Pub. Open University Press. (1992)

12. Hayes N.:Principles of social psychology. Pub. Lawrence Erlbaum Asso. (1993)

13. Weber A. L.: Social Psychology. *Harper Collins.* (1992)

Silhouettell:
Awareness Support for Real-World Encounter

Masayuki Okamoto Hideyuki Nakanishi Toshikazu Nishimura Toru Ishida

Department of Social Informatics
Kyoto University
Yoshida Honmachi, Sakyo-ku, Kyoto, 606-8501, Japan
Tel: +81 75 753 4821   Fax: +81 75 753 4820
E-mail: {okamoto, nuka, nisimura, ishida}@kuis.kyoto-u.ac.jp

Abstract. We have developed a system, called Silhouettell, that provides awareness support for real-world encounters. Silhouettell uses a large graphics screen. People's locations (who and where) are projected as shadows on the screen. The feedback from the shadows allows people to naturally know each other. Silhouettell also selects and presents topics common to two to or more people to make conversations easier to start. The current implementation uses World Wide Web (WWW) pages as the material describing the common topics. Experiments with three users are reported to show how Silhouettell works in practice. We also examined where the system would be best used by polling people from various nations.

1 Introduction

Various electronic meeting support systems have been studied and developed. There are two forms of meetings: formal meetings, such as business meetings, and informal meetings, such as chatting in a hallway or a lobby. Also, there are two ways of supporting these meetings: supporting them in the real world, and supporting them in a virtual space.

Table 1 classifies electronic meeting support systems.

Table 1. Classification of electronic meeting support systems

	Formal Meeting (business meeting)	Informal Meeting (casual meeting)
Real World	Presentation Tools (PowerPoint)	Awareness Support (Silhouettell)
Virtual Space	Conferencing Tools (MediaSpace, etc)	MUD Tools (FreeWalk)

To support formal meetings in the real world, *presentation tools* are commonly used. For meetings between separated people, *video conferencing tools* have been developed. MediaSpace[6], MAJIC[5], InPerson[7], and CU-SeeMe[2] provide virtual spaces through computer networks. To support informal meetings, various *multi-user dungeon (MUD) tools* have widely spread. FreeWalk[3], for example, provides a virtual 3-D space to realize accidental encounters.

It is surprising, however, that almost no research has addressed informal meetings in the real world. Our approach is to provide *awareness support*, which augments the real world, to enable people to become aware of other people who have common interests.

We think that *awareness support* should provide a place for people to come together. For this purpose, we utilize a large graphics screen where people can share displayed information. WebStage[9], a Web browser, actively presents information that users are interested in or need. We introduced this idea into awareness support. We believe that a system that displays common interests to users can enrich their encounters.

This paper describes Silhouettell, a system that finds topics common to the participants and uses World Wide Web (WWW) pages to present the topics by displaying them on the large graphics screen. Section 2 describes the design concept of Silhouettell. Section 3 shows how we implemented Silhouettell. Section 4 reports experiments in real-world encounters using Silhouettell.

2   Design Concept of Silhouettell

2.1   Shadow Play

The following functions are important for awareness support.

- Displaying the presence of others:
   By representing each user as an object (shadow), the system can alert the user to the presence of others.
- Identifying the participants:
   The system displays user profiles (name, affiliation, interests, etc.), so the user can identify the other participants.
- Displaying relations between users:
   The system displays common interests between users to stimulate conversations.

To realize the above functions, Silhouettell uses a large graphics screen. Fig. 1 shows the concept of Silhouettell. Fig. 2 shows an example of it in use.

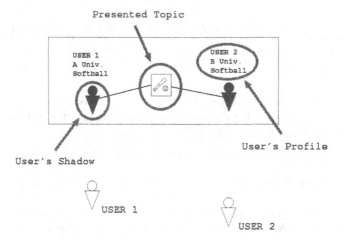

Fig. 1. Concept of Silhouettell

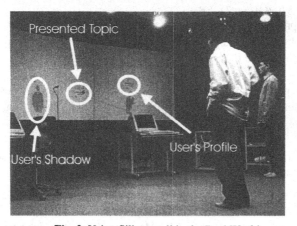

Fig. 2. Using Silhouettell in the Real World

Silhouettell displays the shadows of the other participants as objects, with their profiles above their shadow. The use of shadows is easier to understand than other ways. For example, chatting systems often use avatars or icons, such as in CommunityPlace[8]. When using avatars or icons in a real world, however, users may not be able to identify how avatars or icons correspond to them. If we use shadows, however, the correspondence becomes much clearer. Though mirroring, showing the actual appearance of the other participants, would be clearer than displaying shadows, the user may be uncomfortable at having all the other participants "looking" at him/her all the time. We think that shadows are the best way to signal existence. A comparison of the three approaches is shown in Table 2.

Table 2. Comparison of displaying users

	Avatar or Icon	Shadow	Mirroring
sense of existence	low	middle	high
level of stress	low	low	high

Moreover, Silhouettell enriches encounters and encourages conversation by presenting common topics. The connection lines between each topic and the shadows show groups interested in the same topic.

2.2 Large Graphics Screen

Social Agents[4] supports face-to-face conversation by using a CRT monitor to display the human-like face of an agent. Using a large graphics screen is more effective to support real-world encounters than a CRT monitor.

We find that large screens are better than CRT monitors in the following points.

- *Using functions in a wide sphere*
  If the system provides a small display, users have to use it in a narrow place. A large screen obviously enables users to play with the system in a wide sphere without regarding where they use.
- *Projecting users' shadows at the same size*
  To confirm the profile of a particular person, it is easy if the profile is shown above the corresponding shadow. A large graphics screen enables users to ascertain what people are there at a glance.
- Public display
  Even people far from the screen can see the shadows. They may be attracted and join the conversation.

Table 3 compares CRT monitors to the large graphics screen.

Table 3. Comparison between CRT Monitor and large graphics screen

	CRT Monitor	Large Graphics Screen
Sphere of use	narrow	wide
Shadow size	reduced	full size
number of users who can see the picture	small	large

2.3 Common Topics

It is hard for such media as TV, radio, magazines, etc., to help conversation. Though they surely include various information, they are arranged almost regardless of watchers', listeners' or readers' interests. Each user has to select contents by turning pages or changing TV channels to get information that he/she wants. Silhouettell actively promotes conversation by selecting and presenting common topics among users.

A common feature of electronic conferencing systems is that the system supports conversation by providing a virtual conference room. InPerson and CU-SeeMe, a conferencing room by displaying all participants. MediaSpace and MAJIC connect two or more locations to increase opportunities for encounter among people in distance.

Unlike electronic conferencing systems, Silhouettell increases the opportunities for conversations by presenting topics common to different groups of participants. Table 4 compares electronic conferencing systems to Silhouettell.

Table 4. Comparison of supporting ways

	Conferencing systems	Silhouettell
Provided Object	virtual space	common topics
Place of encounter	increase	no change
Occurrence of conversation	no change	increase

The most efficient way of selecting appropriate topics is to find common terms (affiliation, interest, etc.). Silhouettell compares the terms in the users' profiles and presents topics related to the common terms.

For instance, imagine a conference hall with two (or more) people who do not know each other, but whose research interests are close. To encourage them to start a conversation, Silhouettell provides topics related to terms common in their profiles.

3 Implementation of Silhouettell

We implemented a prototype system of Silhouettell in Human Media Equipment at Kyoto University, following the above policy.

3.1 System Configuration

Fig.3 shows the system configuration of Silhouettell. It consists of two computers, SGI ONYX and a SGI INDY, connected via Ethernet. The ONYX is connected to a large graphics screen with 2880x680 pixel resolution through the SGI Multi Channel

Option (MCO). The INDY is connected to the output of a video camera. The screen is a rectangle some 5 meters in width and 1.5 meters in height, and images are projected on its backside. The video camera is placed at the center of the screen.

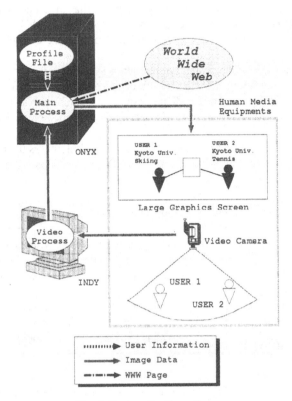

Fig. 3. System Configuration

Images from the video camera are processed by the Video Process in the INDY, and the results are sent to the Main Process in the ONYX. The Main Process generates the screen image from the profile stored in the Profile File, Web pages, and the data from the Video Process.

3.2 Presenting Common Topics

In this section, we describe the selection of common topics and their presentation.

We use WWW pages which can provide multimedia presentation for various topics. The system searches WWW pages for selected topics and displays the found pages between corresponding users as follows, which is performed.

Getting users' profile
We consider the following two ways of inputting the user's profile.

The first one is to have each user wear a small computer[1]. Such systems can collect and present more detailed information to the user. When a user stands in front of the screen wearing a badge that includes his/her information, for example, a sensor could detect his/her profile and location.

The second approach is for the system to store all user profiles. A user enters his/her profile and information for recognition before using the system. If the user stands in front of the screen, the system recognizes him/her by some ways (for example, image processing) and searches and uses his/her profile. After that, no preparation is required.

We adopted the latter approach so as not to burden the user with equipment. The system only needs a projecting device with a large screen and a video camera, and a computer which controls the system, and no special instrument is needed. Users do not have to have any additional device. Before using it, they need to enter their profile only once. Thus, they can use Silhouettell just by standing in front of a Silhouettell screen.

Searching common topics between users
If there are common keywords among several users, system searches a WWW page that matches to them with a search engine on WWW. The page is registered and used at the next time.

Changing the size of displayed topics
The system changes the size of the topic display window to reflect the physical distance between users. When they are far from each other, the topic window is quite size. As they approach each other, the topic window increases in size. This is to encourage users to approach each other with the idea of confirming the topics listed.

3.3 Projecting Shadow

The system generates the shadow of a user by comparing the current image to the background image. This is done in the following three steps.

First, when the system starts, it captures the background image from the pictures taken when nobody is in the room. Noise is averaged over 100 frames. Second, at runtime, the system finds the differences between the current input image and the background image, and displays the areas as shadows if the degree of difference exceeds a predefined threshold. Since the data contain noises mixed when the image is input, the system shades off the picture to diffuse the noises. Shadows must exceed width and height thresholds. It is necessary to consider the difference in the ratio of the width to the height between the image taken by the camera and the screen. The system cuts out the area recognized as a person and pastes it after transferring the coordinates.

3.4 Identifying Users

The system identifies users by the color of their clothes in the following way.

The system averages the value of pixels corresponding to the user's chest area and identifies the participants by the stored values (they are input at the first use).

The system records the locations of all users in the current and the previous frame. The distance of user movement is calculated based on the position difference between the two frames. If it is too large, the system determines that the identification is wrong, and that the detected area corresponds to another person whose value is the second closest to the detected value. The use of both color and location significantly reduces misidentification.

4 Encounter with Silhouettell

4.1 Example of Use

Fig.4 shows an example of an encounter using Silhouettell.

1. One person shows up:
   User SAGAWA enters the media room, his shadow and profile are displayed on the screen (Fig.4(a)). The profile shows, from the top, that his name is SAGAWA Ryusuke, his affiliation is Kyoto University, and his interest is skiing.

2. Another person comes to the room:
   Next, another user (name: TANAKA Hironori, affiliation: Kyoto University, interest: Softball) enters the room. A WWW page related to the common topic, Kyoto University, is presented by Silhouettell (Fig.4(b)). Lines are drawn to link the page and the two shadows to indicate that the topic is shared by SAGAWA and TANAKA.

3. One approaches to another:
   They are motivated by the topic, and one approaches to the other. The WWW page is then magnified (Fig.4(c)). Consequently, conversation about the page occurs.

4. A third person joins:
   The third user (name: MATSUMOTO Hiroaki, affiliation: Kyoto University, interest: Softball) joins, as a result of finding two people talking to each other. The topic of Softball which is also shared by TANAKA is newly displayed, and the page about Kyoto University which is common to all of them moves to the center of the screen (Fig.4(d)).

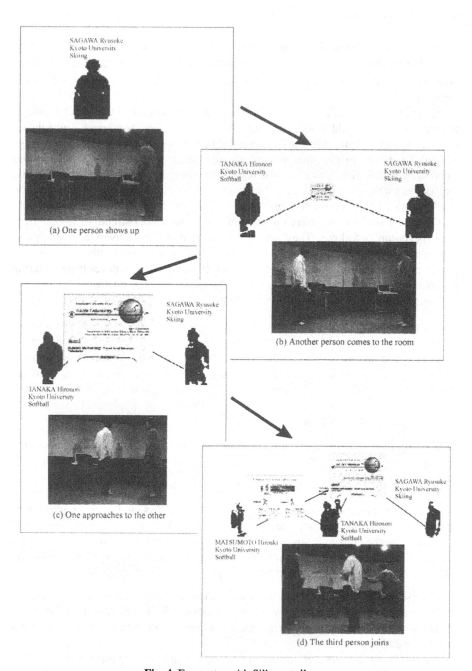

Fig. 4. Encounter with Silhouettell

4.2 Lessons Learned

Through using Silhouettell with three users, we validated our implementation policy. We had three users, who registered their personal profile in advance, spend about ten minutes in the media room with no explicit guidance. They had not been told about the system.

Before this experiment, we expected the following scenario: A user who entered the media room would notice the shadow on the screen first, and immediately understand that it represents himself/herself. The user would then find a WWW page displayed between his/her shadow and another person's shadow. At first, it is too small to be read easily. However, it is magnified when they approach each other, and the user naturally recognizes that the common interest is displayed. Conversation would then occur to discuss the contents of the displayed WWW page.

The actual behavior of users through this experiment was slightly different from our expectation as follows: They saw their own shadows and moved their hands and feet first. Second, they started playing with the shadows: they walked around and passed other users. Finally, conversation about displayed WWW pages began. During the conversation, the users seldom moved and some of them sat down.

Their behavior can be interpreted as follows.

- A user gets interested in the shadow and finds out that it is his/her own shadow because its movement is the same as that of his/hers. Secondly, the user is interested in another user's shadow and interferes by passing, crossing, and so on.
- The user stops moving after understanding the behavior of shadow, becomes attracted by a presented WWW page, and starts conversation about the topic.

Hence, we conclude as follows.

1. Showing their shadows and common interests is effective for attracting users to the system.

2. Presenting topics promotes conversations in real-world encounters.

As we expected, users recognized their own shadows and start conversations related to the WWW pages presented. However, WWW page size often remained static because the change in distance between users was not large after they started a conversation. The content of conversations was not directly concerned to the WWW page, but about the topic suggested by the page.

We also asked 5 Japanese and 25 non-Japanese in Kyoto University to answer a questionnaire. The latter were from Europe, America, Asia, and Africa, and they are mainly research fellows or (under)graduate students. Table 5 shows the nationalities and their numbers.

The following features were obtained from the results of the questionnaire.

Table 5. Rates of Nationalities

nationality	Japan	Asia, except Japan	Africa	Europe and America
number	5	11	3	11
rate (%)	16.7	36.7	10.0	36.7

- *Where would Silhouettell best be used?*
Table 6 shows the results.

Table 6. Where would Silhouettell best be used?

Order (1 means most suited)	1	2	3	4
Public Space	2 (7.1%)	5 (17.9%)	6 (21.4%)	15 (53.6%)
Event Hall	10 (34.5%)	8 (27.6%)	7 (24.1%)	4 (13.8%)
Community Space	12 (42.9%)	8 (28.6%)	8 (28.6%)	0 (0.0%)
Private Party	6 (22.2%)	7 (25.9%)	6 (22.2%)	8 (29.6%)

Over 70% of the subjects selected community space (student union buildings and so on) as being very useful (1) or useful (2). 62% also selected event hall (the site for an international conference and so on). In contrast, over 70% thought that Silhouettell would not be useful in public spaces (i.e. a street corner). The responses for Private Party (home party and so on) varied widely.

- *Contents of profile which a user shows*
Table 7 shows the profile contents that were considered acceptable to the subjects. Most subjects accepted the display of name, affiliation, interest, and nationality. However, few accepted the display of phone number and address.

Table 7. What data should be displayed

content	number
name	25
affiliation	21
nationality	24
address	9
phone number	7
interest	22
birthday	12

– *Cultural Differences*

According to the results of this questionnaire, we found the following cultural differences.

● Places suitable for Silhouettell use

Table 8(a) shows the answers of the subjects from Asia, where the data are the those in Table 6, while Table 8(b) shows the answers of the subjects from Europe and America.

Table 8. Where would Silhouettell best be used?

(a) Asia

evaluation	1	2	3	4
Public Space (%)	9.1	27.3	36.4	27.3
Event Hall (%)	18.2	36.4	18.2	27.3
Community Space (%)	70.0	20.0	10.0	0.0
Private Party (%)	10.0	20.0	30.0	40.0

(b) Europe and America

evaluation	1	2	3	4
Public Space (%)	10.0	20.0	10.0	60.0
Event Hall (%)	27.3	36.4	27.3	9.1
Community Space (%)	20.0	30.0	50.0	0.0
Private Party (%)	40.0	20.0	10.0	30.0

While 90% of Asians have affirmative opinions about the use in community space, only half those from Europe and America shared the same opinion. Though 70% of Asians had negative impressions about its use in private parties, European and American people had various opinions.

● Displayed Profile

Table 9 shows the same data as Table 7, but they are divided into two columns according to the region the subjects were from. The left column shows the number of positive answers for each content from Asian people, while the right column shows those from European and American people. European and American people have negative opinion for displaying their affiliation, while Asians are more liberal on this issue.

Table 9. Cultural differences in releasing data

content	number (Asia)	number (Europe and America)
name	10 (90.9%)	8 (72.7%)
affiliation	10 (90.9%)	4 (36.4%)
nationality	10 (90.9%)	8 (72.7%)
address	5 (45.5%)	2 (18.2%)
phone number	4 (36.4%)	2 (18.2%)
interest	8 (72.7%)	7 (63.6%)
birthday	3 (27.3%)	3 (27.3%)

We summarize these results from three points of view.

1. Utility of Silhouettell

In community spaces where people who have common topics and do not know each other gather, Silhouettell can be an effective tool in helping people to start conversations.

2. Privacy

People hesitate to release their complete details to the public.

3. Cultural Difference

We suggest that there are some differences of sense about presenting topics and privacy between areas. The sense on what topics or attribute one can open to public depends the area he/she come from.

5 Conclusion

We proposed a system, named Silhouettell, for awareness support in real-world encounters. Silhouettell uses a large graphics screen, but does not require the user to possess any additional equipment. It attracts people by projecting their shadows and promotes conversation by presenting common topics based on users' profile. Silhouettell dispays WWW pages as a way of showing common topics. Through a preliminary experience with three users, we validated our implementation policy: the system can support awareness in real-world encounters. We also examined where the system would best be suited through the results of questionnaire collected from people from various nations.

We have developed a series of tools for community computing[10][11]. Community computing supports the early stage of collaboration, or helps various people to organize communities. Awareness support for real-world encounter encourages people to know each other[12].

Future work includes extending Silhouettell to improve of topic selection, and more analysis of the reactions of users from different cultures.

References

1. B. J. Rhodes, "The Wearable Remembrance Agent: A System for Augmented Memory," *International Symposium on Wearable Computers (ISWC-97)*, pp. 123--128, 1997.
2. Cornell University, "Cornell University's CU-SeeMe Page," http://cu-seeme.cornell.edu/, 1997.
3. H. Nakanishi, C. Yoshida, T. Nishimura and T. Ishida, "FreeWalk: Supporting Casual Meetings in a Network," *International Conference on Computer Supported Cooperative Work (CSCW-96)*, pp. 308--314, 1996.
4. K. Nagao and A. Takeuchi, "Social Interaction: Multimodal Convention with Social Agents," *National Conference on Artificial Intelligence (AAAI-94)*, Vol. 1, pp. 22--28, 1994.
5. K. Okada, F. Maeda, Y. Ichikawa and Y. Matsushita, "Multiparty Videoconferencing at Virtual Social Distance: MAJIC Design," *International Conference on Computer Supported Cooperative Work (CSCW-94)*, pp.385--393, 1994.
6. S. A. Bly, S. R. Harrison and S. Irwin, "Media spaces: bringing people together in a video, audio and computing environment," *Communication of the ACM*, Vol. 36, No. 1, pp.28--47, 1993.
7. Silicon Graphics, "InPerson 2.2 Product Guide," http://www.sgi.com/Products/software/InPerson/ipintro.html, 1998.
8. Sony Corporation, "Virtual Society on the Web," http://vs.spiw.com/vs/, 1995.
9. T. Yamaguchi, I. Hosomi and T. Miyashita, "WebStage: An Active Media Enhanced World Wide Web Browser," *International Conference on Human Factors in Computing Systems (CHI-97)*, pp.391--398, 1997.
10. T. Ishida, "Bridging Humans via Agent Networks," *International Workshop on Distributed Artificial Intelligence (DAIWS-94)*, pp. 419--429, 1994.
11. T. Ishida, Towards Communityware," *New Generation Computing*, Vol. 16, No. 1, pp. 5--21, 1998.
12. T. Ishida (Ed.), *Community Computing: Collaboration over Global Information Networks*, John Wiley and Sons, 1998 (in press).

Supporting Network Communities with Multiagent Systems

Fumio Hattori, Takeshi Ohguro, Makoto Yokoo, Shigeo Matsubara, and
Sen Yoshida

NTT Communication Science Laboratories,
2-4 Hikaridai, Seika-cho, Soraku-gun, Kyoto 619-0237 JAPAN
{hattori,ohguro,yokoo,matsubara,yoshida}@cslab.kecl.ntt.co.jp

Abstract. The term "socialware" is used to indicate systems that try
to build a social infrastructure, which is needed to help community activities on the net. Such an infrastructure and systems are needed for
establishing forthcoming network communities, which would become the
core of social activities through the net. This article describes an outline, experimental instances and further directions of socialware. Our
experimental systems reported in this article are: the "Community Organizer" – which aims to support for the formation of new communities,
and the "Community Board" – which aims to support for smooth communications between people by visualizing the structure of discussions.
We believe that socialware will be a promising application for multiagent
systems.

1   Introduction

As the internet is continuous to grow, social activities through the net will become more and more common. Activities entirely on the net have already started:
Virtual factories, virtual markets, virtual malls, network games and so on. The
core of social activities is a network community: Informal group over the network. Various forms of network communities exist and cover a wide range of
subjects: Study group, hobby group, consumer group, research group, local (regional) community and so on. Such network communities are expected to become
more important for all of us in the future.

Although several systems exist for establishing a community over the net,
these systems have limitations which will pose problems in the support of forthcoming network communities. Current problems include:

– Finding people sharing a similar interest.
– Getting to know others better.
– Sharing common contexts in a whole community.
– Identifying the flow of a conversation/discussion.
– Making a decision efficiently over the network.
– Finding what relationships people have.

Such problems also exist in non-network (conventional) communities, but the problems appear much clearly in network communities since they are not constrained by restrictions of time and place. To address these problems, a social infrastructure is needed to help community activities on the net. We call systems that try to build such an infrastructure "socialware".

There are several approaches for building socialware, and they depend on what aspects of communities are to be addressed.

1. Community as an informal communication group.
2. Community as a place for knowledge sharing.
3. Community as a group for performing activities.

First approach can be found in [7], where a new environment is developed for informal communications. Second approach can be found in [9], where systems for sharing mutual knowledge using ontology are discussed. Our approach falls into the last category, that is, to support several network community activities based on interaction between software agents, and between humans and software agents.

There are several characteristics specific to network communities:

- Participants of a network community are widely distributed.
- Most communities have a dynamic nature.
- Each members has individuality.

A multiagent architecture is well suited for such characteristics and therefore we adopt one to achieve socialware.

This article describes an outline, preliminary instances and further directions of socialware, which will be a promising application for multiagent systems.

2   Socialware as Multiagent Systems

2.1   Stages in the Development of a Community and Areas Addressed by Socialware

To explain the issues that we address in the framework of socialware, we roughly divide the development of a community into the following three stages as a working model.

1st stage: Formation of a community.
2nd stage: Activities in the community.
3rd stage: Restructuring the community.

The first stage is the formation of a community. In this stage, we address the issue of how to bring people together. That is, support for linking people with others, or with communities, that share similar interests [1, 8, 10, 13]. For this linking, search engines or directory services for communities can partially help. However, they do have their limitations as they are primarily designed to search for and retrieve information, and not to bring people or communities together. Therefore, more specialized and sophisticated systems are needed.

The second stage involves several activities in a community that has been formed. In this stage, we address the issue of smooth communications [5]. Also included is support for visualizing hidden contexts [11], as well as identifying the stream of a conversation/discussion [6, 12]. To achieve smooth communications, knowing the contexts of the individuals as well as the shared common contexts of the whole community is important. The term "context" includes such aspects as the depth of knowledge of individuals, their attitudes towards the subjects, and mutual knowledge and manners (ethics) for the community. A lack of contexts and/or a failure in identifying the stream of a discussion may cause, for example, "flame wars" [2], which unfortunately often happen in network communications. Another example is where a newcomer possibly has difficulty understanding what is going on in the community.

The third stage is organizing people in a community and/or restructuring a community (or possibly ending a community). In this stage, we address the issue of how to identify the objectives/roles of the community and individuals, and organize them. Revealing human relationships and people networks [4], is important for the issue. Since network communities are amorphous compared to organizations like companies and schools, such relationships and networks are sometimes hidden or unknown. This causes difficulty in finding the "key" person or people suitable for the current concerns, despite such search being needed to restructure the community for the sake of improving current activities or starting a new movement.

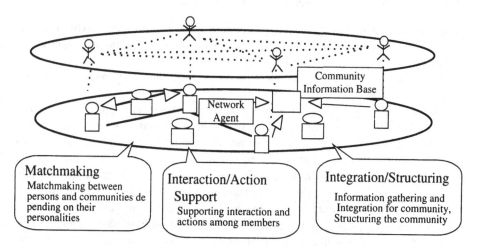

Fig. 1. An image of areas of socialware

2.2 Characteristics of Network Communities

There are several characteristics specific to network communities, for which a multiagent architecture is suited toward. These are: Distributed, dynamic and individuality.

The first characteristic is that the participants of a network community are widely distributed and the number of potential participants is large. Hence no solid, centralized or monolithic system would be adequate: The only feasible way to implement such a system seems to be to create a (set of) personalized agent(s) for each participant, and to have them cooperate with each other.

The second characteristic is that communities have a dynamic nature. The active membership changes over time, in addition to the roles of individuals and objectives, and moreover, the community will likely change its aspect. In other words, there exists no fixed organization nor a clear goal for a network community; people are at an earlier stage, that is to say, a pre-organization. This characteristic contrasts the area of groupware that helps people already organized, work cooperatively, where the members, their roles, and their objectives are rather clearly defined.

The third characteristic is that the individuality of each member is preserved even in one community. That is, each member can have diverse objectives, even if all members share common interests in general. Furthermore, people can be members of several communities at the same time depending on their various interests. Hence, supports need to be personalized to adapt individual objectives and interests. They also need to adapt variations and changes of interests and activities of a person.

2.3 A General Architecture of Socialware

The characteristics described above indicate that a multiagent architecture is suitable for achieving socialware. Here, we propose a general architecture of socialware to illustrate this (Figure 2).

We view a community as a collection of personal units, community-agent(s), and the set of relations between them.

A personal unit consists of a user and his/her personal agent(s). The main functions of the personal agent(s) are to get and maintain user's profile by observing user's activity, and to assist user in communicating with others. This architecture enables the community to spread over the net. It also enables the user's individuality to be maintained: Each personal unit can simultaneously belong to several communities rather than totally included in a community, reflecting the situation that the user has multiple interests and activities.

Community-agents have the function of providing shared information, knowledge and/or contexts within the community and act as mediators for informal communications between people.

The whole system needs to be flexible and adaptive so that it can adapt to the dynamic nature of a community where the community members, as well as their relationships, will likely change over time.

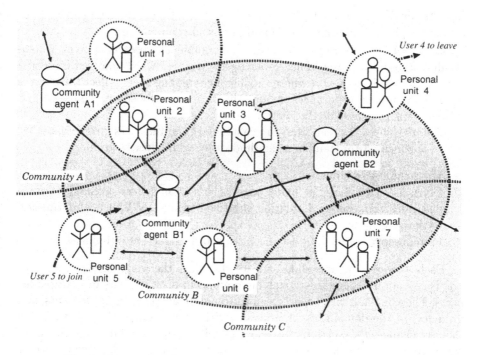

Fig. 2. A general architecture of socialware as a multiagent system

To adapt to multiple aspects of a user and the user's changes in interests, for example, the user may have multiple agents which communicate with each other. These agents communicate with the user either directly or through another agent which acts as a mediator. It is possible for some agents to be domain specific (e.g. an information retrieval agent specialized to financial news), and others more generic (e.g. an interface agent for navigating and reading documents). An individual agent can help the user by, for example, gathering and exchanging information, visualizing contexts, and recommending/assisting the user in making a choice. All of the agents cooperate and act as a whole system, with the user being central to. Adaptation can be achieved by changing the system dynamically and autonomously. For example, a domain specific agent can clone itself to produce a new agent and make additional communication channels when the user's interest has changed.

3 Experimental Systems of Socialware

3.1 Community Organizer

We have developed a prototype application for the purpose of "linking people", which we call the "Community Organizer" [13].

The Basic Function. The basic function of the Community Organizer is to enable people finding other people and potential communities.

Each user has its own viewer agent which graphically presents potential communities around the user. The viewer agent locates users (indicated by icons) in a two-dimensional space, where the distances among users reflect the degrees of common interest (relevances) among them. In any view-space, the user of the viewer agent is located at the center.

The relevances between users are calculated from the users' profile data. We have implemented three different methods in obtaining user's profile.

1. From the user's input.
2. Given a URL for user's "home page", the system collect profile data automatically from user's information published on the WWW using information retrieval techniques.
3. From archives of mailing lists using keyword extraction techniques.

Each viewer agent has slide-bars which adjust the weightings of the viewpoints temporary, since the degree of common interest consists of multiple aspects. These include such aspects as location, date and time, type, contents, and intimacy, in the domain of voluntary activities for example (Figure 3). When the user changes the weightings of the viewpoints using the slide-bars, the agent automatically re-calculates the relevances between users using a weighted cosine measure and reflects the results into the view-space.

In this way, the system enables users to find other people that have similar interests, as well as potential communities among users. Users can also simulate several possibilities of potential communities, by changing their viewpoints.

Additional Functions. Additionally, the viewer agent can learn the weightings from user feedback. When a user finds that a person who does not seem to share common interests is located very close to the center (i.e., to the user), the user can indicate the fact to his/her viewer agent. Then, the agent modifies the weights of keywords permanently to reduce the relevance value between the indicated person and the user. This function enables the user to customize the viewer agent, and personalize the view according to his/her interests.

The viewer agent not only provides the view-space but also communicates with other viewer agents, as well as communicates with a server agent which maintains a database. For example, the learning process involving the weightings can be done cooperatively: Each agent can exchange the weightings that it has learned with others. This cooperation reduces the ability of personalization but improves the speed of learning, especially when profiles of users may be insufficient or erroneous. Therefore, this ability can be regarded as an information sharing method in a potential community.

The system has another function: to multicast a message to other users within a certain distance from the user. This multicast area can be adjusted by the user. The system also has the ability to introduce a user's friend to another friend. These functions enable the user to easily communicate with an amorphous group,

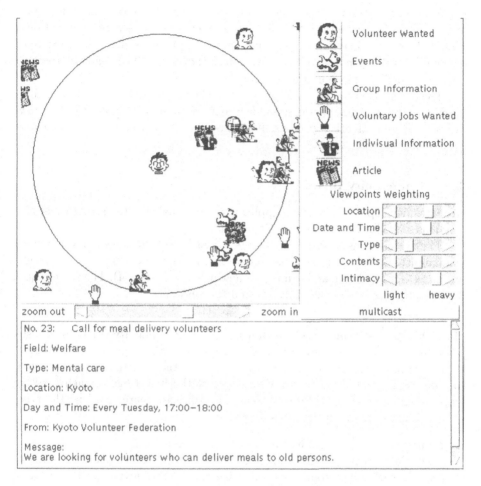

Fig. 3. A screen-shot of the Community Organizer through a viewer agent

leading to the formation of a new community. Furthermore, as an extension, negotiations can be carried out between agents of individual users (under the control and cooperation of the users) when a new community is to be formed.

Extensions. We are now developing several extensions for the system.

One extension is to locate messages/informations in the view-space as well. Besides that user can multicast a message, user can also "locate" a message in the view-space without specifying the recipients. This function enable the users to route the message according to ones interest and intention directly, without first examining who will be interested in. The message located in the view-space has another effect that it can attract other persons near by. Thus, we can expect a positive feedback loop of message/information accumulation and gathering of people.

Another extension is to display an average of profiles of persons in a certain region which is selected by the user. The average of profiles is represented by a simple diagram. Therefore the user can know why there seems to be a group of people (in the region selected), what profiles they share. This leads the user to identify (possible) communities around the user.

The other extension is to exchange user's view-point each other. This enables users to share a common standpoint/context, or enables the users to know new ways of looking at other persons. It is expected to help users in forming new community as well.

3.2 Community Board

We have developed a prototype application for visualizing the structure of discussions, called the "Community Board" [6].

The system consists of board agents for each user and a server agent for a community. Each board agent has functions to display messages as icons, show each messages in detail, and compose a new message (Figure 4). The server agent maintains databases of the messages and the keywords.

The Basic Function. The basic function of the Community Board is to visualize the structure and the context of discussions in an integrated view-space.

Three main dimensions are chosen to express the structure of a discussion: person, topic, and time. In the view-space of the board agent, each message is represented as an icon. Person, topic, and time are represented by the type, position, and shading of the icons, respectively.

Person: Each person has his/her own icon for messages.

Topic: Each message is located according to its topic, with similar topics located nearby. The topic for a message is currently given by the writer of the message as a keyword. We plan to allow multiple keywords or to extract keywords automatically from messages. The relevances between topics are calculated using a database on the server agent. Each board agent decides the locations of the topics from the relevances using a multidimensional scaling method. The locations are re-calculated whenever a message with a new topic arrives.

Time: Icons for messages become dimmer and smaller with time (finally disappearing). The correspondence between the period of time and the icon shading can be defined by the user.

Users can take in the various combinations of these three aspects at a glance, without changing the view-space itself.

Such combinations of information can be used in several ways.

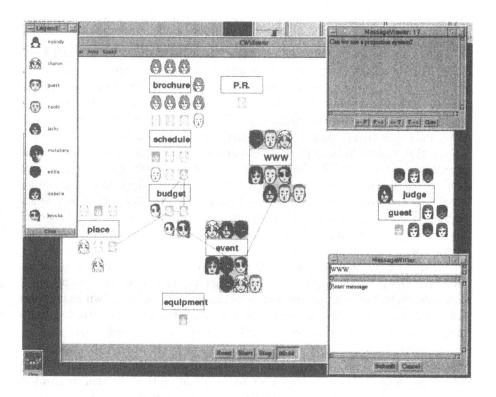

Fig. 4. A screen-shot of the view-space for the Community Board

Person and Topic: A user can decide whether to join a discussion, or can guess to whom a question relating to a topic should be asked, from the information about people and topics.

Topic and Time: Users can grasp the relations between topics, what topics have been discussed (or not discussed), and what topics are current (or old), at a glance, from the information about topics and time. Such knowledge helps the users learn the current context of the discussion and helps them anticipate responses beforehand, e.g., before they join the discussion.

Time and Person: The users can better understand the transitions between topics from the information about people and time. This helps them understand other users and the causal relations between their messages.

In this way, users can obtain and share the contexts of a community. This helps smooth communications between people, helps in revealing relations between people, and helps in finding the role of each person.

Extensions. Beyond the functions described above, we are now developing several extensions for the system.

One extension is to refine the relevance database of topics from user's feedback. This is useful since each community may have its own vocabulary and terminology. By refining the relations between topics, a database that reflects the contexts of a community will be built. Such a database will be valuable especially for newcomers to the community. This also overcomes the drawback that the standard dictionary is hard to capture dynamics of words.

Another extension is to consider the quality of messages. Using evaluations of messages with users' feedback, each user can filter messages of low quality (i.e., less important for the community, or for the user). The evaluations can be used in summarizing and arrangement of the discussion, since they reflect which opinion is dominant or what message is attractive. It can also be used to reveal the trend of "silent majority", or to give users a motivation to improve their discussion.

Further extensions are planned: One is to provide a personal view-space for all users. Except for the basic view-space, which is public to all participants, each user can overlay his/her own personal view-space, using his/her own agent. This gives each user a more closed space, which may be used only by a restricted group of users or privately by the user. The other is to provide multiple board systems for all users, according to their interests. Currently, one board corresponds to one community. Users may set up multiple board systems for each community to which they belong. These systems need to coordinate with each other, to arrange user activities in several communities as they may conflict at times.

4 Future Direction

Socialware is a new concept for network community support [3]. We believe that it opens up new areas of application for a multiagent framework.

In addition to the application systems described above, several research areas may exist in the framework of socialware. Such research areas include:

- Modeling the behavior of communities: How people act in network communities?
- Modeling and describing the relations between people.
- Modeling and efficiently expressing the "contexts".
- Symbiotic media: How to make "community feeling" (or "we-feeling") ?

Further application systems for socialware include:

- Controlling the course of discussions, to help in decision-making in a group.
- Helping to restructuring people inside a community (applications in the 3rd stage of the community).
- Providing much more flexible communication channels (such as self-organizing mailing lists).

– Aiding users in publishing information, so that they can share their knowledge and contexts without much effort (such as semi-automated publishing systems – writing and maintaining, e.g., Web pages, are known to require great effort).
– Integration of these systems.

We are presently trying to develop such systems.

There are several technical challenges in implementing socialware as a multiagent systems.

Flexible multi-agent architecture: There might be a situation that new agents are made dynamically to adapt to changes of a community and a user's interest, or that members (hence their agents) join/leave a community. Finding methods for adapting such situations flexibly, and making coalition of agents which dynamically changes its structure and behavior, are one important direction of technical challenges.

Human-agent collaboration: How human and agents can effectively collaborate as a system? There are several researches that study the collaboration of agents, though new style of collaboration seems to be needed when human is tightly incorporated into the system. Good coordinations of human and agents will be required, and hence effective collaboration in human-agents system is an important technical challenge.

Controlling the complex system: Network communities are very complex systems, since they are distributed and dynamic, and since they consists of variety of users, agents and human-agent systems. Finding ways of controlling, managing and/or get along with such a complex system is an important challenge.

References

1. Foner, L.N.: A multi-agent referral system for matchmaking. In Proceedings of PAAM'96. The Practical Application Company (1996) pp. 245–261.
2. Hambridge, S.: Netiquette guidelines. RFC1855 (Also FYI0028), 1995.
3. Ishida, T.: Towards CommunityWare. In Proceedings of PAAM'97. The Practical Application Company (1997) pp. 7–21.
4. Kautz, H., Selman, B. and Shah, M.: Referral Web: Combining social networks and collaborative filtering. Commun. ACM **40,3** (Mar. 1997) 63–65.
5. LaLiberte, D. and Woolley, D.: Presentation features of text-based conferencing systems on the WWW. Computer-Mediated Communication Magazine. **4,5** (May 1997).
6. Matsubara, S., Ohguro, T. and Hattori, F.: Community Board: Social meeting system able to visualize the structure of discussions. In Proceedings of Knowledge-based Intelligent Electronic Systems (KES'98). IEEE (1998) pp. 423–428.
7. Nakanishi, H., Yoshida, C., Nishimura, T. and Ishida., T.: FreeWalk: Supporting casual meetings in a network. In Proceedings of CSCW'96. ACM (1996) pp. 308–314.

8. Nishibe, Y., Waki, H., Morihara, I. and Hattori, F.: Analyzing social interactions in massive mobile computing – Experiments of ICMAS'96 mobile assistant project –. In Proceedings of IJCAI'97 Workshop on Social Interaction and Communityware. Morgan-Kaufmann (1997) pp. 19–24.

9. Nishida, T., Takeda, H., Iwazume, H. Maede, H. and Takaai, M.: The knowledgeable community. In Proceedings of Knowledge-based Intelligent Electronic Systems (KES'98). IEEE (1998) pp. 23–32.

10. Nishimura, T., Yamaki, H., Komura, T., Itoh, N., Gotoh, T. and Ishida, T.: Community Viewer: Visualizing community formation on personal digital assistants. In Proceedings of IJCAI'97 Workshop on Social Interaction and Communityware. Morgan-Kaufmann (1997) pp. 25–30.

11. Sumi, Y., Nishimoto, K. and Mase, K.: Personalizing shared information in creative conversations. In Proceedings of IJCAI'97 Workshop on Social Interaction and Communityware. Morgan-Kaufmann (1997) pp. 31–36.

12. Uetake, T., and Nagata, M.: A computer supported system of meetings using a model of inter-personal communication. IEICE Trans. Inf. and Syst. **E78-D,9** (Sep. 1995) 1127–1132.

13. Yoshida, S., Kamei, K., Yokoo, M. Ohguro, T., Funakoshi, K. and Hattori, F.: Community visualizing agent. In Proceedings of PAAM'98. The Practical Application Company (1998) pp. 643–644.

Agent Augmented Community: Human-to-Human and Human-to-Environment Interactions Enhanced by Situation-Aware Personalized Mobile Agents

Katashi Nagao[1] and Yasuharu Katsuno[2]

[1] Sony Computer Science Laboratory Inc.
3-14-13 Higashi-gotanda, Shinagawa–ku, Tokyo 141, Japan
[2] Department of Computer Science, Keio University
3-14-1 Hiyoshi, Kohoku–ku, Yokohama 223-0061, Japan

Abstract. An *agent augmented community* is a new framework that uses agent technologies for the augmentation of our community activities by integrating cyberspace, the real world, and personal contexts. We have been developing a mobile agent system that can recognize real world situations, move to remote computers, and process information through communication among agents. The detection of real world situations is performed through the integration of various methods, including location awareness using a global positioning system (GPS) and object recognition through machine-recognizable IDs (barcodes, infrared, etc.). One of our testbeds is a campus navigation system that provides information about the facilities and activities of a university campus environment according to the user's physical location and individual needs. It can be personalized for the user by using user-specific information about her interests and preferences. The other testbed is a new tool for the augmentation of face-to-face conversations. It can exchange participants' personal data through interagent communication.

1 Introduction

An *agent augmented community* is a new framework that uses agent technologies for the augmentation of our community activities by integrating cyberspace, the real world, and personal contexts.

The concept of augmented reality has been extended so that it covers interactive systems that can enhance the real world with additional information. Such systems support real world human tasks by providing information such as descriptions of objects as they are viewed [9, 7], navigational help [8], and instructions for performing physical tasks [3]. Augmented reality systems essentially require the ability to recognize real world objects and situations. There are several approaches for detecting real world objects/situations, such as scene analysis by visual processing, or by using machine-recognizable IDs (barcodes, infrared, etc.), location detection using the global positioning system (GPS), communication with physically embedded computers, and so on. IDs of static objects (e.g., doors, ceilings, walls, etc.) can give clues to a location awareness system.

Integrating augmented reality and agent technologies has created a new research field. This field requires special agents that recognize real world situations, move around in cyberspace, search for information related to the intentions of their users, communicate with humans and with other agents, and perform, on behalf of the users, some tasks in cyberspace.

This kind of agent can support the user's tasks in a real world environment, such as place-to-place navigation, instruction in physical tasks, and the enhancement of human knowledge related to the physical environment. After an agent detects a real world situation and understands the intentions of its user, it can access information worlds (e.g., the Internet) like other software agents. Thus, it can dynamically integrate the real world with information worlds.

We have been developing a mobile agent system that can recognize real world situations and process information using remote computers. Since a wireless network of mobile or wearable computers [13] is unstable, mobile agents are very useful when their users want to access and manipulate information resources on the network. The agents can move to remote hosts, process data, and send results back to the users.

The agent can also be personalized for the user. This personalization is done using a user profile and an agent learning mechanism. Since personalization involves personal information, the agent would also protect the user's privacy using agent authentication and data encryption.

The situation-aware, personalized agent accompanies the user and stays aware of the surroundings and activities of the user. Therefore, the agent has a rich source of nonverbal clues with which to clarify the user's requests and to interpret intentions. The efficiency of communication is affected by situational information, which can also be a cause of ambiguity in messages. Situation awareness can thus play a role in 'disambiguation.'

The agents work to augment interpersonal communication. Situation-aware, personalized agents can add a supplemental context providing personal information and the current status of their users to their messages. This can help receivers of messages to understand their context better, increasing communication efficiency. We call this type of communication *augmented communication.*

The agents can also augment our daily face-to-face conversations by exchanging personal information, i.e., some personal information exchange can be properly managed by the agents. Of course, agents would have to receive their users' approval to send personal information at each exchange, this transfer of personal information might help the conversation participants learn about each other, and could be saved for future use.

In this paper, we discuss the concept and potential applications of augmented communication and an implementation of situation-aware, personalized mobile agents. We also explain two experimental application systems that have been implemented.

2   Augmented Communication

Augmented communication is a new style of human communication that is enhanced via situation-aware, personalized agents.

In this section, we briefly describe several potential applications based on the concept of augmented communication. These have not yet been implemented, but we have enough technology to do so when some issues concerning information and physical infrastructures have been overcome.

The situation-aware, personalized agents can help users make use of previous conversations (within the context of the current conversation), by showing a summary of previous texts. The Remembrance Agent [11] is one such example. This could facilitate conversation by reducing duplication.

Another example is an intelligent telephone operator that checks the current status of the callee before the user makes a call to that person. If the potential callee is very busy or talking to another person, the agent will recommend that the user not call at that time. Again, agents will always take care to protect the privacy of humans and will cooperate to satisfy their users' demands.

Our augmented communication also covers an integrated system of agent-mediated communication and previous asynchronous communication based on electronic mail and bulletin boards. Users can attach their agents to text messages for conveying some contextual information about their physical environments. Also, they can hide messages inside agents by translating the messages into an agent language whose semantics is well defined by the agent's ontology. In this case, more advanced communication will be possible since agents can understand the contents of messages and will be able to convey nuances as well as physical contexts. Futhermore, interactions between the messenger agent and the receiver agent will result in intelligent filtering and summarization of messages.

Community activities will be supported by such an agent-based, intelligent message handling system. This communication among community members will overcome, not only the gap of space but also that of time. Communication will be customized for each agent of each member using personal information. So, received messages will be filtered according to user preferences. Messages being sent can be personalized with the user's situational information (locations, physical environments, current activities, etc.).

Cooperation among agents will work as a social filtering, a type of information filtering based on recommendations given by other users [10]. The agents will exchange users' recommendations with their interests about specific topics. A recommendation will include a user or agent ID, keywords, an identifier of the information resource (e.g., URL), an annotation of contents, and an evaluation value (normalized positive value). The evaluation value is decided considering the frequency of access to the information and counts of usage, reference, and recommendation of the information. The recommendations are generated semi-automatically and stored in a shared database. First, an agent searches for recommendations about a particular topic. Then, the agent tries to contact agents that are responsible for the selected recommendations. Next, the agent tries to assign a credit to each responsible agent contacted. The credit is determined through communication between the requesting agent and the responsible agent, because the credit depends on the task of the requesting agent and the career of the responsible agent. The agent repeats the credit assignment process for all selected recommendations. Then, it gives the user the recommendations that have the higher credits.

The agents can utilize real world information as well as online digital information. For physical environments, respective agents can guide their users to meet at a certain place in the real world. The agents could also negotiate and decide the most appropriate time and place to meet. Since interagent communication includes information on physical environments and personal status/plans, mutual understanding for each other will be established more efficiently than by present-day e-mail or telephone calls.

Our augmented communication also has a role of seamlessly integrating real and virtual community places. Recently, some electronic squares for chatting have been open to the public. There are also virtual cities where inhabitants have three-dimensional figures and can move around a virtual world and talk with one another using speech balloons. Our system tries to reconstruct real community activities on virtual environments. The users can remember their activities by interacting with the virtual environments and change/update their ideas and comments. Our system also supports each individual's memory and extends it to the common knowledge database of the community.

An example application of the integration of real and virtual community places is tracing and re-experiencing real world activities in a virtual environment. Using GPS, the system can trace users as they walk through a real town and then shows the walks on a virtual town that imitates its correspondence. Later, users can re-experience their previous walks using the virtual town and can go so far as to find their favorite items in the stores again. The agent will facilitate their recollection by showing memory cues and guide them to their destination.

3 Implementation of Situation-Aware Personalized Mobile Agents

Augmented communication utilizes mobile agents for personalizing information space by dispatching programs with personal data that are controlled by their responsible users. Mobile agents also give a good solution for information localization. For security reasons, data stored on some hosts might not be accessible from the outside. Only users of authorized mobile agents can access and process such localized information remotely.

Our architecture of mobile agents is based on the design principles of Telescript technology [15]. Here, agents are implemented as migrate-able programs that are interpreted in particular "places." Places can perform the following:

- Places can identify visiting agents using their authorities.
- Places can communicate with visiting agents and supply information service.
- Places can give the right to access resources to appropriate agents.
- Places can mediate communication among visiting agents.
- Places can protect the security of resources from agents.

To implement mobile agents that can move around in cyberspace such as the Internet, we employed a Java-based mobile agent programming system. While Telescript technology provides its own programming environment for mobile agents, it is not easy to use for extending language specification. A Java-based agent programming language such as APSL (Agent Programming System and Language) [5], on the other hand, allows us to easily extend the language so as to include personalization, cryptography, and situation awareness techniques.

The APSL operation environment assumes that agent programs are running on one of three types of hosts: a Customer Host, an Agency Host, or a Service Host. A Customer Host is a user's mobile host that is connected to the network using some type of wireless data communication. Obviously, there are times that it is disconnected from the network and its computational performance degrades accordingly. Therefore, *remote programming* by means of mobile agents is very important. A Customer Host user will access an Agency Host where the agents have been developed and stored, and download an agent customization environment, including templates of agent programs and a user interface. Through the user interface, the user is able to supply some parameters to the agent that can be used during its operation. The user sends the mobile agent to one of Service Hosts where it can obtain various services. After the agent is sent off, the Customer Host will be disconnected. The mobile agent visits several Service Hosts and returns to the Agency Host when it has finished all its tasks. When the Customer Host is reconnected to the network, it accesses the Agency Host again and the mobile agent returns to the Customer Host from an agent repository environment running on the Agency Host. Finally, the mobile agent gives any work results to the user. Figure 1 shows the overall process of a mobile agent operation in APSL.

In APSL, places are implemented as agent programs called *place agents*. However they can not move around the network, in contrast to mobile agents. Place agents provide a variety of services to mobile agents by communicating with them. One of the advantages of this implementation of places as agents is the protection of secured data embedded in the mobile agents, because place agents can access mobile agent information, not by interpreting programs, but by exchanging messages generated by the mobile agents. Place agents also work as mediators that enable several mobile agents to exchange their messages.

APSL also provides a *communication package* that supports communication between a mobile agent and a place agent. The communication package implements a communication protocol according to available resources. Making implementation of communication protocols independent from agent programs is very important since a protocol should be shared by communicators, and implementation depends on the resources that communicators can provide. In APSL, place-mobile agent communication is initiated by supplying the communication

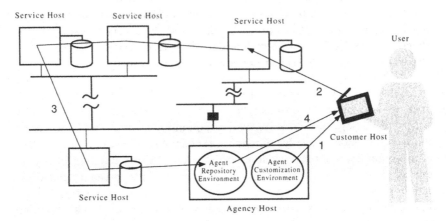

Fig. 1. APSL Operation Environment

package to the recipient agent. The list of resources and their access permissions are checked before initiating each communication, then the initiating agent selects an appropriate communication package. Agents must use a communication package for every message exchange.

Place agents are categorized as personal place agents and public place agents. Personal place agents running on Customer Hosts can access any personal information resources (e.g., ID number of a credit card). Public place agents running on other hosts cannot access such personal information, but can use some public information resources (e.g., product catalogs).

Situation awareness techniques are implemented in place agents. The place agents accept user/object/location IDs from the physical environment and relate these IDs with the appropriate information resources such as customer databases, product catalogs, local area maps, Web pages, and so on. If the information resources are located at remote hosts, then a mobile agent is instantiated and transferred to the remote hosts. The instantiation is done by a parameter setting to a template of agents. So, the place agents have the ability not only to communicate with mobile agents but also to create them. The mobile agents access the information resources that are related with real world situations recognized by the place agents. After communicating with agents at remote hosts, the mobile agents return to their original host and report to the place agents.

Personalization techniques are implemented in personal place agents. The personal place agents can access user profile data. They also have a model of user interests and a statistical learning mechanism for user model modification. A user model will be described using several methods including weighted feature vectors, decision trees, Bayesian networks [2], and Gibbs's distributions [1]. We have to select an appropriate representation, one suitable to a particular task and domain, since a more complex model requires a more time-consuming learning algorithm.

4   Agent Augmented Community Applications

We have been developing two experimental systems using situation-aware, personalized mobile agents based on the above techniques.

4.1   HyperCampus: A Location-Aware Personalized Campus Navigation System

HyperCampus is a system for campus information guidance. It determines a user's location using GPS and infrared beacons, and provides user-specific, context-dependent information on campus and university activities heighten the user's understanding and interest in the university.

Figure 2 shows a snapshot of HyperCampus in use.

Fig. 2. HyperCampus in Use

Figure 3 shows a system configuration of HyperCampus.

The personal place agent detects the user's current position and records his/her activities for personalization. The personal place agent also manages the user's personal data. The user can give orders for the agent to process information on the network. The personal place agent generates mobile agents and dispatches them to appropriate Service Hosts.

HyperCampus Contents Information contents, including a user registration form, are created on using APSL with Java. Personal data, including location information, is managed by the personal place running on mobile or wearable computers. Typical contents are:

1. Campus area information
   Campus map, building locations, information on outdoor services, etc.

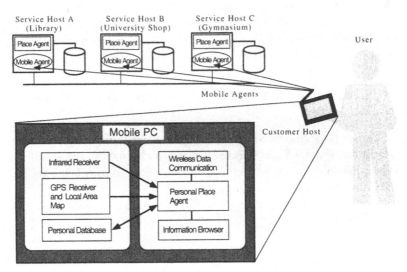

Fig. 3. HyperCampus System Configuration

2. Architectural information
   Outlook images of buildings, history of construction, information on events related to buildings, etc.
3. Indoor information
   Floor plans, laboratory information, room information, information on indoor activities, etc.
4. Class information
   Timetable of classes, lecture room information, etc.
5. University information
   Other university related information
6. User behavior history
   Chronological list of places visited and information accessed

The system shows the user's current position using a campus map with a position indicator (Figure 4), and related information using a simple Java-based information browser that is connected with the location awareness module.

Figure 5 shows an example screen of the user registration form for agent customization. In this screen, the user can give orders for the agent to process information at remote computers located at places the user visits later. For example, user Katashi Nagao asks his agent to make a list of Java-related books by retrieving the data stored at the library. When he arrives at the library, the agent returns and provides information as shown in Figure 6.

HyperCampus Functions The GPS calculates global positions (latitude and longitude) and the system converts them into local map coordinants when the user is outdoors. Inside, each room has an infrared transmitter at the entrance, which transmits the room ID when the door opens. Therefore, the system knows

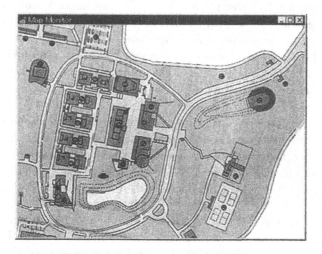

Fig. 4. Map and Position Indicator

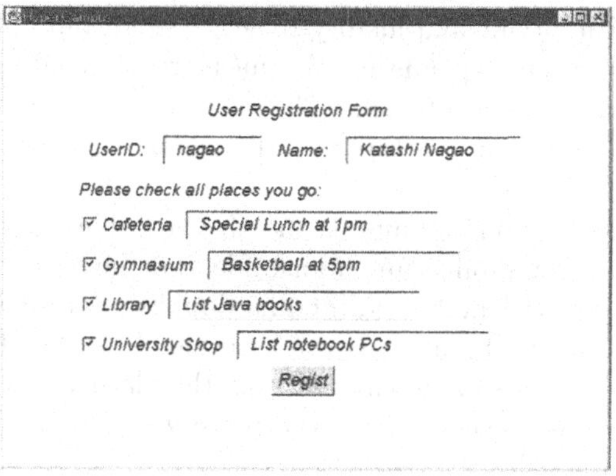

User Registration Form

UserID: [nagao]   Name: [Katashi Nagao]

Please check all places you go:

☑ Cafeteria [Special Lunch at 1pm]

☑ Gymnasium [Basketball at 5pm]

☑ Library [List Java books]

☑ University Shop [List notebook PCs]

[Regist]

Fig. 5. Example of User Registration Screen

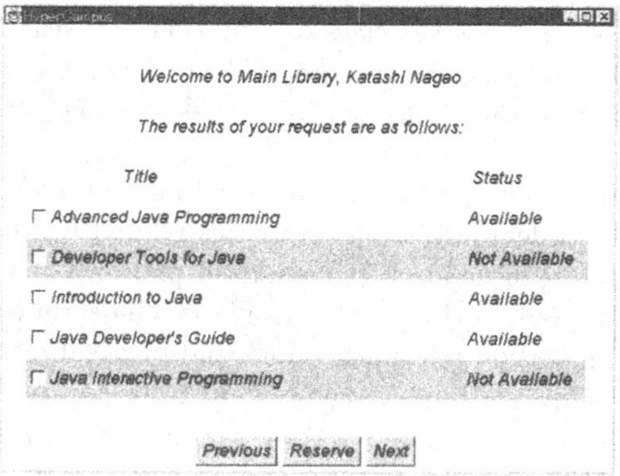

Welcome to Main Library, Katashi Nagao

The results of your request are as follows:

Title	Status
☐ Advanced Java Programming	Available
☐ Developer Tools for Java	Not Available
☐ Introduction to Java	Available
☐ Java Developer's Guide	Available
☐ Java Interactive Programming	Not Available

[Previous] [Reserve] [Next]

Fig. 6. Example of Library Information Screen

its indoor positions by detecting room IDs. The information browser is sensitive to each position and shows related information. Also, the information presentation depends on current time and changes contents according to time. So, when the user is close to a lecture room, for example, the system can present information on the class that is being held at that time. Of course, the user can retrieve information about other events regardless of time.

In order to relate information contents with real world situations, the system prepares some scenarios that specify appropriate information resources that should be selected when the user is on a typical scene. However, it is impossible to predict every interaction that a user could perform at a certain scene. So, we also provided a mechanism that is flexible enough to reduce user confusion and to allow easy recovery of the previous status if the system's prediction function were to fail.

Personalization of this system is done by a predescribed user profile that includes the user ID, subject, research theme, and interested items. History of the user's activities such as places visited and information accessed also contributes to this personalization. The learning mechanism involved will be described later. The system uses the profile and history to select some appropriate scenarios for guidance. The selection depends on the measure of relevance between information and predicted user interests. The relevance value is calculated with a distance of weighted feature vectors that abstractly represent the user's recent concerns.

Since the users of HyperCampus use mobile/wearable computers and wireless networks, the data communication is unstable and the local user-side resources are very limited. So, the mobile agent functionality is essential. After getting user requests, the mobile agent moves to a Service Host, communicates with its place agent, and processes data acquired from the place agent. If some necessary information cannot be accessed from the place visited, the agent can move to another Service Host.

Example Scenarios for HyperCampus To give an example: After identifying the user, the system accesses class information and searches for particular classes related to her subject and interests. Then, the system guides the user to the proper classroom of the next class by considering her current location and the time.

Another scenario demonstrates a laboratory tour. Some visitors and students are looking forward to learning about activities related to their studies and/or interests. The system can create a personalized plan of lab tour for each user. The system will also contact the staff of each lab included in the tour. The order of visits is decided based on relevance values and physical distances.

We are also preparing a library scenario. At a university library, if the user walks around a bookshelf, the system retrieves information on the available books there that are related to her interests. It also will indicate which books are reserved and which can be borrowed. This is an extension of a subscription system that provides its subscribers with information updated since their last visit on the Web. Physical location can be a filtering clue to select appropriate information and timing.

There is a scenario for uninterestedness. If the user has not accessed any information and not moved for a certain period, the system may decide that she is resting for a while. Then, the system will *push* information relevant to her current position and interests. This will encourage the user to become more interested in the campus and the university.

Other scenarios concern community support. An example would be the location notification of other people. If a friend of the user is accessing information in the user's neighborhood, the system informs the user of her friend's location and situation. This function might infringe on the privacy of another. So, the system must solicit agreement before notifying the user of the other person's current location and situation. The system can also support asynchronous communication via physical environments. The user can leave a message at some physical place and other users can read this message when they reach there. The creator of the messages can restrict those recipients by specifying user IDs or group IDs.

We are also designing a human memory supplement system that stores the user's activities connected with physical places. Like Forget-me-not [6], the system works as a memory cue by showing short descriptions of the user's accessed information and places visited in chronological order.

Learning Mechanism for HyperCampus We implemented a learning mechanism for user personalization of HyperCampus. The mechanism uses a weighted feature vector. The feature corresponds to an attribute of concepts related to the user's interests. The concepts include activities, facilities, and social events at the university. The attributes are related objects (e.g., 'book' is an attribute of 'library'), functions (e.g., 'to study' is an attribute of 'lecture'), characteristics (e.g., 'multimedia presentation' is an attribute of 'auditorium'), and so on.

Learning is roughly divided into data acquisition and model modification. The personal place agent acquires user's behavioral data by detection of location change and information access. This data includes the time and duration that the places were visited, the information that was accessed, and the semantic attributes related to the places and the information. Model modification is performed by calculating the relevance value between an input that corresponds to an action of the user and a model of the user's interests that is constructed from previous data, plus parameter adjustments (e.g., weights) of attributes in the constructed model.

First, an initial model is built based on the profile data of the user. The profile consists of the user ID, subject, research theme, and interested items. We defined an initial feature vector (user model) as a one-dimensional array of real number values that implicitly reflect the user's subject, research theme, and interested items. For example, if the user majored in history, features related to historical events and architectures have higher weights than other features.

The model modification algorithm is very simple, because we calculate the average value of all feature vectors. The reason is as follows: Let x be a model of interests, and $\{e_1, e_2, ..., e_n\}$ be a set of feature vectors. A relevance value between a feature vector e_1 and model x is given by an inner product of two vectors $e_i * x$. Then, in order to maximize the sum of relevance values $S(x) = \Sigma_i(e_i * x) = nE * x$, x should be αE, where E is the avarage of all feature vectors and α is a positive constant for normalization.

Considering the task, feature vectors have enough representation power and allow a simple calculation algorithm to be applied for parameter tuning.

HyperCampus is being evaluated by some freshmen at Keio University in Japan. Since they are not very familiar with their campus, the system will prove helpful in finding good lectures, classes, and professors that will interest them.

4.2 HyperDialog: A Tool for Augmented Face-to-Face Conversation

We applied the situation-aware, personalized mobile agents to the augmentation of our daily conversations. The system is called *HyperDialog*. This system would be used at informal meetings or parties. Face-to-face conversations can be augmented through exchanging digital messages in parallel via the participants' agents. Such messages include e-mail addresses and URLs that are more useful if obtained digitally. HyperDialog is a secured digital information exchange tool using mobile agent functions.

Figure 7 shows a snapshot of HyperDialog in use.

Fig. 7. HyperDialog in Use

Figure 8 shows the system configuration of HyperDialog.

The system can also work as a social matchmaker in that it can search for someone who has the same interests as the user at a meeting or a party. The personalized agents retrieve other participants' accessible personal data, and calculate the degree of overlapping interest for each participant.

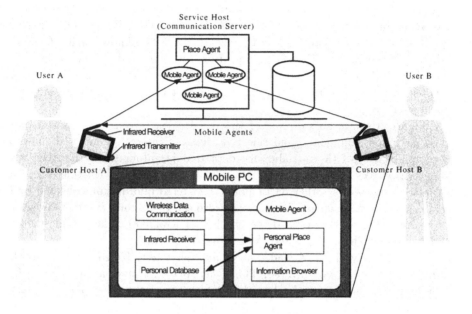

Fig. 8. HyperDialog System Configuration

Example Scenario for HyperDialog A typical scenario might be:

A user receives an invitation to a party and decides to attend. Before going, the user sends her mobile agent to a Service Host that is managed by the party hosts. The agent holds some messages including the person's name, ID, the Customer Host name, comments, items of interest, etc. At the Service Host, the place agent identifies the visiting agents and accepts their holding messages.

At the party, every participants with a mobile computer automatically receives the other participants' information from his/her previously sent mobile agent. Of course, this information can be accessed from outside the party venue by the privileged (e.g., registered) user. However, we think that timely and implicitly conveyed information will be more convenient if the imformation is not so critical.

The personal place agents know where they are by location beacons and can access the Service Host automatically. The agents show the participant list to their users using the information browser. But at this time, the users do not know correspondences between an item in the list and a real person. If the data contains a photo, they might be able to determine the person related to the item. However, in some cases, a photo does not contain enough data to distinguish a person.

The mobile agents calculate affinity values between their users and other participants by checking overlapping items of interest. Then, the agents send the data to the personal place agents. This will facilitate their informal communication. During a face-to-face conversation, participants can exchange personal information such as e-mail addresses and personal Web page URLs via their mobile agents. One person can transmit the user's ID to another person in the conversation via an infrared transmitter like the Active Badge [14]. Thus, the personal place agent can identify the person and get to know his/her Customer Host by receiving the ID through an infrared receiver and retrieving data from the Service Host. The agents can also specify the recipients of any data, be prevented from broadcasting data, and can be instructed to send data only after their users' approval.

Figure 9 shows an example of the registration screen for a user to input his/her name, comments, and selective items of interest. Figure 10 shows an example screen of the introductory data that is automatically received when the user arrives at a party venue. On this screen, the user (in this case, Taro Yamada) can browse other participants' registered information collected by his transferred mobile agent. The user can also see the affinity scores between the user and other participants. However, the participants can keep some personal information such as e-mail and Web addresses private.

At the party, Taro Yamada meets another guest, Hideo Nomo, and they exchange their IDs via infrared. Thus, their personal place agents know whom the users are meeting, and select the profile data of the other person from the introductory data.

After chatting, Taro wants to know Hideo's e-mail and Web addresses. So, Taro's agent asks Hideo's agent for Hideo's e-mail address and URL. If Hideo approves, Taro's agent receives the data and updates the screen as shown in Figure 11.

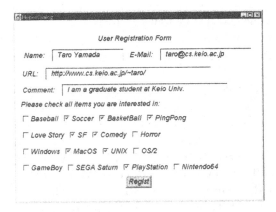

Fig. 9. Example of User Registration Screen

Security Architecture for HyperDialog A security architecture for Hyper-Dialog is based on a public-key cryptosystem [12]. We apply it to agent authentication using a user's secret key as an encrypter of the agent programs. Foner

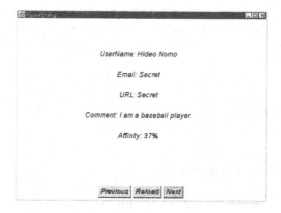

Fig. 10. Example of Introductory Data Screen

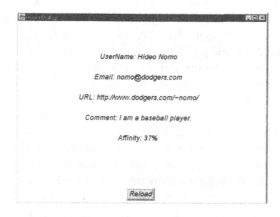

Fig. 11. Example of Filled Data Screen

[4] has discussed another security architecture based on a multiagent system. But it is not applicable to mobile agents.

Since HyperDialog manages personal information, the system must provide privacy protection. This is mainly done at the Service Host maintained by party/meeting organizers. The organizers of a party prepare a listing of invited guests and their public keys obtained from the key repository.

After receiving an invitation, a user A encrypts her mobile agent with her secret key K_{SA}. Expressed mathematically, we can say that $CA_A = K_{SA}(MA_A)$ where MA_A means A's mobile agent and CA_A means its cipher version. Thus, the cipher-agent is computed from the mobile agent via a function of the key K_{SA}.

At the Service Host, the system receives the cipher-agent and tries to decipher it using participants' public keys. This computes $MA_i = K_{Pi}(CA_i)$ where i means any user and K_{Pi} means her public key.

If there is a key K_{Pi} which can decipher the cipher-agent correctly, the user of the agent must be i, since only i's secret key could encrypt her agent MA_i.

The above mechanism is only used for agent authentication. But in Hyper-Dialog, agent authentication is sufficient to protect participants' privacy, because no one other than invited guests can access the party/meeting's Service Host and get the participants' personal information. Since private data not registered to the Service Host will be exchanged during face-to-face conversation, the users can immediately notice what is going on in interagent communication, and, therefore, they can manually control security matters by allowing or disallowing their agents' behavior.

5 Concluding Remarks

We have discussed a new application of agent technologies that supports real world tasks such as campus navigation and face-to-face conversation at a party. The main objective of this research is to integrate the real world and information worlds seamlessly. We think that combining the technologies being pursued in the research areas of augmented reality and software/mobile agents is a very promising approach to this problem.

Interaction between humans and agents is one of the most important issues for software agents. Since the proposed agents detect their users' physical environments, the agents should be aware of users' potential desires and implicitly deduce users' concrete intentions when they say or do something.

We have described two implemented prototype systems based on the concept of an agent augmented community. They are not yet practical because of the lack of adequate technology and open experimentation.

Future research will include a more detailed analysis of agent learning, agent collaboration, security, and personalization. Since we have implemented them in a rather ad-hoc way, a more general mechanism that better realizes the true functions of an agent augmented community needs to be pursued.

We have a lot of work ahead of us to make the concept of augmented communication practical. For example, we have to establish an information and physical infrastructure, that is, a basis of seamless connection between the real world and cyberspace. To implement agent technologies, we have to develop a secured inter-agent communication method, a multimodal human-agent interaction technique, and agent learning and adaptation techniques. We hope that many elegant solutions will be invented in the next decade and that agent augmented community applications will make our personal life more creative and our community life more communicative.

References

1. Adam L. Berger, Stephen A. Della Pietra, and Vincent J. Della Pietra. A maximum entropy approach to natural language processing. *Computational Linguistics*, 22(1):39–71, 1996.
2. Eugene Charniak and Robert P. Goldman. A Bayesian model of plan recognition. *Artificial Intelligence*, 64(1):53–79, 1993.

3. Steven Feiner, Blair MacIntyre, and Dorée Seligmann. Knowledge-based augmented reality. *Communications of the ACM*, 36(7):52–62, 1993.

4. Leonard N. Foner. A security architecture for multi-agent matchmaking. In *Proceedings of the Second International Conference on Multi-Agent Systems (ICMAS-96)*, pages 80–86. AAAI Press, 1996.

5. Yasuharu Katsuno, Ken-ichi Murata, and Mario Tokoro. A Java front-end approach for programming mobile agents. In *Proceedings of OOPSLA '97 Workshop on Java-based Paradigms for Mobile Agent Facilities*, 1997.

6. Mik Lamming and Mike Flynn. Forget-me-not: Intimate computing in support of human memory. In *Proceedings of the FRIEND21 International Symposium on Next Generation Human Interface*, 1993.

7. Katashi Nagao and Jun Rekimoto. Ubiquitous Talker: Spoken language interaction with real world objects. In *Proceedings of the Fourteenth International Joint Conference on Artificial Intelligence (IJCAI-95)*, pages 1284–1290. Morgan Kaufmann Publishers, Inc., 1995.

8. Katashi Nagao and Jun Rekimoto. Agent augmented reality: A software agent meets the real world. In *Proceedings of the Second International Conference on Multi-Agent Systems (ICMAS-96)*, pages 228–235. AAAI Press, 1996.

9. Jun Rekimoto and Katashi Nagao. The world through the computer: Computer augmented interaction with real world environments. In *Proceedings of the ACM Symposium on User Interface Software and Technology (UIST'95)*, pages 29–36, 1995.

10. Paul Resnick and Hal R. Varian. Recommender systems. *Communications of the ACM*, 40(3):56–58, 1997.

11. Bradley J. Rhodes and Thad Starner. Remembrance Agent: A continuously running automated information retrieval system. In *Proceedings of the First International Conference on the Practical Application of Intelligent Agents and Multi-Agent Technology (PAAM'96)*, pages 487–495, 1996.

12. Bluce Schneier. *Applied Cryptography: Protocols, Algorithms, and Source Code in C*. John Wiley & Sons, 1996.

13. Thad Starner, Steve Mann, Bradley Rhodes, Jeffrey Levine, Jennifer Healy, Dana Kirsch, Rosalind W. Picard, and Alex Pentland. Augmented reality through wearable computing. *Presence*, 1997.

14. Roy Want, Andy Hopper, Veronica Falcao, and Jonathan Gibbons. The active badge location system. *ACM Transactions on Information Systems*, 10(1):91–102, 1992.

15. Jim White. Telescript technology: Mobile agents. In Jeffrey M. Bradshaw, editor, *Software Agents*. AAAI Press, 1996.

Community Formation via a Distributed, Privacy-Protecting Matchmaking System

Leonard N. Foner

MIT Media Lab, Software Agents Group,
20 Ames St, E15-305, Cambridge, MA 02139
foner@media.mit.edu

Abstract. Shared interests often serve as the basis for the formation of community. Yet it is often difficult to find others on the net who share one's interests, due to the large size of the network, the difficulty of finding newsgroups, mailing lists, and discussion groups that reflect possibly unusual interests, and because most people do not often post.

To address these issues, I have designed and am implementing *Yenta*, a system that safely and securely introduces people on the Internet who share some similar interests, and that enables the automatic formation of interest groups based on these shared interests. Yenta is a system of distributed, individual agents, each instantiation of which is run by an individual user. Each user's Yenta discovers its user's interests by direct examination of the user's personal files. It then finds groups of similar users without divulging sensitive information.

1 Introduction

Shared interests often serve as the basis for the formation of community. Yet it is often difficult to find others on the net who share one's interests, due to the large size of the network, the difficulty of finding newsgroups, mailing lists, and discussion groups that reflect possibly unusual interests, and because most people do not often post.

To address these issues, I have designed and implemented *Yenta*, a system that safely and securely introduces people on the Internet who share some similar interests, and that enables the automatic formation of interest groups based on these shared interests. Yenta is a system of distributed, individual agents, each instantiation of which is run by an individual user. Each user's Yenta discovers its user's interests by direct examination of the user's personal files. It then finds groups of similar users without divulging sensitive information.

Yenta will be distributed to increasingly larger user populations, and eventually offered to the network at large. I will undertake an initial study of both the operation of its underlying algorithms and the sociopolitical impact of its use as it accumulates a user base. The performance of the underlying algorithms will be studied quantitatively by collecting and analyzing statistics produced by each running Yenta. Yenta's social impact will be studied via qualitative research methods involving interviews of its users.

This paper describes some of Yenta's capabilities in helping to form and support communities, the methodology of its field trials, and how its computational models are designed to facilitate its goals. Research about Yenta bears on issues of community formation, large-scale network discussions, and computer-mediated communication; its use of strong cryptography also bears on the future of the information infrastructure. Thus, this paper describes research that will:

- Facilitate community formation, via automatic determination of user interests and matchmaking users with similar interests into groups of like-minded individuals.
- Deploy such a system to increasingly larger user communities—not only for research purposes, but also as an intended public good.
- Protect user privacy rigorously, and enable large-scale deployment, by careful use of anonymity, pseudonymity, strong cryptography, and a fully-distributed architecture with no single point of compromise.
- Encourage user communication within communities by making a variety of conversational tools available, and prevent abuse of the pseudonymous nature of the system via a built-in reputation system.
- Demonstrate the utility of strong cryptography and the value in designing systems from the outset to protect the civil liberties of their users.
- Enable the study of the resulting system, both technically and sociologically. This includes both the communications between users, and how they make use of the built-in reputation system.

The structure of this paper is as follows. Section 2 describes why we are trying to build community and how matchmaking helps. It then briefly discusses important aspects of the overall architecture of Yenta. Section 3 explains some of the implementation decisions that went into Yenta, how they facilitate community formation, and help users to trust Yenta with private information. Section 4 demonstrates what a user might see in a typical interaction with Yenta. Section 5 describes how Yenta's effects will be evaluated, including both the operation of the software and its effects on its users and the communities they form. Finally, Section 6 describes some related work.

This paper summarizes Yenta's design, but does not provide full details. Interested readers may consult previously-published reports on Yenta's overall architecture and implementation [15] and security model [16].

2 Design rationale

This section discusses why matchmaking is useful for community formation, why it us valuable for studying the formation and maintenance of electronically-based communities, and why Yenta is structured as a decentralized system. It also discusses the implications for user privacy, which can influence user acceptance.

2.1 Why matchmaking?

Yenta is designed to form groups of people interested in similar topics, and to introduce some of these users to each other. This problem is known as *matchmaking*.

There are many reasons why one might want to support interpersonal matchmaking:

- People are often working on similar projects without realizing it—be it two people down the hall from each other reinventing the same wheel, or two doctors doing research on similar cases without knowing that both of them are studying the same literature.

- It is often the case that people need to find an expert in some field, but finding such an expert can be difficult and time-consuming.
- Many people feel socially isolated. Often, someone with a particular, unusual interest may wonder whether there are others who share that interest and, if so, how to find them.

All of these applications are intertwined with the problem of *building community*, which is often poorly-supported by existing tools on the Internet. For example:

- Many matchmaking systems require the user to indicate his or her interests explicitly, either in free text (such as a classified or personal ad), or by selecting from a list of alternatives. In general, however, requiring users to formulate and update a description of current interests is intrusive, timeconsuming, and usually incomplete—and users almost never keep such descriptions updated. Furthermore, lists of alternatives restrict users' descriptions of themselves only to those categories that have been designed into the system.
- Matchmaking often occurs in online communications systems, such as Usenet, mailing lists, and the Web, because one user sees something written by someone else and initiates a dialog based on it. However, this requires that at least one of the individuals involved publish something, be it a netnews post, a letter, or a web page, in order for others to find him or her. Lurkers—people who read, but do not publish—are thus effectively invisible. They form an undiscovered resource, and a huge one, since most people read far more than they publish.

Yenta addresses these problems by determining user interests automatically, without requiring (but not preventing) user intervention, and by constantly attempting to update users' interests and make new matches based on them. It does not require that users publish anything, or, indeed, even write anything in particular of their own in order to do the matching. Yenta operates using a *completely decentralized, peer-to-peer* architecture. The individual Yenta agents thus serve as *facilitators*, acting as *intermediaries* in bringing people together.

This research combines multiagent systems, matchmaking, and cryptographic techniques in a unique fashion. Yenta's automatic determination of user interests, combined with its decentralized, multi-agent architecture, poses challenging research problems. Its method of operation and the interest groups formed of its users facilitate study of a variety of social and political effects.

2.2 Why adopt a decentralized architecture?

One of the simplest ways to implement a matchmaker is to use a *centralized* architecture, in which one system serves a potentially large number of users. Many currently-implemented agents, especially matchmaking agents, are designed this way. Such an architecture has some advantages, including implementation simplicity and the ease of centralized control. Unfortunately, there are problems with a centralized architecture:

- Scaling such a system to large numbers of users is difficult. In systems which must correlate user interests, for example [36], straightforward approaches to this problem generally require a quadratic-order matching step somewhere.

- A system that handles potentially sensitive information requires high trustability. A centralized server provides a single point where either accidental failure or deliberate compromise can have catastrophic consequences. Note that deliberate compromise is not limited to disgruntled insiders or malicious outsiders; a steady flow of subpoenas[1] can be potentially just as time-consuming to deal with for system operators, and can be similarly injurious to users' trust.

Many foreseeable future applications for software agents involve large numbers of agents interacting with each other. Such systems will have to be implemented in a distributed way, rather than depending on a single master server.

2.3 Multi-agent matchmaking

This research focuses on the design and sociology of a *matchmaking* service, one designed to find groups of people with similar interests and bring them together to form coalitions and interest groups. The intended scale of the matchmaking is that of the entire Internet, an environment in which there are potentially millions of users and millions of agents corresponding to them.

Although decentralized, multi-agent systems have several important advantages in such an application, they have problems, too. One of the largest problems is *how agents are supposed to find each other.* Each agent should not have to know about (and, indeed, probably cannot know about) every other agent, user, or resource on the network. Instead, some mechanism by which agents may locate only the useful agents on the network must be arranged. There are several difficult coordination problems, due to the problem being solved and the potentially large number of agents involved. For example:

- There is no obvious a priori hierarchy in this application by which to organize the agents. (Why would any one person's interests be at the top of any hierarchy? How would we know whom to pick, anyway?) This makes the common solution of a single-inheritance tree, which is useful in many other domains, inappropriate here.
- Asking other agents *at random* is quite inefficient, resembling diffusion in a gas— it means each agent could be required to ask every agent on the network, guaranteeing a solution that scales poorly.

Yenta's design addresses these points by using *clustering* and *peer-to-peer referrals.* This approach is outlined in greater depth in Section 3, and is more completely explained in [15].

2.4 Security implications

Yenta's use of personal information—the interests of its users, and their private conversations with each other—raises serious security and user-privacy concerns. There is potential for violating users' civil rights due to inadvertent disclosure. Further, if these

---

1. Subpoenas are not an idle threat—for example, as reported by the Wall Street Journal [41], Federal Express must cope with several hundred subpoenas *a day* of its shipping records. In general, centralized repositories of the activities of large numbers of people must deal with this as a matter of course.

concerns are unaddressed, users may be averse to trying out the software in the first place.

In general, agents are useful because they understand some aspects of their users' goals and can carry out actions autonomously to fulfill those goals. This may require that any given agent know personal or sensitive information about its user. The agent must be robust against revealing this information to third parties and against being subverted by a malicious interloper into carrying out an undesired action.

As the value of the information or the motivation to inflict damage increases, the possibility of inadvertent information disclosure or subversion of an agent's goals by an attacker are very real. This is particularly important in applications that handle highly personal information. People's personal privacy may be violated—and careless handling of this data may violate laws in countries that mandate the safe handling of personal data.

Multi-agent systems require that the multiple agents collaborate to accomplish their users' collective goals. Such systems must often depend, to a greater or lesser extent, on sources of information obtained from others, and must often "leak" information about their own internal state or the goals of their users in order to interoperate with their peers; this makes security and privacy harder to achieve. Further, a trusted intermediary is often an impractical or unavailable solution, which complicates the problem.

Yenta deals with a large amount of potentially personal information, and this information must be protected. A large amount of this protection is obtained by Yenta's decentralization—it is difficult and often pointless to attempt to compromise or subpoena a very large number of sites. Other protections are afforded by the use of strong cryptography. A fuller discussion of Yenta's security strategy can be found in Section 3.3, and a complete discussion appears in [16].

3 Design and implementation strategies

The research proposed here is structured into two primary areas: *design and implementation* of the Yenta system, including algorithms for matchmaking users and algorithms for keeping this data secure, and *evaluation* of the resulting system, including both quantitative evaluation of the algorithms and qualitative evaluation [28][30][40] of the system's utility to its users and its social and political impact for them. An overview of Yenta's design appears in this section, and its evaluation appears in Section 5.

Yenta is concerned primarily with *finding* people who share an interest with each other, and *using* that information to form coalitions and interest groups in which users may communicate among the group. These groups can then be used as the basis for one-to-one introductions. Yenta must also *secure* information about its users to prevent violations of their privacy and civil rights.

Yenta's implementation presupposes that every Yenta is a *persistent* agent that runs most of the time, for long periods. The user does not start up the agent, get an immediate result, and shut it down, but instead runs it in the background for hours or weeks, while it uses the referral algorithm to find and join appropriate groups of agents whose users share the same interests. As the process runs, any given user's Yenta may join several groups simultaneously, because the user may have several interests simultaneously.

3.1 Finding the right cluster of peer agents: the core idea

Yenta's architecture borrows ideas from *computational ecology* [19], in which agents use local knowledge to self-organize into larger units. The *core ideas* in the approach are:

- determine the user's interests,
- compare the agents' information in a *peer-to-peer, decentralized* fashion,
- use *referrals* from one agent to another and an algorithm resembling *hill-climbing* to find other, more appropriate agents when searching for relevant peers, in order to
- build *clusters* or *clumps* of like-minded agents, and to
- *use these clusters* of similar or like-minded agents (whose users therefore share similar interests) to *introduce* users to each other and enable cluster-wide *messaging* between users whose interests match.

Yenta determines the user's interests by scanning all of the user's mail and files and building a statistical representation of what the scanned text is about. This representation is a classic weighted vector of keywords [43], in which common words are dropped and the other words are stemmed. Each document (a single message or a single file) is represented by a single such vector (called here a *grain*) which reflects word frequencies found in the document. These individual vectors are then aggregated using a clustering algorithm into *granules*. Each granule consists of several grains, and represents a single user interest. The user can have an arbitrary number of such grains, reflecting a variety of interests; it typically works out a user has one to two dozen interests.

Yentas cooperate to form *clusters* of users; each such cluster reflects a number of users all of whom share some particular interest. (A cluster is composed of many granules—each granule representing one particular interest of one particular user.) Any given user's Yenta can be in multiple clusters simultaneously, since any given user is presumed to have multiple simultaneous interests.

The Yentas form these clusters by cooperating in a distributed algorithm. Each Yenta remembers, for each cluster that it is in, which other Yentas it has recently talked to—this is its *cluster cache,* and there is one such cache for each interest associated with this Yenta's user. Each Yenta also maintains a list of other recently-contacted Yentas which do *not* seem to share any common interests—this is its *rumor cache.* There is only one rumor cache for any given Yenta.

When two Yentas discover that they share a common interest (two of their granules match better than a threshold), they remember this fact. They also trade the contents of their cluster caches for this interest, hence merging two smaller clusters into one larger cluster. Each Yenta updates its cluster cache to be the union of the initial pair of cluster caches.

On the other hand, consider a Yenta (call it A) which has not yet found a suitable cluster for some particular interest. When this Yenta asks another (B) if it matches this interest, and is told it does not, it then asks for a *referral*—it asks B for some third Yenta (C), from B's rumor cache, which is a *better* match for this interest. Whichever Yenta C is chosen by B does not have to be very good (in particular, it does not have to be good enough to be termed a "good match"); it must only be a better match than B itself. Yenta A then asks C directly about its interests, and this process iterates. Yenta A can follow this chain of referrals in a word-of-mouth algorithm which approximates hill-climbing, and which works better than random search.

3.2 How the resulting clusters can be used

Forming clusters of interests is an ongoing and continuous process for the Yenta agents, due to the scale and constantly-changing environment of the Internet. Once these clusters have formed, how can they be used? The primary application for these clusters is to *use them to send messages to other users*. These messages may go to *single users* or to some *subset of everyone* in a cluster. Some messages may be initiated by Yenta itself, such as the automatic suggestion of an introduction when two users' interests match unusually well. Other messages are initiated by the user, as part of a conversation with either a single other user or the members of a particular cluster.

All messages, introductions, and so forth are identified by *pseudonyms*. These pseudonyms are persistent, and are also unique and unforgeable due to their cryptographic implementation. No Yenta ever transmits actual identifying information about its user to another Yenta—though if its user cares to reveal that information by sending a message to another user, or to a cluster, that is the user's decision. Blinding actual user identities in this fashion is one of Yenta's main defenses against particular sorts of attacks and privacy invasions, and is dealt with more extensively in the discussion of security below.

Clusters are subject to constant change, as Yentas join and leave, and as their users' interests change. Yenta can thus track changes in its environment.

3.3 Security

Since each Yenta handles a large amount of personal information and potentially shares that information with other Yentas under control of arbitrary individuals who are not necessarily all deemed trustworthy, the design must attend to several security and privacy issues.

Many of these issues, at least in theory, affect many distributed applications that handle user information, such as electronic mail. However, such applications traditionally have not been ubiquitously protected, and the use of privacy-protecting technologies, such as cryptography, within them is still very much the exception. Yenta can benefit from being a new application, one created in an era when both the insecurity of the public network is well known and the cryptographic tools to address that insecurity are well-understood.

However, there are unique reasons why protecting users' privacy is an especially important part of Yenta design. In applications such as electronic mail, the user chooses both the recipient(s) and the message text, and thus may exercise at least some control over who is most likely to see the contents, and what those contents are. Disclosure by recipients to unauthorized persons, or by third-party eavesdroppers, is still easily possible, but may be ameliorated somewhat by the sender's choice of subject matter—particularly private matters simply should not be transmitted in the first place. Yenta, on the other hand, transmits a great deal of personal information *automatically* and *to unknown parties*, hence amplifying the potential for disclosure to inappropriate individuals. Further, because it forms groups of users based on their interests, it makes such groups easy to find and could, if improperly designed, make their identities known to outsiders when the group's members wished them concealed.

Attacks on Yenta's security roughly divide into *passive attacks* and *active attacks*. Some of these attacks could be applied to many types of systems, while some are peculiar to Yenta.

Passive attacks do not attempt to modify data flowing between any pair of Yentas; instead, they attempt to obtain data surreptitiously and without permission. They could include eavesdropping on the data being transferred, doing traffic analysis of aggregate data flows among sets of Yentas, reading data stored by each Yenta in its user's file system, and subpoenaing data that may exist in particular locations.

Active attacks are those in which data or the underlying infrastructure is actively disrupted. They can include spoofing (identity fraud of one sort of another), replay of old data, man-in-the-middle attacks, and subverted distributions of Yenta.

Yenta uses accepted and proven cryptographic algorithms and protocols to counter most of these threats. Although the use of these various techniques in Yenta as an application is unique, the actual cryptographic tools employed are *not*, in general, novel, and for good reason—such tools always require a long period of public scrutiny before they can be trusted. Hence, when it comes simply to communications privacy and authenticity, Yenta uses tried-and-true techniques.

Not all the threats posed to users of Yenta are strictly algorithmic—outright fraud and deception by other users are to be expected. Such confidence games require no sophisticated passive or active attacks on Yenta's communications themselves; instead, they prey on user expectations. While this is in general a problem with, e.g., electronic mail, in Yenta it is far worse, because users have no a priori way of either knowing each other or in tracking back a communication to its source. Indeed, since the underlying design emphasizes anonymity and pseudonyms to frustrate such attempts, such fraudulent representations are uniquely important to Yenta. Yenta therefore contains a *reputation system* that allows users to make statements about themselves, called *attributions*. Other Yenta users can then cryptographically sign individual statements with which they agree. Such attributions allow newcomers to judge the character of another user by reading what statements they have made that others agree with, and can be used to determine whether to proceed with an introduction or whether to present communications from another to the user at all.

Reputation systems such as this are extremely unusual in typical applications on the Internet today. How they are used within Yenta may enable interesting sociological study of users' needs for privacy and of how one represents oneself to strangers in a way that one's peers will support.

Yenta explicitly does *not* attempt to deal with certain threats, such as whether the user has a trusted path to his or her binaries, Byzantine failures in which more than a small number of all Yentas have been deliberately compromised by malicious parties, or a large class of denial-of-service attacks (which might well deny service by disrupting the network as a whole, and not just Yenta itself). In general, dealing with these problems are far outside of the scope of this research, and some are fundamental problems in the way most popular operating systems and computer architectures are commonly designed.

4   A typical set of interactions

To lend some concreteness to the discussion above, consider the following typical set of interactions with Yenta. Only a few of the most important parts of Yenta's operation are demonstrated here. In these examples, the user chose the name Greenstalk. We'll use this name for clarity in the discussion below.

When a user starts up Yenta for the first time, she must choose a name and a passphrase. Various cryptographic keys are generated, including a unique, unforgeable cryptographic ID. Yenta then asks where to find the various mail files to start its granule-formation algorithms. When completed, Yenta has a description of the user's various interests. The process of asking for a name and a pointer to the user's filesystem, and of generating cryptographic keys, happens only the first time the user starts Yenta; after that, Yenta remembers all of its information across runs.

Each user runs their own copy of Yenta. Those copies communicate with each other using a Yenta-specific communications protocol known as the InterYenta protocol. Each Yenta also communicates with its owner (only!) via HTTP to the user's web browser, which means that Yenta need not understand every window system in the world, but merely how to speak HTML. We presume that any Yenta user therefore has at least some kind of browser available—a reasonable assumption these days for users on machines that are on the network in the first place. Yenta's user interface thus makes Yenta look like a traditional web server, but do not be fooled—each page is generated on-the-fly by the user's own Yenta, and there is no centralized web server anywhere in the architecture.

Once cryptographic keys have been generated and preclustering is complete, Greenstalk can check on which interests Yenta has deduced by examining a page like that shown in Figure 1, on the next page.

This is a very abbreviated list of interests; typical users find themselves with a few dozen. Each interest is identified by some salient words—those which are most useful in separating out one interest from another. Even though Yenta can make strong guarantees about the privacy of the data, users may still want their Yenta to disregard certain interests for other reasons. In the example above, Greenstalk clicked "Ignore" because she really does not care to be introduced to other people just because they have meetings, too.

Greenstalk can always adjust these listings later if she wishes, and is free to simply allow them all to assume their defaults. Hence, when Yenta starts up, it can immedi-

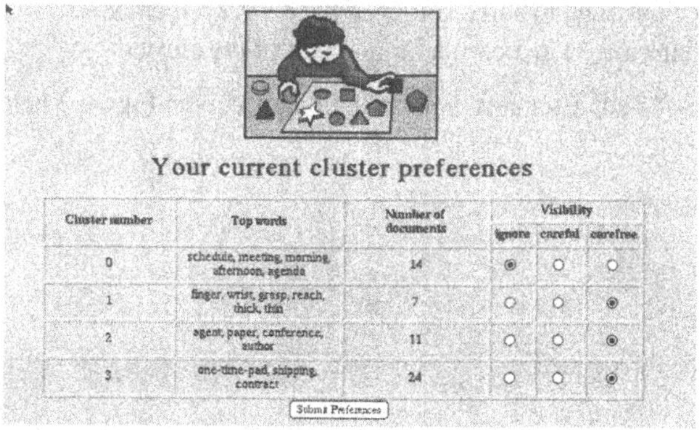

Cluster number	Top words	Number of documents	Visibility		
			ignore	careful	carefree
0	schedule, meeting, morning, afternoon, agenda	14	◉	○	○
1	finger, wrist, grasp, reach, thick, thin	7	○	○	◉
2	agent, paper, conference, author	11	○	○	◉
3	one-time-pad, shipping, contract	24	○	○	◉

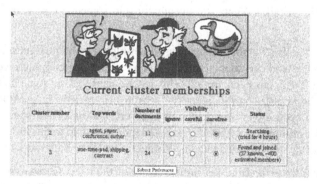

Figure 1. Abbreviated listing of typical interest clusters, as found by Yenta.

ately start trying to find peers, without forcing its user to go through an extensive configuration phase first. This is critical to its success—every minute of configuration required to make Yenta work for a given user cuts down on the number who will be likely to use it at all.

After Yenta has preclustered and is attempting to find peers, Greenstalk can get a rough idea of how the process is going by examining a page such as the one shown in Figure 2 below.

Cluster number	Top words	Number of documents	Visibility			Status
			ignore	careful	carefree	
2	agent, paper, conference, author	11	○	○	◉	Searching (tried for 4 hours)
3	one-time-pad, shipping, contract	24	○	○	◉	Found and joined: (37 known, ~400 estimated members)

Figure 2. Abbreviated listing of Yenta's status while searching for other, similar Yentas.

This particular page shows that Greenstalk's Yenta has already found one cluster of other Yentas whose users share an interest with her—the shipment of one-time cryptographic pads. The number of known peers is computed from the cluster cache for this interest, and the number of estimated peers in the entire cluster is approximated via hearsay from others in the cluster. Her Yenta is still looking for a cluster reflecting a different interest—writing conference papers about agents—but has not yet found any Yentas close enough to be considered peers.

Once Yenta has found a reasonable cluster (or a few such), what might happen? There are two basic operations initially supported for clusters of which we are a member:

- Sending a message to some subset of the cluster's members.[2]
- Getting introduced to a particular member of the cluster.[3]

An example of such a suggested introduction appears in Figure 3 below.

Figure 3. A typical introduction.

In this example, Yenta is suggesting an introduction based on a particular cluster—apparently, Greenstalk's Yenta did eventually find someone else with an interest in one-time pads.

The example details a number of attributes describing the potential introducee, such as Blueshell's name and cryptographic ID,[4] and a cryptographically-derived estimate of how long this Yenta has been around. This latter quantity gives some hints about how much might be invested in this identity—was it just created via an AOL disk in the mail, or has it been around for a while? The very bottom of the page shows which shared interest prompted the introduction, and indicates that, in this case, Greenstalk's Yenta was the one that decided that an introduction might be appropriate.

Note the attestations for Blueshell in the center of the page. Greenstalk might like to take a closer look at them. For example, she might wish to verify that there is some relatively-trusted path back to someone she knows, and hence that the signatories aren't all simply fraudulent alter-egos under Blueshell's control. She can do so by examining a page such as that shown in Figure 4, on the next page.

---

2. Via the attestation system, users may filter which messages are displayed or propagated to other Yentas. Hence, Yenta does not guarantee that messages will get to everyone in the cluster in all cases.

3. These introductions are suggested automatically when two members of the cluster appear to match very closely—more closely, in particular, than most of the rest of the known members seem to match. How often such introductions may be suggested is, like many other aspects of Yenta, a user-settable parameter.

4. Recall that this is a unique, unforgeable quantity, because it is the fingerprint of the key required to communicate with him at all.

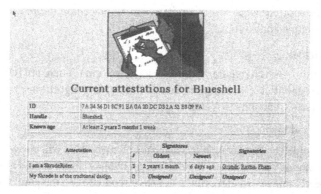

Figure 4. Attestations serves as a word-of-mouth reputation system.

Yenta can give some support in finding paths between the three signatories listed above and someone Greenstalk knows better, if necessary.

Suppose that Greenstalk goes ahead with the introduction. What can she do? One service Yenta can provide involves simply setting up a conversation between the two parties, allowing them to negotiate how much additional information they wish to reveal—a little or a lot. The conversation, like everything else in Yenta, is routinely encrypted, and neither party knows the other's *true* identities unless they tell each other. A typical set of conversations might look like the example in Figure 5 below.

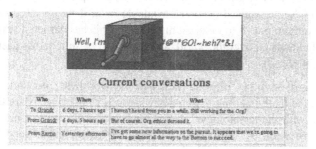

Figure 5. Having a conversation using Yenta. All communications are transparently encrypted.

Note that, in the pages shown here, we assume that the user desires a totally passive interface, in which Yenta never offers information unless the user follows some appropriate link. In fact, for those browsers that support auto-refresh of pages (e.g., Netscape and others), the user can also specify that certain pages should have updates "pushed" out if the page is visible and something noteworthy happens. This allows a user to leave a Yenta page up in some browser window, and be immediately notified when something changes. The choice of interaction styles is up to the user.

Only the high points of Yenta's user interface have been covered here. Advanced users have other ways of controlling Yenta's behavior. For example, Yenta has a large number of configurable parameters to control aspects of its security, how introductions can be made and how often, what sort of limits are to be placed on the resources Yenta is allowed to consume, and so forth.

5 Evaluation

Evaluation of this research requires that real users use Yenta. There are two dimensions to my study: quantitative evaluation of Yenta's underlying algorithms, and qualitative evaluation of users' reactions to Yenta.

5.1 Rollout strategy

Yenta will be fielded to increasingly large groups of users. This will allow investigation of its performance at varying sizes. In addition, a gradual release should allow catching critical bugs early and avoid garnering a negative reputation in the potential user community for items easy to correct.

Initial releases of Yenta will be made available in-house, first to particular interested individuals in the MIT Media Lab and then, more generally, to the rest of the Lab and particular interested sponsors.[5] A later release will target MIT undergraduates via a port to common Athena [2] machines; this provides a relatively large and homogenous set of machines in a user community that is both technically sophisticated and willing to try new software just to experiment with it.

Many details of Yenta's design, including various presented papers about the system, have been available on the Web for upwards of two years. A web form has been available in that interval for readers of these documents to express their interest in using a beta version of Yenta when it becomes available (and, if they wish, to also indicate interest in helping to port it to other architectures). This has garnered several hundred interested individuals all over the world, and these will be solicited as users in the next phase of the rollout.

The ultimate goal involves offering Yenta to the worldwide network, via targeted advertisements to likely mailing lists and newsgroups whose readers are likely to want to experiment with the technology.[6] If Yenta is successful, word of mouth may then enlarge its user base further. This step is not required to complete the research, although it is desirable.

Yenta uses cryptographic algorithms which are currently export-controlled by the United States government [21]. Yenta's deployment is explicitly cognizant of these limitations. Dissemination of Yenta's cryptographic elements will be limited through the use of the same techniques used to make Pretty Good Privacy [42] available on the network.[7]

---

5. In particular, our sponsor British Telecom has been very enthusiastic about collaborating with us on this technology, and will be among the first to try it out. Indeed, the development of their Grapevine system was largely inspired by the author's work on Yenta.
6. Such advertisements will be sent with the cooperation of the moderator of each list; they will not be spammed indiscriminately.
7. The General Counsel for the National Security Administration has stated in a public forum (the 1996 Computers, Freedom, and Privacy conference) that such steps are deemed sufficiently restrictive—since they derail typical commercial export of cryptography simply by their cumbersome nature to corporations.

5.2 System performance

The performance of Yenta's clustering algorithms have a strong effect on the utility of the system as a whole. Therefore, part of the evaluation of the research includes studying the scalability of the algorithms for varying numbers of users, and investigating where performance may be improved.

Yenta can potentially report on a large number of interesting statistics, and Yenta as fielded will do so by extensive automatic logging via the network to a central collection site—being careful to blind such data *before and during transit* so that individual user identities cannot be discovered.[8] Such blinding increases user acceptance of the large amount of data that could potentially be collected, and also makes the collection site a much less attractive one for compromise.

Some of the parameters to be collected from any given running Yenta include, at least:

- Clustering statistics—how many interests does this user have? How many clusters of other Yentas have been found for this user's interests? How much communication did Yenta require to find them? How many interests did the user wish *not* to use for introductions? How much mail or how many files did Yenta scan to determine the user's interests?
- Preferences—how has the user set parameters such as general security and privacy levels? What sorts of resource limits (cache sizes, process and network utilization) has the user imposed on Yenta? Has the user specified a limit on the number of introductions to be made in a particular time period, and if so, what? Is the user filtering incoming messages to him- or herself, from either individuals or the cluster? What filtering parameters are used?
- Usage—how many messages into groups has the user read or written? What about messages to individual users? How often does the user interact with Yenta's user interface? How often is the help used? How many attributions does this user have? How many have been signed, by how many other users?

Since Yenta has not yet had a large-scale trial, many aspects of its basic clustering algorithms have been simulated. The algorithms used to group individual mail messages (grains) into interests (granules) have undergone several revisions, using real mail as input. The algorithms used to group Yentas into clusters have been examined for up to a thousand simulated Yentas.

5.3 Sociology

Part of the impetus for pursuing this research is sociological and political. If provided to users, will they use the sorts of instant interest groups that Yenta can provide? How will they manage their online reputations, and what sort of social signalling systems might develop around them?

---

8. Note that this blinding means that neither the implementor, the server that receives the statistics, nor an eavesdropper to the transmission may obtain user-identity information. Also, since Yenta's transmissions are *always* encrypted, an eavesdropper is denied the contents of the transmission as well.

To investigate these issues, particular individuals in Yenta's user community will be interviewed, either online or in any other communications medium deemed appropriate, and their experiences, attitudes, and opinions will be collected. Users may be solicited at random or may choose to contribute their opinions at their own discretion. The actual identities of those who participate will be protected; those who participate using Yenta itself as the communications medium will have their identities automatically protected unless they take steps to reveal them.

Qualitative evaluation methods [28][30][40] will be employed in pursuing answers to the questions that Yenta raises. I am not interested here in detailed investigations of tweaks to Yenta's user interface or in similar pursuits; instead, I am interested in whether or not Yenta facilitates social change. Such change could consist of enabling conversations among people who otherwise would not have met, or who (even if already known to each other) would not have known of a particular shared interest; it could also consist of changes in attitudes towards the protection of personal information and the use of cryptography in everyday life.

The sorts of communities formed by Yenta users is of prime concern in this sociological research. An interest group is *not* the only thing that makes up a community; the stable, groupwide conversations, social customs, and sense of shared responsibility for the continued evolution of the group are also important. Part of the purpose of fielding Yenta will be to investigate how the affordances it makes available—for example, easy group conversations, easy discovery of people with related interests, a reputation system, and pseudonyms—can be useful in forming and evaluating communities.

6 Related work

A common technique in systems that support computation among a group of users is to centralize a server and have its users act like clients. Such systems are by far the most common organization for this task; Yenta is one of the very few that tries to break this mold. Centralized systems, while unsafe and having scaling problems, do have certain advantages, of course—not only are they easier to build, but web-based centralized systems also offer the possibility of supporting themselves via banner ads and the like in an obvious and straightforward manner. Of course, they have many disadvantages, such as requiring a centralized authority which may not be trustable in the face of crackers or subpoenas, or which may overload and constitute a single point of failure.

Webhound/Webdoggie [35][36] and HOMR/Ringo/Firefly [26], for example, both subscribe to this principle. A central server maintains information about user interests, and users connect to the server (in both cases, with web browsers) to discover whether they have a match. Both systems require the user to be proactive in establishing and maintaining an interest profile, although Webhound/Webdoggie also obtained leverage by using a data source the user already kept updated, namely his or her hotlist.

Kuokka and Harada [24] describe a system that matches advertisements and requests from users and hence serves as a brokering service. Also a centralized server, their system assumes a highly-structured representation of user interests.

Sixdegrees [27] is an interesting idea in matchmaking, generally for professional reasons; this site specializes in *who you already know* and uses this information to find minimal spanning trees to others who you would like to know.

PlanetAll [34] has a somewhat different approach. It concentrates on *finding people you once knew*, rather than on finding new people you might like to know. Like Sixdegrees, it is a centralized, web-based service, and everyone using the service is identified by their real name.

Although romantic matchmaking is *not* an explicit goal of Yenta, there are a large number of matchmaking systems specialized for this application, and they are worth studying. Such systems appear to be invariably centralized. For example, Match.Com [11] is a straightforward romantic-matchmaking service. Similarly, the Jewish Matchmaker [7] (unfortunately also called Yenta, for obvious reasons) is one of several more-specialized systems that function similarly: surveys for filtering, personals for secondary selection, and a centralized server, all backed up by a web-based interface.

Kautz, Milewski, and Selman [22] have taken a more distributed approach to matchmaking. They report work on a prototype system for expertise location in a large company. Their prototype assumes that users can identify who else might be a suitable contact, and use agents to automate the referral-chaining process; they include simulated results showing how the length and accuracy of the resulting referral chains are affected by the number of simulated users and the accuracy and helpfulness of their recommendations. Yenta differs from this approach in many ways, such as using ubiquitous user data to infer interests, rather than explicitly asking about expertise, and in its use of strong cryptography, good user security, and anonymity.

7 References

1. Ackerman, Mark S., and Palen, Laysia, "The Zephyr Help Instance: Promoting Ongoing Activity in a CSCW System," *Proceedings of the Association of Computing Machinery's Conference on Human Factors in Computing Systems (CHI '96)*, pp. 269-275, ACM Press, Vancouver, British Columbia, Canada, 1996.

2. Balkovich, E., Lerman, S. R., and Parmelee, R. P., "Computing in Higher Education: The Athena Experience," *Communications of the ACM*, volume 28, issue 11, pp. 1214-1224, ACM, November, 1985.

3. Chaum, David, "Untraceable Electronic Mail, Return Addresses, and Digital Pseudonyms," *Communications of the ACM*, volume 23 number 2, February, 1981.

4. Cornell, Gary and Horstmann, Cay, *Core Java*, SunSoft Press, 1996.

5. Crabtree, Barry, and Jennings, Nick, eds., *Proceedings of the First International Conference and Exhibition on the Practical Application of Intelligent Agents and Multi-Agent Technology*, The Practical Application Company, 1996.

6. Crowston, Keven and Malone, Thomas, "Intelligent Software Agents," *BYTE*, pp.267-271, December 1988.

7. Cupid Networks, Inc, {http://www.yenta.email.com/}.

8. Dean, Drew, Felten, Edward W., and Wallach, Dan S., "Java Security: From HotJava to Netscape and Beyond," *Proceedings of the IEEE Symposium on Security and Privacy,* Oakland, CA, May 6-8, 1996.

9. Dellafera, C. A., Eichin, M. W., French, R. S., Jedlinksy, D. C., Kohl, J. T. , and Sommerfeld, W. E., "The Zephyr Notification System," *Proceedings of the Winter 1988 Usenix Technical Conference,* February 1988, pp. 213-219.

10. Demazeau, Y. and Müller, J. P., eds., *Decentralized AI, Volumes 1, 2, and 3,* North-Holland, 1991, 1992, and 1993.

11. Electric Classifieds, Inc, {http://www.match.com/}.

12. Feldman, Paul, and Micali, Silvio, "Optimal Algorithms for Byzantine Agreement," *20th STOC,* pp.148-161, ACM, New York, 1988.

13. Foner, Leonard N., "Clustering and Information Sharing in an Ecology of Cooperating Agents," *AAAI Spring Symposium on Information Gathering from Distributed, Heterogeneous Environments,* Knoblock & Levy, eds., Stanford, CA, March, 1995.

14. Foner, Leonard, "Clustering and Information Sharing in an Ecology of Cooperating Agents, or How to Gossip without Spilling the Beans," *Proceedings of the Conference on Computers, Freedom, and Privacy '95 Student Paper Winner,* Burlingame, CA, 1995.

15. Foner, Leonard N., "A Multi-Agent System for Matchmaking," *Proceedings of the First International Conference and Exhibition on the Practical Application of Intelligent Agents and Multi-Agent Technology,* Barry Crabtree and Nick Jennings, eds., The Practical Application Company, 1996.

16. Foner, Leonard, "A Security Architecture for a Multi-Agent Matchmaker," *The First International Conference on Autonomous Agents '97,* Marina del Rey, 1997.

17. Foner, Leonard N., "Entertaining Agents: A Sociological Case Study," *Proceedings of the First International Conference on Autonomous Agents,* W. Lewis Johnson, ed. Also available as "Agents Memo 93-01",{http://foner.www.media.mit.edu/people/foner/Julia/}.

18. Gosling, James, and McGilton, H., *The Java Language Environment,* Sun Microsystems, May 1995. {http://java.sun.com/whitePaper/javawhitepaper_1.html}

19. Huberman, B.A., ed., *The Ecology of Computation,* North-Holland, 1988.

20. Ingemarsson, I., and Simmons, G. J., "A Protocol to Set Up Shared Secret Schemes Without the Assistance of a Mutually Trusted Party," *Advances in Cryptology—EUROCRYPT '90 Proceedings,* pp. 266-282, Springer-Verlag, 1991.

21. *International Traffic in Arms Regulations,* 58 Federal Register 39,280 (1993) (to be codified at 22 C.F.R.§§120-128, 130).

22. Kautz, Henry, Milewski, Al, and Selman Bart, "Agent Amplified Communication," *AAAI '95 Spring Symposium Workshop Notes on Information Gathering in Distributed, Heterogeneous Environments,* Stanford, CA.

23. Kaliski, Bert, "Privacy Enhancement for Internet Electronic Mail: Part IV: Key Certification and Related Services," RFC1424, February 10, 1993, {ftp://ds.internic.net:/rfc/rfc1424.txt)

24. Kuokka, Daniel, and Harada, Larry, "Matchmaking for Information Agents," *Proceedings of the International Joint Conference on Artificial Intelligence (IJCAI) '95*, 1995.

25. Kuokka, Daniel and Harada, Larry, "On Using KQML for Matchmaking," *Proceedings of the First International Conference on Multiagent Systems*, Victor Lesser, MIT Press, 1995.

26. Lashkari, Yezdi, Metral, Max, and Maes Pattie, "Collaborative Interface Agents," *Proceedings of the Twelfth National Conference on Artificial Intelligence*, MIT Press, Cambridge, MA, 1994.

27. MacroView Communications Corp, {http://www.sixdegrees.com/}.

28. Maxwell, Joseph A., *Qualitative Research Design: An Interactive Approach (Applied Social Research Methods Series)*, Sage Publications, 1996.

29. McQuillan, J., "Software Checksumming in the IMP and Network Reliability," RFC528, June 20, 1973, {ftp://ds.internic.net/rfc/rfc528.txt}

30. Miles, Matthew B. and Huberman, A. Michael, *Qualitative Data Analysis: An Expanded Sourcebook*, SAGE Publications, Inc, Thousand Oaks, CA, 1994.

31. Murray, Janet, *Hamlet on the Holodeck*, The Free Press, Simon & Shuster, 1997.

32. Pease, Marshall, Shostak, Robert, Lamport, Leslie, "Reaching Agreement in the Presence of Faults," *Journal of the ACM 27/2*, pp.228-234, 1980.

33. Quist, Anton Braun, *Excuse Me, What Was That? Confused Recollections of Things That Didn't Go Exactly Right*, Dilithium Press, 1982.

34. Sage Enterprises, Inc, {http://www.planetall.com/}.

35. Shardanand, Upendra. *Social Information Filtering for Music Recommendation*, S.M. Thesis, Program in Media Arts and Sciences, 1994.

36. Shardanand, Upendra and Maes, Pattie, "Social Information Filtering: Algorithms for Automating 'Word of Mouth,'" *Proceedings of CHI'95*, ACM Press, 1995.

37. Schneier, Bruce, *Applied Cryptography: Protocols, Algorithms, and Source Code in C*, second edition, John Wiley & Sons, 1996.

38. Thirunavukkarasu, Chelliah, Fini, Tom, and Mayfield, James, "Secret Agents—A Security Architecture for the KQML Agent Communication Language," submitted to the CIKM '95 Intelligent Information Agents Workshop, Baltimore, MD, December 1995.

39. Turkle, Sherry, *Life on the Screen: Identity in the Age of the Internet*, Simon & Shuster, 1995.

40. Wolcott, Harry F., *Writing Up Qualitative Research*, SAGE Publications, Inc, Newbury Park, CA, 1990.

41. *The Wall Street Journal*, page B1, April 11, 1995.

42. Zimmermann, Philip, *The Official PGP User's Guide*, MIT Press, 1995.

43. Zumoff, Joel, "Users Manual for the SMART Information Retrieval System," Cornell Technical Report 71-95.

SYMBIOT: Personalizing Agents in Social Contexts

Chisato Numaoka

Sony Computer Science Laboratory – Paris
6, Rue Amyot, 75005 Paris, France
chisato@csl.sony.fr

Abstract. In this article, we intend to shed some light on the subject of social life in a 3D virtual world. 3D virtual worlds are expected to promote people's interactions over time and space. However something more seems to be necessary to encourage people's activity in a 3D virtual world in which one characteristics of interaction is "anonymity". In anonymous environment, everything is less distinguishable, less trustworthy, and less attractive. It might be interesting to introduce a way to represent our personality. To be compatible with anonymity, we introduce a virtual partner "symbiot". We can use the symbiot to let it represent a part of our personality. Symbiots could develop their personality through interaction with us or through observation of our behavioral traits. We have conducted a series of experiments to develop a personality of symbiot and in some cases, we succeeded in producing a kind of primitive personality.

1 Introduction

It is expected that 3D virtual worlds could easily extend our life over time and space. They provide 3D spaces where we can interact. Unlike text based communication, in a 3D virtual space, we can directly see visual images of a world to which we belong. We can use not only verbal communication but also motions and figures as information media. Due to this characteristic, we have much more freedom of representing ourselves in 3D virtual space interaction than text based interactions. First and foremost, 3D virtual worlds form a "border-less" space: we can free from physical constraints of the real world. When we enter a 3D virtual world, we can meet with people from various countries: US, Europe, Asia, or Africa.

We must create 3D virtual worlds so as to encourage people to interact with others in a group and in motion. Nevertheless, the actual condition does not seem to be as such. In general, people connect to a world and chat with those who have already been in the world. While chatting, avatars do not move so much. Even if there is a function to change a posture of avatars, people do not use it so frequently. This is partially because it is not necessary. It even annoy people when people think of how to and when to use the function. In some sense, for chatting, 3D world images do not help people to interact. A single chatting window may be enough to talk with others.

One apparent contribution of 3D virtual worlds here is that the worlds provide some landscapes about which people can talk. However, because of a rather poor variation of landscapes, the topic about the landspaces will soon become boaring. We could expect future technology that provides more interesting landspaces including more attractive animated objects. Nevertheless, as far as interaction among people is concerned, that does not solve a problem how to encourage people's activity in 3D virtual worlds. This is because 3D virtual world interactions lacks vividness of human society as we have it in the real world.

It is worth thinking about the personality of participants in virtual space interactions. This is related with a subject of "anonymity". This anonymity characterizes one true aspect of virtual space interactions of any style. Because of this anonymity, personality of individuals in a virtual space is less apparent than in the real world. Sometimes, people prefer such anonymity in communication because they can separate their existence in a virtual world from the existence in the real world. We can pretend a person totally different from the reality. From the personality point of view, however, there are some deficits as compared with social interactions in the real world.

Less distinguishable.
In the real world, we have various types of personality. Personality gives us criteria to distinguish people as a group or to distinguish individual people from each other. According to personality, we can assign roles, tasks, and so on. If personality is unclear, it becomes a hard job to purposefully distinguish participants. For example, forming a functional group in a virtual space may be a really difficult subject. It is hard to expect that an organization spontaneously emerges. It may be possible to prepare distinguished characters of avatar. Nevertheless, personality, as we will discuss later, is not only a matter of figures but also and more importantly a matter of consistent pattern of behavior. We may be able to expect sophisticated animation of avatars [1] or facial animation [2]. Then, the next problem is how we can reflect our personality on the expression of those animations. Operationally speaking, it is not easy to let users use such options. There is also an empirical study reporting that people prefers to use voice or text communication rather than animation.

Less trustworthy.
In general, we cannot trust somebody until we know the person very well and unless we are sure that it is the very person. To establish a trust-relationship, we need to look at a person directly as it is. Or, we need a kind of certificate to trust for backup: recommendation, for example, by whom we already trust. In a virtual world interaction such as chatting, such rigorous trust-relationship may not be required[1]. Nevertheless, we want to be sure, at least, if we are talking to a person with whom I really want to talk. If we can obtain some more information on the personality of others, it may be helpful to make a trustworthy conversation. We could present our

---

[1] We may be able to provide a rigorous mechanism for confidential talk. This is another issue from the topic of this paper.

face by using video image transmission as in FreeWalk [3]. It is desirable to present ourselves in a private space where a system can guarantee that nobody else can view our video image. Nevertheless, I suspect that, without such a secure space, most people do not prefer to present their own face on the Internet even if it is technologically possible

Less attractive.
Attractiveness is an important factor in social interactions. The real world is attractive and exciting. It is full of events of various kinds. On the contrary, current 3D virtual worlds are less attractive. One reason is thee reduction of sensory information. In a virtual space, *we lose the sense of touch, of background noise, the scent of odersm kinesthesis, the sensation of taste, and visual cues which give us a peripheral awareness of the presence of others* [4]. The other reason, although it is related with the reason above, is a lack of personality: less variation in characteristics. Imagine an aquarium. If the aquarium is small, it contains less variety of fish, and if the different kinds are separated in individual tanks, then we will soon get bored. This is because they are less attractive and therefore we are not really stimulated. In contrast, if we go to a large aquarium in which many kinds of fish are swimming together in a large tank, then we will be excited to view interactions among different sorts of marine creatures, sometimes in confusion and sometimes in order. Different fishes have different personalities. The same sort of fish tends to school together. This is a natural dynamics of living organisms. However, if we ignore such difference in personality, a world becomes monotonous and boring as seen in a small aquarium. The same words are applicable to current 3D virtual world interactions. This is one reason why virtual world is not so attractive.

In this paper, we will discuss a subject of personality in 3D virtual world. First we investigate what kinds of elements help us to present personality and introduce a way of representing personality as a "partner" avatar, which we call a *symbiot*. Next, we will introduce self-biased conditioning as a learning method to create personality through interactions with a particular user. Finally, this paper reports results of experiment of learning a set of reaction patterns.

2 SYMBIOT: a Representative of Personality in Virtual World

In this section, we will introduce a personalized software agent called *symbiot* and discuss about symbiot's personality. In addition, we will briefly explain self-biased conditioning, as a learning mechanism to train symbiot's personality.

2.1 What is Personality?

A basic assumption here is that we have our own personalities but we do not want to present our personalities as they are. Nevertheless, we need to present any kind of

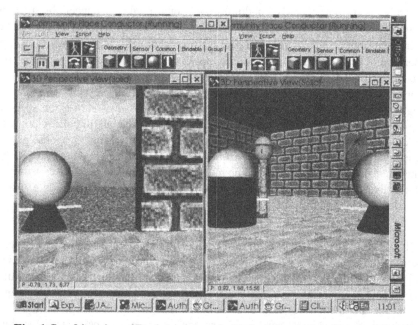

Fig. 1 Symbiots in a 3D virtual world. In the left window shown is one green cone avatar, which represents a remote user. In the right window, three kinds of avatars are shown; a red cone avatar, which is a remote user, a red cylinder avatar, which is a symbiot of the remote user, and a human-like avatar, which is a symbiot of a local user.

personality for making a virtual world interaction more distinguishable, trustworthy, and attractive. How can we achieve this goal? Our solution here is to bring up an artificial agent so that we can find a part of our personalities in behaviors of the agent. We call this type of agent *symbiot*[2] (See an example in Fig. 1).

Then, what is personality for symbiot? Personality, as one definition by a psychologist, represents those characteristics of the person that account for consistent pattens of behavior [5]. This is a very concise human-specific definition. To apply the notion of personality for artificial agents, Moffat arranged the definition by Pervin as: *Personality is consistent reactive bias within the fringe of functionality* [6]. Then, the question is how we could have such consistent reactive bias. Personality has a close relationship with emotion because, as Frijda emphasises, emotion can be seen as changes in activation of behavioral dispositions caused by relevant stimulus events [7]. It can be thought that personality and emotion are supported by the same underlying mechanisms[3]. A significant function of emotion is action readiness by

---

[2] Symbiot is a synthesized word derived from "symbiosis" and "robot". This word represents the nature of an agent which forms a symbiotic relationship with users.

[3] Moffat classifies emotion, sentiment, mood, and personality, with respect to focus and duration [6]. Emotion is a focused and short-term response while sentiment is a focused but long-term response. Mood is a generous and short-term response while personality is a generous but long-term response. Here, he addressed emotion and personality in both side of extremes.

which we can prepare body conditions for some predicted danger. In situation of danger, it is very useful to respond quickly. *It is better to have treated a stick as a snake than not to have responded to a possible snake* [8]. So, emotion is essentially this type of consistent reactions. Furthermore, we can find a relevant topic in primate social intelligence such as alarm call learning, attachment behavior, or deceiving [9]. For example, in the case of eagle alarm call learning in monkeys, a young monkey's eagle alarm call is initially nonspecific [10]. But, they soon learn to be specific by observing their peer's lack of reaction to their false eagle alarm call. A point to be noted is a fact that young monkeys originally have a "nonspecific" response pattern of reacting to any bird. This is interesting because personality, emotion, and social intelligence seems to root to the same mechanism, which is to produce consistent bias or reactive patterns. In some sense, personality or social intelligence is a matter of decision making of an attitude based on perceived inputs.

If we think so, a process to form a personality could be the same as a process to train social intelligence. According to our previous study on social intelligence [11,12], a conditioning system helps to develop social intelligence. The conditioning here denotes classical conditioning by which more than two stimuli originally irrelevant are associated in a conditioned reflex. We could explain this fact by conditioning, an originally very generic response pattern becomes specific, as this can be seen in young monkey's eagle alarm call learning. Resulting specific patterns may differ among individuals due to their different experiences. This variation, we believe, is a root of personality. Therefore, we could summarize that personalities come out through a process of specialization of given generic and consistent response pattens. We could say, in turn, that personalities could be consistent reactive bias because they are bounded by fundamental generic and consistent response.

In our study, based on the above consideration, we are going to use the same conditioning system used for developing social intelligence as a basis of personality. In the next section, I will briefly explain the self-biased conditioning.

2.2 Self-biased Conditioning

We have developed a self-biased conditioning system for the purpose of developing social intelligence in interaction with others. This is basically an unsupervised learning method. This method presumes that there is a set of primary response networks, each of which responds to any definite pattern of inputs with a definite pattern of outputs. Each response network should be as general as possible. This means that only a few sensor inputs are originally considered. Each primary response network contains at least one expectation node which detects whether an expected input is received. If the expectation fails, it forces the learning system to learn to produce a negative reinforcement signal so as to suppress the output of the primary response network. This learning is done with an associative network by incorporating some sensors which were active at the moment when the expectation failed. This learning of a negative reinforcement signal may result in a situation where the output

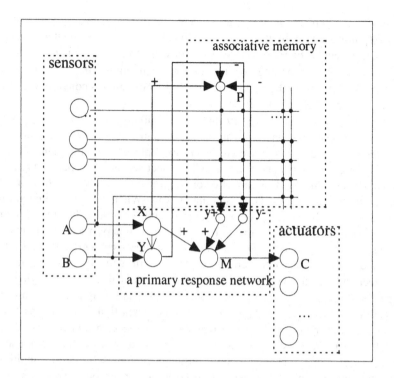

Fig. 2 An example of self-biased conditioning system. A conditioning system is composed of two elements: a set of primary response networks and a single associative memory shared by all the primary response
networks. A primary response network consists of three types of nodes: a
single activation node X, at least one expectation node Y, and at least one
motor center M. A motor center takes a pair of inputs: y+ and y-. These
are a positive and a negative reinforcement signals which come from the
associative memory. A system takes a set of sensor inputs, among which
A is connected to X and B is connected to B, directly. A system also has a
set of actuators (or effectors), among which C is directly connected to M.

is suppressed even when the expectation is satisfied. This, in turn, forces a learning of
a positive reinforcement signal in order to activate the output from a corresponding
primary response network.

Let me explain more concretely how it works, with an example shown in Fig. 2.
Initially, the primary response networks produce a definitive response pattern that if X
is activated, then M fires (namely, if A, then C). This direct activation of M by X
corresponds to what Frijda calls a *concern*, which is a major need or preference. There
is at least one expectation node. This denotes an expected input to be perceived while
a corresponding primary response network is activated. When it perceives an
expectation failure, then it triggers a conditioning of a corresponding negative
reinforcement signal, which is to update weights of those nodes on the line connected
to y-. As it experiences this negative perception, the amplitude of y- becomes such
larger as it suppresses the output of M. After that it will face with a situation where X

is activated and a perception at Y is as expected but M does not respond. Because a primary response network by itself represents a consistent response pattern, behaviors against the expected pattern has to be adjusted. So, this situation triggers a conditioning of a corresponding positive reinforcement signal so that it promotes an activation of M. These are the basic processes happening on this conditioning system[4] and mostly fitting to Frijda's theory of emotion [7][5].

The action on associative memory during conditioning is to let sensors, initially irrelevant to a primary response network, participate in a motor center response of the primary response network. Let's consider an example of learning eagle alarm call [12]. In this case, sensors A and B are a flying object sensor and a peer's eagle alarm call detector, respectively. C is an effector to produce an eagle alarm call. Other sensors could be yellow object sensor and so on. When we give three different samples to a conditioning system randomly and continuously, the system is conditioned so as to make a better response with respect to a peer's eagle alarm call.

Three samples are given: S1 gives a set of sensor inputs saying that there is a flying object and a yellow object but there is no peer's alarm call. S2 says that there is a flying object and a peer's alarm call. And S3 represents that there is no flying object but a peer's alarm call. Expected conditioned reflexes are to ignore a yellow flying object and to respect a peer's alarm call unless there is a flying object. The result is shown in Fig. 3. The success rate is a number of the same response as peer's eagle alarm call for simulation steps. A success rate in its early stage decreases and then increases. This tendency characterizes a basic process of self-biased conditioning. This conditioning begins with a negation of a definitive response when it perceives that a situation does not support an expectation, represented by an expectation node. Then, it gains positive reinforcement when it perceives that a motor center response is inconsistent with an expected input. As we expected, the resulting conditioned reflexes are to ignore a yellow flying object and to respect a peer's eagle alarm call over a perception of a flying object.

2.3 Symbiot's personality

Then, what do we think of symbiot's personality in consideration of self-biased conditioning? Personality determines a way of reaction in a given situation. Emotional responses is one way of reaction. Emotional responses support personality. In fact, Self-biased conditioning represents emotional responses by its primary

---

[4] For more details on system's behavior, please refer to [12].

[5] According to Frijda's theory of emotion, emotion arises as a result of two-stage appraisal of the stimulus. Primary appraisal is a continuous relevance detection procedure to see if stimulus events are relevant to one or more of the concerns. Secondary appraisal is the context evaluation of the event, to identify features of the surrounding situation that are significant of the right behavioral mode. In self-biased conditioning, primary appraisal is embodied as activation nodes and a part of secondary appraisal is implemented in mechanisms to trigger conditioning of an associative memory.

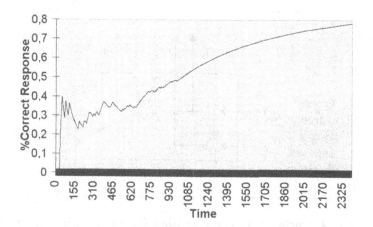

Fig. 3 Success rate in eagle alarm call experiment

response networks. Primary response networks enables a system to produce immediate response whenever they perceives a definitive pattern of inputs.

However, personality is a characteristic made of a collection of tendency of responses, including not only emotional responses but also more sophisticated cognitive responses. Nevertheless, we can assume that emotional responses as the most fundamental reactive mechanisms restrict a tendency to develop a unique personality by producing conditioned reflexes and by creating more deliverative way of thinking in a higher level. For example, social intelligence affects the personality. If we cannot develop social intelligence, which is an intelligence required for social life, we will have a personality disorder. Self-biased conditioning can explain how some basic types of social intelligence could be developed by making specific conditioned reflexes. A conditioned reflex in this case is a specialization of a more generic response. It is ineffective to systematically respond to a certain pattern of inputs after we experienced that we did not meet any danger when we perceived the very same pattern. This is why young monkeys can soon learn not to produce an eagle alarm call when they do not hear any peer's eagle alarm call.

In this paper, we focused on personality of this level, namely, personality supported by conditioned reflexes. In addition, we are interested in such conditioned reflexes as being created through interaction with others[6]. This is because our objective in this study is to personalize a software agent so that it can exhibit a part of our personality. If we succeed in helping an agent to develop its personality through interaction, then it must show such a personality that we prefer. Because a personality is supported by our concerns, which can be thought as preferences, our preferences reflect our own

---

[6] An example of this is a monkey's eagle alarm call. Here, we can suppose that young monkeys have a unconscious expectation of listening peer's eagle alarm call when they produce an eagle alarm call.

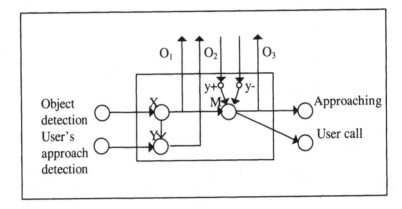

Fig. 4 A primary response network for one experiment. This network defines a fundamental personality which is open, extremely conscientious, extrovert, agreeable, but not neurotic. If a symbiot detects any object in its sensing area, it produces two behaviors: one is to approach the object and the other is to let a user know the object by which this symbiot was attracted. The expectation node Y represents an expectation that, during this particular primary response network is activated, it must detect a user's approach. Otherwise, it causes an expectation failure.

personalities. Then, the personality that we prefer may represent a part of our personality. This is a fundamental idea of this study.

3 Experiment

In this section, I would like to introduce an experimental system to demonstrate a development of simbiot's personality.

3. 1 Foundation of Personality

First of all, we are going to define very fundamental primary response networks that enable agents to exhibit personality. Here let us consider the Big Five theory in psychology. In the Big Five theory, which accounts for human personality with five major traits: Openness, Conscientious, Extrovert, Agreeable, and Neurotic (which are abbreviated by mnemonic OCEAN). *Openness* covers natures of curious, broad interests, creative, original, imaginative, and untraditional. *Conscientious* includes organized, reliable, hard-working, self-disciplined, honest, and clean natures. *Extrovert* is a trait to contain natures of sociable, active, talkative, optimistic, fun-loving, and affectionate. *Agreeable* mentions good-natured, trusting, helpful, forgiving, gullible, and straightforward natures. Finally, *Neurotic* considers natures of worries, nervous, emotional, insecure, inadequate, and hypochondriac.

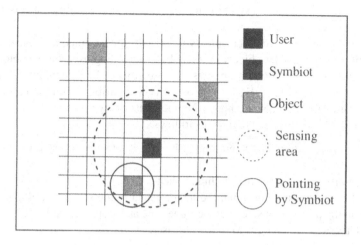

Fig. 5 A simulation environment. A user and a symbiot can move in a 2D lattice space. The symbiot has a sensor to detect any object within a certain range. If an object is sensed, then the symbiot can also detect the properties of objects (e.g. color, size, and so on).

For Openness, we initially define a symbiot as curious entity by giving one primary response network. This primary response network illustrated in Fig. 4 lets a symbiot approach any object. The same primary response network can represent sociable and talkative nature by letting the symbiot call a user to the location of the attracted object. If a user does not show any interest in any object, the symbiot may become indifference. A symbiot is in some sense agreeable. Namely, it does not know doubt correctness of perceived inputs.

It is possible to condition a symbiot so as to believe that a user prefers a particular type of object if we intentionally pretend to do it, despite we do not like it. With respect to a trait of Neurotic, it is a matter of conditioning sample. If conditioning samples are inconsistent, it may produce a purely emotional symbiot, which means that the symbiot is faithful to its original implementation of primary response network. A matter of conscientious, we could say that symbiots is conscientious to its low level responses by primary response networks.

There is no cognitive process to estimate future benefit so it is not possible to make mercenary behaviors. In summary, a symbiot that we define is initially, open, extremely conscientious, extrovert, agreeable, but not neurotic. However, some possibilities exist to develop a closed and/or neurotic personality. Note that a user is a special object and there is a stationed routine that lets a symbiot be near the user unless it detects any object.

3.2 Simulation Environment

Our target system is a 3D virtual world. However, a 3D world visualization is computationally expensive. In addition, for our objective in this particular experiment, a 2D environment is sufficient. Therefore, we use a 2D-world, as an approximation of

3D world, where a user and a symbiot are modeled as square mobile objects as shown in Fig. 5.

Basic units are provided: user unit, symbiot unit, object units, and world units. A world unit registers all the objects in a database, including user and symbiot avatars and maintains all the exported properties of these objects. Each symbiot has a limited range of sensors as in Fig. 5. Each symbiot can access attribute information of objects, which is maintained in the world unit, within its sensor range.

Behaviors of a symbiot are defined as follows:

1. If the distance to a user is more than D, then it attempts to catch up with the user.
2. If the distance to the user is within D, then
2.1. If it detects any object and the motor center outputs 1, then it draws a circle on the object on a screen at the same time as it approaches the object.
2.2. Otherwise, it attempts to follow the user.

Attributes of objects have three categories: color and size. Color is either red, green, blue, or yellow and size is either large or small. For all of these, the symbiot has sensors to detect them. The symbiot has two other sensors: one to detect an object near them and the other to detect an approach of a user to an object by which the symbiot is attracted. In total, the symbiot has 7 sensors to detect all the attributes. Some experiments may not use all the attributes.

3.3 Simulation Results

In this experiment, note that simulations are not repeatable. This is because a user is controlling movement of user avatar and it is difficult for a user to repeat the same movement. Many trials of experiment were attempted. Self-biased conditioning was successfully able to produce a consistent attitude to a particular attribute of object when user's attitude was consistent. Otherwise, it is regarded that user's attitude was neutral to a certain atribute of object. Typical examples of personality we have obtained through simulations were: 1) a presentation of a strong preference, 2) a presentation of a strong aversion, and 3) a neutral attitude. In case 1, a symbiot presents a behavior to hesitate to leave an attracted object even if it perceived that a user went away from the symbiot. In case 2, a symbiot no longer shows any interest for a detest object even it passes near the object. In case 3, a symbiot produces an action as it is designed. Namely, it approaches an attracted object whenever it detects the object.

Fig. 6 depicts a result of one particular experiment involving a strong preference to yellow objects. This shows a very good example when a symbiot develops such a strong preference. In a framework of self-biased conditioning, by its nature, it is not possible to develop solely a positive preference. It first needs to have a conflict between a perception as is expected and an unexpected output of a motor center. As seen in Fig. 6, WYOP, which is an intensity of preference for yellow objects grows up, between 1800 and 2000 time steps, abruptly while a value of negative reinforcement signal is high.

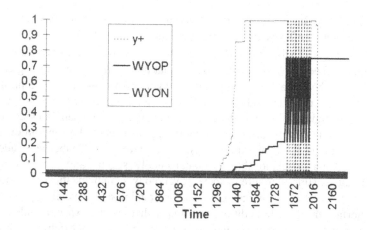

Fig. 6 Preference to yellow objects. This figure depicts a result of an experiment to investigate a relationship between a negative reinforcement signal and a development of positive preference to yellow objects. In this figure, symbols y-, WYOP, and WYON stand for a negative reinforcement signal, an intensity of preference, and an intensity of aversion, respectively.

4 Related Work

One strong motivation of this study is to make our life in 3D virtual worlds more attractive so as to promote people's interaction. It is sure that attractiveness is a property of entertainment. For example, it is possible to introduce artificially tailored personalities or characters of agents. A typical example of this is Bate's believable agents [13]. Bates' believable characters have attracted people because they can imitate human-like expressions of emotion and present an "illusion of life." People will feel them as living if we can feel any kind of sympathy. For this objective, Bates emphasizes the role of the emotional state of the character. I agree with him in a sense that software agents must show behavioral patterns, even if only partially, with which we are familiar in human society. By so doing, people can project their own feelings onto the agents. Some studies emphasize this point (e.g. [14, 15]). Our point of view is slightly different from those views of "directed personality" as in believable agents. Agents can attract people not only because their behaviors are human-like but also and more importantly because their behaviors are personally familiar to us. In other words, we need to emphasize a process to develop personality rather than an appearance of personality. In this sense, it is important to develop personality, in a way of training conditioned reflexes, through run-time interaction with ours.

Nass, Steuer, and Tauber has conducted a set of experiments on human-computer interaction [16]. They have picked up some social psychological or sociological theories and applied these theories by replacing humans with computers. The purpose of this set of experiments is to study whether human users recognize computers as social actors or not. Computers are provided with characteristics of human: language output, responses based on multiple prior inputs, the filling of roles to play, and production of human voice. As the result of experiments, Nass, Steuer, and Tauber concluded that "the human-computer relationship is fundamentally social" and "many principles drawn from the existing literature in social psychology, communication, and sociology are relevant to the study of human-computer interaction and have clear implications for user interface design". In addition, they imply that we can expect a wide range of social responses from computer agents, even if the agents are not rich enough to represent themselves. With respect to their remarks, introduction of personality for software agents behaving as ours partners is expected to contribute to human's devotion to 3D virtual worlds or to human's pleasure in 3D virtual worlds.

Some researchers have developed systems on which personality was implemented (e.g. [6, 17]). Moffat's Will is an implementation of Frijda's theory of emotion. It is a symbolic architecture, based on traditional AI techniques, and consists of some components: perceiver, executor, planner, predictor, and emotor. All the components are connected through memory. It is not a learning agent. The personality of Will is determined by programmable parameters. The parameters include the number of concerns, the relative importance of the concerns, the factor of surprise, the factor of uncertainty, the appraisal categories, the appraisal value, the action tendencies, the relative strengths of the action tendencies, and the built-in sentiments for particular objects. In our current study, we only consider the action tendencies and the strength of action tendencies are learned through conditioning. In a future study, we may extend our work so as to include the above parameters. Moffat discusses how Will fits to the Big Five theory. In conclusion, Will can model about a half of the Big Five (Conscientious and Neurotic, for sure, and Extrovert, somehow). In addition, Moffat notes that Will's awareness of other agents as social beings is non-existent. In contrast, self-biased conditioning always presupposes the involvement of social beings for their development. By using an expectation node to represent somebody's attitude, we can let systems learn social intelligence as is the case of young monkey's eagle alarm call learning or attachment behavior [12].

5 Conclusion

In this paper, we have discussed about a subject of personality of agents in 3D virtual worlds. The current 3D virtual world is less distinguishable, less trustworthy, and less attractive. This is partially due to the fact that 3D virtual world does not contain enough variation. As well as other possible ways to increase variation, introduction of personality will lead to more distinguishable, more trustworthy, and more attractive

3D virtual world interaction. We have introduced symbiots, being our representatives in a 3D virtual world, which can exhibit personality.

Personality can be defined as consistent reactive bias within the fringe of functionality. In other words, personality is produced by a collection of consistent tendencies or preferences to do something or to choose one of many. Personality of a symbiot can be obtained through interaction with a particular user if it is consistent. To acquire personality, we have used self-biased conditioning, which was originally designed for developing social intelligence. This self-biased conditioning supports to create emotionally motivated fundamental personalities.

In this paper, we have conducted a series of experiments to investigate how the self-biased conditioning works for creating a symbiot personality through interaction with a user. Experiments were done by using a simplified 2D virtual space. The self-biased conditioning has succeed in producing a unique personality of a symbiot which reflects user's preference. When the user consistently avoids objects with certain attributes, the symbiot starts to averse object with such attributes. When the user shows a strong preference for objects with certain attributes, then the symbiot also shows a strong preference for them. In this case, even if the symbiot perceives that the user went away from it, it exhibits a certain persistence to one of them, by which it was attracted for the moment.

It is true that an acquisition of personality by self-biased conditioning illustrates just one possible way of personality development. In the case of human beings, a much higher level of cognitive processes such as planning or prediction for the future is also affecting a personality formation. Nevertheless, we would like to mention that primary responses (or emotional responses) must provide the most fundamental generic consistent biases. Namely, primary responses are also a part of personality. Self-biased conditioning gives a way to specialize such generic consistent biases through "presupposed" interaction with others. This is just a beginning of our study of symbiots as our representatives in virtual worlds. Once we successfully create our own symbiots, we could imagine that, while we are meeting in a virtual space, our symbiots can interact with each other so as to examine other's personality. This is one of our future studies in this direction.

References

1. Thalmann, D. Noser, H. and Volino, P. 1997. Autonomous Virtual Actors based on Virtual Sensors. In *Creating Personalities for Synthetic Actors* (Eds. R. Trappl and P. Petta): 120-165. Springer-Verlag.
2. Takeuchi, A. and Nagao, K. 1993. Communicative Facial Displays as a New Conversational Modality. In *Proceedings of INTERCHI'93*: 187-193. ACM Press.
3. Yamaki, H., Wellman, M. P., and Ishida, T. 1996. A Market-Based Approach to Allocating QoS for Multimedia Applications. In *Proceedings of Second International Conference on Multi-Agent Systems (ICMAS'96)*: 385-392. AAAI Press.
4. Mark, G. and Voss, A. 1997. Attractivity in Virtual Environments: Getting Personal with Your Agent. In *Proceedings of 1997 AAAI Fall Symposium on Socially Intelligent Agents*: 81-86. AAAI Press.

5. Pervin, L. A. 1993. *Personality: Theory and Research* (6th edition). New York: Wiley & Sons.
6. Moffat, D. 1997. Personality Parameters and Programs. In *Creating Personalities for Synthetic Actors* (Eds. R. Trappl and P. Petta): 120-165, Springer-Verlag.
7. Frijda, N. H. 1987. *Emotions.* Cambridge University Press, Cambridge, UK.
8. LeDoux, J. 1997. *The Emotional Brain.* Simon & Schuster.
9. Worden, R. P. 1996. Primate Social Intelligence. *Cognitive Science,* 20: 579-616.
10. Seyfarth, R. M. and Cheney, D. L. 1980. The ontogeny of vervet monkey alarm calling behaviour: A preliminary report, *z. Tierpsychology,* 54: 37-56.
11. Numaoka, C. 1997. Innate Sociability: Sympathetic Coupling. *In Proceedings of 1997 AAAI Fall Symposium on Socially Intelligent Agents:* 98-102. AAAI Press.
12. Numaoka, C. 1998. Innate Sociability: Self-biased Conditioning. CSLP-1997-21-01. To be published in Journal of Applied Artificial Intelligence in 1998.
13. Bates, J. 1994. The role of emotion in believable characters, *Communications of the ACM* 37(7): 122 -125.
14. Becheiraz, P. and Thalmann, D. 1996. The Use of Nonverbal Communication Elements and Dynamic Interpersonal Relationship for Virtual Actors. In *Proceedings of Computer Animation'96.* IEEE Computer Society Press.
15. Maes, P. 1995. Artificial Life Meets Entertainment: Lifelike Autonomous Agents. *Communications of the ACM* 38(11): 108 - 114.
16. Nass, C., Steuer, J., and Tauber, E. R. 1994. Computers are Social Actors. In *Proceedings of CHI'94:* 72-78. ACM Press.
17. Sloman, A. 1997. What Sort of Control System Is Able to Have a Personality? In *Creating Personalities for Synthetic Actors* (Eds. R. Trappl and P. Petta): 166-208, Springer-Verlag.

Author Index

Asakura, T.   218
Axelrod, R.   16

Bekkers, D.   108
van den Besselaar, P.   11, 108
Bowker, G.C.   11, 231

Chan, M.   201
Cohen, M.D.   16
Contractor, N.S.   201

Deguchi, H.   61

Etani, T.   137

Fels, S.   137
Foner, L.N.   359

Hattori, F.   330
Hirata, T.   183
Hurwitz, R.   155

Ishida, T.   1, 316
Ishiguro, Y.   218

Jirotka, M.   249

Katsuno, Y.   342
Kida, K.   218
Kobayashi, K.   137
Koch, M.   77
Kurahashi, S.   43

Luff, P.   249

Maeda, H.   183
Mallery, J.   155
Mase, K.   137
Mason, J.   11, 125
Matsubara, S.   330
Minami, U.   43
Miyashita, T.   11, 218
Mizuno, H.   267

Nakanishi, H.   316

Nakatsu, R.   94
Nagao, K.   11, 342
Nishida, T.   11, 183
Nishikawa, N.   267
Nishimura, T.   11, 316
Nishio, G.   170
Numaoka, C.   377

Ohguro, T.   11, 330
Okamoto, M   316

Schlichter, J.   77
Sidhu, C.   11, 299
Simonet, N.   137
Star, S.L.   231
Sumi, Y.   11, 137

Takeshima, Y.   218
Tanaka, T.   267
Terano, T.   43
Tsuji, H.   267

Wexelblat, A.   281

Xu, C.   77

Yajima, H.   267
Yamakami, T.   170
Yokoo, M.   330
Yokozawa, M.   11
Yoshida, S.   330

Zink, D.   201

Vol. 1498: A.E. Eiben, T. Bäck, M. Schoenauer, H.-P. Schwefel (Eds.), Parallel Problem Solving from Nature – PPSN V. Proceedings, 1998. XXIII, 1041 pages. 1998.

Vol. 1499: S. Kutten (Ed.), Distributed Computing. Proceedings, 1998. XII, 419 pages. 1998.

Vol. 1501: M.M. Richter, C.H. Smith, R. Wiehagen, T. Zeugmann (Eds.), Algorithmic Learning Theory. Proceedings, 1998. XI, 439 pages. 1998. (Subseries LNAI).

Vol. 1502: G. Antoniou, J. Slaney (Eds.), Advanced Topics in Artificial Intelligence. Proceedings, 1998. XI, 333 pages. 1998. (Subseries LNAI).

Vol. 1503: G. Levi (Ed.), Static Analysis. Proceedings, 1998. IX, 383 pages. 1998.

Vol. 1504: O. Herzog, A. Günter (Eds.), KI-98: Advances in Artificial Intelligence. Proceedings, 1998. XI, 355 pages. 1998. (Subseries LNAI).

Vol. 1505: D. Caromel, R.R. Oldehoeft, M. Tholburn (Eds.), Computing in Object-Oriented Parallel Environments. Proceedings, 1998. XI, 243 pages. 1998.

Vol. 1506: R. Koch, L. Van Gool (Eds.), 3D Structure from Multiple Images of Large-Scale Environments. Proceedings, 1998. VIII, 347 pages. 1998.

Vol. 1507: T.W. Ling, S. Ram, M.L. Lee (Eds.), Conceptual Modeling – ER '98. Proceedings, 1998. XVI, 482 pages. 1998.

Vol. 1508: S. Jajodia, M.T. Özsu, A. Dogac (Eds.), Advances in Multimedia Information Systems. Proceedings, 1998. VIII, 207 pages. 1998.

Vol. 1510: J.M. Zytkow, M. Quafafou (Eds.), Principles of Data Mining and Knowledge Discovery. Proceedings, 1998. XI, 482 pages. 1998. (Subseries LNAI).

Vol. 1511: D. O'Hallaron (Ed.), Languages, Compilers, and Run-Time Systems for Scalable Computers. Proceedings, 1998. IX, 412 pages. 1998.

Vol. 1512: E. Giménez, C. Paulin-Mohring (Eds.), Types for Proofs and Programs. Proceedings, 1996. VIII, 373 pages. 1998.

Vol. 1513: C. Nikolaou, C. Stephanidis (Eds.), Research and Advanced Technology for Digital Libraries. Proceedings, 1998. XV, 912 pages. 1998.

Vol. 1514: K. Ohta, D. Pei (Eds.), Advances in Cryptology – ASIACRYPT'98. Proceedings, 1998. XII, 436 pages. 1998.

Vol. 1515: F. Moreira de Oliveira (Ed.), Advances in Artificial Intelligence. Proceedings, 1998. X, 259 pages. 1998. (Subseries LNAI).

Vol. 1516: W. Ehrenberger (Ed.), Computer Safety, Reliability and Security. Proceedings, 1998. XVI, 392 pages. 1998.

Vol. 1517: J. Hromkovič, O. Sýkora (Eds.), Graph-Theoretic Concepts in Computer Science. Proceedings, 1998. X, 385 pages. 1998.

Vol. 1518: M. Luby, J. Rolim, M. Serna (Eds.), Randomization and Approximation Techniques in Computer Science. Proceedings, 1998. IX, 385 pages. 1998.

1519: T. Ishida (Ed.), Community Computing and Support Systems. VIII, 393 pages. 1998.

Vol. 1520: M. Maher, J.-F. Puget (Eds.), Principles and Practice of Constraint Programming - CP98. Proceedings, 1998. XI, 482 pages. 1998.

Vol. 1521: B. Rovan (Ed.), SOFSEM'98: Theory and Practice of Informatics. Proceedings, 1998. XI, 453 pages. 1998.

Vol. 1522: G. Gopalakrishnan, P. Windley (Eds.), Formal Methods in Computer-Aided Design. Proceedings, 1998. IX, 529 pages. 1998.

Vol. 1524: G.B. Orr, K.-R. Müller (Eds.), Neural Networks: Tricks of the Trade. VI, 432 pages. 1998.

Vol. 1525: D. Aucsmith (Ed.), Information Hiding. Proceedings, 1998. IX, 369 pages. 1998.

Vol. 1526: M. Broy, B. Rumpe (Eds.), Requirements Targeting Software and Systems Engineering. Proceedings, 1997. VIII, 357 pages. 1998.

Vol. 1528: B. Preneel, V. Rijmen (Eds.), State of the Art in Applied Cryptography. Revised Lectures, 1997. VIII, 395 pages. 1998.

Vol. 1529: D. Farwell, L. Gerber, E. Hovy (Eds.), Machine Translation and the Information Soup. Proceedings, 1998. XIX, 532 pages. 1998. (Subseries LNAI).

Vol. 1530: V. Arvind, R. Ramanujam (Eds.), Foundations of Software Technology and Theoretical Computer Science. XII, 369 pages. 1998.

Vol. 1531: H.-Y. Lee, H. Motoda (Eds.), PRICAI'98: Topics in Artificial Intelligence. XIX, 646 pages. 1998. (Subseries LNAI).

Vol. 1096: T. Schael, Workflow Management Systems for Process Organisations. Second Edition. XII, 229 pages. 1998.

Vol. 1532: S. Arikawa, H. Motoda (Eds.), Discovery Science. Proceedings, 1998. XI, 456 pages. 1998. (Subseries LNAI).

Vol. 1533: K.-Y. Chwa, O.H. Ibarra (Eds.), Algorithms and Computation. Proceedings, 1998. XIII, 478 pages. 1998.

Vol. 1538: J. Hsiang, A. Ohori (Eds.), Advances in Computing Science – ASIAN'98. Proceedings, 1998. X, 305 pages. 1998.

Vol. 1540: C. Beeri, P. Buneman (Eds.), Database Theory – ICDT'99. Proceedings, 1999. XI, 489 pages. 1999.

Vol. 1541: B. Kågström, J. Dongarra, E. Elmroth, J. Waśniewski (Eds.), Applied Parallel Computing. Proceedings, 1998. XIV, 586 pages. 1998.

Vol. 1542: H.I. Christensen (Ed.), Computer Vision Systems. Proceedings, 1999. XI, 554 pages. 1999.

Vol. 1543: S. Demeyer, J. Bosch (Eds.), Object-Oriented Technology ECOOP'98 Workshop Reader. 1998. XXII, 573 pages. 1998.

Vol. 1544: C. Zhang, D. Lukose (Eds.), Multi-Agent Systems. Proceedings, 1998. VII, 195 pages. 1998. (Subseries LNAI).

Vol. 1546: B. Möller, J.V. Tucker (Eds.), Prospects for Hardware Foundations. Survey Chapters, 1998. X, 468 pages. 1998.

Vol. 1548: A.M. Haeberer (Ed.), Algebraic Methodology and Software Technology. Proceedings, 1999. XI, 531 pages. 1999.